Schooner II

1 *Two-masted topsail schooner*
2 *Two-masted schooner* Elsie, *1910*
3 *Two-masted gaff-rigged schooner* Romp, *1847*
4 *Five-masted Vinnen two-topsail schooner*
5 *Three-masted barquentine*
6 *Schooner* America, *1851*

7 *Body plan of the* America
8 *Schooner-brig or 'true' brigantine*
9 *Six-masted barquentine*
10 *Seven-masted gaff-rigged schooner*
11 *Hand winch*
12 *Grating*
13 *Capstan*
14 *Mast partners*

17 *Deckhouse with skylight*
18 *Four-masted topsail schooner*
19 *Galiot*
20 *Eighteenth-century brigantine*
21 *Two-masted fore-and-aft schooner*

DICTIONARY OF SHIP TYPES

DICTIONARY
OF
SHIP TYPES
SHIPS, BOATS AND RAFTS UNDER OAR AND SAIL

Alfred Dudszus & Ernest Henriot

Translated from the German edition
Das Schiffstypen Lexikon
by
Keith Thomas

CONWAY

MARITIME PRESS

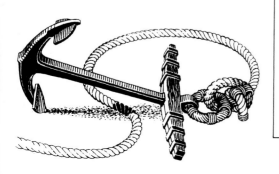

First English language edition, published in 1986 by
Conway Maritime Press Ltd,
24 Bride Lane, Fleet Street,
London EC4Y 8DR

First published in 1983 under the title
Das Schiffstypen Lexikon
© Transpress VEB Verlag für Verkehrswesen 1983

ISBN 0 85177 360 5

Translated by Keith Thomas
Designed by Tony Garrett

Typeset by Witwell Ltd, Liverpool
Printed and bound in Great Britain by
the Bath Press, Bath

CONTENTS

Forword 7
Chronology 8
Basic Tenets 14
Dictionary of Ship Types, A–Z 38
Bibliography 241
Appendices 247

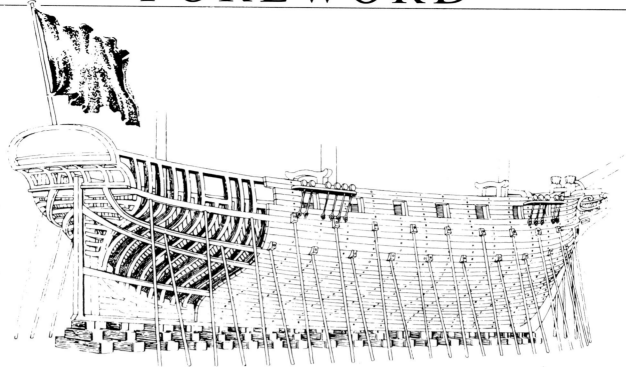

The *Dictionary of Ship Types* has been written for the many friends of maritime literature, and for everyone who has an interest in ships and sea travel from earliest times to the present. The history of sea travel and shipbuilding can be traced back about 5000 years. From the early, highly developed civilizations on the Nile, the Euphrates and the Tigris, through the periods of the ancient Phoenicians, Greeks and Romans, and right up to our own time, the development of the ship has reflected the conditions and requirements of the societies which it served, as well as the development of the skills and experience which enabled man to build vessels to higher and higher standards.

We felt that it was important to describe the links and relationships between many of the important ship types, and for this reason decided against giving this work a strictly lexical form, which would have necessitated giving equal weight to all entries, in favour of devoting more space to the more important types. With this decision in mind, it was clearly not possible, or even sensible, to attempt to cover in its entirety the vast number of types of ship which have been produced worldwide throughout history. We wanted to have enough space to describe noteworthy vessels of our own time, and to avoid weighing down the volume with unnecessary ballast.

The authors have at their disposal a maritime library which is the result of decades of collecting and collating. The collection details more than 4,000 ship types, of which roughly one half were deemed significant enough to earn inclusion in this dictionary. The remainder includes more than 1000 types of vessel which have special designations, are of local significance only, differ only slightly from other types, or whose characteristics are no longer known. We hope that our readers will understand if a particular term or type of ship has been omitted which they would have wished to see included.

Bearing in mind the potentially broad range of interests of our readers, we have made considerable efforts to avoid using obsolete or highly specialized terminology; when there was no alternative we have explained the terms in the text.

Although the book's title — *Dictionary of Ship Types* — was of our choosing, this reference work also contains information on boats, rafts and other floating devices in addition to the ships themselves.

The alphabetical arrangement of the work means that the ship types are necessarily discussed in isolation. With this in mind, it seemed necessary to provide supplementary information on aspects which certain groups of vessel had in common, whether chronological, geographical or technical. For this reason we decided to include a number of broader terms which cover groups of ships rather than individual types, such as Roman ships. We also decided to include details of items such as archaeological finds of ships, boats and models, stone carvings and wall drawings, reliefs and other forms of historical evidence, which provide essential information on the development of ships and other vessels. In many cases this evidence provides valuable historical data, and illustrates how developments were interrelated in a way which, once again, we did not want to omit, even though only part of the material is directly applicable to individual ship types.

One further decision which we made was to include a limited number of famous ships, which either typify a ship type, played a significant rôle in historical development, or which have an interesting history of development in their own right.

We would like to express our appreciation to the illustrators Herr Freitag and Herr Rost for their work in compiling the drawings. We also owe a special debt of gratitude to the experts Dr Meyer, Herr Oesterle and Dr Fethke for their work, which was of immense value. We are very obliged to our publishers, who encouraged us in every way and made it possible to achieve our ambition, and to their employees who have been involved in the work's production.

Publisher's Note

Dictionary of Ship Types was translated from the German book *Das Schiffstypen Lexikon* and every effort has been made to retain the flavour of the original. To this extent the strong emphasis on German and Dutch craft has been retained, particularly because of the unavailability of comparable material in English.

Nevertheless, some changes and revisions were necessary and we would like to acknowledge and thank John Harland, Eric Kentley and Adrian Morgan for their help and suggestions.

The origins of the construction and use of water borne vessels lie thousands of years in the past. Regions close to inland waters, rivers and the sea provided favourable conditions for early settlements, and invited the use and adaptation of naturally occurring buoyant objects. Areas of the world such as Southeast Asia, Indonesia, the Indian and Arabian coasts, the Near East, Mesopotamia, the riverside and costal regions of the eastern Mediterranean, the Nile region, the Caribbean, certain parts of South America and Polynesia are among the regions where it is probably that the first crude forms of raft and boat were developed. These areas had relatively favourable climatic conditions, but it was not possible for man to make permanent settlements in northern Europe until relatively late, when a milder climate set in around 10,000 BC, after the last Ice Age.

Our knowledge of the early development of sea travel, and of the construction of rafts, boats and ships, is based on the results of various ethnographic studies. Although clear evidence of human activities in the earliest times is very scanty, research into ancient civilizations has provided us with indisputable proof that the development of early sophisticated cultures was closely linked with the availability of water for drinking, fishing, and transport. Significant stages in the development of boats and ships in different civilizations are reflected in the many historical finds and pictures of ships and boats from the ancient Egyptian civilization on the Nile, from the early settlements on the Euphrates and the Tigris, from the coasts and islands of the Mediterranean and the Black Sea, from the rivers which flow into the North Sea and the Baltic, and especially from the coasts of Scandinavia.

We also owe much of our present knowledge to the fact that river deposition and swamps preserved the remains of a large number of boats and ships from rotting for thousands of years.

Boats and ships were a regular feature of the cult activities of early civilizations, and our overall view of early times is based very largely on burial items, burial ships, model ships, and sculptures, relief pictures and scored rock drawings on temples, buildings and rocks.

Underwater research and maintenance work on inland waters, canals, harbours, and coastal installations often provide further evidence which allows us to check earlier assumptions.

A wide variety of floating craft, rafts, boats and ships was developed long before the essential laws of physics, relating to flotation, buoyancy, water resistance and the strength of boat and ship hulls were understood. They were based entirely on their constructors' experience and skills. Gradually, man learned to make larger rafts, by bundling together bamboo, bushes and reeds, or using a large quantity of hollow fruit shells, clay pots or animal skins. Around the same time, or

slightly later, rafts consisting of one or more layers of tree trunks bound together were developed. Wickerwork boats, bark boats, framed boats covered with animal skins, and dugouts were also developed, the type depending on the requirements and skills of the people, and the materials and tools available for bundling, plaiting, covering, sewing and sealing the craft.

The next stage was the dugout with added side planks; this led eventually to the fully planked boat, consisting of planks assembled using a number of different methods, and producing craft in a variety of shapes. Certain types of raft and boat made of various materials, depending on the conditions and facilities in the areas of settlement, proved effective vessels for thousands of years. The larger, more durable, sea-going vessels, however, were built exclusively of timber from very early times, where a suitable supply of trees was available.

The significant stages in the development of boat and ship types until the middle of the nineteenth century were as follows: the constant refinement of planked construction, the development of strong, watertight joints, the inclusion of transverse and fore-and-aft structural timbers to stiffen and subdivide the ship's hull, and the invention of effective methods of joining keel, stem and stern timbers. All the important ship types of the Egyptians, the Phoenicians, the Carthaginians, the Greeks, the Romans and the Arabs, including the galley, the nao, the carrack, the caravel, the junk, the dhow and many other ancient and medieval types, were timber-built vessels, as were the Norman and Viking ships, the cogs, the hulks and the flutes, Dutch, English and French two and three-deckers, frigates and full-rigged ships, brigs, clippers and barques, and the large sailing ships which were built up to the second half of the nineteenth century. The general transition from wood to composite construction, and subsequently to the ship built of iron and steel, started around the year 1850. Modern materials such as light alloy and fibre-reinforced plastics have only assumed a significant role since the middle of the present century, but are now used in various types of vessels.

As boats and ships grew larger, and ship

design and methods of construction improved, developments in methods of propulsion, both by muscle power and natural forces, advanced apace. It is certain that man the observer must have noticed and exploited the natural power of flowing water for journeys down-stream very early on. Against the current he set his muscle power, via punt poles, paddles and oars. Men or draught animals also towed vessels upstream from tow paths.

In ancient times there were the great oared ships: the pentekonte, diers, triers, biremes and triremes. Norman ships, Viking ships and galleys of the early Middle Ages were primarily rowing ships with supplementary sails, as were the galleys of the later Middle Ages.

Our first evidence of the sail dates from about 5000 BC. The route from the simple animal skin or matting sail to the eventual multitude of sail forms passed through many stages from the oared vessel with supporting sail up to the towering sail plans of the great multi-masted sailing ships, and the tall sails of modern yachts.

Much of interest could be written on the development of the ship's rudder, on ships' guns and their range, on the historical background to the development of particular ship types, or on the outstanding contributions mady by many nations. Among the tools which man has created over centuries of development, the ship has always held a position of special significance, right up to our own time. Ships have allowed man to discover, open up and colonize new areas of the globe, to explore the world's oceans, to hunt for food and raw materials in the sea, and to trade goods.

The development of a new ship type, the refinement of its design, and its eventual eclipse by a further new type, is a relentless process which has continued unabated for several millennia, and remains in force to this day.

In spite of the large number of important developments, and the large number of ship types in existence today, it is still the case that each ship bears its own individual name. There is hardly a single ship which is exactly identical in all characteristics to another, and even today a crew frequently develops a special relationship with its ship.

Significant stages in development, events, ship finds and progress from the beginnings of sea travel and shipbuilding to the end of the nineteenth century.

Ca 9000 BC

In favourable settled areas such as Southeast Asia, Mesopotamia, the Nile region and others, the first craft might have been made, consisting of bundled reeds and bushes, and primitive forms of wood rafts and dugouts.

Ca 8000 BC

Coastal areas of the North and Baltic Seas and also of Scandinavia become ice-free in the second half of the fourth Ice Age. The remains of sea fish (cod and haddock) are found at the sites which the hunting and fishing tribes of Northern Denmark colonized; the fish were probably not caught from the shore.

Ca 7500 BC

The oldest northern European find of the remains of original wooden paddles, used as a means of propulsion on water. Paddles from Star Carr, Seamer, in Yorkshire, have been dated by the radio carbon method as coming from the year 7535 BC ± 350 years.

Ca 6300 BC

Oldest northern European dugout found, in Pesse, Groningen, Netherlands, dated as from the year 6315 BC ± 275 years.

Ca 6000 BC

Find of a dugout made of a pine trunk in Perth, Scotland on the Firth of Forth.
Seal hunters from Scotland and Scandinavia use skin boats with lightweight supporting frameworks. Wickerwork boats, covered with animal skins, are known on the Indian, Mesopotamian and African rivers.

Ca 5000 BC

First evidence of a sail in a rock drawing from Hodein Mogall in what is now the Nubian desert. The picture of a boat consisting of a bull's body with mast and square sail is ascribed to Hamitic shepherd tribes, which emigrated from Arabia to what was then fertile North Africa between the seventh and sixth centuries BC.

Ca 4200 BC

Unification of Egypt under a central government.

Ca 4000 BC

Boat-shaped papyrus rafts and the first planked boats in the Egyptian pre-dynastic period on the Nile.

Ca 3500 BC

Eridu model boat, made of clay. The model, found in present-day Iraq about 60km south of the Euphrates-Tigris confluence at the burial site of the Eridu temple, dates from the Obed civilization around 3500 BC, and includes a mast socket and attachments for mast stays.

Ca 3000 BC

Dümmersee dugout find. The 5.5m long, lightweight dugout, made of softwood, is one of the oldest dugout finds in north Germany.
- Egyptian settlements on the Nile develop into city states.
- Picture and first model of Egyptian sepulchral ships dating from the second Negade civilization.
- Phoenicians settle in Syria and northern Palestine

Ca 2880 BC

Development of city states of Eridu, Ur, Uruk and others in Mesopotamia.

Ca 2800 BC

Ship pictures on the Aegean Cyclades island of Skyros. The ships feature a bow ram and a tall sternpost.

Ca 2650 BC

Cheops burial ship. The oldest find in the world of a complete ship. The planked ship is of considerable size at 43.6m long and 5.9m beam. The refinement of the timber construction infers a long period of prior experience. The predominant use of cedar wood proves that there were sea connections with Lebanon.
- In Egypt, whole fleets are built for trading and for fleet expeditions to Syria.
- Egyptian oared sailing ships about 30m in length are built, with bipod mast, square sail, cable belts and fore-and-aft tension cables.

Ca 2500 BC

Pehenuka relief. The grave plate from the tomb of Pehenuka (Vth Dynasty (2770–2270 BC) shows a large, long-distance ship with a planked hull, about 80 Egyptian Ells (roughly 42m) in length, with a bipod mast and tall, narrow sails.
- Ships on the Sahu Re relief. The reliefs found at Abussir depict Egyptian ocean going oared sailing ships about 18m long and 4m wide. Pharoah Sahu Re sent around 2500 ships to Syria, Somalia and east Africa.
- Introduction of steering rudder supported in rotating mount on Egyptian ships.
- Ship pictures on containers on the Cyclades islands, dating from the early Aegean civilization.

Ca 2400 BC

Sakkara relief. Detailed representation of the construction of vessels, including tools made of copper and wood, on the grave of the senior Egyptian official Ti (2480 – 2350 BC) from the Vth Dynasty.

Ca 2300 BC

The rapids of the first Nile cataract become navigable for larger ships in the downstream direction.

Ca 2200 BC

- General use of sails in Nile shipping.
- Frequent construction of fully-equipped wooden model ships in Egypt.

Ca 2040 BC

- Expedition to the land of Punt under Pharoah Mentuhotep in the XIth Dynasty. To achieve this, dismantled ships were transported from Koptos on the Nile through the Hammanat Wadi to the coastal city of Kosser.
- The Sumerians dig a 15km long canal from Ur to the sea in Mesopotamia.

Ca 2000 BC

- Jang-Shao find proves that transverse bulkheads were known in China by this time.
- Pharoah Senwosret has a canal dug from the Nile to the Red Sea capable of navigation by ships.

Ca 1900 BC

Letters of loading found on clay tablets in Mesopotamia; cuneiform writing.

Ca 1870 BC

10m wide canal makes first Nile cataract navigable in upstream direction.

Ca 1850 BC

Dashur boat. Wooden boat found near Sesostris' III pyramid (1878–1844 BC); about 10m long, stiffened with transverse beams.

Ca 1700 BC

The Mesopotamian trade centres (Mari and others) maintain extensive trade connections with Cyprus and Crete and become chief loading points between south Mesopotamia and the Mediterranean.

1694 BC

The ruler Hamurabi orders a yard to be built in Babylon for the construction of cargo ships.

Ca 1500 BC

Fresco found on the Cyclades island of Thera, showing ships with tall stems and sterns and spur-shaped keel extensions.

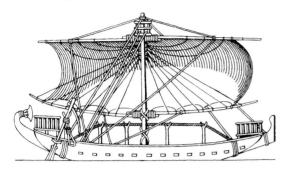

Ca 1490 BC

Hatshepsut ship relief. Relief picture of five Egyptian ships, some of them under sail, on the rock temple Deir el Bahari in Thebes, shown after a successful voyage to the land of Punt, carried out during the reign of Queen Hatshepsut around 1490 BC. The ships are based on a keel and feature deck beams to stiffen the hulls, thus obviating the cable belts, but still including a full-length fore-and-aft tension cable.
- Obelisk transport ships on the Nile, to carry obelisks up to weight of 1200 tons.

Ca 1300 BC

Fore-and-aft sails in common use in the Mediterranean.

Ca 1190 BC

Naval battle between Ramses' III (1198–1167 BC) of Egypt and 'peoples from the sea'.

1184 BC

Destruction of Troy at the end of the Trojan war (1193–1184 BC).

Ca 1150 BC

Greek settlements in Asia Minor with subsequent building of cities (980 BC).

Ca 1000 BC

- The Phoenicians build the trade centre of Kition on Cyprus.
- Karstad stone tablet. Rune stones found by the Nordfjord in Norway showing a number of boats or ships with double stem and stern.
- Brigg dugout. The dugout found at Brigg in Lincolnshire, England, was cut from an oak trunk, is 14.80m long and 1.37m in breadth.

Ca Ninth century BC

Greek and Phoenician civilizations extend their influence: further colonization of the coast of Asia Minor from Troy to Smyrna.

814 BC

Founding of Carthage on the Gulf of Tunis by Phoenicians from Tyre. With the founding of further colonies the Phoenicians grow to be the dominant sea power in the Mediterranean in the first half of the first century BC.

Ca 800 BC

Lubljana ship. The remains of a carvel-built river cargo ship, 40m long, found in a moor near Ljubljana in Yugoslavia, date to this period.

Eighth century BC

- Kukjundschik relief. The relief found on the temple ruin on the bank of the Tigris shows Assyrian river boats and rafts.
- Nineveh relief, showing the bow of a Phoenician warship the Assyrian service.
- Differentiation between the Phoenician cargo ship (Gaulos) and warship (Hippos).

750 BC

Greek cities founded on Sicily.

734 BC

Greek colony founded on Corfu.

705 BC

Khorsabad relief showing Phoenician oared sailing ships; warships built with bow ram.

704 BC

The Corinthian shipbuilder Ameinokles, to whom the invention of the oar outrigger is ascribed, is appointed to Samos.

681 BC

Naples developed as a Greek colony.

680 BC

Foundation of the Macedonian state in northern Greece.

660 BC

- The Corfu Fleet defeats the Corinthian fleet in Greek power struggles.
- Twin fluked metal ships' anchors are made.

658 BC

Foundation of Byzantium.

537 BC

Carthaginians and Etruscans defeat the Greek fleet in a naval battle off Alalia, present-day Algeria, off the eastern coast of Corsica.
- End of Greek colonization in the western Mediterranean.

518 BC

Sparta unites the southern Greek cities in the Peleponesian Federation.

Eighth – sixth centuries BC

Rowing warships from single-row vessels (moners) up to fifty-oar types (pentekonte) form the main force of the Greek city state fleets.

Sixth – fourth centuries BC

- Acropolis relief. Attic triers with outriggers.
- Triers become the principal fighting ships in the Mediterranean from the sixth to third centuries BC.

429 BC

The first Persian campaign against Greece is accompanied by a Phoenician-Ionic fleet of 600 ships.

490 BC

- Athens victorious over the Persians at Marathon.
- Egyptian canal extended from the upper course of the Nile to the Red Sea.

483–480 BC

Athens builds a large number of triers (triremes) in rapid succession.

480 BC

Athens defeats the Persian-Phoenician fleet at Salamis. Three hundred Attic triers, most of them newly built, defeat the Persian fleet, consisting of around 400 ships.

477 BC

Attic maritime federation; Athens dominates in the eastern Mediterranean with its triers.

463 BC

Construction of grain ships for supplying Athens. By 440 BC Athens has a population of 100,000.

433 BC

Corfu and Athens fight naval battle against Corinth.

Fourth Century BC

- Kyreneia shipwreck. Greek freight ship about 15m in length.
- Triangular lateen sail becomes established in Mediterranean.

334–325 BC

Defeat of Persia by Alexander the Great.

Ca 300 BC

Hjørtspring boat. A slim, paddled boat with double stem and stern, 13.28m long; one of the oldest boat finds in northern Europe.
- Use of magetic iron ore as direction finder in China.

284–212 BC

- Archimedes of Syracuse discovers basic laws of hydrostatics.
- Rome victorious over Syracuse (212 BC).

264 BC

Start of the First Punic War against Carthage and the rise of Rome as a maritime power.

260 BC

- Naval victory by Rome over the Carthaginian fleet off Sicily at Mylae.
- Roman triremes are fitted with boarding bridges.

Ca 200 BC

Rome rules the Mediterranean.

150 BC

North Ferriby boat. River boat found in the mouth of the Humber; 15m long, 2.6m beam.

146 BC

Destruction of Carthage and Corinth at the end of the Third Punic War.

First Century BC

- Albenga ship. Roman freight ship, around 35m long, and 12m in breadth.
- Use of water power for corn mills.

Ca 50 BC

Pompei graffito. Scored picture of a Roman freight sailing ship with ship's boat towed behind.

31 BC

Sea battle at Actium, victory of Octavius over the fleets of Marcus Antonius and Cleopatra; Rome again rules the Mediterranean.

Ca O BC

Ostia Fresco. Picture of a Roman freight ship in the port of Ostia, shown as cargo of grain is discharged.

40 AD

Lake Nemi ships. State house ships of the Roman Emperor Caligula (37–41); 70m long and 17.5m in breadth.

First to Second century

Torlonia relief. A corbita (Roman freightship) in Rome's port of Ostia.

First to third century

Blackfriars boat. River boat found in the Thames, dating from the Roman occupation of England (43–400).

Second century

New Guy's House boat. Shallow-draught, carvel-planked oak boat found in the Thames, 12m long. From the period of the Roman occupation of England.

Third century

Nydam boat. Oak planked rowing boat, with no keel, found in Schleswig-Holstein; 22.84m long, for 28 oarsmen.

Fourth Century

Björke boat. Eastern Swedish dugout with side planks added; 7.22m long.

Fourth to fifth century

Frombork boat. Boat of 17.4m length with beam keel and a sail, from the central Baltic region.

Fifth to sixth century

Wood saws first used in central and northern Europe.

Sixth to seventh century

Bruges ship. Single-masted, flat-bottomed shoalwater sailing ship found in Belgium. 14.5m long.

645

Build-up of Arabian fleet.

655

Byzantium looses naval supremacy in Mediterranean to the Arabs.

673–678

Unsuccessful attack on Constantinople by the Arabian fleet; Greek fire used to defend the city.

Seventh century

Kvalsund ship. Norwegian clinker-built, 20-oar ship 18m long.

Eighth century

Äskekarr ship. Remains of a Viking ship found near Gothenburg.

762

Baghdad founded on the Tigris; subsequently develops into an important trade and shipping centre.

Ca 790

Utrecht ship. Flat-bottomed river ship of 17.20m length, possibly a primitive form of hulk.

Ca 800

- Boro Bodur ship picture. A three-masted, multi-storey raft from the Far East, possibly with an original form of direction finder.
- Vikings and Normans build fast, sea-going, keeled ships for oar and sail propulsion.

820

Vikings land in Ireland.

844

Vikings penetrate to the west coast of Spain.

Eighth to ninth century

- Angkor boat. Large rowing boat from Cambodia.
- Roskilde ship. Wrecks of Viking ships found on the Danish island of Seeland in the Roskildefjord.

850

Oseberg ship. Large royal oared sailing boat (Karfe) 21.44m long, belonging to the Viking Queen Asa, daughter of King Harald Redbeard.

851

Vikings land in England, capture London and Canterbury, plunder, then withdraw.

901

Vikings discover Greenland.

941

Russian fleet suffers great losses in attack on Byzantium.

Tenth to eleventh century

- Charbrow ship. Remains of a 13.5m long boat found by Lake Leba.
- Baumgarth boat. Slim doubled-ended boat 11.90m long found on the Pomeranian Baltic Sea coast.

990

The city state of Venice builds a strong fleet of galleys.

1000

Possible first discovery of America by the Viking Leif Erikson.

Eleventh century

- Original form of the single-masted clinker-planked cog.
- Angkor relief: Far-Eastern large 'dragon ship'.

Ca 1066

Bayeux tapestry. Depiction of the invasion of England (1066) by William the Conqueror, showing Norman ships.

1098

Start of the First Crusade.

Ca 1200

Brösen ship. Clinker-planked cargo ship with iron rivets and wood nails, but still with side rudder.

1242

First proof of a stern rudder on a ship type; the cog.

Mid thirteenth century

- Kalmar ship. Open sailing boat 11.2m long and 4.6m in breadth, with fitted ribs and transverse beams.
- Bergen ship. Large find of wrecked old Norse and medieval ships.

1270

End of the Crusades. For the eighth and last Crusade most of the ships are built in Venice and Genoa.

1291

Attack on Japan by a Chinese-Mongolian fleet.

Ca 1300

Falsterbo find. Six prahm-like cargo barges of varying size, between 13 and 27m in length.

1306

First proven magnetic compass, consisting of magnetic needle and direction-finding disc.

1340

Cog the most common ship type in northern Europe.

1358

- Naval battle at Sluys; Edward III of England defeats the French fleet in the first year of the Hundred Years' War.
- First mention of the use of powder cannon on ships in Aragon.

1370

The Hansa holds power in the Baltic.

1372

A French-Castillian fleet defeats the English fleet in a naval battle off La Rochelle.

End of fourteenth century

Bremen cog. Hull of a cog built of oak planks; 15.5m long, 6m in breadth and 3.5m depth.

1401

The Hamburg Hansa defeats the fleet of the Liekedeeler.

1418

Prince Henry the Navigator of Portugal founds a maritime college and begins sending reconnaissance ships to the west coast of Africa.

Fifteenth century

First drawings of ship sheer plans and designs.

1460

Portuguese reconnaissance ships reach what is now Sierra Leone on the African coast.

1462

First large carvel-built ship *Peter von Rosels* in the Baltic (Gdansk) marks the start of the transition to the carvel method of construction.

1492

Discovery of America (Bahamas) by Columbus.

1497–98

The Portuguese explorer Vasco de Gama sails round Africa and reaches India.

1498

John Cabot discovers Labrador, New Caledonia and Newfoundland, and takes possession of them for England.

1500

A Portuguese fleet of 12 ships sails to South America under Pedro Cabral, and establishes the Portuguese claims to power over Brazil. After this the fleet sails on to India to form trade links.

1509

Victory over the Arabs by a Portuguese fleet in Indian waters.

1514

The *Great Harry*, a four-masted English carrack of around 50m length, equipped with 184 cannon of all calibres, is launched at Woolwich in the County of Kent; the biggest warship of its time.

1517

Andrade reaches south China by sea, starting from Portugal.

1519–1522

An expedition under Ferdinand Magellan (1480–1521) attempts to sail round the world for the first time, discovering the Philippines and the Marians.

1552

Portuguese ships land in Japan for the first time.

1566

Large Hanseatic four-masted warship *Adler von Lübeck* is launched.

1571

Naval victory by the allied 'Holy League' over the Turkish fleet at Lepanto.

Sixteenth century

Introduction of extended masts, consisting of lower mast, topmast, and topgallant topmast.

1577–1580

Francis Drake (1540–96) circumnavigates the world for the first time during his voyage on the *Golden Hind*.

1585

John Davis reached the Davis Strait, named after him, in the search for a northwest passage.

1588

Victory of the English fleet over the Spanish Armada in the Channel.

1594–97

The Dutchman Willem Barents (1550–1597) reaches Novaya Zembla in the search for a northwest passage; this part of the ocean between northern Europe and Spitzbergen now bears his name.

1597

The attempted Spanish invasion of England ends with the loss of the Spanish fleet.

1600

Foundation of the English East India Company.

1602

Foundation of the Dutch East Company,

1605

Discovery of Australia by Jansson.

1606

Henry Hudson (*ca* 1550–1611) searched for a northwest passage to the Pacific.

1609

H Hudson lands on the island of Manhattan at the mouth of the Hudson River (named after him) on his third attempt.

1612

England takes possession of Hindustan (port city of Surat).

1618–48

Thirty Years' War.

1620

– The *Mayflower* lands close to what is now Boston.
– Investigations into the stability of ships by Simon Stevin.

1625

Holland takes possession of Guayana.

1628

The Swedish warship *Wasa* capsizes in Stockholm harbour.

1634

France takes possession of several Antilles islands.

1636

Construction of the French two-decker *La Couronne* with 46 broadside guns.

1637

The *Sovereign of the Seas* is the first three-decker to be launched for the English navy. One hundred and four cannon on three decks.

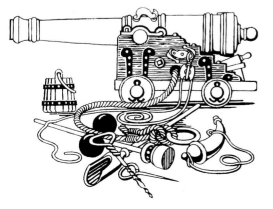

1639

Dutch-Spanish naval battle of the Downs, off Dover.

1640

Portugal disassociates itself from Spain and becomes an independent kingdom under João IV.

1642

Tasman discovers the Fijian islands.

1648

Sweden is granted German coastal regions.

1650

– Start of the emigrant tide, which continued for centuries.
– Holland gains monopoly for slave deliveries to Spanish America.

1651

England forbids the import of goods on foreign ships with the Navigation Act.

1659

Spain forfeits dominance in western Europe to France.

1662–1683

Colbert modernizes and extends the French fleet.

1663

Colbert founds the *Academie des Sciences* in Paris.

1664

French East and West Indian trade company founded.

1672

The Royal African Company of England is granted the monopoly for the slave trade in Africa.

1673

First model towing experiments in France.

1676

Greenwich observatory built.

1691

The Swede Ake Classon Rålamb describes ship types, tools, dock equipment and weapons in *Skepsbyggeriet*.

1692

First French triple-decker, *Royal Louis*, built in Toulon.

1695

Build-up of Russian Fleet.

1698

Barras de la Penne publishes a description of the galley in *Frabrica di Galere*.

1720

For the first time prizes are offered by the Paris Academie des Sciences for significant work on the theory of stability and resistance in ships.

1728

The Danish polar explorer Vitus Bering (1680–1741) crosses the sea passage between Alaska and Siberia (the Bering Straits) on his voyage of discovery commissioned by Tsar Peter I, and proves that there is no land connection between the land masses of Asia and America.

1749

Leonard Euler publishes technical investigations on ship resistance, stability and displacement calculations in *Scientia Navalis*.

1755–63

English-French colonial war, battle for domination in the overseas colonies.

1765

Fredrik Hendrik af Chapman publishes plans and drawings of various ship types in his technical work *Architectura Navalis Mercatoria*.

1768–71

James Cook undertakes his first three-year voyage of discovery in the Pacific, with the *Endeavour*.

1775–83

North American War of Independence.

1787

Construction of the first iron harbour boat, 21.5m long, by J Wilkinson in England.

1791

A paper by Louis de Hamel du Monceau 'Elements de l'architecture navale' appears in an extended German language version by C G D Muller: 'Anfangsgründe de Schiffbaukunst', 'The basic elements of the art of shipbuilding'.

1798

Horatio Nelson destroys a French fleet in the port of Aboukir.

1799

Lloyds Register of British and Foreign Shipping (LR) founded in London.

1805

Nelson leads English to naval victory over the combined Spanish/French fleet at Trafalgar.

1810

First attempts at building composite ships, with iron frames and timber planks.

1811

School of Naval Architecture in Portsmouth founded.

1812

North American states gain the lead in the development of small, high-speed sailing ships with the Baltimore schooner.

1827

Victory over the Turkish fleet by English, French and Russian squadrons in the battle off Navarino.

1828

Bureau Veritas founded in Antwerp.

1830

Royal shipbuilding school founded in Stettin

1831

Geographical position of the magnetic North Pole defined by JC Ross.

1832

Bureau Veritas in Paris.

1845

The clipper *Rainbow* is launched in New York.

1849

- Repeal of the English Navigation Act. Ships of any flag can import and export goods to and from England and all European and overseas countries.
- Expansion of world shipping, carrying bulk cargoes of the world's products: grain, coal, iron, saltpetre, cotton etc.

1851

Launch of the clipper *Flying Cloud*, developed by Donald McKay.

1853

Launch of the largest timber-built clipper, the *Great Republic*.

Mid nineteenth century

The three-masted barque becomes the most commonly used ship amongst the northern European merchant fleets.

1861

Royal Professional Institute opened in Berlin.

1869

Opening of the Suez canal, reducing the distance between London and Bombay by almost a half: Built under the direction of the French Engineer Ferdinand de Lesseps.

1870–71

First model towing experiments carried out in Torquay by W Froude. Towing experiments involved the corvette *Greyhound*.

1873

First manufacture of steel by the Siemens-Martin process.

1893–96

F Nansen spends the winter locked in the ice in the research ship *Fram*.

1904

The *Preussen*, the only five-masted full-rigged ship in the world, is built at Geestemünde for the Laeisz shipping company.

BASIC TENETS

Ships are the combined result of the labours of many individuals and groups of tradesmen. With the increasingly powerful and complex ships now being built, shipbuilders have to be able to co-operate very closely with each other and with the future owners of the vessel. Once a ship is in service, the security of the ship, cargo and the crew requires that communication and command arrangement should be efficient and unambiguous. This is especially true when narrow shipping lanes, canals and locks have to be negotiated, the ship has to be manoeuvred within the ports of the world, cargoes are to be loaded or discharged, or ship's supplies embarked. At such times the wide-ranging duties of the crew members demand that they are well versed in the vessel's design, its capabilities at sea, its control characteristics, and the operation of its many items of equipment.

When a ship is in danger, either at sea or in port, from heavy seas, listing, fire or structural damage, then the crew's intimate knowledge of the ship's responses in every condition from fully loaded to empty, and a lightning fast command system, are of crucial significance to their survival. Over the centuries, the fundamental importance of effective communication has resulted in the coining of a large number of maritime terms – both basic and specialized – which relate to ships, their dimensions, their fittings and ambient conditions, and which alone could fill several volumes. This book includes a bibliography, with notes on specialist maritime dictionaries which include more or less complete explanations of this terminology.

In this book we have made great efforts to make the information as comprehensible as possible, at the same time using those expressions which are still in general use today. Explanations of specialist terms have been included in the text where necessary.

With this in mind, the following section just covers a few of the fundamental principles in order to form an introduction to the subject. The subjects covered are:

METHODS OF DIFFERENTIATING BETWEEN TYPES

METHODS OF TIMBER CONSTRUCTION

PRINCIPAL DIMENSIONS AND COEFFICIENT OF FINENESS SHIP MEASUREMENT

ARMAMENTS

SAIL RIGS

METHODS OF DIFFERENTIATING BETWEEN TYPES

Differentiating between principles of flotation

The vast variety of water-borne vessels can be sub-divided and categorized in a number of different ways. The primary characteristic of a vessel is its buoyancy, and the method by which it remains afloat represents our primary means of differentiating between types. These are the main categories:

Rafts,

Partially submerged boats and ships,

Completely submerged bodies.

A raft is a buoyant vessel which floats because of the structural material is of lower density than the water. The low-density material may be reeds, bushy material, bamboo or timber logs, or other individual bodies bundled or rigidly joined together. In general terms, rafts are not watertight vessels, and usually do not even have sides.

The buoyancy of the partially submerged boat or ship rests on the fact that the submerged body of the hull, and at least part of the hull located above the surface, has a watertight outer skin. The outer skin may consist of animal pelts (as in animal-skin boats), sealed woven materials (wickerwork boats), or wooden planks, metal plates, or fibre-reinforced plastics, as in the majority of all types of ships and boats. In every case the vessel is submerged to the point where the mass of the displaced water equals the mass of the entire floating body, including all cargo. Partially submerged boats and ships can be further sub-divided into multi-hull vessels (outrigger boats, catamarans, trimarans) and the more commonly built single-hull ships.

The final category is the fully submerged vessel, which has no reserve of upthrust, unlike the boat or ship, which has excess buoyancy proportional to its draught. In this case the vessel's mass has to be equal to that of the water displaced; this is always achieved by altering the vessel's own mass. In early diving boats ballast could be ejected to increase upthrust, while more modern types can pump water in and out of tanks.

Differentiating according to size and purpose

In seamen's terms the difference between boat and ship is not universally acknowledged. In the navy, various types of vessel are designated 'boat', even though they have the characteristics of ships in terms of size and construction. In general terms, boats are smaller, usually uncovered (open) vessels, or are fitted with partial decks or a cabin. Although a ship's size, its construction, and its intended purpose are the principal means of differentiating between ship types, their range of operation is also a factor, whether they are used on inland waters, around the coasts, or on the open sea.

In terms of their intended purpose, ships carry out a broad range of tasks, which can be roughly categorized as transport, the acquisition of food and raw materials from the sea, technical work and military duties. The main groups can be differentiated as follows: merchant ships, research and fishing ships, tenders and naval vessels. Each of these main groups embraces several sub-groups; merchant ships, for example, are used for carrying livestock or goods, bulk goods and liquid loads, and also as passenger ships, cattle transporters, freighters for mixed cargo or bulk goods, wine, gas and oil transporters, and hybrid types.

The necessity of tailoring ships to the changing requirements of commerce and sea transport leads to a continual development of new types of vessel, to their subsequent obsolescence and on to further new types, as well as to increasingly specialized types on the one hand, and hybrid forms on the other. Amongst passenger ships, for example, we can sub-divide further according to the vessel's size, its level of comfort, its intended range, the variety of climatic zones it can cope with, whether it caters for combined passenger and freight transport, and other factors. Such subdivisions can be applied in a similar fashion to all other type groups.

Differentiation according to material and method of construction.

Differentiation between vessels according to the characteristics described above overlaps with categorization according to the principal material employed to make the hull. Although primitive forms of boat were constructed using a wide variety of materials, the main shipbuilding material used for thousands of years has been wood of various types. In the first half of the nineteenth century composite vessels of wood and iron were built, followed by ships made of iron and, a few decades later, of steel. Until the middle of the twentieth century, the riveted steel hull was the dominant design. Fully welded steel hulls, light alloy hulls and fibre-reinforced plastic types, with the exception of few experimental types, were not developed until the second half of the present century.

The structural material, type of construction and manufacturing methods adopted, although useful as aids to categorization, are not sufficient in themselves. Thus the number of decks, the design of the ship's structural timbers, the hull openings, the sub-division of the hull by means of bulkheads, the arrangement and position of the superstructure and deckhouses, the vessel's steering equipment and cargo-handling gear, amongst many other features, are further important factors by which the vast number of ship types can be separated.

Differentiation according to type of propulsion

Boats and ships differ fundamentally according to their basic means of propulsion: muscle, natural energy, and engine power. This book covers those types which are driven by paddles, oars, punt poles, draught animals (towed ships), water currents or sails. Rowed ships are sub-divided according to the type of oar, and the number of oarsmen and banks of oars, as in the case of the diers, triers, galleys and other types. In a similar way, sailing ships are differentiated according to the type, number and arrangement of the masts and their sail complement.

METHODS OF TIMBER CONSTRUCTION

The origin of the development of the large, timber-built sailing ship can be traced back to the dugout. This was a tree trunk or log, hollowed out and tapered at either end. The need for larger and more seaworthy vessels led to the addition of bound-on side planks, a development which represents the crucial step towards vessels consisting of a large number of wooden components. This line of development came to its natural conclusion in the planked boat or planked ship, in which the hull has a skin of wooden planks, joined together and rendered watertight. This method of construction demanded that the planks be worked as accurately as possible, first using the adze and axe, then the saw. It also demanded a strong, durable means of joining them, and a means of sealing the butt and edge joints.

As an example, the ancient Egyptian wooden ships such as the Cheops burial ship (around 1650 BC) had the butt joints of its planks scarphed together, with the longitudinal joints joined by dowels. For thousands of years, right up to the time of the Hjortspring boat (around 300 BC), and even into the Middle Ages (fifteenth century) planks were joined or 'sewn' together with fibres, rope or thongs. At a later stage the 'sewn' joints were reinforced with dowels, wooden rivets, split and wedge-shaped wooden nails and – later – metal nails and rivets, which had spreader washers or rooves under the rivet heads in order to spread the load to a greater area of plank. Eventually, the 'sewn' joints disappeared altogether. As shipwrights' skills improved, so the fit of the planks became more accurate, and the methods for sealing the plank joints were refined, using natural bitumen, non water soluble resins, bast fibres, animal hair and other materials, culminating in tar-soaked oakum.

Within the category of timber planked construction we have to differentiate between clinker and carvel planking. In a clinker-built boat the longitudinal planks overlap in the manner of roof tiles. In contrast, the longitudinal edges of the planks in a carvel-built hull are butted together to form a smooth outer surface. For a variety of reasons carvel planking was the standard method adopted in the Mediterranean from earliest times, but in northern Europe it only came into use in the course of the fifteenth century, when its advantages in the construction of large ships became apparent.

The larger the timber-built ships grew, the more important became the structural timbers whose task was to stiffen the hull, and thus prevent the ship's planking from moving. In ancient times the Egyptian ships had ropework belts wrapped round the ship's hull, and fore-and-aft cables stretched fore and aft, supported on forked posts set up on deck. Shipwrights continued to address the problem of sagging and consequent leaks into quite recent times (Chapman 1768, Snodgrass 1791, Seppings 1820), seeking to solve the problem with diagonal bands of planking, until the steel members of the skeleton frame design solved the problem by substantially increasing the longitudinal strength of the hull.

Research has shown clearly that the very earliest shipbuilders used their experience to tailor the design of structural timbers to match the loads placed on them. This is evident from the size of the main frames of early vessels. Initially, the topmost plank – the gunwale plank – was left thicker than the rest of the planking. Later on the lowest plank – the keel – was also thickened. The keel, stem and stern gradually altered in form from the hollowed-out block stem via the flat keel to the more or less pronounced stem- and stern-post of the oared sailing ship, and the pure sailing ship. Full-length decks, whose planking contributed to the vessel's longitudinal strength, were already in use in some Greek and Roman warships and the Roman cargo ship, the Corbita. Weatherproof deck planking, however, only came into general use in the Middle Ages with the introduction of the covered cog.

The ancient Egyptians knew of one method of building transverse strength into the hull, which enabled them to omit the ropework belts. This is shown in the picture on the Hatshepsut relief (around 1490 BC), illustrating ships with deck girders, which pass through the outer planks at the sides. A number of early dugouts also feature ribs which were left projecting when the boat was hollowed out. In northern European boats' cleats were left projecting on the inside of the planks, to which the natural curved ribs were attached, before methods of joining the planks directly, by means of nails or rivets, were developed.

The design of the transverse hull timbers also changed in the course of time, from curved ribs cut from naturally grown timber of roughly the correct form, via ribs which were roughly hewn to the correct shape, to the built-up frames of large ships, which consisted of many components. On large sailing ships with several decks the lower part of the transverse stiffening structure evolved into the floor plates. To these were fitted up to three futtocks linking the floor to the sides, with a top component running from side to side. This basic frame shape was further stiffened by the transverse deck beams at the height of each support rib. Deck knees were used to reinforce the joints between the horizontal transverse deck beams and the support ribs.

Good shipbuilding timber was very much in demand even amongst the ancient Egyptians and Greeks, but the demand peaked in the eighteenth and nineteenth centuries during the period of the great timber-built sailing ships. The massive wood components required for the outer skin and deck planking, the fore-and-aft and transverse timbers, and not least the masts, topmasts and yards of these ships, which were built every year in their hundreds, give some idea of the acreage of forest which disappeared in the era of timber shipbuilding.

PRINCIPAL DIMENSIONS AND COEFFICIENT OF FINENESS

The size of a ship and certain other characteristics are related to its principal dimensions such as length, beam, depth and draught, and their inter-relationships.

L	Length of the ship, determining its overall size; usually expressed as L_{DWL} or L_{pp}.
L_{OA}	Overall length; generally the horizontal length between the forwardmost and aftermost fixed point of the ship's hull or deck, less bowsprit or sternsprit.
L_{pp}	Length between perpendiculars, measured between the centre of the rudder shaft or the rear edge of the sternpost, and the front edge of the forestem with the waterline at the design draught. The design draught is the draught which results at the design displacement; it is close to the fully-loaded line on ship.
L_{DWL}	Length at the design waterline at the design draught (T_{DWL}), ie the length between the front edge of the stem and the rear edge of the sternpost at the design waterline (DWL).
L_K	Keel length of the straight keel.
B	Beam of the ship, determining the overall size; usually the beam at the DWL or the beam across the mainframe (B_{DWL}).
B_{OA}	Overall beam of the ship, ie beam across all fixed side members, including gunwales, rubbing strakes etc.
B or	Beam across the outside edges of the frames at the broadest point at the DWL. On wooden ships the beam across the inside edges of the outer skin planking.
B_{SPT}	
B_{DWL}	Beam at the design waterline.
B_{WL}	Beam at the waterline at any particular time.
B_D	Beam on deck.
D	Depth of the ship, measured from the bottom edge of the main deck planking to the top edge of the keel, generally equal to the depth of the hold.
D_{FB}	Freeboard; the prescribed minimum dimension by which the sides of the ship must be clear of the water surface in calm water at full load, measured at half the ship's length (0.5 L_{pp}) from the top edge of the deck.
T	Draught of the ship at any load; distance from the bottom edge of the keel to the waterline, measured at half the ship's length.
T_{DWL}	Design draught; distance from the bottom edge of the keel to the design waterline measured at half of ship's length.

The form of a ship's hull is characterized by a number of degrees of fullness as well as its principal dimensions. These factors represent the relationship between the area included by a frame, or by the waterline outline, and the rectangles which enclose them. The alternative term is volume ratios. The most important degrees of fullness are as follows:

C_M	Degree of fullness of the midsection area; the ratio of the submerged portion of the midsection area to the enclosing rectangle, calculated by the formula: $B_{DWL} \times T_{DWL}$.
C_{DWL}	Degree of fullness of the design waterline area; the ratio of the design waterline area to the enclosing rectangle, calculated by the formula: $L_{PP} \times B_{DWL}$.
C_B	Degree of fullness of the displacement, or the block coefficient; the ratio between the displacement of the submerged portion of the ship's hull and the enclosing cuboid, calculated by the formula: $L_{PP} \times B_{DWL} \times T_{DWL}$.
C_P	Prismatic coefficient or cylinder coefficient; the ratio of water displacement to the enclosing prismatic body formed by the main frame area and the length L_{PP}.

THE MEASUREMENT OF SHIPS

Since shipbuilders usually construct vessels under contract to shipping companies, they are not usually the owners of the ships they build. The future owners need to know the principal dimensions, coefficients of fineness, displacement, carrying and loading capabilities in respect of various types of cargo, and also the costs which depend on these factors. Therefore, the shipping company needs to obtain the most accurate information possible about the ship before construction begins. This information must cover building and operating costs, canal, harbour, anchorage and loading and unloading fees, wage costs, insurance and depreciation.

The medieval unit for the cargo capacity and, therefore, indirectly for the size of a ship, was the barrel, or tonne (tun). Larger than the amphorae of the Greeks and Romans, barrels were the most important transport vessels. Oils, fats, fruit, wine and beer, even spices and skins were packed and securely sealed in barrels. Next to the shipwrights, the coopers were numerically the largest guild in the

Gouden Leeuw *(Golden Lion), flagship of the Dutch*
Admiral Cornelius Tromp, in the port of Amsterdam
in 1660. Painting by van de Velde (1663– 1707).
Rijksmuseum, Amsterdam

Painting by Nicholas Pocock showing four English
warships and the Victory, the three-masted flagship
of Admiral Horatio Nelson (1758– 1805) on the right
of the picture National Maritime Museum,
Greenwich

Sea battle in the Downs off Dover, 1639, painting by
Cornelisz Verbeeck. The flagship Amelia (to the
right, flying red, white and blue flag) of Marten
Tromp (1529–1653), and a further Dutch three-
master, engage two Spanish ships. National
Maritime Museum, Greenwich.

dockyards and ports.

The Hamburg Commerz Last (commercial unit of cargo) was 3000kg. The Danzig and Bremen rye Last was about 2000kg and occupied a volume of about 3.25m³. In the Hanseatic period the Rostock ton was another generally recognized measure, in this case for salt herrings. The volume of a herring last was about 0.8 rye lasts.

In the Mediterranean and in western Europe, the wine barrel (tonneau) was the usual unit of measurement of storage space. This barrel was about half a rye load, or 1000kg.

In 1872, the former method of quoting ship freight in Lasten, or load units, was superseded in the German Baltic and North Sea areas by the metric tonne, (t) of 1000kg. Stowage space is now quoted in m³, and the ship's useable hold volume in NRT (see below).

The standard international unit for measurement of volume on ships until now has been the register ton (RT). This is the equivalent of 100 English cubic feet (1 English foot = 0.3048m) and is equal to 2.832m³. In terms of ship volume we have to differentiate between the Gross (Brutto) Register Tonnage (BRT) and Net Register Tonnage (NRT). The gross volume of the ship, stated in BRT, includes the entire volume below the measurement deck as well as the volume of the hatches, shafts and superstructure. In contrast, the net volume includes only the profitable volume, ie all cargo holds and passenger compartments. The net volume can be calculated by subtracting all navigation and operation rooms, crew living quarters, messes, store rooms, drinking water tanks, other provision rooms, supplies and loads from the gross volume. As ship fees generally relate to the net volume, there is a constant effort to keep his figure as favourable as possible in relation to the cargo capacity. New measurement regulations are at present being introduced.

The cargo capacity of a ship defines the maximum volume of cargo in cubic metres (m³) and its mass in Net Register Tons (NRT), and the effective load in tons (t) which can be carried. In contrast, the deadweight DW is that mass in tonnes (1000kg) which a ship can carry in terms of cargo, supplies, crew and passengers in accordance with the safety regulations.

In the case of warships it is usual to state the mass of water displaced – in short, the displacement – in English tons (ts – 1016kg) instead of the useable volume.

The displacement or water displacement V defines the volume of water displaced by the submerged portion of the hull, less appendages (rudder etc), measured at the outside edge of the frames, in cubic metres. In the case of wooden ships the displaced mass of water refers to the outside of the outer skin.

The displacement is the mass of water displaced by the submerged hull in tonnes (1000kg), and equals the total mass of the ship including its current load, tank contents and supplies. The magnitude of the current displacement varies according to the displacement volume, taking into consideration the outer skin and the varying density of the water in different parts of the world. The difference between the displacement and the deadweight is equal to the mass of the empty, but operational ship.

ARMAMENTS

Before the introduction of gunpowder, ships' main armaments were the bow ram, whose origin can be traced back to the Phoenicians and Greeks; catapults; light, medium and heavy slings; and Greek fire. In the thirteenth century, thunder barrels, sparrowhawks and Falconetts came into use; these were light front or rear loading guns, which were mounted in yokes on the railings, or fired from the tops. In the fourteenth and fifteenth centuries the first real ship's guns came into use: these were the kammerbuchsen. They were breech loaders, with a barrel reinforced with wrought iron rings, and were mounted in a block carriage. Swivel guns, mounted on the bulwarks came into use and were maintained well into the eighteenth century. The main light gun from the fourteenth to the middle of the sixteenth century was the bombardelle, a front or breech loader mounted on a two-wheeled carriage. The heaviest ship's gun at this time was the heavy calibre bombard, mounted on a massive block. In the fourteenth and fifteenth centuries such bombards were the preferred weapons on galleys, in front or breech loader form. Breech loading bombards were built in two parts, to enable them to be fired in rapid succession. The gun barrel was lashed down firmly on the block mount, but the fired chamber could be exchanged for a freshly loaded one.

The effective range of the guns made earlier strategies of naval warfare obsolete. Rowing ships were now too clumsy, owing to their great mass. The ships became larger, were fitted with more sails, and increased beam or a greater mass of ballast became necessary to balance the mass of the guns at the higher level. Originally, ships' guns were set up forward and aft to serve as pursuit and defence guns, and in consequence could only fire approximately in a fore-and-aft direction, but by the fifteenth century the broadside arrangement had been adopted. At first, a simple circular opening was cut in the external planking to accommodate the gun barrel, with no means of sealing the hole. Around the year 1500 hinged gunports were introduced, an innovation which is ascribed to the Dutch masters and the French master shipwright Descharges. In the course of the seventeenth century the broadside arrangement of the guns led to the adoption of a new battle tactic, in which the warships sailed in line ahead. The large 'ships-of-the-line' each sailed in the wake of the preceding vessel, and attempted to destroy the enemy ships, also sailing in line astern, parallel and within firing range, by broadside fire.

After the seventeenth century, cannon were categorized according to the mass of the cannon ball in pounds, one pound equalling roughly 0.5kg. The double cannon had a mass of more than two tons and a calibre of 177mm. The 'demi-cannon' was a 24-pounder, the culverin an 18-pounder, and the demi-culveran a 9-pounder. Until about 1750, most ships' guns were cast in bronze, but the manufacture of iron cannon barrels was gradually mastered after that date.

With the guns distributed over several decks, specially reinforced structural timbers were called for to absorb the mass and recoil forces of the weapons. The cannon were lashed to rings in the sides with ropes called breechings, intended to absorb the recoil shock. The considerable camber of the gun deck also helped to prevent the gun running back far when fired, and made it easier to push the cannon back into the firing position. To reduce the effect of the enemy's fire, the ship's timbers were very strongly built. New methods of building lighter and faster unarmed sailing ships only became feasible once the problems of piracy and armed power struggles at sea had been resolved.

SAIL RIGS

In addition to the factors already discussed, sailing ships are categorized according to the type of sail they carry and the number and arrangement of the masts. The following tables show these variations graphically, and list the most important terms.

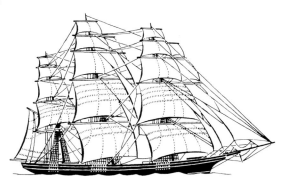

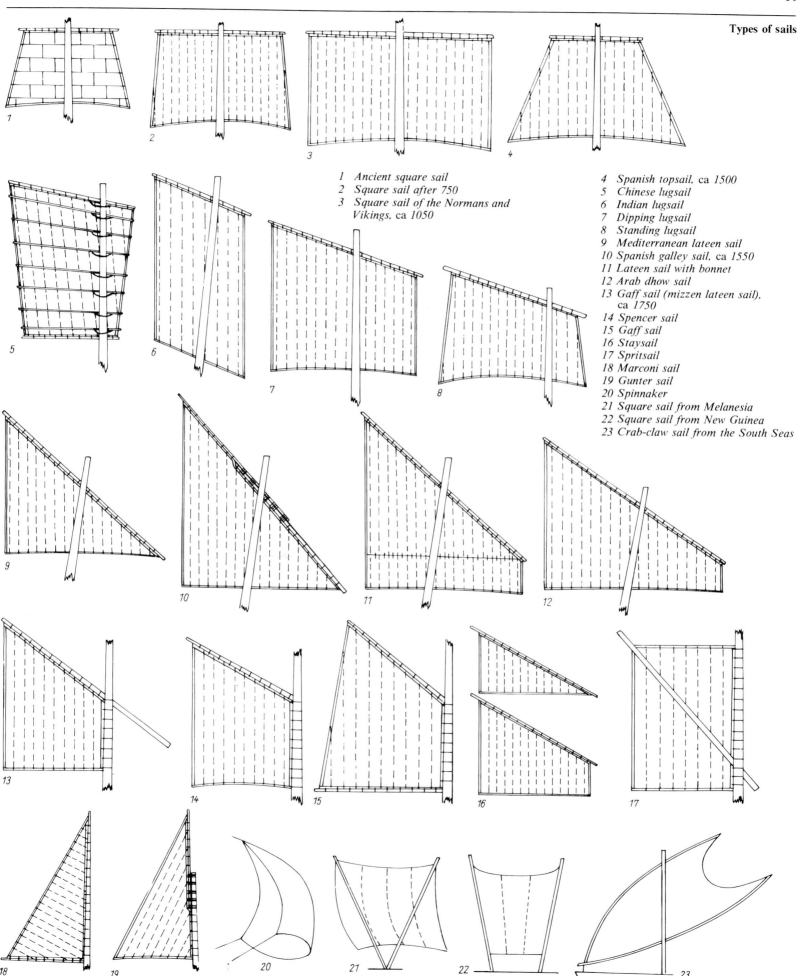

1 Ancient square sail
2 Square sail after 750
3 Square sail of the Normans and Vikings, ca 1050
4 Spanish topsail, ca 1500
5 Chinese lugsail
6 Indian lugsail
7 Dipping lugsail
8 Standing lugsail
9 Mediterranean lateen sail
10 Spanish galley sail, ca 1550
11 Lateen sail with bonnet
12 Arab dhow sail
13 Gaff sail (mizzen lateen sail), ca 1750
14 Spencer sail
15 Gaff sail
16 Staysail
17 Spritsail
18 Marconi sail
19 Gunter sail
20 Spinnaker
21 Square sail from Melanesia
22 Square sail from New Guinea
23 Crab-claw sail from the South Seas

Two-masters and three-masters

1 Brig
2 True brigantine
3 Hermaphrodite brig or brigantine
4 Snow
5 Two-masted two-topsail schooner
6 Two-masted topsail schooner
7 Two-masted fore-and-aft schooner
8 Two-masted staysail schooner
9 Full-rigged ship
10 Three-masted barque
11 Three-masted barquentine

Three-masters and four-masters

1 *Three-masted jackass barque or 'polka-barque'*
2 *Three-masted topsail schooner*
3 *Three-masted fore-and-aft schooner or 'Tern'*
4 *Three-masted staysail schooner*
5 *Four-masted full-rigged ship*

6 *Four-masted barque*
7 *Four-masted barquentine*
8 *Four-masted jackass barque*

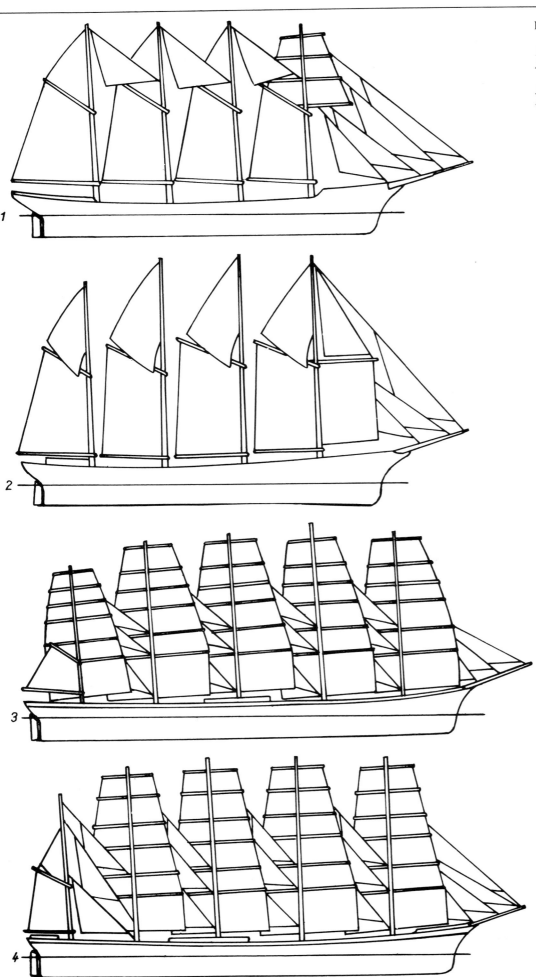

Four-masters and Five-masters

1 *Four-masted topsail schooner*
2 *Four-masted fore-and-aft schooner with square foresail*
3 *Five-masted full-rigged ship*
4 *Five-masted barque*

Five-masters

1 *Five-masted barquentine*
2 *Five-masted two topsail Vinnen schooner*
3 *Five-masted gaff-rigged schooner*

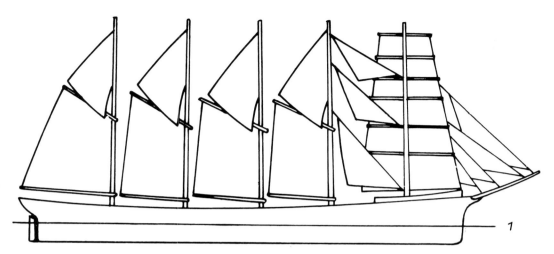

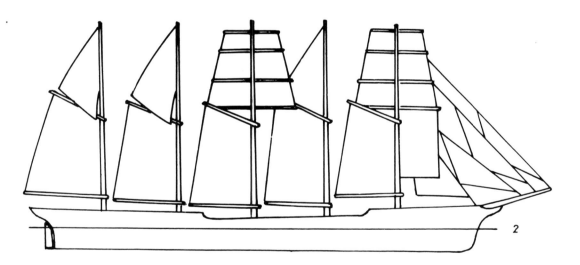

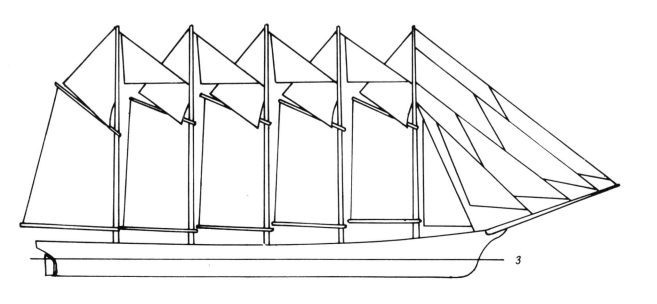

Mast names from the two-master to the six-master

a Brig
b Brigantine
c Two-masted gaff-rigged schooner
d Two-masted staysail schooner
e Three-masted barque
f Three-masted full-rigged ship
g Three-masted barquentine
h Three-masted gaff-rigged schooner
i Four-masted barque
j Four-masted full-rigged ship

k Four-masted gaff-rigged schooner
l Five-masted barque
m Five-masted gaff-rigged schooner
n Five-masted full-rigged ship
o Six-masted barquentine
p Six-masted gaff-rigged schooner

1 Foremast
2 Mainmast
3 Mizzen mast
4 Mizzen mast
5 After mast

6 Middle mast, also Laeisz mast on five-masted full-rigged ship
7 Jigger mast
8 Driver mast

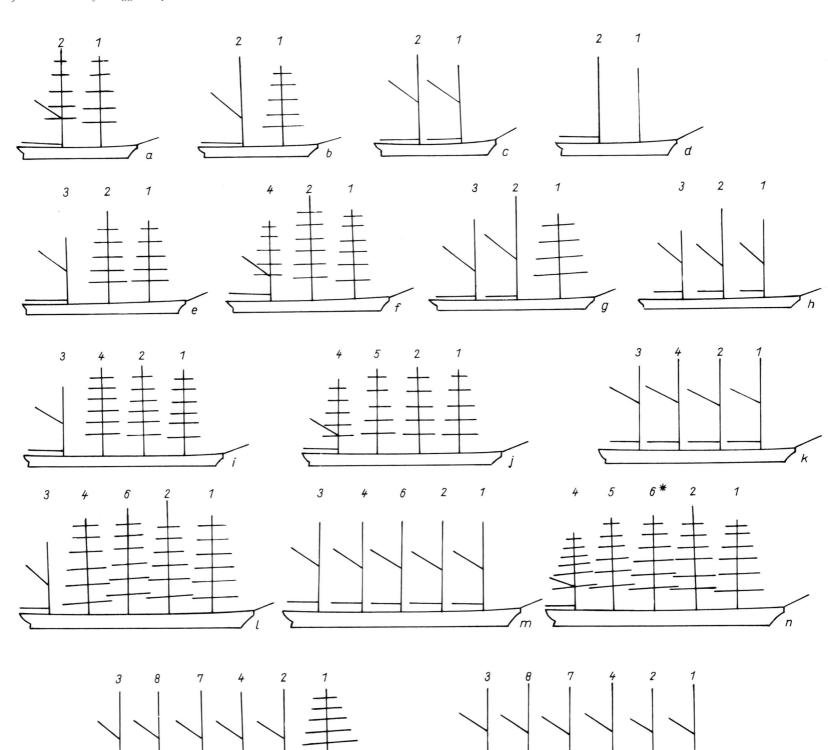

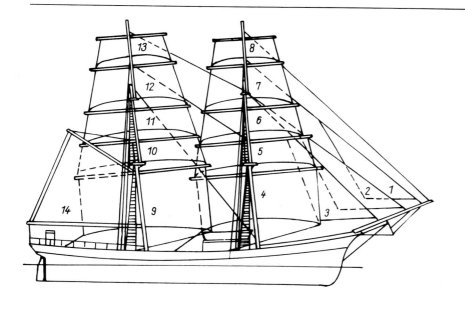

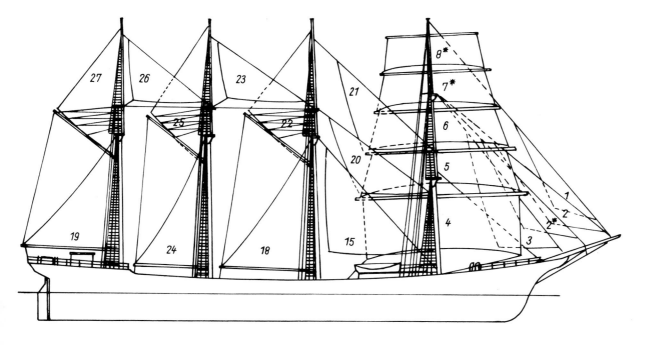

Sail names

BRIG

1 Outer jib
2 Inner jib
3 Fore topmast staysail
4 Foresail
5 Fore lower topsail
6 Fore upper topsail
7 Fore topgallant sail
8 Fore royal sail
9 Mainsail
10 Main lower topsail
11 Main upper topsail
12 Main topgallant sail
13 Main royal sail
14 Spanker or brig-sail

THREE-MASTED STAYSAIL SCHOONER

3* Fore staysail
15 Main staysail
16 Foresail
17 Mizzen staysail
18 Mainsail
19 Mizzen sail

FOUR-MASTED BARQUENTINE

2* Inner jib
7* Fore lower topgallant sail
8* Fore upper topgallant sail
20 Middle staysail
21 Main topmast staysail
22 Main gaff topsail
23 Mizzen topmast staysail
24 Mizzen
25 Mizzen gaff topsail
26 Jigger topmast staysail
27 Jigger gaff topsail

Sail names of a full-rigged ship

1 Outer jib
2 Jib or inner jib
3 Fore topmast staysail
4 Fore topgallant studding sail
5 Fore topmast studding sail
6 Fore lower studding sail
7 Fore royal sail
8 Fore topgallant sail
9 Fore topsail
10 Foresail
11 Main royal staysail
12 Main topgallant staysail
13 Main topmast staysail
14 Main royal sail
15 Main topgallant sail
16 Main topsail
17 Mainsail
18 Mizzen topgallant staysail
19 Mizzen topmast staysail
20 Mizzen royal sail
21 Mizzen topgallant sail
22 Mizzen topsail
23 Crossjack
24 Spanker
25 Outer jib tack
26 Foot
27 Sail seams
28 Outer jib sheet
29 Luff
30 Cringle
31 Leech
32 Downhaul
33 Outer jib halyard
34 Gaskets
35 Yard arm
36 Fore royal buntline

37 Leech
38 Foot
39 Clew
40 Fore topgallant buntline
41 Fore topsail reef tackle
42 Fore topsail buntline
43 Leech line
44 Foresail buntline
45 Outer jib-sheet pendant
46 Outer jib-sheet
47 Gaskets
48 Reef band with reef
49 Reef point
50 Reff-tackle cringle
51 Head of fore royal sail
52 Fore royal brace
53 Fore topgallant brace
54 Fore topsail brace
55 Foresail reef tackle
56 Foresail brace
57 Main tack
58 Fore sheet
59 Main royal staysail sheet
60 Main topgallant staysail sheet
61 Main topmast staysail sheet
62 Main royal buntline
63 Main topgallant buntline
64 Main topsail buntline
65 Leech line
66 Main buntline
67 Main royal brace
68 Main topgallant brace
69 Mizzen royal brace
70 Mizzen topgallant brace
71 Main topsail brace
72 Main topsail reef tackle
73 Downhaul
74 Mizzen topgallant staysail sheet

75 Main brace
76 Mainsail reef tack
77 Mizzen topmast staysail sheet
78 Main sheet
79 Mizzen royal buntline
80 Gaskets
81 Mizzen topgallant buntline
82 Mizzen topsail brace
83 Gaskets
84 Mizzen topsail reef tackle
85 Head of spanker
86 Peak
87 Mizzen topsail buntline
89 Crossjack reef tackle
90 Leech line
91 Spanker reef
92 Spanker sheet
93 Foot
94 Crossjack buntline
95 Crossjack sheet

Rigging of a full-rigged ship

1 Fore royal stay
2 Fore topgallant stay
3 Jib halyard
3a Main royal stay
4 Forestay
5 Main topgallant stay
6 Footropes
7 Flagmast with truck
8 Royal truss
9 Peak
10 Royal yard
11 Footropes
12 Lift
13 Fore royal topmast
14 Fore royal brail
15 Fore royal halyard
16 Topgallant truss
17 Hand ropes
18 Peak
19 Fore topgallant yard
20 Footropes
21 Fore brace pendent
22 Fore topgallant brace
23 Fore royal sheet
24 Fore brace block
25 Fore topgallant lift
26 Fore topgallant topmast
27 Fore topgallant cap
28 Fore topgallant shrouds
29 Fore topgallant masthead
30 Fore topgallant halyard
31 Cross-trees
32 Topgallant trestle trees
33 Backstay outrigger
34 Cheeks
34 Barrel truss

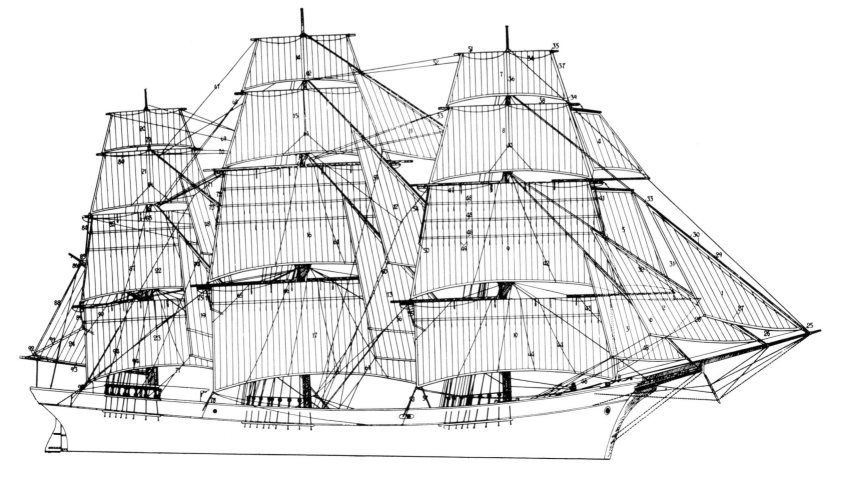

36 Hand ropes
37 Fore topgallant brail
38 Studding sail iron
39 Fore topgallant studding sail spar
40 Flemish horse
41 Peak
42 Reef tackle block
43 Brace pendant
44 Footropes
45 Fore topsail yard
46 Stirrup
47 Fore topgallant sheet
48 Reef tackle
49 Brace block
50 Fore topsail lift
51 Topsail brace
52 Tye
53 Topmast shrouds
54 Fore topmast
55 Cap
56 Carrier
57 Mantle
58 Masthead
59 Fore spreader
60 Trestle trees
61 Cheeks
62 Futtock stave
63 Futtock shrouds
64 Hand ropes
65 Foresail lift
66 Fore topsail brail
67 Studding sail iron
68 Studding sail spar
69 Peak
70 Reef tackle block
71 Flemish horse
72 Reef tackle
73 Brace pendant

74 Brace block
75 Stirrup
76 Fore yard
77 Footropes
78 Fore topsail sheet
79 Truss band
80 Truss
81 Reef tackle
82 Fore brace
83 Foremast
84 Stay cleats
84a Main topmast stay
84b Mizzen royal stay
84c Mainstay
84d Mizzen topgallant stay
85 Fore mast partners
86 Fore royal brace
87 Sling
88 Outhaul
89 Fore topmast backstay
90 Fore topgallant backstay
91 Fore royal backstay
92 Fore topsail halyard
93 Top tackle
94 Runner
95 Standing part
96 Hauling part
97 Fore clew-garnet
98 Pendant
99 Main masthead with main royal
     yard
100 Main royal topmast
101 Main topgallant yard
102 Main topgallant topmast
103 Main topgallant studding sail boom
104 Main topsail yard
105 Main topsail brace
106 Main topmast

107 Main topsail clewline
108 Mainsail lift
109 Truss of mainyard
110 Main yard
111 Main topmast studding sail boom
112 Main topsail sheet
113 Main brace
114 Main clew-garnet
115 Main royal brace
116 Main royal clewline
117 Main topgallant spreader
118 Main topgallant clewline
119 Main topgallant brace
120 Main topsail
121 Main topsail halyard
122 Ratline
123 Sheer pole
124 Deadeye
125 Deadeye lanyards
126 Mainmast
127 Mizzen royal brace
128 Mizzen royal clewline
129 Mizzen royal topmast
130 Mizzen topgallant brace
131 Mizzen topgallant mast
132 Mizzen topgallant clewline
133 Mizzen topgallant spreader
134 Mizzen topsail brace
135 Mizzen topsail clewline
136 Crossjack lift
137 Mizzen top
138 Crossjack brace
139 Jaws with throat halyard
140 Crossjack yard
141 Crossjack clew-garnet
142 Mizzen topmast stay
143 Mizzen stay
144 Main topmast backstay

145 Main topgallant backstay
146 Main royal backstay
147 Mizzen topsail sheet
148 Mizzen mast
149 Chain plates
150 Channel
151 Mizzen masthead with truck
152 Mizzen royal yard
153 Mizzen topgallant yard
154 Monkey gaff
155 Flagline
156 Mizzen topmast yard
157 Spanker gaff
158 Peak
159 Spanker outhaul
160 Peak halyard
161 Flagline
162 Vang
163 Topping lift
164 Mizzen topsail halyard
165 Spanker boom
166 Mizzen topmast backstay
167 Mizzen topgallant backstay
168 Mizzen royal backstay
169 Spanker sheet
170 Brace bumpkin

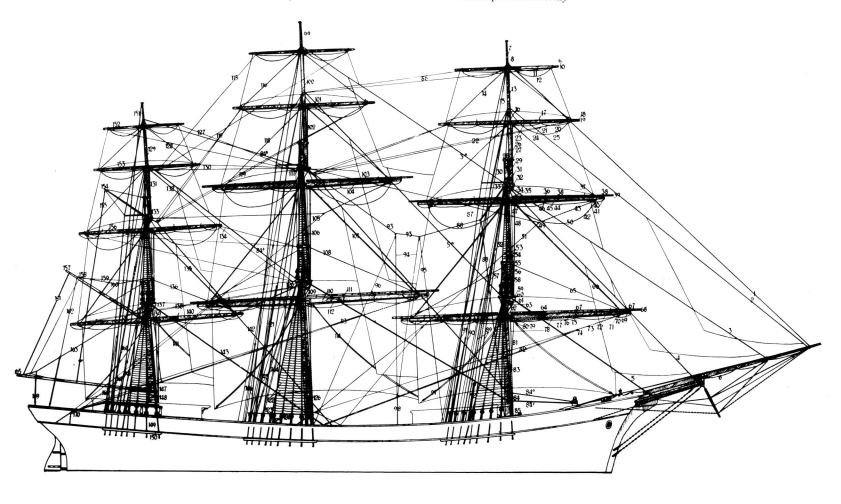

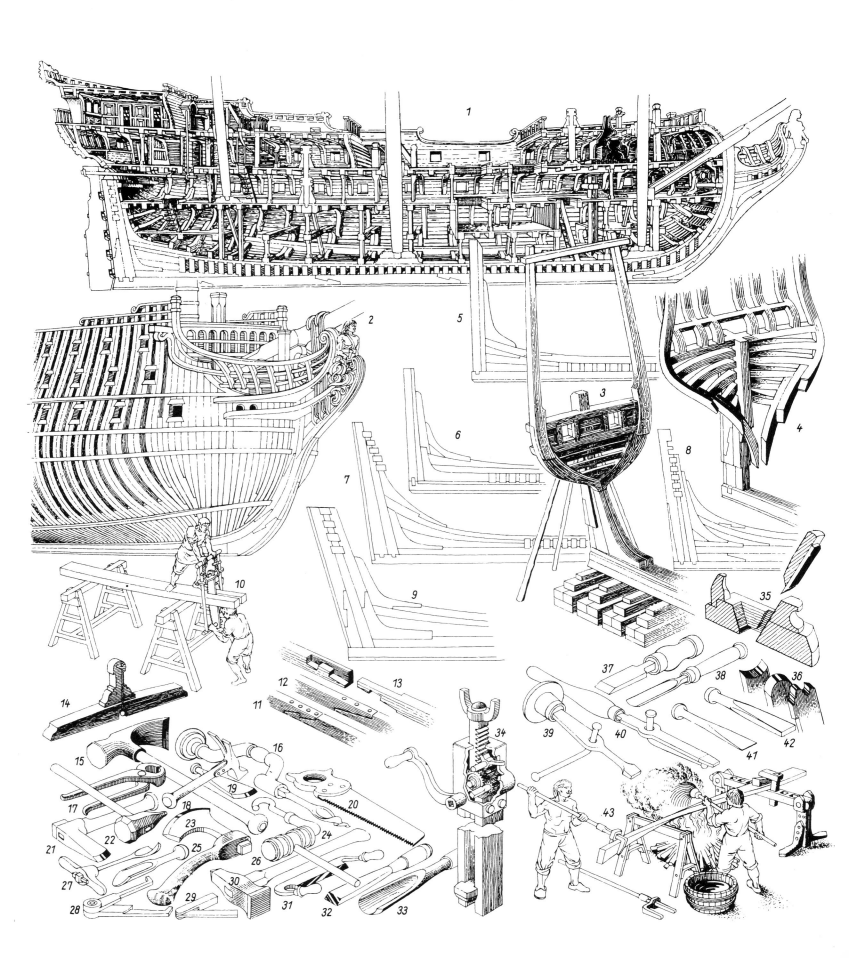

Wood shipbuilding II

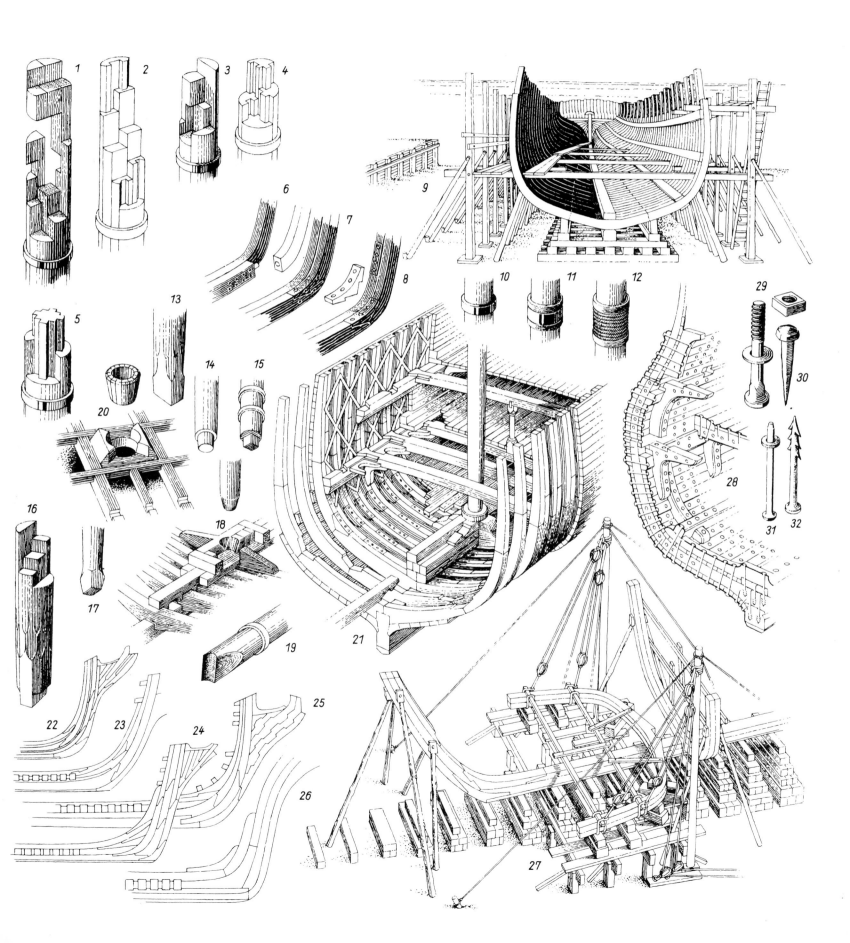

Wood shipbuilding I

1	Fore-and-aft section through an eighteenth-century frigate
2	Bow of a first-rate ship of the line, framed up
3	Stern and transom formation of a square-sterned ship
4	Counter timbers, transom timbers and hawse pieces for transom timbers and filing pieces
5–9	Stern forms
10	Sawyers at work
11–13	Hook scarphs for joining beams and planks
11	Lock scarph
12	Standard scarph
13	Lock scarph
14	Level for checking the horizontal
15–42	Tools, measuring instruments, jigs
15	Adze
16	Dutch brace and bit
17	Pincers
18	Claw hammer
19	Caulking iron
20	Handsaw
21	Swedish hammer-axe
22	Hammer
23	Carpenter's hand axe
24	Oakum hook
25	Small gouge for marking hole positions
26	Caulking hammer
27	Drill
28	Dividers
29	Angle protractor
30	Punch hammer
31	Draw knife
32	Chisel
33	Large gouge
34	Rack and pinion jack
35	Plane, longitudinal cross-section
36	Various forms of plane blade
37	Chisel
38	hallon gouge
39, 40	Screwdrivers
41	Cold chisel
42	Rebate chisel
43	Carpenters bending a plank

Wood shipbuilding II

1–5	Construction of made masts
1, 3	First half seventeenth century
2, 4, 5	First half nineteenth century
6–8	Assembling frames
6	Eighteenth-century method
7	Hook scarph
8	Early method showing butt-chocks
9	Stocks and jigs in eighteenth–nineteenth centuries
10–12	Methods of clamping made masts
10	Iron rings
11	Combination of iron and wood rings
12	Combination of wood rings and woolding
13–17	Various forms of mast tenon and socket
18	Mast tenon and mast socket, partly dismantled
19	Mast tenon of bowsprit
20	Mast junction consisting of: mast beams, half-beams, mast blocks, with ring of wedges at deck level
21	Hull of a wooden clipper
22–26	Stem forms
27	Setting up the frames
28	Assembling an eighteenth-century ship using nails, bolts and rivets
29	Bolt with nut
30	Spike
31	Rivet with spreader washer
32	Barbed spike

Ships' guns

1	English design of carriage, dismantled, with quoin
2	68-pounder
3	Breech loader, 1585, from a Danish artillery manuscript
4	Culverin, sixteenth century
5	Arrangement of on deck gun
6	Arrangement of breech tackle of cascabel; top: English method, bottom: French method
7	24-pounder, first half seventeenth century
8	Galley gun on mount, sixteenth century
9	Breech loading swivel gun (with separate chamber piece), fifteenth century, Tower of London
10	Mount for a galley gun, 1697, after Pâris
11	Swivel gun with chamber piece
12	Mortar on rotating bed
13	Gun bed for a mortar on a bomb ketch
14	Gun lashed down for heavy weather, English-type carriage
15	Thirteenth-century sperber. [sparrow hawk]
16	Swedish gun with accessories, ca 1630
17	Half-port vertically hinged
18	Half-port horizontally hinged
19	Wreathed gunport, seventeenth century
20	Various gun types: Greek fire, chain shot, rod shot, etc.

Ships' guns

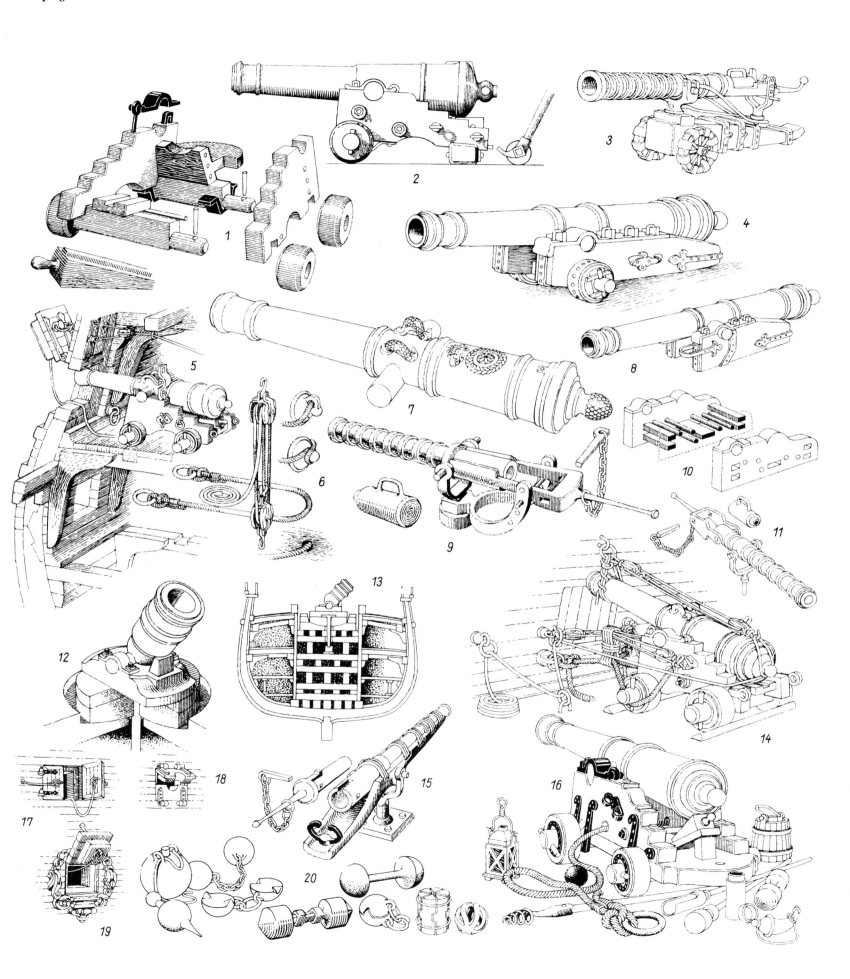

Ships' equipment I: capstans, knots, blocks

1	*Windlass, seventeenth and eighteenth century*
2	*Pump capstan, nineteenth century, dismantled*
3	*Anchor bitts, Dutch, ca 1690*
4	*Anchor bitts, French, ca 1690*
5	*Bitts on the forecastle deck, topsail halyard bitts*
6	*Bitts with pin rail, eighteenth-century French warship*
7	*Sheave timber, ca 1690, for the running rigging of the jib and spritsail*
8	*Small English capstan*
9	*Capstan with barbotin ring to engage chain*
10	*Dutch capstan, early seventeenth century*
11–14	*Knots*
11	*Type of fisherman's hitch*
12	*Reef knot*
13	*Overhand knot*
14	*Stopper knot*
15	*Single sheet bend*
16	*Clove hitch*
17	*Double sheet bend*
18	*Slip knot*
19	*Two half hitches*
20	*Midshipman's hitch*
21	*Toggle*
22	*Anchor bend*
23	*Figure-of-eight knot*
24	*Bowline*
25	*Reef laced with single line*
26	*Reef laced with two lines*
27–29	*Cringles on sail leeches*
27	*Cringle up to ca 1600*
28	*Cringle with thimble*
29	*Simple rope cringle*
30	*Double block with iron stop*
31	*Belaying a rope with a by-the-wind-hitch*
32	*Procedure for belaying to a belaying pin*
33	*Shroud cleat*
34	*Staghorn for mainsail halyard in section*
35	*Kevel for foresail sheet*
36	*Cat block with iron reinforcement*
37–40	*Eye bolts*
37	*Eyebolt with nut*
38	*Eyebolt with split pin*
39	*Old form of threaded eyebolt*
40	*Modern form of eyebolt with baseplate*
41	*Snatch block*
42	*Pelican hook*
43	*Peak cringle*
44	*Sheet block with cleat and double hook, twentieth century*
45	*Single-sheave stropped block with groove*
46	*Simple snatch block with strop rove through*
47	*Snatch block with external hook, nineteenth century*
48	*Lift block*
49	*Viol block, seventeenth century*
50	*Euphroe*
51	*Single-sheave block with double strop and thimble*
52	*Oval stay block*
53	*Three-sheave viol block with external bail and pointed thimble.*
54	*Triple block*
55	*Double block with grooves for double strop*
56–58	*Forms of clew*
56	*Served clew; boltrope encloses a thimble*
57	*Clew with external strop*
58	*Clew with ring*
59	*Bowsprit of an eighteenth-century warship, with jibs and spritsails, and appropriate standing and running rigging*

The Dutch flagship Amelia *before the Dutch-Spanish sea battle of 1639 in the Downs off Dover.* National Maritime Museum, Greenwich.

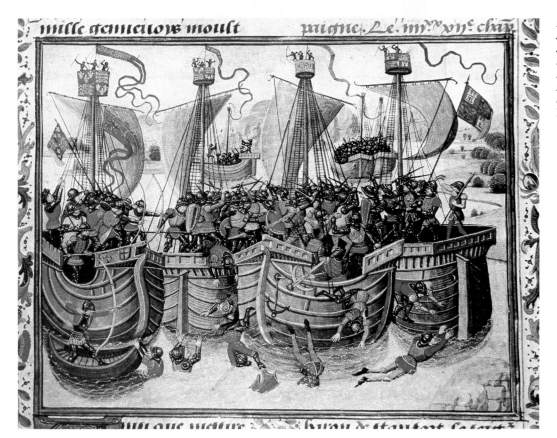

Page from the Chronicle of the French miniaturist Jean Froissart, showing the battle near Sluys on 24th June 1340 between the English and French fleets at the beginning of the hundred years' war (1339–1440). The single-masted ships have a deck and castle-like superstructures fore and aft. In these ships, elements of the Norman ship, the nef and the cog are combined. Bibliotheque National, Paris

Grosser Adler von Lübeck (1566), a sixteenth-century Hanseatic four-master, (model). Rostock Maritime Museum

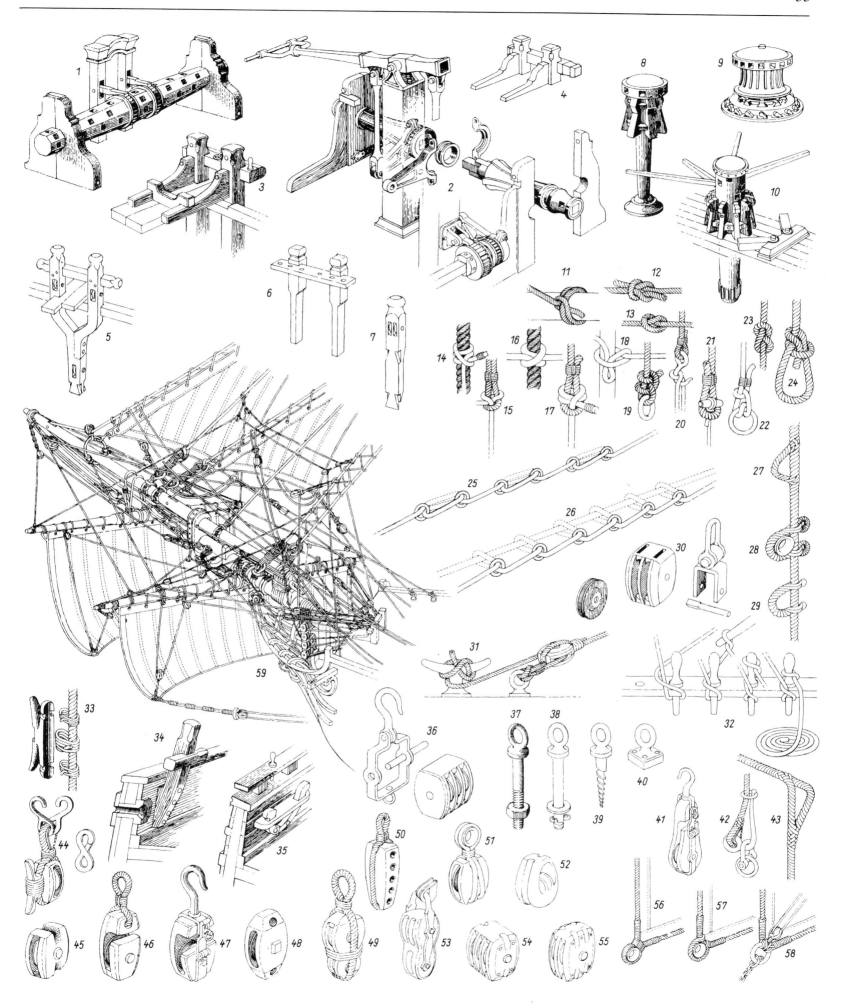

Ships' equipment II: halyards and parrels

1   English type of halyard, seventeenth-century version; rove over cheek block
2   Topsail yard tie of 1650; a hauling part runs downward
3   Topsail yard tie of 1650; standing part below
4   Masthead with cap and topmast, English
5   Swedish cap, ca 1630
6   Dutch cap, seventeenth century
7   Cap, French type
8   Topgallant halyard, English
9   Centre section of yard: cleat for tie
10   Centre section of an English yard, early nineteenth century
11   Variant on halyard attachment
12   Spanker halyard
13   Mast of a seventeenth-century ship, with sheathing and mast cheeks
14   Heel of a topmast, with sheave for heavy tackle and fid
15   Belaying the topmast yard halyard
16   Tie and halyard, French type, seventeenth and eighteenth centuries
17–23 Chain plates for shroud deadeyes
17   Chain plate, sixteenth century
18   Chain plate, ca 1660, Dutch
19   Chain plate, after 1670, English
20   Chain plate of an eighteenth-century barque
21,22 Nineteenth- and twentieth-century chain plates
23   Reinforcement for chain plate (channel iron)
24   Centre section of yard, late nineteenth century
25–34 Parrels
25   Truss with hinged band
26   English method of attaching parrel on lower masts
27   Mizzen parrel with block, for lateen yard
28   Simple topmast parrel
29   Parrel for spritsail yard and upper spritsail yard
30   Simple parrel for topgallant and upper topgallant yards
31   Patent truss for lower yard on an iron mast
32   Truss parrel on a lower yard, with three rows of ribs with trucks
33   Chain parrel
34   Truss with sleeve, for upper topmasts

Ships' equipment III: tops and stays

1   Stay crow's foot with euphroe and tackle for setting up the stays, sixteenth and seventeenth centuries
2   Top, 1630–50
3   Top, 1600–20
4   Top, 1600–1700
5   Top, ca 1700
6   Top, fourteenth and fifteenth centuries
7   Foretop, 1700–1800
8   Top, 1670
9   Top with curved crosstrees, seventeenth century, northern Europe
10   Fore lower mashead, Dutch, ca 1630
11   Clipper top, 1870
12   Nineteenth-century spreader, with outriggers to guide the running rigging rising from the deck
13   Topmast stay eye on a late nineteenth-century sailing ship
14   Mast cheeks, trestle trees, crosstrees, seventeenth century English
15   Maintop (partial cross-section), and main masthead, Dutch ca 1630
16   Top of a French frigate, 1780
17   Crosstrees of an eighteenth-century barque
18–24 Staysail lacing methods
18   Wooden stay runners or cringles
19   Lacing using a running line
20   Simple iron stay runners
21   Stay runners similar to carabiners
22   Stay runners similar to split shackles, open and closed
23   Runners with metal springs
24   Simple double hook
25–27 Devices for setting up the stays
25   Deadeyes
26   Blocks, sixteenth and seventeenth centuries
27   Hearts
28   Method of fixing the mizzen stay to the mainmast
29   Method of fixing the mainstay to the deck, nineteenth and twentieth centuries
30   Method of fixing the main topmast stay to the foremast
31   Method of fixing the mizzen topmast stay to the main topsail eye
32   Fore topmast stay, pre-1600
33   Fore topmast stay, Dutch, ca 1600, with crow's foot and euphroe
34   Fore topmast stay, English, ca 1690
35   Fore topmast stay, Danish, ca 1650

Ships' equipment IV: sheets, braces, brails, lifts

1   Upper topsail sheet
2   Lower topsail sheet
3   Square sail sheet, seventeenth century, bulwark omitted at kevel position
4   Square sail sheet, eighteenth century, section through hull wall at the sheave position
5   Lower sail sheet
6   Sheet block for sail with bonnet
7   Fore brace
8   Lower topsail brace
9   Bowline bridles
10   Leech lines, continental form
11   Buntlines
12   Topsail clewline
13   Footropes, stirrups fixed to the jackstay on this nineteenth-century yard
14   Lower sail clew-garnet
15   Lacing a square sail, using robins
16   Lacing a lateen sail with running rope
17   Tack; section through the bulwark at the tack hole position
18   Lateen sail brails
19   Topping lift of a mizzen yard with crow's feet
20   Jib sheet (always double)
21   Lifts, Dutch, seventeenth century; the hauling part runs over a sheave in the yard arm sheet block; English method, eighteenth century
22   Lifts, nineteenth and twentieth centuries
23   Old form of two-part lateen yard
24   Simple yard arm cleat
25   Yard arm wth roller guide to studding sail spar
26   Topsail yard peak on old ships
27   Made lower yard, seventeenth century
28   Yard arm with studding sail boom iron
29   Yard arm with roller for studding sail boom

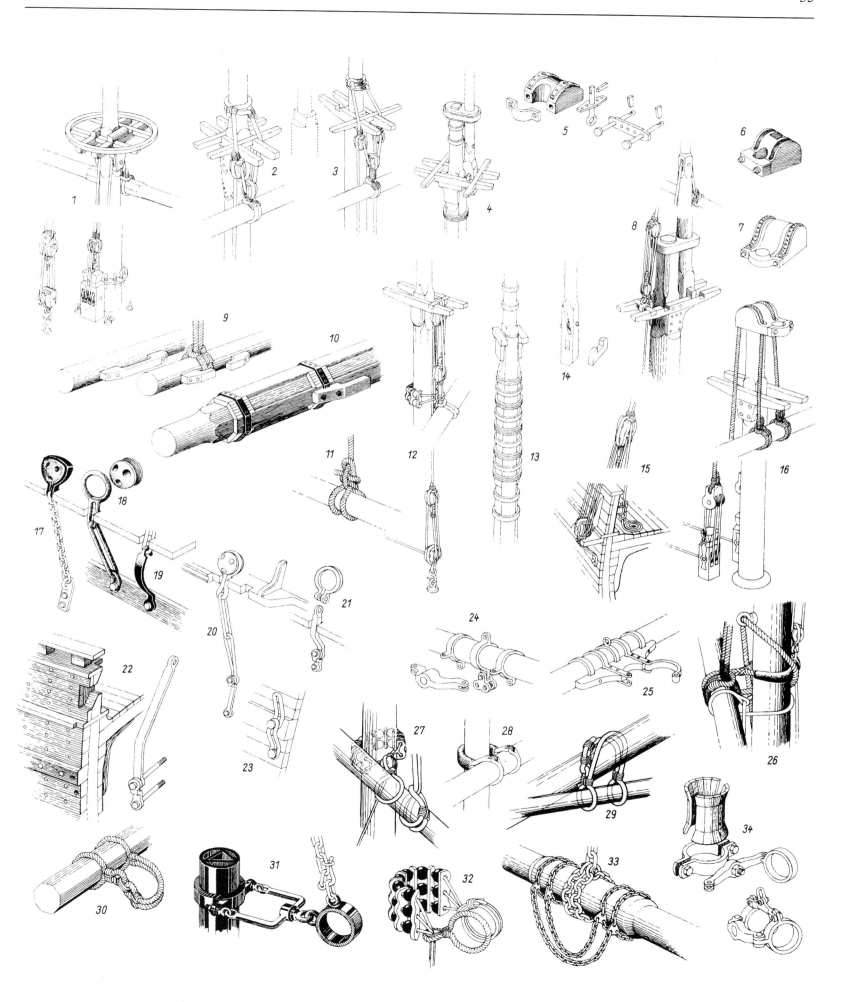

Ships' equipment III: tops and stays

Ships' equipment IV: sheets, braces, brails, lifts

A

AAK, *aake*: A ketch-rigged sailing cargo ship used from the Middle Ages to the end of the nineteenth century for river and coastal transport. Aaks varied regionally in size and construction. In the main they were used on the rivers Rhine (Rhine-aak), Maas (Maas-aak) and Lahn (Lahn-aak), to transport the wine produced in the vineyards of those areas. To cope with the conditions encountered in river and coastal work, they were flat-bottomed, generally had no keel, and featured a less full hull shape than other northern sailing cargo ships. The hull was initially built of timber, but was later of composite wood and steel construction. This ship type often had a very noticeable sheer. Smaller aaks were mostly open, while larger ones were decked. The Steven-aak differed from other forms in that its stem and stern were reminiscent of a clipper. The aaks usually had leeboards. The vessels were built in German, Dutch and Belgian yards, depending on where they were to be used (eg the Dorsten aak in Dorsten an der Lippe, the Brabanter aak in Brabant, the Hasselt aak in Hasselt in Belgium). A Kahn-aak, or barge aak, displacing 240 tons was 40m long and 6m wide. The mainmast was 24m long, and the gaff up to 20m long, while the sail area was around 420m². Aaks were also built with steel hulls after wood had been superseded by steel as the principal ship-building material.

AB-GOOZAR: A ferry boat used on the Ganges river in Hindustan around 1800.

ACATIUM: A shallop or boat used by pirates in ancient times.

ACCOMMODATION SHIP: a ship used for the temporary accommodation of ship's crews. The rules obtaining in the majority of navies prohibited the crew of a ship staying on

Acropolis relief

Large kahn aak ca 1900

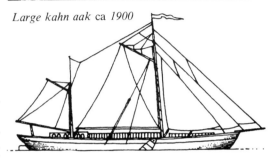

board when it was being fitted with cannon, fitted out in the arsenal, or during a period in dock.

ACON: A flat-bottomed boat for mussel fishing in Gascony (southern French coastal region in the southern part of the Garonne basin), which has been in use since the eighteenth century.

ACROPOLIS SHIP RELIEF: A representation of an Attic trireme dating from between the sixth and fourth centuries BC. The

surviving portion of the stone bas-relief was discovered and salvaged by Lenormand from the ruins of the Acropolis in Athens in 1852. This historically valuable relic is today in the Louvre.

ACTUARIA NAVIS: A fast, low freeboard, shallow draught, oared sailing ship of the ancient Romans, with up to 30 oarsmen. Because of its manoeuvrability and shallow draught this ship type was best suited to fairly short coastal journeys in the Mediterranean; its particular task was to transport troops, and more rarely horses and war equipment. The low freeboard limited the vessel's stability as a warship, but some actuariae were fitted with a bow ram, and were used for acts of piracy, exploiting their high speed and manoeuvrability.

ACTUARIOLUM: A small Mediterranean vessel mentioned by Cicero, fitted with oars and sails. They were built in large numbers and were still in use in Genoa in the sixteenth century.

Dutch aak ca 1800 *(model)*

Adler von Lübeck, a sixteenth-century Hanseatic four-master (model)

Admiralty yacht, late eighteenth century

Dutch aviso, late eighteenth century

ADLER VON LÜBECK, *Der Grosse Adler von Lübeck*: One of the great four-masted ships of the sixteenth century. The ship was known as the Lübscher Adler, and is mentioned in various contemporary sources under different names. She was a large ship in comparison with the vessels preceding her. The fore- and mainmasts were square-rigged, while the mizzen and jigger masts carried lateen sails. The *Adler von Lübeck* was originally laid down in 1565 as a warship, and launched in March 1566. Her dimensions were as follows: length of keel 62 Ells (36m), length from stem to stern 85 Ells (49m), length from the figurehead to the gallery lll Ells (64m), inboard beam 48 feet (13.84m), height of the stem 24.5 Ells (14.13m) height of the stern 20 Ells (11.55m), height from keel to sternboard 37.5 Ells (21.50m). The subdivision of the masts was an innovation for the sixteenth century. When assembled, the lower mast, the topmast, the topgallant topmast and flagstaff of the mainmast stood 108 Ells (62.15m) above the keel. The main yard was 57 Ells long (34m), several times longer than the ship's beam. The armament, comprising 122 small cannon and the wartime complement of over 1000 men became an embarrassment after the signing of the peace treaty in 1570. The ship was then transferred to a commercial shipping consortium. Accordingly, the ship's very high superstructures were cut down by 4m, but she proved too complex for a cargo vessel, however, and she was broken up in Lisbon for her timbers.

ADMIRAL'S FLAGSHIP: *see* FLAGSHIP.

ADMIRALTY YACHT: A fast, yacht-like seventeenth-century sailing warship, flying a naval ensign and used for fleet command duties, transfer of orders, reconnaissance work, and also for fleet reviews. A few Admiralty yachts were fitted with leeboards for work in shallow coastal waters.

ADRYA: The Greek name for the Cypriot-built bark or boat made from a hollowed-out tree trunk, and still in use in the eighteenth century.

Stern gallery of a Dutch warship ca 1650

ADVICE BOAT, *aviso, abiso, advieso*: A small, fast sailing ship of yacht-like appearance used for carrying dispatches and orders, and also for patrol work and reconnaissance. (French 'avis', Spanish 'aviso': news, information). In the transitional period from sail to steam this ship type remained fully rigged but was also fitted with paddle wheels. After the propeller had been introduced, the yacht-like design was retained along with the name aviso, although the ships were then built much larger, and used in particular for duties abroad.

AFTER: A medium-sized towed Weser kahn, or barge, dating from the mid-nineteenth carrying about 50 tons. The terms achterhand and hinterhand were also commonly used for these vessels.

AGEN BOAT: see ARGEN BOAT.

AGGUB: A heavy, single-masted, flat-bottomed sailing craft with a square sail, used exclusively for carrying stone on the Nile. The vessel survived into the nineteenth century.

AGITAKI: An eighteenth-century term for the canoes used in great numbers in the East Indian Archipelago for communal fishing.

AKTOS: An ancient term for a small boat.

ALBENGA SHIP: The remains of a Roman trading ship dating from the first century BC. Fishermen working close to the port of Albenga in the Gulf of Genoa repeatedly brought up ancient amphorae from the sea bottom in their trawl nets. Archaeological research and salvage work on the wreck, which lay in 42m of water, began in the 1960s. The work was carried out by divers working from a

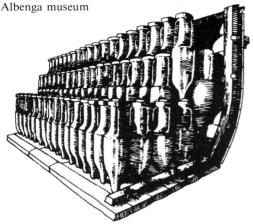

Albenga ship, reconstruction of amphorae storage, Albenga museum

Alster schuten in Hamburg canal ca 1890

diving bell, a salvage ship and a floating crane. The vessel's cargo had consisted entirely of amphorae. Although virtually nothing remained of the ship's hull, it proved possible to reconstruct a section of the cargo hold with some certainty. From the dimensions of the amphorae and the surviving components of the cargo hold, and also from studying the method of stowing the amphorae, it was possible to estimate that the ship had been capable of carrying 4000 to 5000 amphorae, indicating a ship length of around 35m and a beam of 12m. Since many other ancient amphorae have been salvaged in the Mediterranean region, it has been possible to trace the the voyages of the sunken ships and to determine their age.

ALLÈGE: The French term for a lighter, which was used to lighten ships in the roadstead, and so allow them to proceed up river into port. Auxiliary boats carried on large river barges were also known as allèges.

ALLIGATOR: A type of boat used by North American timber raftsmen. The boats were equipped with winches and tackles.

ALS BOAT: see HJORTSPRING BOAT.

ALSACE KAHN, *Alsace barge*: A specialized nineteenth-century river barge, originally from the Alsace region, designed to cope with frequent passages through restricted locks. As the locks could only accommodate a ship length of about 35m and a maximum beam of 5m, the vessels were built rectangular with a beam of about 5m, and a total length of around 50m, divided into two hulls of equal length. The two sections of the barge were joined at the centre by chains. When a lock had to be negotiated which was shorter than the overall length of the two vessels, the connections were undone, so that the barge halves could be taken through one by one. To improve the control of such unwieldly vessels, the stern of the trailing barge was fitted with three rudders instead of a single long central rudder, which could not be accommodated by the short locks. The main rudder was fitted on the centreline, and a smaller rudder on each side of it.

Allège ca 1840

Ambatch raft on the upper Nile

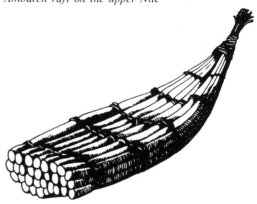

ALSTER SCHUYT: An open, flat-bottomed cargo barge, around 15 to 20m in length, with no means of propulsion, used for transporting persons, bulk goods, bales and packing cases around the Hamburg region. The Alster schuyt was propelled by a punt pole, or pulled along the canals and waterways with a pek rod.

ALTENLÄNDER JOLLE: A nineteenth-century open boat used mainly for transporting fruit and vegetables from Altenland to Hamburg.

AMBATCH RAFT: A small, boat-like raft made of the buoyant wood of the ambatch bush. The forward portion was bundled together to form an upward-curving bow, widening into a broader, trough-shaped mid section. It was very light in weight, but only suitable for fairly short passages, such as for fishing, because of the fairly rapid rate at which water was absorbed. Because of the high level of tannin in the wood, however, it was more resistant to rot than papyrus rafts. Such rafts were used on the upper Nile, and are still found in Angola.

AMMONIA: Ancient Greek ships, mentioned around 425 BC, which were used for cult/religious or state ceremonial purposes.

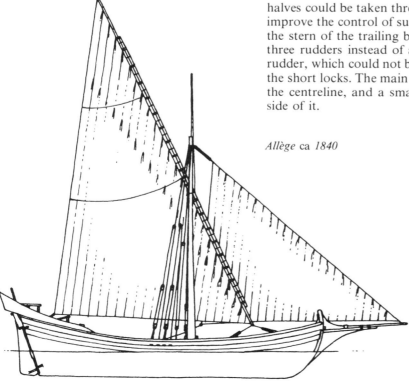

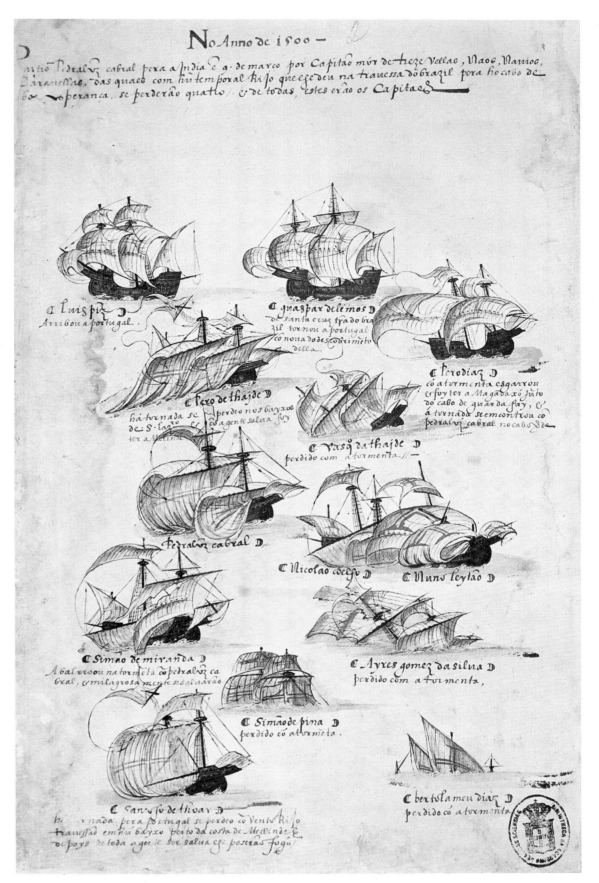

Pictorial table from the Livro das Armadas *by the Lisbon Academy of Science, showing the 12 ships of the Portuguese expeditionary fleet, which sailed to India under Cabral on 9th March 1500, after Vasco da Gama had discovered the sea route. Five of the ships were wrecked.* Horacio de Sousa, Lisbon

East Indiaman Oostrust, *Amsterdam, 1721 (model)*

Painting by Antoine Roux 1801. The Bella Aurora, *a Greek polacre with slender hull, hybrid rig and lowered topsail yards, off Marseille.* Jos Mel, Marseille [1]

Reconstruction of the Santa Maria, *1492, flagship of Colombus*

AMPHIDROME, *ámphiprora*: Eighteenth-century sailing ships whose hull and rigging were arranged in such a way that they could sail in both directions without having to go about. The hull was of very similar shape underwater at bow and stern, and a rudder was fitted at both ends. Corvettes were sometimes built as amphidrome ships for special purposes.

ANAN: A birch bark boat up to 8m long, still used around 1900 by Tierra del Fuego Indians. Individual bark strips were sewn together using whalebone needles, and the joints were sealed with seaweed. A wooden gunwale was fitted over the frames, which were bound in place. *See also* BARK BOAT.

ANCHIROMACHUS: General term used in the Middle Ages for a fast, sailing ship with speedy hull form, said to have been used for carrying anchors and equipment to larger vessels.

ANCIENT EGYPTIAN SHIPS: *see* ANCIENT SHIPS OF EXTREME DIMENSIONS, CHEOPS BURIAL SHIP, DASHUR BOAT, SEWN SHIPS, HATSHEPSUT SHIP RELIEF, PEHENUKA RELIEF, SAHU – RE RELIEF and SAKKARA RELIEF.

ANCIENT GREEK SHIPS: *see* ACROPOLIS SHIP RELIEF, AMMONIA, DIER, MONER, NIKE STATUE and TRIER.

ANCIENT NORDIC SHIPS: *see* BJÖRKE BOAT, HJORTSPRING BOAT, KVALSUND SHIPS, NYDAM SHIP and STONE TABLET SHIP PICTURES.

ANCIENT SHIPS OF EXTREME DIMENSIONS: The dimensions and load-carrying of some special-purpose Egyptian and Greek ships far exceeded those of ordinary ships (120 to 200) tons) in common use even up to the early Middle Ages. These vessels provide clear evidence of early shipbuilding skills.

In the Ancient Egyptian burial temple of Queen Hatshepsut (around 1500 BC) at Deir el Bahari (Thebes) a representation of an obelisk transport ship was found. The original dimensions of this freight vessel were about 84m in length, 24m beam and 2600m³ displacement. This order of size was necessary to transport large obelisks, like the rough-hewn Syenite (reddish granite) obelisk found in a quarry at Syene (Aswan); this was 41.7m long, 4.2m in breadth, and had a mass of 1168 tons. According to contemporary reports, a water-filled trench was dug under at right-angles to the obelisk, so that either a single ship or two ships close together could be manoeuvred under the stone block. In order to achieve the required draught, the carrier ships were loaded with stone ballast beforehand, the

mass of which was greater than that of the obelisk to be raised. After the stone ballast had been removed, the buoyancy of the hull would raise the obelisk. Historical sources also indicate that specially large ships were built for transporting elephants several centuries before Christ. These strongly built open ships had to be broad enough, and of sufficiently shallow draught, to allow easy loading and unloading of the animals, and to allow the vessels to navigate shallow coastal waters.

The Greeks also built large ships. Around 250 BC the Macedonian army chief, Ptolemeus, is said to have built a mighty oared ship with rows of 40 oars, the vessel being 124m long with a beam of 17m. *See also* TESSACONTER.

One of the most famous of these large ancient ships was developed by the Greek mathematician, engineer and shipbuilder Archimedes of Syracuse in 230 BC. The Greek writer Athenaois reported that Archimedes designed and supervised the construction of the giant ship *Syracusia* as a gift for the Egyptian king Ptolemeus Philadelphus, commissioned by King Hieron II of Syracuse (306 – 215 BC). This vessel was said to be 180m long, and 31m broad. As wood was virtually the sole shipbuilding material at this time, these gigantic dimensions are almost unbelievable. The ship's hull, divided into several decks, is said to have had eight five-storeyed battle towers. In the centre of the ship there was a giant statue of a god with a large burning-mirror, which was intended to set distant targets on fire. The ship was equipped with two large catapults which could hurl lumps of rock weighing 75kg a distance of 150m; there were also a number of smaller

ballistae catapults. There was a space on board the ship for 3000 soldiers, 4000 oarsmen and a large number of horses. Guests of high standing were housed and entertained in luxuriously appointed dining halls, libraries and kitchens with fish ponds. The giant ship was said to be able to carry a cargo of more than 2600 tons. The load was stated as 60,000 keramia (around 1320 tons) of grain, 10,000 keramia (around 220 tons) of salt meat in barrels, 20,000 talents (around 524 tons) of wool and 20,000 talents (around 524 tons) of other goods. The ship's boat, towed behind the ship, as was customary, was said to have a load capacity of about 80 tons. As the ship was too large for any Sicilian and Italian ports, it can be assumed that Alexandria was intended to be the vessel's permanent base from the outset.

Another 'giant ship' with a length of 128m, a beam of 17m and a height of 22m was built as a state ship by the Egyptian king Ptolemeus Philopater (231–204 BC). The dining hall and apartments were said to have been fitted out with scarcely imaginable splendour, decorated with ivory and rare hardwood carvings. This pleasure vessel, built solely for celebrating glorious occasions, was a tessaconter, ie a ship with rows of 40 oars.

The Greek writer Lucian (AD 165) has provided us with information on the Egyptian wheat-transporting sailing vessel *Isis*. This sailing ship is said to have carried out regular voyages between Alexandria and Rome. According to Lucian, the ship was 55m long, 14m wide, 13.3m high and displaced more than 1200 tons.

The pleasure ships built by order of the Roman Emperor Caligula (AD 37–41) for use on Lake Nemi were also unusually large for

Representation of a rowing boat on one of the bas reliefs on Angkor temple

the time at 70m long and 17.5m broad. One of these ships was a state houseboat, known as Thalamegi by the Romans. It was fitted out like a palace, with columned halls, luxuriously decorated dining halls, temples, sleeping apartments, and artistically laid out gardens and ponds. *See also* LAKE NEMI SHIPS.

ANGKOR BOAT RELIEF: A relief on the southern gallery of the ruined temple at Angkor showing a boat in an eleventh-century naval battle between Cham and Khmer. Angkor Wat, in Kampuchea, not far from the border with Thailand, is one of the oldest and most famous historical sites in the Far East. The ruins of this Buddhist temple of pilgrimage feature numerous inscriptions, and provide glimpses into a great past. One relief shows a large dragon boat, carrying 26 oarsmen and a helmsman, the later operating the side rudder at the stern, as well as a number of soldiers wielding weapons.

ANGNLA: A Sri Lankan double boat, whose two identical hulls are linked by a connecting platform. Large versions have an arched roof formed by a woven mat. It was used principally as a ferry.

ANTUNG TRADER: One of the two basic types of northern Chinese junk (the other being the PECHILI TRADER). It was flat-bottomed and flush decked with a bluff bow and stern and considerable sheer fore and aft

and about 21m in length. For two-thirds of its length ran a high hatch coaming giving access to its hold. Built of Fukien pine, it was strongly constructed, having 12 closely spaced bulkheads extending from the bottom to the main deck. It hoisted a foresail, a mainsail and two light mizzen sails. Like most Chinese junks (a few examples from Kwangtung being the only exceptions), there was no standing rigging, the masts being stepped into straight-sided tabernacles.

APHRAKTE SHIPS: Ancient Greek open, oared ships of an earlier design (pre-fifth and fourth centuries BC), which were only fitted with a narrow central strip of deck (gangway); the oarsmen's seats on both sides of the ship were left uncovered. Later designs developed from the aphrakte ships included the KATAPHRAKTE ships.

ARBE: An ancient Adriatic ship type.

ARK: A box-shaped ship, whose name comes from the latin arca meaning box. Noah's Ark is the famous example. According to the Bible, this was built by Noah before the great flood, to save his family and all species of animals. According to tradition the ship was built of cypress wood. The ark was said to be 300 Hebrew Ells long and 30 Ells wide and high, of three-storey construction and with many chambers, sealed inside and out with pitch. The dimensions are quite realistic in

shipbuilding terms, as demonstrated by the Scottish merchant, Livern, who built a copy of it in 1694.

ARGEN BOAT, *agen boat*: A simple vessel used for east Friesian coastal fishing. It was box-shaped with a swim-headed bow, and was about 5m long and 2m wide. It was propelled by sweeps.

ASKE: An oared boat used in the Frankish empire and the Anglo-Saxon kingdoms from the fifth to the ninth centuries. The aske was probably a dugout made of oak (aske meaning 'esche', the German for oak), with gunwhales added. The crew were called askenmen.

ÄSKEKÄRR SHIP: The remains of a Viking ship dating from around 800 AD, found in 1933 near Äskekärr to the north of Gothenburg on the Göta river in Sweden. The vessel was accurately dated, but it proved impossible to preserve or restore the remains.

ASLAMKA: A single-masted river cargo ship used on the lower Volga and the Caspian Sea in the mid nineteenth century. The rig consisted of a tall, narrow square sail, with shrouds attached half way up the mast. The ship measured about 10 to 12m at the waterline, and had a transom stern and quite strongly raked stem.

ASPING: *see* ESPINK

ATTIC TRIER: *see* TRIER.

AVISO: *see* ADVICE BOAT.

Medieval picture of the building of the ark from Weltchronik *(World History) by H Schedel, 1493*

BAARTZE, *baardse*: A Dutch sailing ship with one to three masts plus auxiliary oars (up to 40 oars), which existed from the fourteenth to the sixteenth century. It had a virtually identical bow and stern, similar to an early cog.

BACHOT: French term for a small river ferry. The ferryman is called the bachoteur.

BAGGALA, *baghla*: A two-masted Arabian dhow used as a fishing vessel, freight carrier and warship, displacing between 100 and 400 tons, in use from the end of the sixteenth to the nineteenth century. A few ships of this type even survived into the mid-twentieth century. The baggala carried settee sails on the mainmast and a small mizzen mast. The hull featured rounded frames and a sharply raked, projecting prow, which accounted for up to one-third of the ship's length. The stern superstructure was fitted with windows, galleries and balconies and decorated with carvings and bright paintwork. On warships and pirate ships the carronades (light cannon without recoil-absorbing carriages) were set up on deck. The bulwarks were pierced by gunports. In order to emphasize the threatening appearance, a second row of false gunports was often painted on the hull sides. Guns could not be set up below deck, however, because of

A baleinier lowering of one its boats. Painting by F G Roux, ca 1850

the low freeboard. Similar Arabian craft differing in size, included the SAMBUK, PATTAMAR and GHANJA.

BAGGALOW: The Maldivian term for a KOTIA.

BAIDA, *baidarka*: A nineteenth-century, ferry boat carrying 10 to 12 persons, used on the River Don. The vessel's bow and stern curved gently upwards, so that it could be run up onto river banks. The boat was propelled by punt pole or sailed with a form of lateen sail set on a long angled spar mounted on a short mast.

East Siberian baidara

BAIDARA: The Russian term for an open eskimo boat of the Koryaks of eastern Siberia, similar to the UMIAK.

BAIKAK: A type of wooden inland cargo barge of around 20m length, as used on the Dniepr around the middle of the nineteenth century. The baikak was steered either by a long, shallow rudder or very long steering oars. The vessels had either one or two masts, which were variously gaff-, square- or spritsail rigged.

BAKINKA: A high-sided, two-masted cargo ship working on the Volga and the Caspian Sea in the mid-nineteenth century.

BALEINIER: French term for a sailing whaler, which carried small whaleboats onboard.

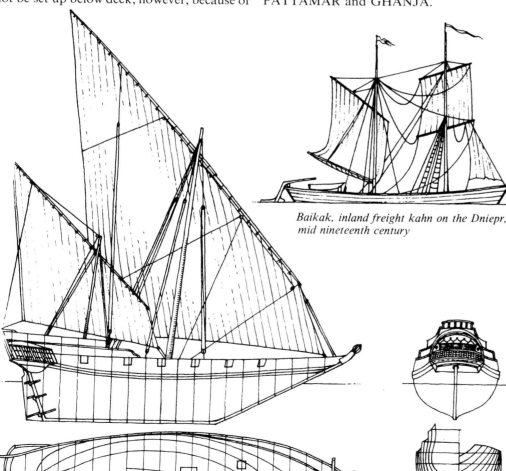

Baikak, inland freight kahn on the Dniepr, mid nineteenth century

Early nineteenth-century bagalla in the gulf of Oman

BALINGER: A sailing ship used for a variety of purposes by the Hanseatic League and other northern nations in the fifteenth century, especially in the North Sea. Its cargo capacity was around 160 tons. This ship type was frequently used as a whaler, and sometimes also as a warship.

BALLANTRAE BOAT: A clinker-built boat with steep, upward-curving stem and rounded stern from the west coast of Scotland at the end of the nineteenth century for fishing on the Ballantrae Banks.

BALLAST LIGHTER: Broad, flat-bottomed lighter, used mainly for loading and unloading ballast. Sailing ships required extra ballast to achieve adequate stability when lightly loaded. Whenever possible this ballast took the form of bulk goods, such as bricks, pit coal, chalk, salt or fertilizer. Loose ballast had the advantage that it could be distributed evenly throughout the cargo holds, but it did call for additional measures to prevent the cargo shifting. Ideally, the ballast took up as little space as possible, so as not to soil the cargo holds. Ballast which shifted easily, such as sand, and combustible and fusible materials, were only used as a last resort. Stones were the most common form of coarse ballast, but worn-out cannon, cannon balls and other old materials were also pressed into service. Later, purpose-made cast-iron pigs weighing up to 50kg each were used.

The ballast was taken to the sailing ships by small vessels, which came alongside the ships and transferred the ballast via small ports above the waterline, known as ballast ports. The harbour authorities always had to be vigilant to prevent excess ballast from the ships being simply dropped overboard, resulting in a steady reduction in available depth of water. For this reason the authorities designated special areas outside the port limits where the ballast vessels could take on or transfer ballast. On the continent special versions of ewers and schuyts were used for the carriage of ballast.

BALONE: A luxurious river ship used in Indo-China (especially Burma, Thailand, Laos) from the seventeenth to the nineteenth century. Its bow and stern were richly decorated, and there was a kind of covered throne in the central area. The ship's length could be up to 30m. The term balone also applied to long slim, oared boats from Siam with a tower-like superstructure. These balone were said to be made from a single tree trunk, and were very light in weight. The French priest Choisy reported in 1685: 'all these balone were clad in gold leaf, and had very finely worked, heavily gilded bells. There were 60 oarsmen on each side, working with small, gilded oars, all of which moved up and down together in rhythm.'

In Burma, honoured guests were received on gilded balone and heavily decorated barks similar to the balone. These splendid ships were embellished with many brightly-coloured mythical beasts from Burmese legends. Some balone were also built without oars or sails. These vessels were towed by several rowing boats, themselves up to 15m long, in which the oarsmen stood, using a special rowing technique. The development of the balone was presumably influenced by the development of the Chinese DRAGON BOAT.

BALOR, balour: One of the larger pirate ships of the Moluccan region, armed with 6- to 8-pounder bow and stern chasers plus a few cannon on the ships' sides. The balor could carry up to 300 armed men. These large pirate ships were generally accompanied by smaller boats, known as piahiaps, which the pirates used as landing boats for plundering on shelving coastlines.

BALSA: Light, buoyant vessels and boats made of clay, animal skins, reeds and rushes by the south American Chimu tribe (north Peruvian coastal civilization of the pre-Inca period). The balsa was sometimes so small that the sailor sat astride it. At the other extreme they could be large enough for the Spanish conquistadors to transport their horses on them. The smaller vessels were called caballitos (sea horses) by the Spanish. Excavations have discovered pictures of caballitos, also commonly called huampu, on drinking vessels dating from the ancient Peruvian period. Larger vessels were made from the Totora reed, on a similar principle to the ancient Egyptian papyrus rafts. According to the pictures on drinking vessels, the ends of the balsa were bound together to form a kind of double stem/stern arrangement. Bundled reed boats (totora), fitted with mast and sail, are still in use today on lake Titicaca. Larger balsa were also used to form floating bridges. Until 1857 a floating bridge consisting of many reed rafts was situated at the influx of Lake Titicaca, over which vehicles could travel. The individual rafts were bound to each other, and covered with a dense grass mat. The bridge was maintained by replacing some of the rafts every two years. The American copperplate engraver G Squier made a drawing of this pontoon bridge in 1875 shortly before it was destroyed.

Balsa reed bundle raft on Lake Titicaca

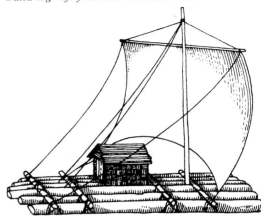

Balsa log raft from the Peruvian coast

BALSA RAFT, balse: A Peruvian tree-trunk raft fitted with a sail and sometimes a deckhouse. On the coasts of Peru, rafts made of the wood of the balsa tree were built and used for coastal travel by the indigenous indians centuries before the discovery of America. The wood of this tree, which grows in the humid tropical forests of Ecuador, is less than a sixth the weight of other timbers. The raft was generally constructed of an odd number of dried trunks lashed together in two or more layers, with a simple palm leaf-covered deckhouse, a mast carrying a rectangular sail and a hearth. In 1947, the Norwegian researcher T Heyerdahl built a balsa raft following the ancient pattern, which he named the Kontiki after an indian sun god. The raft consisted of nine trunks of unequal length (greatest length around 13.5m) surmounted by a second layer about 8m long set at right-angles. He wanted to establish whether it would have been possible to sail from east to west 1500 years earlier, and thus found settlements. This he set out to do by undertaking the voyage from the west coast of South America to the Polynesian islands. On 28 April 1947 the vessel left the port of Callao, close to the Peruvian capital of Lima, with a crew of six men, and, using the Humboldt current, landed 101 days and 4300 nautical miles later on one of the Tuamotu islands. In 1970, the Frenchman E de Bischop undertook an equally successful voyage from Ecuador to Australia with a similarly constructed balsa raft.

BALTIC EWER, ever: see EWER.

BALTIMORE SCHOONER, Baltimore clipper: A type of SCHOONER developed around Baltimore, in the Chesapeake Bay area of the USA); the first vessels were built about the beginning of the nineteenth century with a tonnage of 90 to 200 tons and a hull of particularly slender form and very sharp waterlines, all aimed at increasing speed. The sloping keel (draught deeper aft than forward), flat floor with marked deadrise, a V-shaped mid-section instead of the usual rounded or U-shaped form, marked out this vessel as a major step forward in the evolution of the first sailing

Baltimore schooner, sheer draught plan

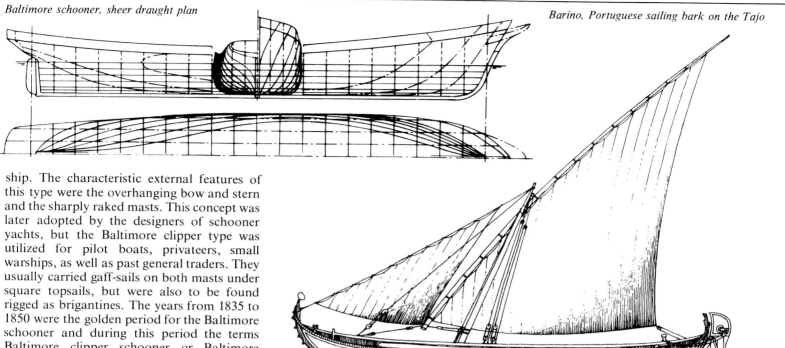

Barino, Portuguese sailing bark on the Tajo

ship. The characteristic external features of this type were the overhanging bow and stern and the sharply raked masts. This concept was later adopted by the designers of schooner yachts, but the Baltimore clipper type was utilized for pilot boats, privateers, small warships, as well as past general traders. They usually carried gaff-sails on both masts under square topsails, but were also to be found rigged as brigantines. The years from 1835 to 1850 were the golden period for the Baltimore schooner and during this period the terms Baltimore clipper schooner or Baltimore clipper also came into use, though they were not related to the china or tea clippers, except in their emphasis on speed.

BALUK, *caïque*: A light and fast oared boat used in Turkish waters into the 19th century for personnel transport. The vessel was propelled by up to six standing oarsmen.

BAMBOO RAFT: A raft consisting of bamboo stems lashed together, and found principally in Southeast Asia. *See also* TEK-PAI.

BARCANE, *barcone*: A two- or three-masted fishing sailing ship of the Mediterranean, around 20m long. The term is a derivative of the Italian barca.

BARGE: This term has been used in a variety of closely-related forms over the course of the history of shipbuilding. It was initially applied to a European oared boat with powerful wales (specially reinforced upper strakes). In the eleventh century, the names of bardinn, and later bargiea, bardza and barsa evolved. Around 1350 a bardze was a boat with 12 thwarts. In English Hanseatic documents

dating from 1403 there is reference to bargea, bargiza and bardisa as different types of boat. In the fifteenth century, the barga was a Mediterranean ship's boat. In the sixteenth century, small warships of around 100 tons were termed barges. In the eighteenth century, the captain's personal boat, with eight to 12 oars, carried on board English warships was termed a barge. Later a barge was a larger oared boat, usually only carried on flagships, for the use of admirals and their staff. The same term was used in France for flat-bottomed general-purpose river barges with sail and oars, of 7 to 10m length. The Thames barge is a flat bottomed sailing vessel with leeboards, setting foresail, spritsail mainsail and topsail, often with a spritsail jigger. Nowadays, this term is used generally for dumb lighters and transport vessels, which can also be carried as units of cargo on special lighter transport ships known as barge carriers.

BARINO: A river barge of around 20m in length and up to 4m wide, which was used up to the beginning of the twentieth century on the River Tagus (Portugal). It carried a lateen sail or a lugsail on a short, raking mast.

BARKAROLE, *barcarole:* A small Mediterranean rowing boat used for pleasure jaunts; it could carry four to six persons, and was particularly popular in Italy (Venice). The name was also adopted for the songs of the Venetian gondoliers.

BARKE: A general term for small boats without sails used for centuries in the Mediterranean and on the Nile (Nile barke). The term can be traced back to ancient times (Greek barika, latin barca). At the end of the

Spritsail barge, late nineteenth century

nineteenth century small Sicilian boats used chiefly for sponge fishing were still termed barke. The term barke has been in use in the North Sea area since the fourteenth century, mostly for light, three-masted, flush-decked pirate ships with a cargo capacity of around 100 tons. This type of barke often featured two masts only: a large foremast and a smaller mizzen. In the Mediterranean, barkes were also used in war fleets, although as a rule they only operated as tenders, carrying a few signalling guns. *See also* STATE BARGE.

Three-masted barque Singapore, *built in Sunderland in 1864, 922 BRT*

Barketta, oared sailing boat

BARKETTA, *barquette, barquetta*: A fairly small oared sailing boat mostly encountered in the eastern Mediterranean. In French usage the barquette is generally a rowing boat used within the harbour. In the seventeenth and eighteenth centuries similar small boats were also used for fishing.

BARK BOAT: A common type of river boat built by forest tribesmen using local materials varying from the simplest possible form of vessel to those needing sophisticated constructional skills. Bark boats were paddled like dugouts, punted or sometimes even sailed. The basic material was tree bark cut in complete half-round shells. Several pieces of bark were sewn up at the ends, using prepared roots, vegetable fibres or leather thongs, and the seams sealed with resin, asphalt or other waterproof substances. *See also* SEWN BOAT.

The American indian tribes in the north of the continent used the bark of the pine and the

fir, while the indians who settled further south preferred birch bark. Indians of Hudson Bay and Labrador also built boats of birch bark, sewn with prepared split pine roots, the seams sealed with resin. We know that the Iroquois built their artistically constructed boats from elm bark. The bow and stern portions of the indian boats curved upward when the bark was pulled together, and this shape became the pattern for modern Canadian canoes.

The bark boat was also commonly used in the northeast of Siberia between the Yenisei and the Ochotsk Sea, and also in the Amur region. There are certain design similarities with the North American bark boats, but the Siberian vessels were usually built with a stiffening of frames and stringers. They were sewn or bound together with woven osiers or willow.

A simple form of bark boat evolved in the Zambezi and Kuneno regions of Africa, and in the coastal areas of East Africa. On the coasts of Mozambique quite large bark boats were built, incorporating frames, thwarts, mast and sail. The original inhabitants of the island of Borneo also built boats of tree bark for use on the mountain streams, as did the aborigines of northwest Australia. The lightweight bark boats — one-man vessels made of birch bark weighing about 20kg — could be carried over land for long distances and also offered protection from bad weather.

BARK-KUFF: A hybrid ship type built in Holland at the beginning of the nineteenth century, combining the hull of a KUFF with the rig of a three-masted barque (two square-rigged and one gaff-rigged mast).

BARQUE, *bark*: A sailing ship with at least three masts, of which only the aftermost mast (the mizzen mast) carried fore and aft sails, the

remaining masts being square-rigged. The three-masted barque was especially common. Additional fore and aft sails could be set between the foremast and the bowsprit and between the fore- and mainmasts. The matching of sail area to hull side area (area of the projected side of the submerged portion of the ship's hull — roughly length × depth) permitted more advantageous, full-bodied forward sections and more slender after sections. The three-masted barque became one of the most important types of ship in the northern European merchant fleets, especially for transporting goods over long distances, for which the BRIG had formerly been used. The origins of the barque rig stretch back into the fourteenth century, with the difference that the third mast then carried a lateen sail instead of a gaff sail. The undivided gaff topsail yards of the earliest true barques were later developed into divided topsail yards and divided sails, in the interests of simpler operation. The usual tonnage was between 240 and 600 tons.

This merchant ship was built in large numbers for it could be sailed reliably with a relatively small crew of 15 men, principally because of its simple sail handling. The later large sailing ships, including the clippers, were often cut down to barque rig in later life to save on crew size and maintenance costs.

At the end of the nineteenth century and the beginning of the twentieth century the development of the barque continued with the transition from timber construction to composite steel/timber construction. Composite construction, larger dimensions and greater tonnage led to that well known sailing ship of the final golden period of sail: the four-masted barque. These ships were up to 95m in length with a beam of 14m, displacing 3000 to 3400BRT and with a sail

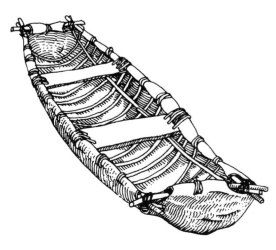

South American bark boat

Barque: sails and rigging of a three-masted barque (masts, yards and sails)

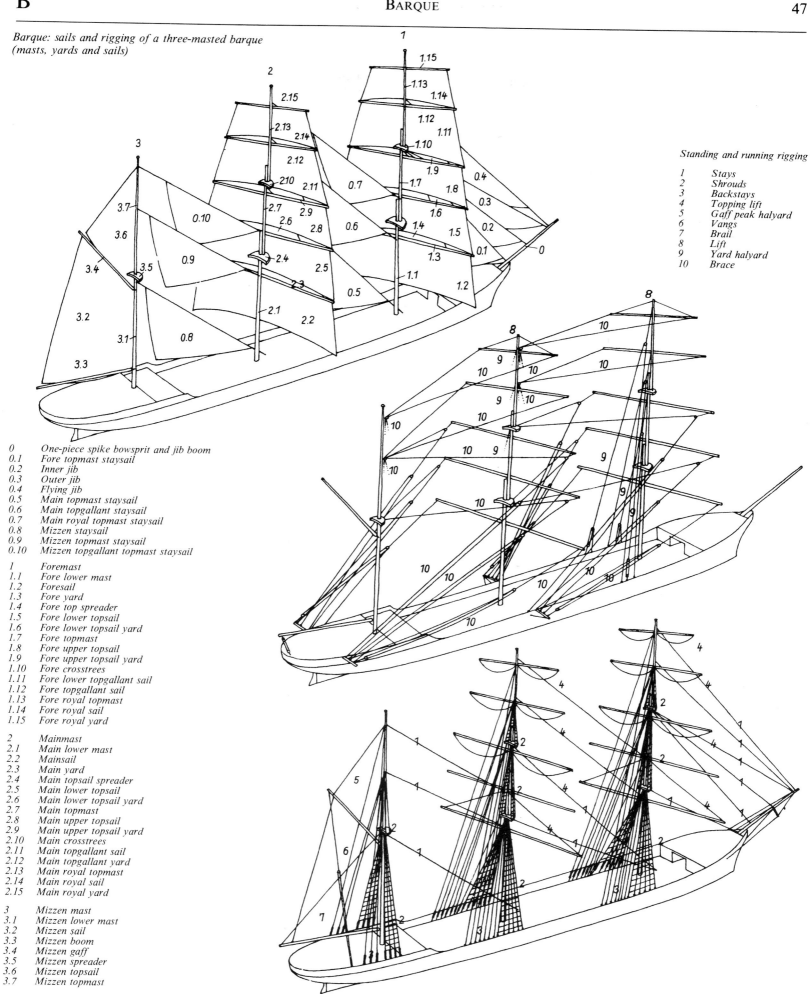

Standing and running rigging

1	Stays
2	Shrouds
3	Backstays
4	Topping lift
5	Gaff peak halyard
6	Vangs
7	Brail
8	Lift
9	Yard halyard
10	Brace

0	One-piece spike bowsprit and jib boom
0.1	Fore topmast staysail
0.2	Inner jib
0.3	Outer jib
0.4	Flying jib
0.5	Main topmast staysail
0.6	Main topgallant staysail
0.7	Main royal topmast staysail
0.8	Mizzen staysail
0.9	Mizzen topmast staysail
0.10	Mizzen topgallant topmast staysail

1	Foremast
1.1	Fore lower mast
1.2	Foresail
1.3	Fore yard
1.4	Fore top spreader
1.5	Fore lower topsail
1.6	Fore lower topsail yard
1.7	Fore topmast
1.8	Fore upper topsail
1.9	Fore upper topsail yard
1.10	Fore crosstrees
1.11	Fore lower topgallant sail
1.12	Fore topgallant sail
1.13	Fore royal topmast
1.14	Fore royal sail
1.15	Fore royal yard

2	Mainmast
2.1	Main lower mast
2.2	Mainsail
2.3	Main yard
2.4	Main topsail spreader
2.5	Main lower topsail
2.6	Main lower topsail yard
2.7	Main topmast
2.8	Main upper topsail
2.9	Main upper topsail yard
2.10	Main crosstrees
2.11	Main topgallant sail
2.12	Main topgallant yard
2.13	Main royal topmast
2.14	Main royal sail
2.15	Main royal yard

3	Mizzen mast
3.1	Mizzen lower mast
3.2	Mizzen sail
3.3	Mizzen boom
3.4	Mizzen gaff
3.5	Mizzen spreader
3.6	Mizzen topsail
3.7	Mizzen topmast

Barque: sheer draught plan

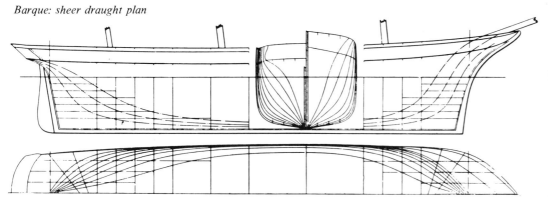

Barquentine Carl Max, *built in Rostock in 1873*

Five-masted barque Maria Rickmers, *1892. Length 115m, beam 14.5m, 3822 BRT. From a drawing by Arenhold.*

area of around 3000m². The four-masted barques of the 'Flying P' Line included the famous vessels *Pamir* (built in 1905, 3102BRT), and *Padua* (built in 1926, 2064BRT). The four-masted barques *Herzogin Charlotte* and *Herzogin Cecilie*, commissioned in 1900 to 1902 by Norddeutsche Lloyd for training purposes, were also good fast sailing vessels.

The first five-masted barques built in German yards were the *Maria Rickmers* (built in 1892, 3822BRT) and the *Potosi* (built in 1894, 4026BRT). The *Potosi* was one of the fastest sailing ships, and could log consistent speeds of more than 16 knots. Six-masted barques were built, but only in small numbers (only six ships can be traced).

BARQUE SCHOONER: *See* BARQUEN-TINE

BARQUENTINE, *barkentine*: A sailing ship developed around 1800, usually with three masts, and similar to the barque in size and construction. While the barque was rigged with square sails on the foremast, and a gaff sail on the mizzen, the barquentine carried square sails on the foremast only, the two remaining masts carrying fore and aft sails (gaff sails and topsails).

One variant of the barquentine carried two square sails and one gaff sail on the foremast and the mainmast. Because of this combination of top square sails and schooner-type gaff sail this hybrid was also known as a topsail schooner. Sicilian barquentines, which carried lateen sails on the two after masts, were termed vellaciers.

BARSE: A single-masted cargo ship used in the Weser estuary in the seventeenth and eighteenth centuries for laying out navigation buoys and other sea marks.

BATEAU, *batteau*: As well as being the French word for boat, this term is also applied to a number of craft in the Americas. The Canadian bateau was a lumberman's flat- and rocker-bottomed river boat, with flaring sides, marked sheer and raked stem and stern posts.

Such boats were rowed and ranged between 4 and 28m. It was possibly the ancestor of the DORY. On the Chesapeake Bay a bateau is a half-decked SKIPJACK. On the rivers of the Mosquito coast in Nicaragua a bateau is a dugout which has been split lengthwise and has had planks fastened between the two halves.

BATEL, *batil*: A dhow from the northwest coast of India, usually with only one mast, although large batels may also have a mizzen. It is an open boat, similar to a small SAMBUK. *See also* DHOW.

BATTELA: An Indian coastal and ocean-going dhow used for freight transport and fishing. The hull form of the two-masted, ocean-going Arab battela was similar to the small single-masted ZARUK. The mainmast has a marked forward rake (about 20°) while the mizzenmast is raked forward about six degrees. Settee sails are carried on the main- and mizzen mast.

The battela was used especially in the coastal region between Bombay and Karachi. Various Arabic and European influences are evident in this ship type, including the bowsprit configuration and the transom. *See also* DHOW.

BATOS: A narrow dugout used by the fishermen and hunters of northern Siberia and Kamchatka.

BAUMGARTH BOAT: A small, single-masted boat without oar or rudder fittings found on the Pomeranian Baltic coast at

Baumgarth boat

The Zeven Provincien *(centre, flying the Admiral's flag on the mainmast) under Cornelius Tromp in the sea battle off kijkduin on 21st August 1673, during the third Dutch – English war*

The Zeven Provincien, *the flagship of the Dutch Admiral de Ruyter (centre, flying red, white and blue flat) in the second Dutch – English war during the four-day long sea battle (1st – 4th June, 1666). Painting by Abraham Stork.* National Maritime Museum, Greenwich

Baltimore armed schooner Rambler, *built at Medford, Massachusetts, in 1812.* Peabody Museum, Salem

Barque Peter Suppicich, *Rostock, built by J H Wilken, Ribnita 1869, 442 RT.* Museumsheft, Rostock Maritime Museum

Bazaar caique from the Bosphorus

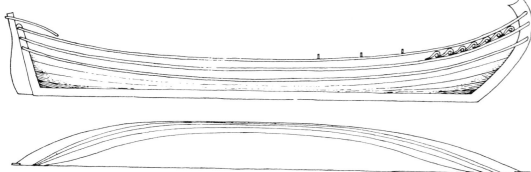

Bagart in 1899. The length of the boat was 11.90m, the beam 2.52m. It was a slender double-ended vessel, with pointed bow and stern. The construction was based on a keel, to which the strakes were fitted clinker-fashion. The frames were cut in a saw-tooth pattern to match the internal overlapping of the planks (a technique known as jogging), in similar style to the boat found at Kvalsund dating from the sixth or seventh century, to the ninth/tenth century Ladby boat, and the Kalmar boat from the thirteenth century. The strakes were rivetted to the frames and also along their edges. The boat's design is typical of Baltic vessels used in the tenth and eleventh centuries.

BAWLEY: A single-masted fishing boat, principally of the Thames estuary, which trawled for shrimps. The hull was broad-beamed with a vertical stem and a raking transom stern. Its tall sail plan was its most distinctive feature: the gaff mainsail was boomless, and above this on a long topmast, was set a large jib-headed topsail. A staysail, a jib and a number of other headsails were also carried. The bawley was around 12m in length.

BAZAAR CAIQUE: A large rowing boat used in the Bosphorus in the seventeenth and eighteenth centuries. Its primary use was for the transport of up to 30 persons, or appropriate quantities of goods to and from market.

BECASSE: A luxurious, highly decorated nineteenth-century Spanish barque boat with a strikingly high prow but no deck, especially common in the Cadiz region. The becasse had a single mast carrying a square sail. The vessel could also be rowed by up to 16 oars and was between 10 and 13m long, with a beam of up to 3m.

BELEM, *bellum*: A long, gondola-like oared boat used in Iraq for personnel transport. The stem and stern were coiled, like a snail shell.

BERGANTINE, *bergantin*: An Italian, seventeenth-century oared sailing ship, whose origins can be traced back to the thirteenth century. The ship was one of the smaller types of galley used for dispatch duties, propelled by up to 16 oars on each side, with one oarsman

per oar. In the sixteenth and seventeeth centuries a version evolved with two oarsmen per oar. The rig consisted of one mast with lateen sail.

BERGEN SHIP: The remains of various ancient Nordic and medieval ships, recently discovered in the old port area of Bergen in Norway. The majority of the finds date from the mid thirteenth century, as the Hanseatic League established a trading post there in 1278. Two of the shipwrecks are similar to the KALMAR BOATS. Various other wrecks are of uncertain classification. For the thirteenth century these are very large ships, with lengths of 26m and widths of 9m. Some historians claim that the vessels are those of Haakonsson. There is documentary evidence that this man had the famous 37-thwart ship *Kristsudin* or *Kristaudin*, built at Bergen in 1262 and 1263. An earlier ship, discovered in 1925 in a swamp near Möre, dates from around 800. A characteristic feature of this relic is that the strakes were worked exclusively with axe and adze; the tool marks are still clearly recognizeable. At that time the saw was not known in Nordic countries.

BERMUDA SLOOP: A single-masted late-seventeenth century sailing ship which, also known as a Jamaica sloop, was used mainly by pirates and smugglers in the waters around Jamaica. In Europe, the bermuda sloop survived until the end of the nineteenth century as a flush-decked boat around 20m in length with a reverse-raked stem and an extra-ordinarily long bowsprit which almost doubled its length. The mast, with pronounced rake, carried a large gaff sail, a big foresail, a gaff topsail as well as a staysail, jib and flying jib.

BERMUDIAN SAILING YACHT: A yacht setting a tall, triangular mainsail. Similar rigs, common around Bermuda, gained recognition in Europe in the first half of the twentieth century. Designers learnt from the triangular lateen sails on high-speed Mediterranean sailing ships, that mainsails with larger luff and leech would be more efficient, especially when sailing to windward, and this feature became more and more widespread on yachts which, in Europe, had retained their gaff rig into the twentieth century. On small boats the gaff rig with gaff topsail evolved into the gunter rig with its steeply angled upper spar, which is still encountered to this day, and the transition to the present-day bermudian mainsail was completed by extending the mast upwards, thus eliminating the gunter spar. The gunter rig was seldom used on larger vessels and on them there was a transition straight from gaff to bermudian rig. The famous Royal yacht, *Britannia*, began life as a gaff cutter but was given a bermudian rig in her later years. Ocean-going yachts with bermudian sails have taken part in racing since the late 1920s. In 1936, a race between Bermuda and

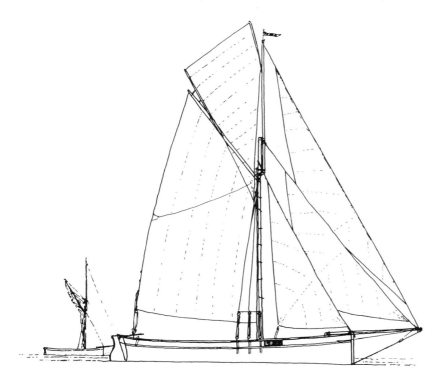

Bawleys in the Thames Estuary

the lightship *Elbe I* was held for yachts conforming to a special Bermuda measurement formula.

BESAN EWER: A ewer, fitted with a mizzen mast and leeboards, used for coastal work and fishing in the North Sea. The small ewer which was this vessel's predecessor had a single pole mast, and was known as the pfahlewer (pole ewer) or giekewer. Its successor, the besan ewer, which is known to have been built after 1849, had a second mast: the besan, or mizzen. The besen ewer carried a total sail area of about 170m². *See also* EWER.

Besan ewer rig: –1 Mainsail. –2 Staysail. –3 Jib. –4 Flying jib. –5 Mizzen. –6 Main gaff topsail. –7 Mizzen gaff topsail.

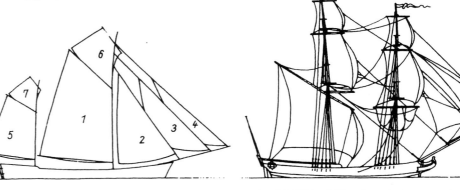

Bilander, mid eighteenth century

BILANDER: *billander*: A two-masted, flat-bottomed merchant ship similar to the brig, which was built widely in Holland, Sweden and England for transporting goods in the shallow waters of the coastal and inland regions. The foremast was fully square-rigged, while the main or after mast set upper square sails above the 'bilander sail', which was a four-cornered lateen. The small bilander is a different ship type, also with two masts, but rigged with lugsails. At the end of the nineteenth and the beginning of the twentieth century inland freight barges were also termed bilander. *See also* BRIG.

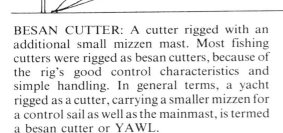

Besan Ewer ca 1880

BESAN CUTTER: A cutter rigged with an additional small mizzen mast. Most fishing cutters were rigged as besan cutters, because of the rig's good control characteristics and simple handling. In general terms, a yacht rigged as a cutter, carrying a smaller mizzen for a control sail as well as the mainmast, is termed a besan cutter or YAWL.

BESAN YACHT: A small seventeenth-century Dutch yacht. It had one or two masts, and was rigged as a schooner. An interesting feature was the very short gaff, sometimes curved rather than straight, carried high up on the mast. The gaff sail on the mizzen was named the bezaan by the Dutch.

BETTE: A small, flat-bottomed boat common to the Rhone estuary region in the nineteenth century. The vessels were 3 to 6m long, carried a lateen sail, and were used for pleasure sailing and fishing.

BILANCELLA, *bilancelle, balancela*: A coastal fishing boat found on the west coast of Italy, southern France and Spain, setting a lateen sail. The vessel was partly decked, up to 20m long and with a beam of around 4.5m.

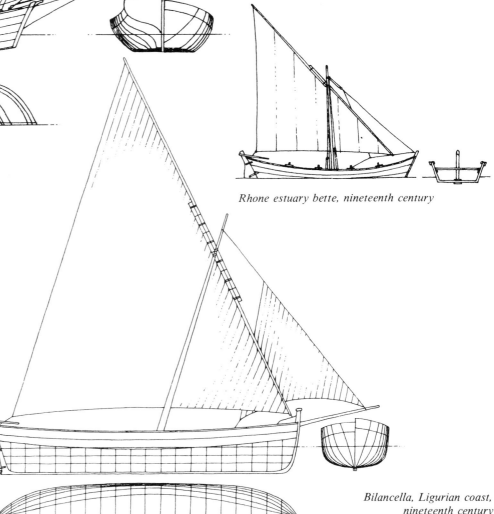

Rhone estuary bette, nineteenth century

Bilancella, Ligurian coast, nineteenth century

Binta, Malayan pirate ship, nineteenth century (model)

Björke boat

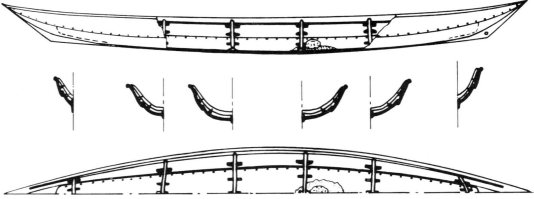

Roman bireme, relief dating from ca *30 BC*

Roman bireme, relief on the Trajan column, Rome

BILLY BOY: *see* HUMBER SLOOP

BINTA, *bintak*: A two-masted ship used primarily by pirates in the eighteenth and nineteenth centuries around the Malayan archipelago. It features oars to supplement the sails, and had two steering oars at the stern.

BIREME: An ancient Roman warship of the Mediterranean region. The bireme was propelled by oars arranged in two rows set one above the other, each oar operated by one or two oarsmen. The wide geographical distribution of the bireme in ancient times is indicated by pictures of the vessels in the Sanherib palace in Lebanon (dating from 704 – 661 BC), on the Trajan column (Trajan 53 –117), and in Greek scultpures. *See also* DIER.

Bisquine, early nineteenth century

BISQUINE: A combined oared and sail-driven vessel used in the Mediterranean for fishing and coastal transport, with a cargo capacity of around 30 tons. It featured two masts and a bowsprit; the foremast was usually raked forward, and the taller pole mast carried a flying topsail.

BJÖRKE BOAT: In 1947, a dugout dating from the fourth century was found at Björke in east Sweden in a canal bed between the Hille and Jus lakes. This is a dugout with side strakes added on both sides of the hull. The trough-shaped bottom plant is 5.22m long, has a maximum beam of 0.7m and is around 40mm thick. At both ends of the bottom member there are 1.5m long ribs, approximating to a

Blackfriars boat

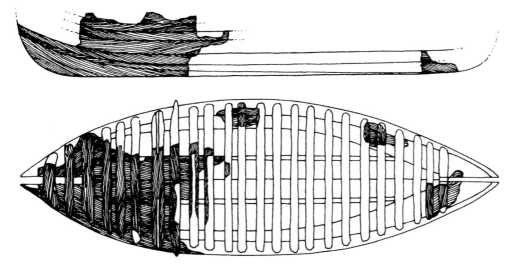

Keel-plank joints

1.1   Dugout
1.2   Dugout with added planks
1.3   Hollowed floor shell with floor planks
1.4   Flat beam keel
1.5   Beam keel

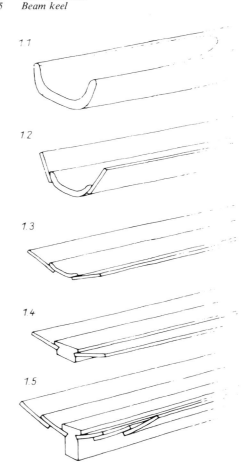

keel, which were left projecting when the hull was cut. The limewood side strakes, set overlapping in CLINKER style, feature cleats which were again left projecting when the strakes were hewn; a feature shared with the NYDAM BOAT. These were used as an attachment for the side strakes. The strakes were bound to fir thwarts with willow twigs. The dugout with side planks represents a primitive form of the ancient Nordic sailing ships called scaiths in the sagas. There is no trace, however, of a mast step on the Björke boat. One strake 0.35m wide and 20mm thick was fitted on each side of the boat. The strake components were fixed to each other by iron rivets with roves under their heads. All the planks were worked with axe and adze; they were not sawn. In the bilge there was 67kg of rough stone ballast. This ballast may have served to increase stability or been used as anchors. The boat was 7.22m long including the side strakes, with a beam of 1.24m and a depth of 0.94m. With a crew of four men including weapons and provisions the draught might have been around 150mm.

BLACKFRIARS BOAT: The remains of an oak boat found in the Thames in London during dredging work in 1962. After detailed examination of the relic, the vessel was dated from the time of the Roman occupation (43–400 AD). Hundreds of pieces of Roman ceramics were found close to the wreck. The hold contained stone which came from a quarry on the Medway river near Maidstone, Kent. The boat had a flat bottom, consisting of two full-length planks, 650mm wide and 7.5mm thick. There was no keel. The side planks were up to 50mm thick, and were connected to each other and to the bottom planks by 20mm thick oak plugs and iron nails in the plugs. Some of the floors nailed to the planks were massive: up to 210mm thick and 300mm wide. The longitudinal joints between the side strakes were caulked with hazel twigs pressed into place. The mast step was sized well forward; no evidence of any other masts

found, and it is assumed that the ship was probably propelled by a single square sail.

BLAZER: A single-masted Dutch fishing vessel which eventually developed two masts. The hull of the single-masted vessel was squat and featured massive timbers. The rig set on the thick, unstayed pole mast was made up mainsail, staysail and jib. It is probable that the blazer did not evolve until the second half of the nineteenth century, but opinions vary on the craft from which it was developed. It could have been a development of the very old KAAG or a variant of the Texel lighter, which transported cargo from sea-going ships on the Texel roads. Another possibility is that the blazer was a form of BOTTER enlarged for fishing on the northern sections of the Zuidersee. The dimensions of the blazer vary. The largest two-masted ships were those based at Texel, and were 17m long overall. The blazer type spread from the northern part of the Zuidersee to Zeeland and Antwerp.

BOAT: The general term for a small, usually open vessel, propelled by muscle or wind power. Different types are usually categorized according to the principal material used: eg leather or hide boat, bark or planked boat, or according to shape and type of construction: eg circular boat or outrigger boat, or planked boat depending on the conditions and materials available in any one region. In some areas skin and bark boats have remained unchanged for centuries, or millennia even, manufactured from the same materials, using the same methods of joining, and employed for the same purposes. On the other hand, some types of boat, such as planked and keel boats, represent a development of the original simple forms. The methods of joining the components of the boat vary widely. The frames may be fixed by nails or by rivets, while the floor components may be connected to the planking by sewing, tying or treenailing.

Hide-covered boats were used primarily in the Arctic regions. Bark boats evolved mainly

on the east coast of Australia, on the central and South American west coast as well as in the northern regions of North America. Planked boats appeared wherever suitable timber and the knowledge required to work it were available.

Punting and paddling do not require any fixed supports in the boat, whereas the use of oars and sweeps requires inset or raised rowlocks or thole pins. If sails are used as the means of propulsion, supports for the mast at gunwale level are needed in addition to a mast step, and due consideration has to be given to providing extra rigidity to the hull.

Stem/stern – keel joints

2.1   Overlap joint
2.2   Hook joint
2.3   Simple corner joint

2.4   Hollowed block stem/stern
2.5   Sloping stem/stern
2.6   Block stem/stern
2.7   Stem or stern post

Planked boat

3.1   Fore-and-aft floor planks
3.2   Transverse floor planks
3.3   Vertical side planks at the hull ends

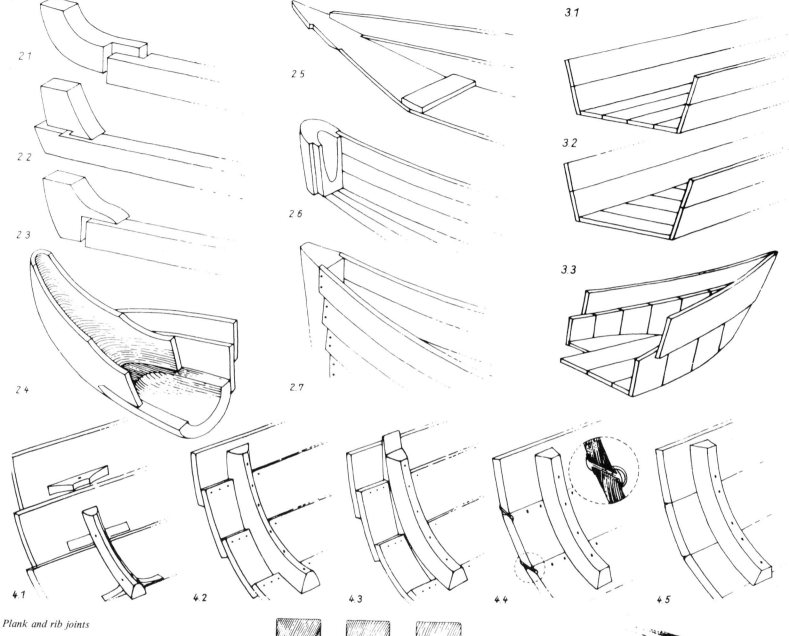

Plank and rib joints

4.1   Clinker planking with cleat joints
4.2   Rivetted or nailed clinker planking with ribs notched to fit
4.3   Rivetted or nailed clinker planking with separate wedges
4.4   Carvel planking with angled rivets
4.5   Carvel planking with caulked seam
4.6   Carvel joint with angled nails
4.7   Dowelled carvel joint
4.8   Bound or sewn carvel joint
4.9   Nailed clinker joint
4.10   Bound or sewn clinker joint
4.11   Diagonal double carvel planking

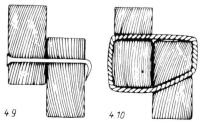

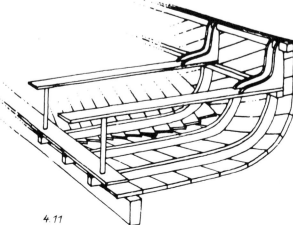

Handling of sculls, oars, paddles and punt poles

5.1   Seated, one pair sculls
5.2   Seated, single oar
5.3   Standing aft, single oar supported in rowlock
5.4   Standing forward, unsupported single paddle
5.5   Standing, crossed sculls
5.6   Two-man paddle boat
5.7   One-man double-paddle
5.8   Standing aft, punt pole
5.9   Standing aft, sculling oar supported in rowlock

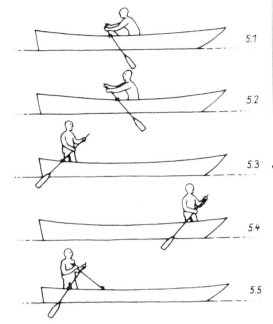

5.1
5.2
5.3
5.4
5.5

5.6
5.7
5.8
5.9

Two-masted boier with sprit and lateen sails, sixteenth century

Boier yacht, early eighteenth century (model)

BOATSCHIP: An eighteenth-century three-masted Dutch ship type which was also known simply as a boat with a flat transom stern. The ship was primarily used as a commercial coaster and for herring fishing. Its rig represents a hybrid between the GALIOT and FLEUTE. The term boatschip was in use as early as the fifteenth century, and by the sixteenth century the term was applied for various types of coastal ships. In the course of the seventeenth century larger boatships of around 28m length and 7m beam appeared.

BOCK: The largest of the nineteenth-century Weser barges were around 36m long and 2.7m wide, and could carry up to 80 tons. The medium-sized barges were termed 'after' (achterhang or hinterhang), because they were towed behind the bock. The smallest or the Weser barges were known as bullen. The three types of barge, when loaded and coupled together, made what was known as a full load, ie one cargo-carrying unit for a deep-sea sailing ship. The freight barges were towed from Bremen to Hameln by 40 to 70 leinlooper (runners) and from there to Minden by horses.

BOIER, *boi, bojer, boeijer, boieier*: A small, shallow-draught, bulbous, Dutch sailing ship with flat bottom and wide leeboards, used for laying buoys and for freight transport in coastal waters and over the sand banks. Originally single-masted, carrying a spritsail only, it later sometimes added a spritsail under the bowsprit and a small lateen mizzen. In this

Dutch boatschip ca mid eighteenth century (model)

Single-masted boier with short curved gaff, mid nineteenth century

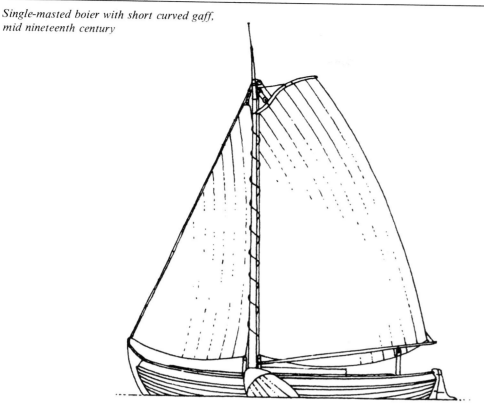

Boier with straight gaff and vangs

form the bojer became one of the best known coastal sailing ships on northern European waters in the sixteenth century. Among the characteristic features of this fairly large sea-going boier were the lack of leeboards, the more rounded hull bottom, the flat transom stern and a small deckhouse. Later, a small top square sail was added on the mainmast. At the beginning of the seventeenth century the spritsail on the mizzen mast was superseded by a gaff sail. At this time the ship type was in widespread use along the Friesian and German North Sea coasts. Its broad, full shape clearly influenced the succeeding ship types KUFF, TJALK, GALIOT and others. Gaff-rigged boiers called boier yachts, remain in use today.

BOMBARDE, *bombard, bombardiere, bomb galiot, mortar prahm, bomb ketch, bomb vessel*: Originally a mortar-carrying Mediterranean vessel with a mainmast and square sails and a mizzen mast with a small gaff sail. Bomb vessels feature in the fleets from the sixteenth to the eighteenth century, and were originally ketch-rigged vessels fitted with several small mortars. In the eighteenth century the mortar prahm, a barge, evolved in France. These full-bodied prahms, devoid of mast and sail, were towed behind rowing boats or other ships. A French report dating from 1787 describes a prahm of this type. It had 26 36-pounder cannon (36 French pounds = 16.4kg), and two mortars each of 12in (305mm). Prussian mortar prahms of the eighteenth century had 20 to 22 24-pounders (each around 11kg) and six 6-pounders (each around 2.75kg) plus various mortars. The bombardier prahm was principally used for bombarding shore targets.

The bomb vessel was supposedly invented by the Frenchman Renaud, and it was first used in action in 1682 during the siege and bombardment of Algiers. The bomb ketch had two heavy mortars, the size of which exceeded that of any previous ships' guns. Projectiles of around 200 pounds (around 90kg) were fired from these weapons, while the ships' guns of that time did not exceed 42-pounders (around 20kg). To cope with the heavy mortars, which fired upward like a grenade launcher, in contrast to the direct bombardment of a gun, the ship's timbers had to be specially reinforced. At a later stage bomb galiots were mainly two-masted ships of medium size, flat-bottomed with shallow draught, so that they could work close inshore. The mortars were set up on specially strengthened mortar beds in the forward section of the ship, and were fired over the bow, so that the ship's side was not exposed to the shore during firing. The rig was basically a mainmast and mizzen mast, but had certain idiosyncratic features linked with the mortar equipment. The mainmast was set very far aft, sometimes aft of the centre of the ship. Even so, before the mortar was fired, all the fore-rigging except for a forestay consisting of strong chain, had to be removed.

From the mid eighteenth century three-

Nineteenth-century Dutch bomschuit (model)

but relatively narrow bottom. The bow was pointed and the stern rounded. The vessels were up to 24m, with a beam of up to 6m. This gave a carrying capacity of 30 to 50 tons.

BORO-BUDUR SHIP RELIEF: A relief picture of a two-masted ship or raft with outriggers, on the outside walls of the Boro-Budur temple in central Java. The temple was built between the eighth and ninth centuries and decorated with several kilometers of relief pictures. One of the sculptures represents a multi-decked ship after a successful voyage, in similar style to the Egyptian relief pictures. It is rigged with a kind of lugsail.

BOTE: A whalboat of the Azores, between 7 and 9m in length with a beam of between 1.77 and 1.90m. The design is similar to the whaleboats of New England, whose ships visited the islands from the eighteenth century onwards. It was CARVEL-built, with imported pine planking and frames of a local species of acacia. The hull was painted white with a coloured topstrake: the colour identifying the island from where the boat came. The boat was nearly double ended with a sharp V midship section. It hoisted a high peaked gaff mainsail. However, when a whale had been spotted the craft relied on six oars, which were exchanged for paddles when a quieter approach was required. Once a whale was harpooned the rudder was quickly unhinged and for greater manoevrability a large steering oar — over 7m long — swung into position.

BOTTER: A single-masted, shallow-draught coastal sailing vessel with leeboards, similar to the Dutch BOIER. In contrast to other types of ship the transition from the flat bottom to the lower part of the sides was abrupt with

masted ship-rigged bombs were built and ketches gradually disappeared from service. In the nineteenth century, freight sailing ships with POLACCA rig were also known as bombards.

BOMSCHUIT, *bom*: A Dutch fishing vessel of the seventeenth and eighteenth centuries with a flat bottom which enabled it to be beached. They usually carried a mizzen mast and were gaff rigged. The ship's length could be up to 10m and the load capacity up to 32 tons.

BONS: A small, flat-bottomed fishing boat used on the Zuiderzee, up to 10m long, and rarely seen nowadays. It had certain similarities to the schokker, and was used for catching anchovies and herrings.

BOOM: *see Bûm.*

BOOPA: A small South Seas PIROGUE with outrigger.

BORDING, *Bordinger*: This term referred to a flat-bottomed lighter used on the lower Weichsel until the early twentieth century. In the pre-Viking and Viking periods the term byrdinger signified a trade and freight ship, while the term bordinger came into use after the fourteenth century. During the Hanseatic period the bording was known as a coastal freight ship and lighter in north Germany. *See also* BYRDINGER.

BORNACHEN, *Bohrnachen*: Barges once used for transporting wine grapes on the Moselle. They were strongly built, with a flat

Small nineteenth-century Dutch botter (model)

Reconstruction of the Bounty, *1960*

pronounced chimes, although the bow was rounded off as it curved upwards. The term may have evolved from the Dutch bot which means bluff or blunt. This ship type first appeared in the sixteenth and seventeeth centuries in the southern part of the Zuidersee, but was later to be seen in virtually all Zuidersee ports. The vessels were not uniform; botters from the south, north or east coast were all different. The smaller botter was used primarily for fishing close to the coast. A larger version up to 15m long was called the North

Botter yacht, complete with traditional leeboards and short, curved gaff (model)

Sea botter. This vessel had a tall, broad fort section with a curving, projecting stem and a relatively narrow aftership with a low freeboard, in order to make it easier to haul the nets in and out.

In its yacht form the botter had more generous freeboard; among its special features was the larger foresail, known as the botter or sailor's foresail. Most botters were constructed

Relief on the temple of Boro-Budur, Java, showing an oared sailing ship, eighth century

of timber, but steel versions were also made. Because of its good seagoing qualities and fine sailing characteristics, the botter is still in use today for recreational boating.

BOTTER YACHT: A flat-bottomed, full-bodied boat fitted with a cabin. Boats similar to the botter yachts are still in common use today as sailing yachts. Leeboards are still used, as on the original.

BOUNTY: A ship which is famous for its commission to transport breadfruit cuttings from Tahiti to Jamaica and notorious for the mutiny carried out on 28 April 1789 by part of the crew against Captain William Bligh. The ship was originally built in England in 1784 as the merchant ship *Bethia*, with a cargo capacity of 200 tons. With a length on deck of 27.5m and a beam of 7.3m, the full-rigged three-master carried a crew of 45 men. It was bought by the English Admiralty and left Spithead in December 1787 under Captain Bligh. After the cuttings had been loaded in Tahiti, the voyage continued in April 1789 until the mutiny.

Captain Bligh and 18 men were abandoned on the open sea in the *Bounty*'s longboat in the region of the Tonga islands, and the boat reached Timor after a voyage of 3600 nautical miles. The *Bounty* sailed first to Tahiti, commanded by the first officer Fletcher Christian and then continued to the island of Pitcairn, where it was beached in 1790. After salvaging all the useable equipment and components, the crew burned the ship to destroy all evidence. The last survivor of the eight crew members, six Tahitians and 12 women was discovered in 1808 by the frigate *Topaze*. He was allowed to live out the rest of his life in peace on Pitcairn, but three of the 14 mutineers who were captured in Tahiti by the English frigate *Pandora* after news of the mutiny became known, were condemned (by court martial) to death by hanging.

In 1960, a reconstruction of the lightly-armed ship (four 4-pounders and 10 half-pounders swivel guns) called the *Bounty II* was built for filming. The full-rigged ship had a sail area of around 950m² with a displacement of

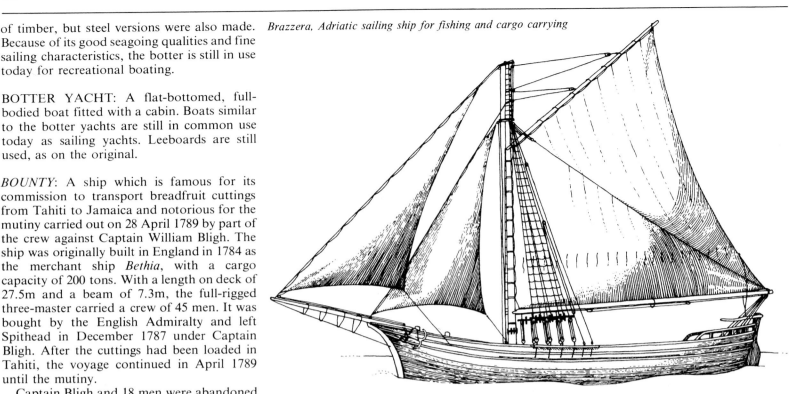

Brazzera, Adriatic sailing ship for fishing and cargo carrying

about 120 tons. Length overall was 51.4m, length between perpendiculars 33.6m, beam 9.2m and the depth 6.3m. While the original crew in 1789 had consisted of 45 men, only 26 men were required on the later version. The ship is now a museum ship in St Petersburg, Florida.

BOVO: A Sicilian coastal ship with mizzen-mast in use up to the end of the nineteenth century. The vessel was also known as a bull boat (Italian bove meaning ox). It was 12 to 18m long, had very fine lines, and could carry up to 40 tons as a cargo vessel. It was also used for fishing, however, and was even used on odd occasions by the navy, fitted with a gun mounted in the bow. Both masts were rigged with lateen sails, plus a jib set flying on the long bowsprit.

BRAGOZZO, *bragazzi*: A decked, two-masted fishing vessel used in the Adriatic, especially by the inhabitants of Chioggia, on the southern inlet of the Venice lagoon. These shallow-draught vessels had rounded fore and aft sections, and their length varied between 9 and 15m. Both masts were rigged with lugsails and booms.

BRANDSKOG BOAT PICTURE: One of many rock drawings of boats to be found on the Scandinavian peninsula. This one shows a boat propelled by paddles, with six paddlers on the port side. The bow and stern curve upwards and end in horses' heads.

BRAZZERA: A small to medium-sized fishing vessel used by the Venetians and Dalmatians in the Adriatic region into this century. It had one or two masts, and usually set a dipping lugsail and jib. The crew consisted of four to six men, and the vessels could carry between 15 and 80 tons of cargo; if necessary, the brazzera could also be rowed.

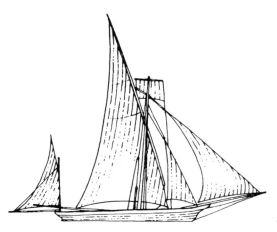

Sicilian Bovo, nineteenth century

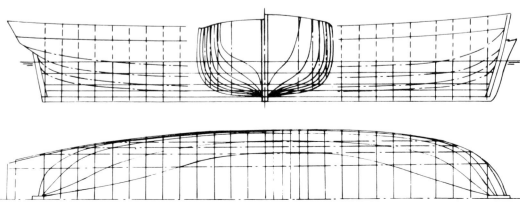

Sheer draught plan of a Russian merchant brig, ca 1860

BREMEN COG: During dredging work on the Weser near Bremen in 1962, a ship's hull was discovered. It turned out to be a Hanseatic cargo ship, 25.5m in length, 6m wide and with a depth of 3.5m. The vessel, a cog dating from the end of the fourteenth century, was carried away from its moorings by a catastrophic flood, and sank before launching. Divers initially salvaged parts of the ship then, in 1965, a diving bell ship was used to continue the salvage operation. The bed was examined systematically over an area of 1400m² using modern equipment capable of locating metal parts in the river bed to a depth of one metre. After removing a layer of sand 3 to 4m thick, around 550 individual components were salvaged.

Bremen cog, side planking

18-gun armed brig, first half of the nineteenth century

Reconstruction of the salvaged components indicated that the cog could carry a load of around 130 tons. The primary construction material was oak, which was the preferred timber in northern Europe because of its durability and resistance to rotting as well as its good working qualities. Danish and Swedish experts had considerable experience in the preservation of ancient ship relics, and this knowledge was drawn on to conserve the cog. The ship was reconstructed at the Deutsches Schiffahrtsmuseum, Bremerhaven, and is currently undergoing conservation, using water-replacing polyethylene glycol to prevent shrinkage.

BRIG: A two-masted, square-rigged sailing ship. The after mast (mainmast) also carried a large gaff sail (brig sail or mainsail). Studding sails could also be set off the wind on studding sail booms (extensions to the yards). Special features of the brig from the mid nineteenth century onward were the narrow hull and clipper bow. These relatively small sailing ships were economical to operate because of the small harbour dues.

Brigs between 140 and 340BRT and with one and two decks were in use. In 1834, for example, a 340BRT brig with a crew of 11 men was able to carry 100 emigrants to America in addition to its cargo. In spite of its relatively small tonnage, the brig was not ony used in European waters, but also for long-distance voyages, for whaling and for seal hunting. The great navies of the time, such as those of England, the USA, France and the Netherlands, also adapted the brig as a warship, carrying up to 20 guns. In the decades before the turn of the century, brigs were rigged with double topsails and other changes were made to make them easier to handle with a small crew. In the 1860s the brig began to give way to the larger, three-masted barque.

BRIGANTINE, *brig-schooner, schooner-brig*: Originally a sixteenth-century, half-decked, oared sailing warship used in the Mediterranean region, with eight to twelve banks of oars on each side, and rigged with lateen sails.

Brig Wustrow, *built in Rostock in 1885 by W Zeltz, 288 tons*

Mediterranean brigantine, ca *1650*

Brigantine Peter I, ca *1700*

Russian Black Sea brigantine, 1859

Northern European 'true' brigantine with square topsails on mizzen mast, Newfoundland sailing ship, 1860

This ship type was favoured by pirates because of its manoeuvrability. Its raised ends resulting from the pronounced deck sheer offered better facilities for attack and defence than the flatter galley, and also allowed better handling. From the end of the seventeenth century the term has been adopted in northern Europe (Netherlands, France, England) for two-masted sailing ships which were initially square-rigged on both masts. Later on, the square sails were removed from the mainmast leaving the fore-and-aft canvas. In France the term brigantine has survived for the mizzen sail, as brigantines often carried a lateen sail on the aftermast, after the Mediterranean custom. In contrast, the fore-mast was square-rigged, in whole or in part.

At the start of the nineteenth century, the terms brigantine, schooner-brig and brig-schooner were almost synonymous, but nowadays, a distinction could be made between a true brigantine — that is, one having a square main topsail — and a HERMAPHRODITE BRIG or brig schooner with no square canvas on the mainmast. However, the term brigantine has replaced hermaphrodite brig for a vessel with a brig-like fully-rigged (square-rigged) foremast without gaff sail, combined with a gaff-rigged mainmast.

BRIXHAM TRAWLER: A specialized English, ketch-rigged trawler about 20m long; its heyday was the mid nineteenth century. These fishing vessels were based in Devon, and a few of them have survived to this day, now serving as training ships, because of their excellent handling and outstanding sailing characteristics.

200-ton brigantine or hermaphrodite brig, late nineteenth century

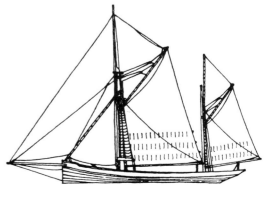

Rig of a Brixham trawler

BROADSIDE SHIP: The standard term used from the seventeenth to nineteenth centuries for a ship with its guns arranged along the sides ('in line') and firing at right-angles to the ship's centreline. In contrast the bow-mounted guns on galleys and oared gunboats were fixed in the direction of travel. On broadside ships the guns were mounted along virtually the whole length of the battery deck on each side. It was not until the second half of the nineteenth century that the turret ship evolved, whose guns were placed amidships in rotating, armoured barbettes or turrets. Two of the first turret ships were launched in 1861.

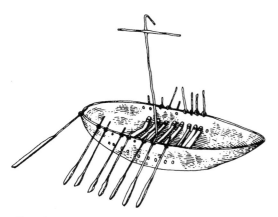

Broighter boat model, first century

BROIGHTER BOAT MODEL: A model of a boat made in gold, and discovered at Broighter in County Derry in Ireland. The model dates from the first century AD and formed part of a votive deposit. The model is of a barrel-shaped boat with seven oars on each side, fitted with thwarts and a single steering oar at one side at the stern. There is a central mast with a yard, which was not yet a common feature on northern ships of this period.

BRÖSEN SHIP: This is a ship's hull, found at Brösen near Gdansk in 1872 during harbour work. The CLINKER-built hull was in good condition. An illustrated report dated 1873 states that the hull consisted of 40mm oak planks which were split not sawn. The strakes were joined to each other by iron rivets and

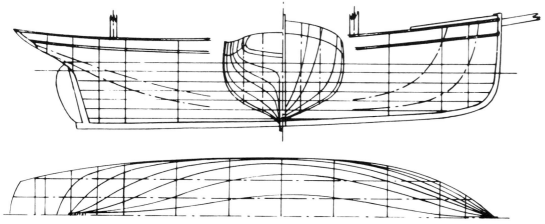

Brixham trawler, sheer draught plan

fixed to the frames with treenails. There was no trace of a stern rudder, which indicates that the hull dates from before 1240 (first evidence of a stern rudder on northern ships). The bottom of the boat was flat. There were also signs that the ship had been used for transporting corn, and had been fitted with inner planking. The ship was about 17.5m long with a beam of 4.9m. The wide beam suggests that this was a cargo vessel.

BRUGES SHIP: A flat-bottomed ship found at Bruges in Belgium in 1899, during harbour construction, probably dating from the sixth or seventh centuries. It was a single-masted sailing ship with a 4.3m-long steering oar. The bow and stern were of identical form (double-ended), both of them moderately raked. The ship was around 15m long, with a beam of 3.5m. The mast was 8.3m high and presumably square-rigged. The ship might have had a draught of around 1.35m. This vessel is now considered as a primitive form of the low-German ewer. It was certainly intended as a freight sailing ship for shallow sand flats, judging by its size and flat bottom.

Bruges ship, sixth and seventh centuries

BRÛLOT, *brulotte*: This is the French/Italian term used in the sixteenth to eighteenth centuries for fireships which were driven towards enemy ships by the current or by the wind.

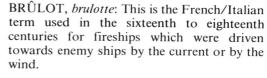

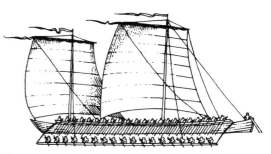

Buanga, fast Malaysian ship, eighteenth and nineteenth centuries

BUANGA, *bonanga*: A two-masted pirate ship based in the Malayan archipelago. It was about 30m long, and had large, square sails of matting which could be rolled up. The ship had three rows of auxiliary oarsmen, the rows stepped in height, the higher ones towards the outside. Each row of oarsmen comprised 25 men, one behind the other. In addition there were outriggers on each side, beyond the reach of the oars, each carrying 20 men with paddles. The result was that 190 men could work simultaneously on oars and paddles. The oarsmen sat on a three-tiered framework extending outside the hull proper. This kind of vessel was first encountered by French expeditionary exploration ships in 1767.

BUCINTORO, *bucentoro, bucentaur*: The famous medieval state galley of the Venetian republic. Every year on Ascension day the Doge of Venice travelled to the entrance of the St Nicolas lido on board the bucintoro. There, amid great ceremony and applause from the onlookers in the accompanying boats and gondolas, the Doge would hurl into the sea a

Bucintoro, early eighteenth century (model)

Budarka, nineteenth-century Russian kahn

BUDARKA: A shallow-draught barge with one or two masts used in the Volga region and the Caspian Sea in the nineteenth century. The stem of the budarka was raked forward and upward at a shallow angle.

BUG DUGOUT: A dugout found in 1937 by the Soviet researcher RA Orbeil in the lower course of the river Bug. Around 2500 years old, it is now in the central naval museum in Leningrad. The dugout was hewn and burnt out from a 7m long oak trunk.

BULL BOAT: A skin boat made from an open framework of willow rods and covered with buffalo or bison hides, used by North American Indian tribes. It is a lightweight boat, used solely for crossing rivers, and is circular or oval in shape, somewhat similar to the British coracle.

BULLE: This was the smallest of the Weser barges. Special-purpose barges which were used to careen sailing ships were also called bulle. *See also* BOCK.

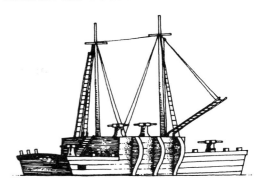

Bulle, prahm used for careening ships

The Bucintoro Leaves the Quay, painting by Antonio Canale (1697–1768)

ring carrying the symbolic inscription: 'O sea, we marry ouselves to thee, and acknowledge your unbounded mastery over us!' This custom can be traced back to the tenth century, and the pillaging of Istria, Dalmatia and various islands by the people of Narant. A campaign by the Venetians under the Doge Orseola, brought victory and each year since then its anniversary, the Sensa, has been celebrated. The battle was fought by various types of warship, amongst which the bucintoro played an important rôle, as it was a particularly powerful type of galley used to combat pirates.

Before the first custom-built bucintoro in 1311 ordinary warships (galleys), albeit specially decorated, were used to celebrate the anniversary. The name derives from 'bu-cin-toro' meaning ship with the golden belt. The last bucintoro was built in 1729 and destroyed in 1798. The remains of this state ship are now in the Civico Correr museum and the Venice Arsenal. The bucintoros of 1520, 1605 and 1729 are the most famous, the main differences being in the lavishness of their decoration.

BÛM, *boom*: A common type of DHOW, originally from Kuwait, usually with two masts hoisting settee sails. The boat has some similarities with the DHANGI — the stem post is straight and the stern pointed — but can be most easily distinguished by the shape of the stem post head which is rounded at the top. In size, bûms range between 12 and 37m. As with perhaps the majority of dhows still operating, many bûms are now fitted with inboard engines, carrying sails for emergencies only. Some, however, are not equipped with masts. In 1980, a bûm was built in Oman by traditional sewing techniques, rather than the more modern method of metal fastening. This vessel, *Sohar*, made a successful voyage under sail from the Persian Gulf to Canton.

Egyptian buriel ship, ca 1300 BC (Model)

BUMBOAT: An early English term for a boat which sold home-grown provisions and products, and also foreign goods to ships lying in harbour, at the roads or in rivers. The term bumboat was also frequently used for a boat which supplied ships with drinking water.

BURGHELLO: A small nineteenth-century BUCINTORO with a central gallery. It was a popular vessel for pleasure trips in Venice.

BURIAL SHIP: The generic term for ships and boats, both models and full-size, which were buried with the dead in order to honour them and speed them on their way on their final voyage.

Symbolic burials of these ships formed a part of religious ceremonial in various early cultures, especially when important figures died, and had to be prepared for their journey to the next world and the after-life. To this end the corpse was provided with equipment, weapons, draught animals, domestic articles, jewellery and food to help him on his way. Amongst the oldest known royal graves which contains a ship is the Sumerian royal grave near Ur, which is 5000 years old. This was a grave for a king and his fallen warriors. As well as 74 human skeletons, which before their burial were richly decorated with gold, silver

and precious stones, there were two model ships just over 60cm long. The one model, made of copper, was practically destroyed, but the other one, made of silver, had survived well. This 5000-year old model features a slender hull with tall bow and stern, thwarts, and a roofed area in the centre of the vessel. A rudder blade also survived. The model is thus similar to the vessels which were used until recently on the lower course of the Euphrates.

Egyptian grave sites have yielded many significant burial ships and models, made of wood, clay and metal. In the ancient Egyptian religion of sun worship, burial ships had the task of bearing the soul of the deceased person over the earth through the path of the sun from east to west by day, and through the under-world from west to east by night. A large collection of the rich haul of Egyptian grave artefacts, also known as sun ships or barks, is on show in the museum in Cairo. The oldest models from upper Egyptian graves are made of red fired clay, and were consigned to the grave in about 4200 BC. Some of these rough, clumsy-looking boats already feature a type of canopy or deck-house. Another burial ship, placed in an Egyptian grave around 3000 BC, is a model of a boat-shaped papyrus raft, carved in bone.

Among the most significant Egyptian full-

size burial ships are the CHEOPS BURIAL SHIP (around 2650 BC) and the DASHUR BOAT (around 1850 BC).

The journey to the next world, over the ocean to Valhalla (the resting place for warriors fallen in war) was also a feature of German mythology. Amongst the best known German burial ships, which were buried in burial mounds, and which have remained at least partially preserved because of favourable ground conditions, are the OSEBERG and GOKSTAD ships. In all Norse ship graves the orientation of the ship was the same: the bow always had to face south, because that was the direction in which lay Valhalla.

In northwest Borneo, 18 artistically worked wooden rafts dating from the third century were discovered in a limestone cave. The corpses were placed on the rafts, and were sent out to sea as part of a nocturnal burial ceremony, after the rafts had been set on fire. Small burial ships are also known from Kalimantan and Sumatra, and these were allowed to float down river carrying the ashes of the dead.

BUSHNELL DIVING BOAT: A diving boat developed and built by the American David Bushnell (1742–1824). Bushnell, one of the pioneers of submarine vessels, created his egg-shaped underwater craft in 1775 during the War of Independence. It was 2.5m in diameter, and was called the *Turtle*. The vessel, propelled by means of two hand-driven screw wheels, (arranged horizontally and vertically) was developed to attach an explosive charge to the bottom of the English flagship. The first experiment in 1776 off New York was unsuccessful, as Bushnell evidently had not reckoned on the copper-sheathed hulls of the British ships, and could not secure the charge to them.

BUSS: *büse, buse, busse, buise, buyse, busa, bussa:* A small merchant ship with a particularly long history of development. In the Mediterranean in the twelfth century the terms buza, bucia and bucius meant a cumbersome, oared trading ship. This type of ship is, however, thought to be of much older origin in the Mediterranean, and the term was brought to the north in tenth or eleventh century. Since the beginning of the eleventh century the terms buza or buzur have been applied to a type of Scandinavian longship. The ship of this name built around 1060 for Harald Hardrada is particularly famous, although it was also known as a skeid or dreki meaning ship with a dragon's head. In twelfth-century Scandinavia the buza was a pure sailing ship without auxiliary oar propulsion. In the thirteenth century the bussa was widely used for trading. The first written reference dates from 1303 in Kings Lynn (England), where it was used as the term for a Wismar ship. During the Hanseatic period (fifteenth century) the büsse is often mentioned in inventories for the North Sea region. At this

Merchant buss, late eighteenth century

Herring buss, ca 1800 (model)

time their cargo capacity was between 60 to 100 tons. The buss survived almost to the end of the sailing ship era, as a full-bodied, rounded-stern merchant ship with two masts. The buss, with the same or modified sail rig, was also used widely as a fishing vessel, and at times even as a warship. It survived in Holland into the nineteenth century as a herring fishing ship.

The numerous combination names, covering the different methods of construction and regions in which the ship were used, such as Enkhuyser buis, Vlardinger buis, Emder büse and others, and also the large number of similar terms which exist, indicate how widely the type was distributed. These ships, with their full bow and stern forms, carried a variety of rigs. The smaller büssen, such as the Emder büse of around 1805, carried a removable mainmast with a simple square sail and a smaller mizzenmast with a gaff sail. The largest büsen had up to three masts and were square-rigged, with the mizzen mast carrying a fore-and-aft mizzen sail. As herring and mackerel fishing ships the büsen displaced around 80 tons. We can also assume that the famous Dutch herring buiser was a development of the büse. Herring büsses were also used by the English fishing fleet.

BUTT-AAK: A flat-bottomed fishing vessel with a rounded stern, a fishwell and a removable mast, carrying a gaff mainsail. The ship carried a staysail and a jib on a running bowsprit. The bow curved up strongly and was decked in.

BUTTJOLLE: A nineteenth-century sailing fishing boat from the Lower Elbe fitted with leeboards and a fishwell. It was around 8m long and 2.50m wide, and was decked up forward. The rig consisted of a tall, pointed lugsail and staysail. The mast was raked forward slightly. Originally, two leeboards were used, but later they were replaced by a centreboard.

BYRDINGER: A Scandinavian merchant and freight ship of the Viking period. The name comes from the old Nordic byrdingr, which in turn comes from byrdr (burden, or load) or even from bord or bording (planks), as the ship's upper section was built from planks. It was originally a dugout with additional side strakes. The BJÖRKE BOAT (east Sweden) might have been a byrdinger. This type of ship was used principally around the coasts, but occasionally for sea voyages, eg to the Faroes or Iceland. It was similar in construction to the KNARR, which was probably its predecessor. Its crew is said to have numbered ten to 12 persons. Larger byrdinger may have carried 20 to 30 men. They were also used to accompany warships as supply and transport vessels (vista byrdingr). After the fourteenth century the name byrdinger was no longer used in the north, having been displaced by the terms bording and bordinger.

BYRSOPAGIS: A leather vessel used by Romans and Armenians.

Four-masted barque Krusenstern, *built in 1926. 114.5m length overall, 14.0m beam and 3247m² sail area.*

Barquentine Mönchgut, *of Thiessow on Rügen, oil painting, 1877.*

Brig Marye und Betty, *Rostock, 1844*

Turkish caique with square and lateen sails

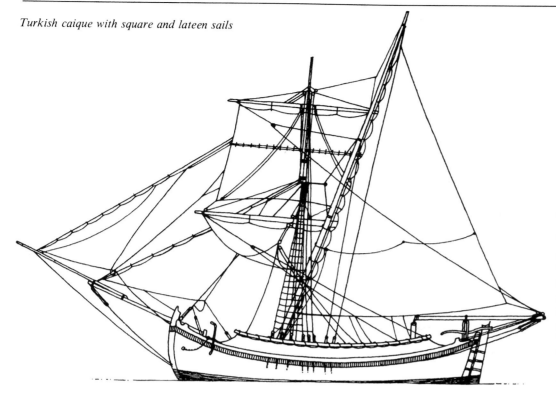

CABILLITO: *see* BALSA.

CABLE FERRY: A specialized predecessor of the later engine-powered chain towing ship. Cable ferries were sketched as early as 1438 by J Mariano. The cable ferry was fitted with a transverse shaft carrying large paddle wheels on each side. One end of a cable was affixed to a drum mounted on the shaft, the other was staked down further upstream. The paddle wheels were driven round by the current causing the cable to wind itself up on the drum, and thus the ship moved up the river. Sometimes the drum was helped round by muscle power.

CABOTEUR, *cabotier*: A one or two-masted, fast sailing coastal freighter used in the Mediterranean region in the nineteenth century. Cabotier is also the French term for a ship used for cabotage (coastal trading).

CAGH, *kagh, kaag*: A Dutch river and coastal vessel of the seventeenth and eighteenth centuries. It was about 15m long, flat-bottomed, and featured leeboards and a single mast. Originally, the vessel was rigged with a spritsail, but later with a gaff sail. In the nineteenth century these were built to carry between 80 and 100 tons.

CAÏQUE, *caic, kaik, kaike, daiak, kajik*: An oared boat in use in the Black Sea and the Eastern Mediterranean region since the sixteenth century. It is a plank-on-frame vessel with a keel. Larger boats were similar to the Arab dhow and could be rowed or sailed, with lateen sails on the main and mizzen masts.

In the seventeenth and eighteenth centuries these manoeuvrable vessels (also known as half-galleys) were often used by Turkish and Cossack corsairs in the Black Sea. At the beginning of the nineteenth century the term was applied to a galley/shallop, which was also more often known as a barke. The name is also applied to a small Turkish single-masted coaster.

CALABASH RAFT: *see* GOURD RAFT.

CAMARA: A light vessel used in the Mediterranean, especially for ferry duties in the Bosphorus and the Black Sea. The boat's hull was of timber with a rudder at bow and stern, to avoid turning round. An arched deck was provided to give protection from high seas. Similar vessels, in various states of development, have been used in the Mediterranean since the first century.

CAMEL: A pontoon, similar to a floating-dock, which was used to reduce the draught of ships. The two wooden tanks or pontoons, fitted on either side of the ship to be raised, may have reminded somebody of the two-humped camel, itself a beast of burden.

The use of buoyant containers to overcome the problem of shallow water was one of the most significant Dutch inventions of the seventeenth century. Because of the shoals and silting in the river estuaries, larger sailing ships could only put into Dutch ports if lightened, or with the help of camels. The camels employed were strong, hollow timber structures, stiffened and sub-divided into compartments. The width between the inner sides of the pair

had to be greater than the beam of the ship, while the length of the pontoons was about 40 to 50m. The camels were first submerged by flooding the compartments. Heavy hawsers were passed under the ship, or under beams passed through the gunports. The camels were emptied using manually-operated pumps until they and the ship floated sufficiently high. The first camel is said to have been built in Amsterdam in 1688, and they remained in use until 1825.

CANADIAN CANOE: A light, open bark or skin shelled canoe, similar to those used by North American indians. The sections of the boat's skin were cleverly sewn together at the ends, resulting in a streamlined form with tapering ends, concave waterlines, convex sides and a quite marked sheer forward and aft. The craft was propelled and steered in similar fashion to modern sports Canadian canoes with a paddle, used kneeling or sitting. The specifications for modern competition Canadian canoes are as follows:

RCI — One-man racing Canadian:
Length 5.20m
Beam 0.75m, 20kg

SIC I — One-man slalom Canadian:
Length 4.00m
Beam 0.08m

WRC I — One man wild-water racing craft:
Length 4.30m
Beam 0.80m

RC II — One-man racing Canadian:
Length 5.20m
Beam 0.75m, weight 20kg

WRC II — Two-man wild-water racing craft:
Length 5.00m
Beam 0.80m

RMC — Team racing Canadian:
Length 11.0m
Beam 0.95m

The wild-water canoe has a rockered keel, and is covered. It is paddled with a single rather than a double blade, unlike a kayak.

CANGIA, *cange*: A small, narrow sailing boat used on the Nile in the nineteenth century. Sometimes the boats had two masts, but usually only one, carrying a lateen sail. The boats were about 16 to 20m long and there was often a small deckhouse at the stern of the boat.

Canadian canoe, forerunner of the open Canadian canoe

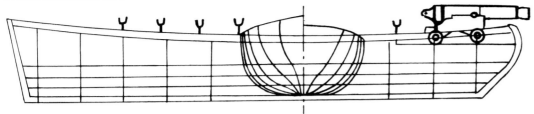

French canonnière, 1792

CANOE

CANOE: *canoa, canot*: Originally a dugout, of the Caribbean region. The term was adopted for small, paddled craft of different construction, such as the Canadian canoe. The original inhabitants of Haiti had boats up to 30m long, capable of accommodating 80 oarsmen. Since the turn of the century the CANADIAN CANOE has been one of the most popular water sport craft on the rivers and lakes of Europe. The term canoeing today embraces canoes, folding boats and KAYAKS. In canoe racing, the boats are propelled by paddles, either single or double, in contrast to the oars used for rowing. The term is applied to a large number of canvas, aluminium and glassfibre canoe-like derivatives.

CANONNIÈRE: The French term for gunboat. They were rowing or sailing vessels in use from the seventeenth to the nineteenth centuries, while in the nineteenth and twentieth centuries they came to be propelled by steam.

CANOT: French term for barge or small boat.

CANTON FLOWER BOAT, *hua ch'uan*: A luxuriously decorated and furnished pleasure boat on which the rich of Canton entertained their guests. The accommodation consisted of two large saloons, below which were smaller apartments where one could sit on the flower-bedecked verandas and enjoy the evening air.

The hull of the boat was massive and squat, quite unsuitable for normal navigation. The only means of propulsion were oars on the bow and long poles which could be thrust into the muddy river bottom. Flower boats were noted by Marco Polo not only in Canton but also on the magnificent lake at Soochow. They were still in existence in the 1940s.

CARABUS: A Roman leather or hide-covered boat used for crossing rivers, especially in the Roman army at the time of Caesar. The keel and frames were made from light wood, with willow woven into the structure, and covered over with leather or animal skins. The boat is supposed to have originated in the region of the River Po, although various parts of the world have produced similar craft, amongst them the Eskimo boats and the Irish curraghs.

CARAVEL: In thirteenth-century Portugal this was a fishing boat with lateen sails. By the beginning of the fourteenth century, before the time of the great Portuguese voyages of discovery, the term had been adopted for a two-masted, lateen-rigged merchant ship with forecastle and deckhouse, which was used for Mediterranean and coastal work. When the Turks overran the land routes to India, at a time when Mediterranean commerce had lost its importance, Portugal was the nation which began to search intensively for a southern sea route to India. The far-sighted Prince Henry, known as Henry the Navigator (1394–1460), promoted shipbuilding and sea travel. To him is due the credit not only for the continued development of the caravel, but also for the foundation of a state-supported observatory and school of navigation.

The first development of the two-masted caravel, aimed at making it more suitable for longer voyages, was the caravela latina, which had a relatively slender hull and three masts, carrying lateen sails exclusively. A typical feature of the ship, to which the name alludes, was the CARVEL style of planking in which the strakes were butt-jointed together along their long edges, resulting in smooth surfaces to the ship's sides inside and out. The seams were caulked, so that the ships took in little water even in heavy seas. The smooth, outside skin was also easier to protect against fouling and worm attack. A further characteristic of the caravel was the relatively high poop.

The next stage of development produced the three-masted square-rigged caravel (caravela redonda), on which the bowsprit, foremast and mainmast carried square sails. Above the mainsail on the mainmast was a further square sail, the topsail. On the mizzen mast, square-rigged caravels continued to carry lateen sails, because of their advantages as an aid to manoeuvring. Caravels were amongst the most sea-worthy sailing ships between the fourteenth and sixteenth centuries, and even four-masted versions were produced.

Vasco da Gama's ships were also caravels. Of the three ships with which Columbus discovered America in 1492, *Santa Maria*, *Nina* and *Pinta*, the latter two were probably caravels, while *Santa Maria* was probably a somewhat more full-bodied, beamier NAO. In his logbook, Columbus gave his speed at up to 15 Italian mph, which corresponds to about 11 knots. Standard Portuguese caravels could carry 50 to 100 tons, but later versions could carry much more. For example, among the ships of Ferdinand Magellan there were quite large, four-masted caravels.

Because of its advantages, the carvel method of planking soon spread to Holland and the whole of Europe, to become the standard method of construction for timber ships. Thus in Holland the first 'karvielscheepen' of substantial size were built in 1460, with a

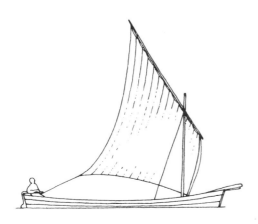

Canot, French sailing kahn with lugsail

Spanish fore-and-aft rigged caravel, sixteenth century, watercolour by Monleon

Caravel

1 French caravel after Jacques Devaulx, 1583
2 Swedish caravel, ca 1560
3 Bonnet, laced with running line
4 Spanish caravel
5 Lateen caravel, 1520
6 Portuguese caravel, 1492, with square and lateen sails, after Fernando Colombo
7 Square-rigged caravel from a Portuguese chart, fifteenth century

8 Portugese caravel, 1492, after Fernando Colombo
9 The caravel Redonda, 1570, from the atlas Theatrum Orbis Terrarum, by Abraham Ortelius
10 One of Emperor Charles V's caravels off Tunis, 1535
11 Keel, frames and counter timbers of a caravel, after Fernandes, 1616
12 Lateen-rigged caravel, 1490, after Simão Bening
13 Longitudinal section through a lateen-rigged caravel
14 Lateen yard parrel, after Quirino de Fonseca
15 Lateen-rigged caravel after de Cosa's atlas, 1500

Carrack

1   Carrack from Breydenbach's Pilgrims' journey, 1486
2   Hull of a carrack, after B Bonfigli, Perugia, mid fifteenth century
3   Sixteenth-century armament: breech loading cannon in timber bed

4   Carrack ca 1475
5   Masthead of a carrack
6   Breton caracca, sixteenth century

length of around 43m., a beam of 12m, and a cargo capacity of 800 tons. In the first half of the sixteenth century Lübeck and Danzig assumed a leading role in the building of large carvel ships.

CARRACK: From the fourteenth to the seventeenth centuries this was one of the most important sailing ship types of the Mediterranean region. An early Genoese reference to a caracca occurs in the first half of the fourteenth century. Throughout the period, these ships were operated as trading vessels and warships in the Mediterranean area, and also, to a lesser extent, in northern European waters.

Originally, the carracks were rigged with one large square sail on the fore- and mainmasts, but by the first half of the sixteenth century topsails were in use. Carracks were heavily built, with a castle-like superstucture forward, and a relatively long after superstructure, starting as far forward as the mainmast and ending in a gallery above the straight sternpost. Carracks were longer and broader and much heavier than CARAVELS, but shared the CARVEL style of planking typical of Mediterranean ships. In terms of rig they were primarily three-masted ships, although four-masted examples were built in the sixteenth century, with square sails on the fore- and mainmasts, and a lateen sail on the mizzen mast which served as a steering sail. If a fourth mast (the bonaventure or jigger mast) was fitted, then this also carried a lateen sail. Carracks did not usually carry a spritsail (square sail) on the bowsprit.

From various sources it is clear that the carrack was one of the larger, if not the largest, ship types of its time. It is reasonable to consider this ship type — the three-masted carrack in particular — as the real predecessor of the large three-masted ships, whose development continued up to the middle of the nineteenth century.

In 1501, the *La Charente*, a large French carrack, carried a total of 1200 fighting men (without servants, pages etc) and an armament of 200 guns of various calibre. In spite of the inevitable regional differences in shipbuilding, F Olveira, the Portuguese master shipbuilder, comments in a document dated 1450 that Portuguese caracas (carracks), Portuguese-Spanish NAOs or NAVE and German HULKs were very similar ships from the mid-fifteenth century on. Carracks transported the Portuguese and Spanish between their homelands and Brazil and India in the sixteenth century.

CAREBE: A two- or three-masted nineteenth-century Arab sailing ship, around 12 to 15m long and 3m in beam. The mast arrangement was quite peculiar. The mainmast was strongly raked aft and carried a form of lugsail. The fore- and mizzen masts were almost vertical, or raked forward, and carried lateen sails.

CARTEL SHIP: A ship used for negotiating

Carebe, Tunisian coast, nineteenth century

or for exchanging prisoners of war. One of the early meanings of the word cartel was written agreement. The cartel ships sailed under a flag of truce and carried a single cannon, but no apparatus of war or no goods.

CARVEL-BUILT SHIP: *karweel*: Vessels on which the hull strakes are butt-jointed along their top and bottom edges, instead of being overlapped as in the CLINKER method. In the Mediterranean, and especially in Egypt, this method was known 4000 years ago. Carvel planking permits the use of shorter, thicker planks, and, where necessary, of double planking. Various sources state that the frame method of construction was not known to the ancient Egyptians, but this is open to doubt, as the carvel method works well when frames and planking have to be joined. In northern Europe carvel planking was adopted much later in the middle of the fifteenth century. The first large carvel-built ship to appear in the Baltic during the Hanseatic period caused a considerable stir, and led to a rapid transition from clinker to carvel style. *See also* CHEOPS BURIAL SHIP.

In the nineteenth century we can distinguish between the standard parallel carvel planking and diagonal or double-diagonal carvel planking. In diagonal carvel planking the strakes on the outside skin run horizontally, and the internal strakes run at an angle of, say, 45°. In double-diagonal planking the outer planks are also set at an angle to counterbalance the angle of the internal planking. Diagonal planking techniques were adopted in particular for certain areas of the outer skin of large, usually highly stressed, boats and ships.

The first large carvel-built ship to sail in the Baltic Sea was *The Great Caravel* or the *Grosse Kraweel*. In 1462, the *Peter von Rosseel* put into Danzig from La Rochelle carrying a cargo of salt. She had been built by Breton shipbuilders, and was one of the first large carvel-built ships in northern Europe. The vessel needed repairs,

Carvel ship, ca 1480 (model)

Carvel construction

including a new mainmast to replace that destroyed by lightning in a storm, but the owner could not pay, and the ship was mortgaged to Danzig citizens on 19 May 1464. The ship's equipment was gradually sold off to cover the costs which accrued; this included the ship's six anchors. However, hardly anyone bothered about the ship itself until 1470. In that year the ship was completely rebuilt and caulked and fitted out to accommodate soldiers. On 19 August, the *Grosse Kraweel* set to sea from Bruges as the *Peter von Danzig*; its task to counter the attempts to disturb the Hanseatic trade by the English and French. In 1472, Paul Beneke took over the ship and operated it successfully as a pirate vessel.

In 1478, the *Peter von Danzig* was scrapped after sustaining damage. From surviving information and the data in the inventory lists, the size of the ship can be estimated as follows: deck length around 43m, beam at the upper deck around 12m, cargo capacity around 800 tons. A key dimension for ships of this period is, in general terms, the length of the keel, and in the case of the *Peter von Danzig* this was 31.0m, whereas the keel length of ordinary ships was less than 28m. It was not until 1488 that the first ship was built with a greater keel length — by half a metre — than the *Grosse Kraweel*. The total sail area, consisting of mainsail, foresail and mizzen, was around 760m². The number of soldiers and crew was around 350 men. The armament consisted of 17 guns, 15 crossbows, a wallbuesche or swivel gun and a blunderbuss and spears for hand-to-hand combat, according to the inventory lists.

CAT BOAT: The cat boat was developed in the mid nineteenth century in North America for fishing in shallow waters. It had a particularly shallow draught, broad beam and large centreboard. This vessel was further developed into a single-masted racing boat with a mast stepped very far forward, often right at the stem, with a large area of sail. This cat boat carried a high peaked gaff sail, but no jib. The very large sail area and unusual mast location restricted the boat's sailing and manoeuvring ability.

CATAMARAN: Originally a raft from the east coast of India consisting of three to five shaped logs bound together. The central trunk was longer than the side ones, and curved upwards at the bow. The word catamaran comes from the Tamil language and means, approximately, bound timber.

More recently, the term catamaran has come to mean a vessel with two hulls. The two hulls are connected by some suitable means, and fitted with a platform suiting the purpose of the vessel, be it for sport, transport, lifting from the seabed or fishing. A racing catamaran, the 80ft-long *Formule Tag*, holds the record for the greatest noon-to-noon sailing run with an average speed of nearly 22 knots. The 60ft-long *Crossbow II* holds the world sailing speed record. There are a growing number of smaller racing and cruising catamarans of all kinds.

CATAPHRACT: An ancient Greek open oared ship with fixed bulwark, but with no fixed deck on the transverse beams, which doubled as oarsmen's seats. Areas of the ship which were not required for oarsmen were covered in with loose deck planks.

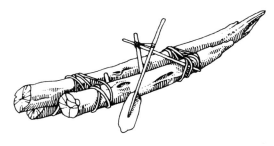

Rowing catamaran

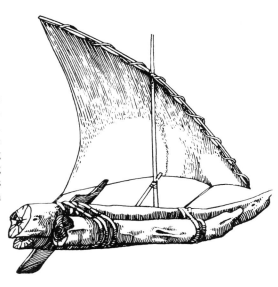

Log catamaran from the Indian Coromandel coast

A North American cat boat

Sailing catamaran

CELOX: A fast Mediterranean oared ship dating from around AD 400 to 1000, used for carrying despatches, but often employed as a pirate ship. This small vessel carried up to ten oars. The type designation comes from the Latin celer meaning fast and also alludes to the Greek verb kelevein meaning to drive, and thus to the command given to the oarsmen.

CHALAND: A French term for a barge or lighter used on rivers and coastal waters for transporting goods, and sometimes fitted with a small mast. The term is now applied generally to freight barges and SCHUYTS.

Chalands with different mast arrangements

French chaland

Russian chaland

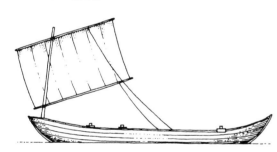

Modern racing catamaran

Chasse-marée, nineteenth century

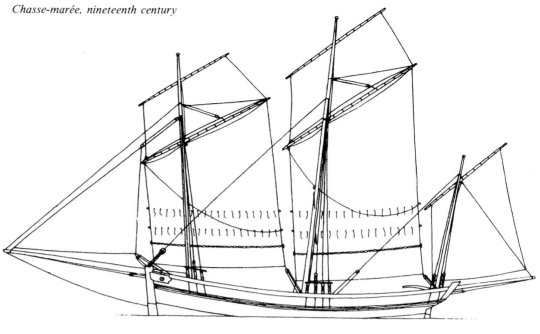

CHALUTIER, *chaloutière*: French term for a fishing boat using nets. Later used generally for modern types of fishing ship such as trawler or seiner.

CHASSE-MARÉE: A French two- or three-masted, fine-lined sailing ship with flush deck. It was used as a coaster, as a privateer or small warship, and for fishing, especially in the Brittany region, although chasse-marées also sailed as far afield as the Antilles. In their heyday, in the eighteenth and nineteenth centuries, these ships could carry cargo of up to 100 tons. On the three-masted ships the central mast was sharply raked aft, and carried an extremely large lugsail, which could be lowered on deck in bad weather. Above this

was a topsail. The foremast was almost vertical and stepped very far forward and carried the same type of rig, but with a much smaller sail area. The origins of this ship type can be traced back to the fourteenth century. The French term means, literally, tide chaser. Ships of Brittany are dependent on the tides, because of the huge tidal ranges which dictate when ships can leave or enter harbour.

CHAT: A Mediterranean ship similar to the galley used in the eleventh century and during the crusades. The vessel carried up to 100 rowers, with two men to an oar.

CHATTE: A lighter and coastal sailing ship of about 60-ton cargo capacity, used in France in the seventeenth century, similar to the French CHASSE-MARÉE. By the eighteenth and

Chatte, early nineteenth century

nineteenth centuries it had became a common coastal ship based mainly in Norway, and had the following features: a flat-bottomed hull, a large central mast, foremast and mizzen mast. Square sails were carried on all masts. The usual length was between 20 and 25m, the beam between 6 and 7m, and the draught around 2.5m.

CHATTY RAFT: A raft found in the Euphrates and Tigris region and in India formed by binding clay pots to a wooden framework. Rafts of this type were in use several thousand years ago, and they are still on rare occasions, encountered today.

CHELINGUE: *see* MASULA

CHEOPS BURIAL SHIP: Discovered at the great Cheops pyramid in Giza in 1954, this is the oldest surviving ship. Built more than 4600 years ago around 2650 BC as one of the burial ships for the Pharaoh Cheops (second Pharaoh of the fourth dynasty). This ancient vessel is of immense importance to ship-building history, and offers powerful testimony to the sophistication of the early civilization on the Nile, giving us insights into the Egyptians' religious philosophy concerning eternal life, sun worship, and the corresponding burial customs.

Kings and other important people were buried accompanied by those earthly goods which were believed to be of use in the coming life. Massive, elaborate royal stone graves were built, sometimes supplemented by additional structures, and decorated with jewellery, paintings, reliefs, model ships etc, and in some cases accompanied by the full-size ships themselves.

Three ship graves on the eastern side of the Cheops pyramid were already well known, but they contained only remnants of wood and ropework. During building work however, and excavations which began on the south side of the pyramid in 1952, a long, low wall was discovered, under which two further graves were located. The graves were covered with carefully and precisely hewn limestone blocks, each 15 to 20 tons in weight. Gypsum had been used to provide an extra seal, and this, together with the sand lying over the graves had produced watertight, airtight compartments which survived for four millennia with scarcely any change in temperature and humidity.

One of the graves, 31.2m long, 2.6m wide and 3.5m deep, was opened revealing a total of 407 ship components, including planks, beams, oars, steering oars, doors and the remains of hawsers made of Halfa grass, fabrics and carpets, either already dismantled or fallen apart, rather like a ready-to-build kit. Further dismantling during the restoration work showed that the ship consisted of 1224 timber components in all. Most of the parts were made of cedar wood from Lebanon and had survived in good condition with a water content of 10 per cent, which is close to the normal figure for dried timber. Various smaller parts were made of mulberry or figtree wood. The largest ship planks are 22.72m long, 520mm wide and 100mm thick, while the smallest parts were only 100mm long.

The ends of the planks were scarfed together, while their edges were secured with dowels. The floor and side strakes were connected by holes drilled through both parts

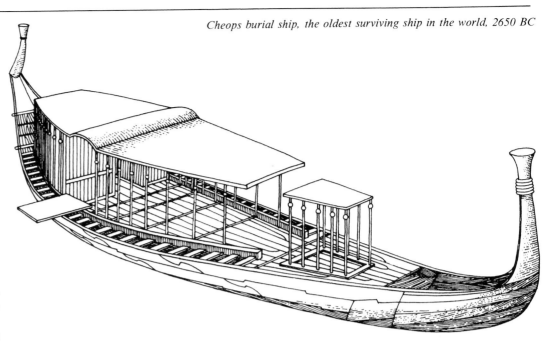

Cheops burial ship, the oldest surviving ship in the world, 2650 BC

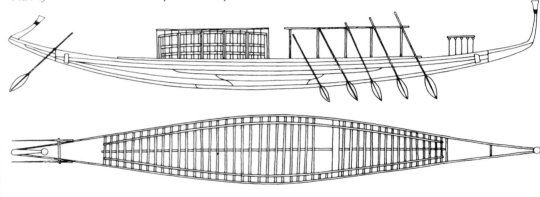

Plan of the reconstructed Cheops burial ship

Cross-section and construction of the Cheops burial ship

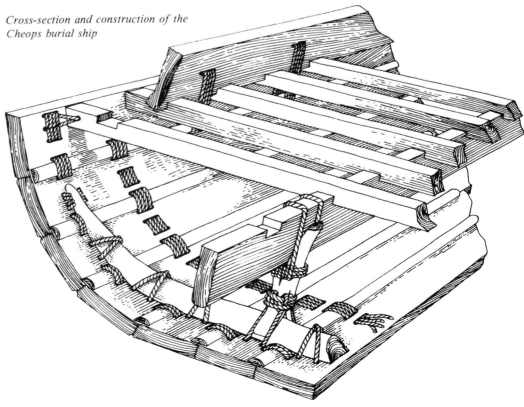

and wooden pieces glued in — similar to the still current method utilizing wood dowels. During the salvage operation the glue on these wood plugs was discovered to have retained its adhesive quality in spite of the long period of storage. The high resin content of the timber used may have prevented it drying out completely.

Six pairs of oars were also found in the grave, the longest pair 7.8m long and the shortest 6.8m. These oars were used mainly to steer the ship, which would have been towed by rowing boats. Thwarts for oarsmen, or other oar fittings were not present. There was also no sign of a mast, or any form of mast attachments or rigging, as the vessel's intended use did not call for any form of propulsion, although the design of the ship's hull would have allowed the fitting of oars or sails. Reconstructing the ship accurately presented many difficulties. After the original components had been treated to preserve them, they were measured precisely, and a 1:10 scale model was built to exact scale. In assembling the model ship the various possible arrangements of the individual components were carefully checked. The restoration workshop near the pyramid now houses the original ship, partially assembled. It has a slender hull with tall ends and a flat keel. The ship is 43.6m long, 5.9m wide, and would displace about 40 tons.

The discovery and the reconstruction of the Cheops burial ship extends significantly our knowledge of early Egyptian shipbuilding techniques and Egyptian sea travel, and has also led to the alteration of some earlier assumptions. The high degree of technical refinement and the sophisticated design and workmanship of the ship force us to recognize that there must have been an extended period of development prior to its construction, during which the Egyptians gained the experience and perfected the technical expertise required for the design of timber ships, the manufacture of individual timber components and their assembly into large structures.

The extensive use of cedar wood in the ship also proves that it had been possible to transport cedar wood from the Lebanon or other Mediterranean regions to Egypt at least as early as 2650 BC, either overland or - more probably — by sea. The transport of such large baulks of timber by sea required ocean-going cargo ships, or strongly built oared boats to tow the timber. We may suppose, then, that Egypt's fleet not only sailed the Nile, but also the eastern Mediterranean and the Red Sea, even earlier than is commonly supposed.

CHITIHA: Arab term for PINKE.

CISTERN SHIP: An eighteenth- and nineteenth-century ship whose holds were divided up into cisterns (tanks), for the transport of liquid cargoes such as drinking water and, later, petroleum and other liquids,

in place of the loose barrels previously used. The cistern ship is thus a predecessor of the tanker. Special boats for transporting drinking water have existed since the Middle Ages. *See also* PETROLEUM CLIPPER.

CLASS BOAT: A racing boat which meets certain dimensions and design criteria in order to place limits on its performance, and which is usually raced over short distances on inland and coastal waters. Boats of the one-design classes are, as far as possible, identical, ie all the design characteristics are prescribed and strictly uniform, while in the development classes, intended to promote further development, the designer has some room for manoeuvre.

The rules for international class boats are laid down by the international Yacht Racing Union (IYRU). The various classes are distinguished by the recognized class symbols which have to be clearly displayed in the upper part of the mainsail for international regattas.

CLINKER-BUILT BOAT: A vessel in which the fore-and-aft outer timbers are overlapped like roof tiles, in contrast to a CARVEL-BUILT hull, in which the strakes are butt-joined along their long edges to form a smooth surface inside and out. The strakes are joined to each other along their long edges by bolts, rivets or nails, or in the case of sewn boats by twisted fibres or leather thongs.

In northern Europe the clinker method was standard from the birth of shipbuilding until the fifteenth century. As the historic Nordic ship relics show, even very long strakes were worked exclusively with axe and adze. Sawing, for the production of straight plank seams, did not appear in northern Europe until very late. The clinker style of construction was particularly suited to the tools and shipbuilding knowledge of an earlier era, as the planks were joined not along their long edges, but on their overlapping surfaces, and thus thinner or slightly uneven strakes could be rendered sufficiently watertight by suitable non-water-soluble, flexible sealing materials. Clinker-built boats and ships were usually built from the bottom strake upwards, successive planks being added, and the overlapping joints sewn together, joined with wooden dowels or, later, iron nails or rivets. A variant of this method of construction is that used on the Chinese junk, whereby the strakes are overlapped in the reverse order, ie from the top towards the bottom. This is only possible if the framework is built before the planks are fixed.

In the early Nordic method of construction, relatively few frames were employed; they were of natural grown wood, and were fitted after the planking was in place. Extra hull strength was gained by means of doublers along the plank seams.

The first carvel-built ships, introduced in the Netherlands around 1460, for example, soon rendered clinker planking obsolete for large ships, but not before some extraordinary

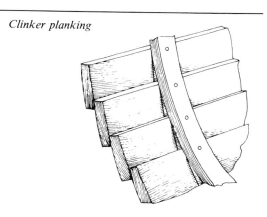

Clinker planking

clinker-built vessels had been tried. Probably the largest was the English *Grace Dieu* of 1418 which was as big as Nelson's *Victory* and constructed of triple-skinned clinker. However, stronger frame/plank joints, better sealing, easier maintenance and the lower water resistance were convincing advantages of carvel building.

CLIPPER, *clipper ship*: The famous, high-speed merchant sailing ship from the golden age of sail. The boom in sea trade at the start of the nineteenth century called for faster ships for longer sea voyages. Thus, in the period between 1815 and 1830 a new type of freight ship was developed in the New York and Boston yards on the American east coast. The starting point was the shipbuilders' experience in the construction of fast schooners, specially designed for higher sailing speeds. The result was the American clipper.

Among the characteristic features of this ship are the reduced freeboard and lack of superstructure, so that the dimensions and underwater shape could be designed for minimum resistance. The first ships, which were constructed of timber, had a length to beam ratio of between 5:1 and 6:1. With the transition to composite wood/iron construction, and later to iron and steel construction, the ships could be built even narrower at up to a ratio of 8:1.

The principal dimensions and proportions were chosen to reduce resistance to forward motion, but retain adequate surface for lateral resistance. The result was that the waterlines were particularly fine, and even concave in the forward part of the ship. The long, sharp, curving clipper stem characteristic of this ship type contributed to the vessels' racy appearance, reduced the wave-making resistance by dividing or clipping the waves (hence clipper), and extended the ship's length (useful for increasing sail capacity) whilst keeping the bowsprit short. The clipper bow has remained popular for yachts and passenger ships. Fine, tapering waterlines round the after body, and a narrow, rounded stern blended harmoniously with the refined forms of this high-speed sailing ship.

Even more pronounced was the increase in sail area. Clippers were usually three-masted full riggers, although the occasional four-

Clipper Lightning *under studding sails*

Clipper Lightning, *1854 (model)*

masted clipper was built. In its basic form, the sail plan was similar to that of the full-rigged ship, with square sails on all masts. The clipper had tall masts, up to three quarters of the ship's length, often setting staysails and moonsails above the royals. On the three-masted type the foremast was quite far aft, to allow a short bowsprit, and the number of staysails between the masts few, in order to favour the square sails. Ths sail area could be increased dramatically by adding studding sails to increase the width of sail, these carried on studdingsail booms on both sides of the vessel.

The 750-BRT clipper *Rainbow*, designed by John Griffith and built in 1845, was one of the first clippers in which all the typical features were brought together. Around this time American clippers began to travel the oceans of the world carrying tea, wool and grain between India, China, England and America. A large number of efficient clippers were then built in rapid succession, achieving worldwide fame for their extraordinary sailing speed, and their impresive appearance under full sail.

The American master shipbuilder Donald McKay built a large number of successful and famous clippers at his East Boston yard,

Clipper Lightning, *waterline length about 75m, sheer draught plan*

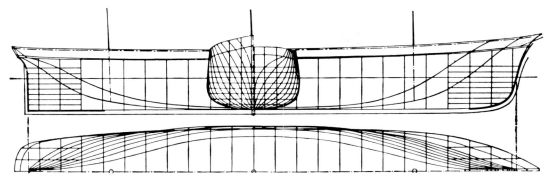

Four-masted clipper Great Republic, *1853 (model)*

Race between the clippers Ariel *and* Taeping, *1866*

founded in 1845, during the two decades between 1850 and 1868, among them the *Flying Cloud* (1851), the *Lighting* (1853), the *Great Republic* (1853), and the *Glory of the Seas* (1953).

The 1783BRT *Flying Cloud* made a noon-to-noon run of 433 nautical miles (roughly 800km). The *Great Republic* of 4000BRT had a cargo capacity of 5400 tons, a length of 100m and carried 1253m² of sail when fully rigged. The *Lightning* had a top speed of 18 knots. The clipper *Oriental* set up a record time for the voyage from New York to Hong Kong, covering the distance in 81 days. Famous clippers of this period also included the *Sovereign of the Seas* and the *Westward Ho*.

With the transition to COMPOSITE iron and steel shipbuilding, the centre of clipper building shifted to England, favoured by the advances made there in steel production and manufacturing methods. The size of the clippers varied according to the year in which they were built, the country of origin, the number of masts and their original purpose. The average dimensions of the clipper were 1200 to 2000BRT, 60 to 70m in length and 10 to 12m wide, and they could achieve an average speed of around 14 knots.

The clippers built in London yards competed directly against the American clippers and amongst each other, particularly in races to bring home the new season's tea from China; these races aroused great public interest. One of the most famous races started from the Chinese port of Foo-Chow in 1866. Five large clippers left the port at almost the same time, and reached London in 99 to 101 days, with the two clippers *Ariel* and *Taeping* arriving on the same tide, finishing in an exciting final sprint up the English Channel.

With considerable foresight, a well-known English clipper from the second half of the nineteenth century, the *Cutty Sark*, was preserved as a museum ship. The vessel can be viewed at Greenwich as a reminder of that epoch.

The term clipper came to be associated with speed and excellence and so was adopted for various other ship types when individual clipper features were adopted, eg on the clipper barque or clipper aak. In the nineteenth-century Russian navy the terms clipper frigate or clipper corvette were used, depending on size and rig, for particularly narrow, high-speed sailing warships. Fast tuna fishing ships, using hand lines, also adopted the clipper terminology, the vessels being known as tuna clippers. The term was sometimes used in connection with the trade involved, thus there were tea-, opium- and wool-clippers.

COASTAL LIFEBOAT: Heavy rowing boats with auxiliary sail were the most important shore-based means of aiding stranded ships until the 1930s. In 1798, the sailing ship *Adventure* sank in the Tyne estuary, and in spite of the proximity of land, the entire crew was lost. This turned out to be a direct stimulus for founding a Society for Rescue of the Shipwrecked. Nevertheless, the rescue service was of little account for a further few decades, until the foundation of a new society on 24 March 1824, which then received the title Royal National Lifeboat Institution for the Preservation of Life from Shipwrecks in 1854. By 1884 the institution possessed 284 lifeboats.

In France, private companies maintained lifeboats from 1825 onward, and in 1846 the first mortars were used to fire life-saving lines to shipwrecked persons. A French society, similar to the English lifeboat institution, was set up in 1865.

In Germany, the Gesellschaft zur Rettung Schiffbürchiger (Society for the Rescue of the Shipwrecked) was founded in Kiel on 29 May 1865. By 1885 there were 99 rescue stations on German coasts, 35 among them fitted with the principal means of rescue of the time (boats and rescue lines).

Two specialized boats were developed for coastal rescue: the Peake boat, named after its English developer, and the Francis Boat, named after its American designer: In Germany, the decision was made to adopt the Francis boat, which was the latest design at the time.

Coastal rescue boats were exceptionally stable and strong, had to have excellent sea-going qualities, and were meant to be unsinkable, with extra buoyancy incorporated in the form of cork inserts, air chambers etc. The boats were stored in the rescue stations on trolleys, and were taken to the launching site by teams of horses. The rescue crews, who had to be volunteers, then frequently placed their own lives at stake in the hazardous rescue operations.

Today the emergency rescue services are often state-run, while others, like the RNLI are purely voluntary organizations.

COASTER: An English term for a coastal sailing ship, although the designation was later adopted for powered ships.

COBLE: A distinctive type of boat from the northeast coast of England. It is CLINKER-built with marked tumble-home and a raked transom stern, almost oval in shape. A centre plank (ram) is the principal longitudinal member and to this a forefoot, extending roughly half the length of the boat, is fastened. The rudder projects well below the bottom of the boat and is unshipped for beaching. The coble is always beached stern first. Cobles are fishing boats and are of a number of sizes, up to around 13m. The length is four times the beam. Traditionally, they were fitted with a dipping lugsail. The larger versions had a bowsprit and a mizzen mast. Today most are fitted with inboard engines. The same name is applied to a flat-bottomed open rowing boat on Scotland's west coast, used for salmon fishing. It has a very broad transom and a marked sheer forward.

Cog, reconstructed model, based on the vessels depicted on the city seals of Stralsund (1329) and Elbing (Elblag), 1350

COG, *kagh*: One of the most significant early northern European sailing ship types, developed through many stages over a period of centuries. These were quite different from the sleek, oared and sailing Viking ships. Thus the broad-beamed knorren, which were cargo ships propelled mainly by sail, featured in large numbers in the nineth-century Viking fleets. In the early Germanic language kuggon or kukkon might have meant a curved, arched vessel or arched ship. There is another early reference in a report by King Alfred (871–900), in which it is clear that Friesian ships differed in design from the Scandinavian and English ships in use up to that time. In 948 the term kogge (cog) appeared for the first time in ships' inventories from Muiden near Amsterdam. The Norman ships which appeared a century later in William the Conqueror's fleet, and which became famous in Europe after the invasion of England in 1066, could hardly have

failed to influence the development of the cog.

Initially, two different basic types evolved. On the western French coast a CLINKER-built, rounded and full-bodied type known as the NEF was developed from the Norman ship, and although it shared various features with the original cog, the typical Friesian cog evolved as a separate type.

In the initial stage the obvious external features of the sea-going, single-masted cog were the straight keel, the squat, short hull with rounded sections, a keel length to beam ratio of 3:1, the almost straight, moderately raked stem and stern and the high-sided, clinker-built hull. Fittings for occasional oar propulsion were retained for a long period. The vessel's great beam and depth contributed greatly to its stability and cargo-carrying capacity. A fixed, full-length deck was sometimes fitted so that the cargo could be protected effectively from the weather. These

Cog

1 Single-masted cog on the La Rochelle seal, ca 1200
2 Hythe seal, thirteenth century
3 Stern of a cog, partially planked
4 Early form of cog, ca 1250
5 Cog on the seal of the English town of Rye, fifteenth century
6 Cog on the Elbing seal, from 1350

7, 8 Cog seals
9 Sheer draught plan of a cog, ca 1350
10 Stern of a cog, sectional view
11 Cog with after castle, seen from forward
12 Clinker and carvel planking
13 Hulk, ca 1480

modifications marked the gradual transition from a ship which could still be rowed, to the true sailing cargo ship. In this early form the cog was a single-masted sailing ship with one strong mast on which a large, rectangular square sail was set. Timber frameworks, later of castle-like form, were built at bow and stern in wartime to accommodate archers whose task was to defend the ship. Steering was originally by the standard side rudder on the starboard side.

Among the important innovations introduced on the cog was the first verifiable centreline rudder, in 1242. This was fitted on the sternpost and pintles and could be swivelled on a system of hinges called gudgeons. The introduction of the stern rudder greatly improved the sailing and steering qualities, and hence the seaworthiness of the cog. The stern rudder has remained the most effective means of steering ships to this day (albeit in a highly developed, streamlined form).

The development of the cog into a reliable sailing cargo ship was a most important technical advance, opening the door to the foundation of the city federation known as the Hanseatic league, and the resultant expansion of trade in the Baltic and North seas. Details of ship dimensions are contained in the calculations and customs reports of the Lübeck customs archives. According to this, cogs were classified into three sizes in 1227. Class 1: up to 10 tons, class 2: from 10 to 24 tons, and class 3: over 24 tons cargo capaity. The single-masted cogs could achieved speeds from 5 to at best 8 knots in favourable conditions. Smaller cogs were built for fishing.

By the beginning of the fourteenth century the normal size had already risen to 80 tons. A classification made in 1358 only differentiates between two sizes: under and over 120 tons. In parallel with the steady increase in ships' sizes came further developments; some were adopted for use on other ship types, especially the original Dutch HULK. In 1315, a great concentration of the two ship types occurred prior to a military campaign carried out by William III of Holland, in which the Friesian and Ijssel cities transported their entire contingent by means of cogs, while their allies from the Lower Rhine used hulks.

As a result of the intense trading activity by the Hansa, which at its zenith included about 90 cities, cogs travelled the entire Baltic Sea region and to Flanders, France, England, spain and occasionally as far as the Mediterranean. At this time cogs were built in large numbers in various countries. In 1386 alone, a total of 846 vessels left the then important Hanseatic port of Lübeck, with 598 leaving Hamburg, most of them cogs. The Hanseatic cogs, when undertaking long voyages, sailed in convoy, to guard against armed attack, and defenced themselves with archers, slings and catapults. By the end of the thirteenth century the Hanseatic cogs always flew a pennant, known as the Flüger, denoting

Reconstruction of the Santa Maria *in harbour at Barcelona*

Santa Maria *(model)*

their home city; for Lübeck it was red and white, for Hamburg red, for Rostock blue, white and red, and for Riga a black pennant with white cross. Around 1360, the castles were fitted with light guns.

Until the start of the fourteenth century cogs were clinker-built. The BREMEN COG, discovered during dredging work in 1962, is one of the few surviving examples of the type. It is probably one of the larger cogs from the last two decades of the fourteenth century. The length is 23.5m, the beam 6.20m and the depth 3.50m. The hull is clinker-built at the sides, but the bottom is carvel-planked with oak. Five powerful deck beams project through the outer skin, to stiffen the hull. The keel is 15.6m long, and reinforces the ship's bottom, which is almost flat in the central section.

The usual dimensions for a cog of 200 tons cargo capacity were around 15 to 16m in length and 4m in beam. The crew numbered up to 20 men. Around 1400 there was a further increase in size. From the single-masted cog evolved the single-masted hulk or holk, a sea-going ship with cargo capacity of over 200 tons.

The hulk combined those features of the original lower Rhine ship which provided good stability and load carrying ability, (flat, broad bottomed, with full, rounded sections) with the advantages of the later cog developments (keel, superstructure, extended prow, centreline rudder, improved sailing qualities). One of the external differences of the two ship types, which were very similar at this stage, was the design of the forward and aft superstructures, and the method by which they were incorporated into the ship's body, by means of upward-curving side strakes, running up to the appropriate level. Both ship types were still clinker-planked. These vessels represent the limit of clinker-style construction in respect of the difficulty of achieving sufficient strength in the frame/planking joints, and adequately watertight seams. The carvel method, which was in general use in the Mediterranean, was certainly known in northern Europe because of the sea connections between Brittany, Spain and southern France, as is clear from the inventories of Bruges in 1412. The rapid transition to carvel construction in the north did not occur, however, until the second half of the fifteenth century.

At the end of the fifteenth century the number of Hanseatic ships was estimated at about 1000, with a total tonnage of 60,000 to 80,000 tons. With three or four fairly short voyages per year with a full load, about 200,000 tons of goods could be transported annually. For example, Schonen alone exported up to 300,000 barrels of fish per year. In 1481, 1100 ships sailed from Danzig to Holland and Flanders carrying grain.

As is clear from the *Grosse Kraweel* (*see* CARVEL-BUILT SHIP) this late type of cog was really a two-masted or three-masted hulk, with three-masted ships predominating. In

Table from the Livro das Armadas showing Portuguese ships

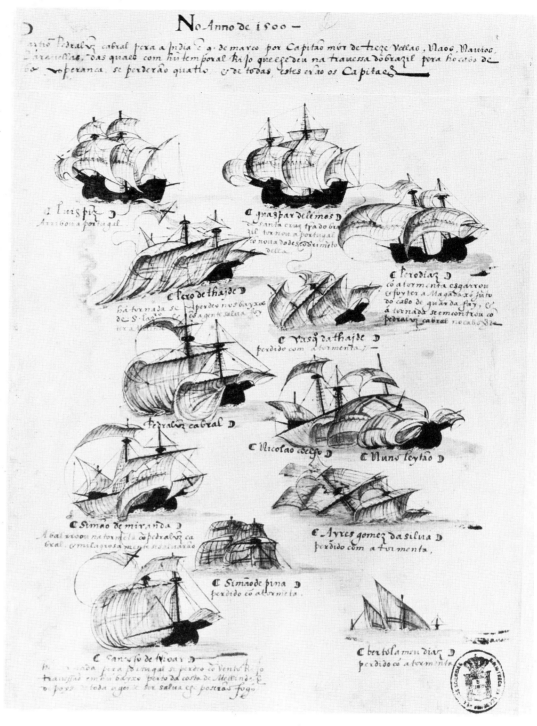

these three-masted vessels the mainmast was steped amidships, with the foremast on the forecastle. Square sails were set on the two forward masts, while the mizzen mast standing on the after castle carried a lateen sail.

COLUMBUS' SHIPS: The small fleet, consisting of the three ships *Santa Maria*, *Pinta* and *Niña*, with which Christopher Columbus reached America in 1492. His flagship *Santa Maria* is generally thought to have been a NAO while the two other ships of the little squadron, *Pinta* and *Niña* are usually termed CARAVELs. No authentic documents concerning these ships and their rig have survived, with the

exception of a few of Columbus' own log book notes. The standard contemporary Portuguese-Spanish term nao (lat. navis meaning ship) covered all three-masters of heavy construction, while caravels were ships under about 100 tons cargo capacity. Contemporary pictures and other research have provided the basis for various reconstructions and copies of the vessels, amongst which the Spanish and Italian designs are the best known.

The lack of authentic information is the reason for the differences in the reconstructions. It is thought that the *Santa Maria*, for instance, which was around 100 tons, would have been 18 to 24m on the waterline. She was Columbus' flagship. The *Niña* was probably about 90 tons while the smallest, the *Pinta*, was about 50 tons. They probably did not vary all that greatly in their lengths.

According to later research, the caravels were what are known as square-rigged caravels, although they probably carried a combination of lateen sails and square sails. Some latter-day designs show lateen sails on the main and mizzenmasts and square sails on the foremast; others show square sails on fore and mainmast and a lateen sail on the mizzenmast only.

A painting dating from 1500 shows various ships of C Cabral's fleet assembled for the voyage to India. The two three-masted ships in the upper part of the picture could be similar to the *Santa Maria*.

COMPOSITE SHIP, *composite clipper*:

A ship constructed of timber in combination with iron or steel framing. Iron was not adopted as a shipbuilding material until the 1820s, and even then only gradually, probably because of its limited availability, the necessary extensive modifications of yard equipment and working arrangements, the highly developed state of established timber construction, plus the problem of the effect of iron hulls on magnetic compasses (this was solved in 1839). Iron had been used to a limited extent as stiffening since the later eighteenth century, but the Royal Navy's Surveyor (head of ship design) Robert Seppings was the first shipbuilder to adopt iron bracing for timber in a systematic fashion.

Despite the disadvantages outlined above iron (and even more to steel) was much stronger for a given weight, so longer, lighter hulls were more easily constructed. Therefore, in an attempt to combine the best qualities of both materials, composite construction was evolved. Keel, frames and deck beams were built of iron for maximum structural strength and the outer skin and the decks planked with timber. Since the problem of fouling and weed growth on iron hulls had not been solved, wooden planking held the additional advantage that the traditional copper sheathing could be directly applied to the hull. As it was not until the middle of the nineteenth century that it became standard practice to use steam to bend timber (before this wood could only be bent by dry heat, warmed over an open fire), and as natural-grown curved timbers were only available in limited quantities, the constant increase in iron production resulted in the eventual dominance of iron and steel construction even in the building of the larger sailing ships.

The stiffest competition between traditional timber construction and composite construction developed between the American and English clipper shipyards at the beginning of the second half of the century. On the light high-speed sailing ships, every reduction in the vessel's displacement, every refinement in line and every improvement in stability had a

Frigate Constitution, *United States, launched 1797; museum ship at Boston (USA) since 1934*

marked effect on the ship's sailing qualities. The English yards' exploitation of English advances in steel production and manufacturing techniques resulted in their American competitors being outstripped. The composite clipper *Cutty Sark*, built in Dumbarton, Scotland in 1869, has survived from this period.

CONSTITUTION: An historic frigate, designed by J Humphrey, and one of the most famous ships of the US Navy. The *Constitution* was launched on 21 October 1797 at Boston. Originally, the armament consisted of 28 long 24-pounders and 10 12-pounders on the forecastle and quarterdeck. The vessel was first used against the French in the Caribbean in the 'Quasi-War' of 1802 and in 1804 against the Mediterranean CORSAIRs.

During the war of 1812 against Britain, the ship took part in the victorious battle against the British frigate *Guerriere* on 19 August 1812. The ship's crew gave the vessel the nickname *Old Ironsides* around this time, since the ship was said to have the scantlings of a line-of-battleship. In December 1812, the frigate captured and destroyed the frigate *Java*, and in 1815 succeeded in capturing two British sloops at the same time. After a long Mediterranean voyage, the *Constitution* was withdrawn from active service in 1828. The ship avoided the scrapyard two years later through a poem entitled 'Old Ironsides' by OW Holmes, as the resultant publicity raised enough money to preserve the vessel. In 1844–45, the *Constitution* undertook a world voyage. After extensive restoration work in the years 1927 to 1931 the ship visited numerous US ports, and in 1934 the ship finally came to

rest in the naval yard at Boston. The principal dimensions of the ship are: length overall 62.2m, beam 13.6m, depth 6.85m. The crew consisted of 22 officers and 378 petty officers and crew.

CONVICT SHIP: From the beginning of the eighteenth century to the end of the nineteenth century this term was used in England and France for a decommissioned warship which was used as a prison ship. Term also applied to vessels transporting convicts to Australia. *See also* HULK.

CONVOY SHIP: An early term for a warship which was specifically allotted to a merchant ship fleet as a protective escort. With the increase in merchant shipping in the fourteenth and fifteenth centuries, the Hanseatic League, the Venetians and the Genoese were the first to introduce purpose-built convoy ships, but the French and English employed regular warships. In the seventeeth and eighteenth centuries, Hamburg still maintained several convoy frigates. After the piracy problem had been overcome towards the end of the eigthteenth century, and as sea trade turned into a worlwide business, the convoy ships became obsolete. In English the term convoy originally meant the escort, but later was transferred to the ships under its protection.

CORACLE: A small boat, used principally for salmon fishing, found on a few rivers in Wales and England. It consists of an open framework

Contemporary print of the sea battle near Flamborough Head in 1779. On the left there is the English 44-cannon frigate Serapis, *on the right the American squadron coming from Brest, including the* Bonhomme Richard *(centre), a converted east Indiamen with 40 cannon.* National Maritime Museum, Greenwich

Fireship attack on the Spanish armada 1588 off Calais. Painting attributed to Aert van Antum. National Maritime Museum, Greenwich

Napoleon III receives Queen Victoria on board the Bretagne *in the harbour of Cherbourg.* Musée de la Marine, Paris

Coracle from Ireland (1) and Wales (2)

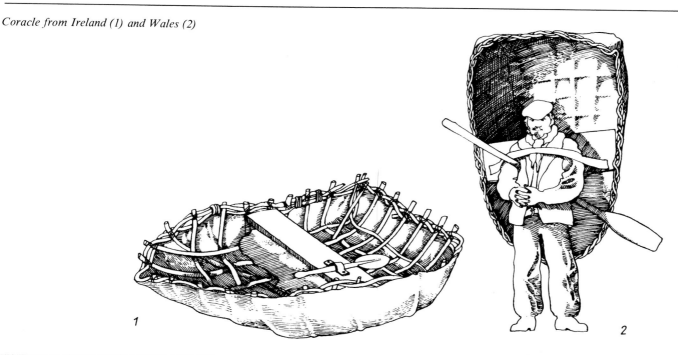

1   2

of wooden laths covered by canvas, calico or flannel, coated with pitch and tar to render it waterproof. Originally, the framework was of natural branches and the covering of hide. Coracles are generally one-man boats, paddled downstream and carried upstream. Although there is considerable variety in shape, even in some cases on the same river, all coracles have a set of longitudinal laths crossing a set of transverse laths at right angles (some types also have additional diagonal laths) and all have a seat fitted across the middle. Similar craft were found in Scotland and in Ireland on the River Boyne. The BULL BOAT of North America shows the same basic constructional pattern. However, the skin boats of India, known as paricil, although bearing a marked resemblance, have three sets of laths, each crossing at 60°.

CORBITA: A Roman cargo ship dating from around the first century, whose name has it origin in the Latin corbis (basket). They were squat, round-bodied, single-masted sailing ships (Latin naves onerariae; onus meaning freight) carrying 100 to 200 tons, and used primarily to supply Rome with grain. The ship size was limited mainly by the handling capacity of Rome's port of Ostia. The port was extended during the reign of the Emperor Claudius (proclaimed Emperor in AD 41), which enabled larger sizes of ship to be built. The freight ship depicted on the TORLONIA RELIEF is probably a medium-sized corbita. Smaller corbitae, which could be used for grain transport on rivers, are shown on the OSTIA FRESCO and the SALERNO RELIEF.

Wappen von Hamburg, *1688, Hamburg convoy ship of Admiral Karpfanger*

Corbita, Roman freight ship, first to third century

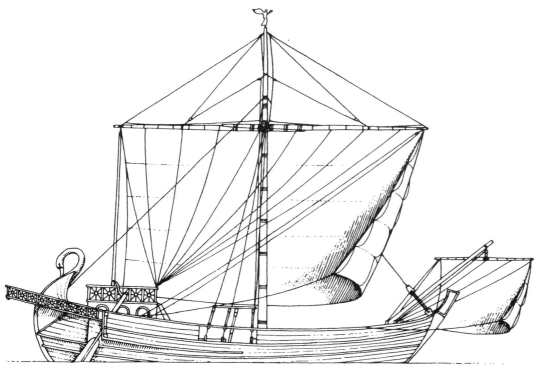

Curagh from the Irish Aran islands, ca 1920

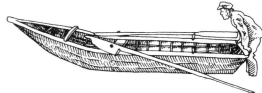

CORSAIR: In general terms a pirate, and hence his ship; however, the term was applied in particular to the Mediterranean corsairs which used to operate from Algiers, Tunis and Morocco. Originally, these were ships which were fitted out by their owners to harrass the merchant shipping of their government opponents, with official approval, or 'letter of marque'. *See also* PRIVATEERS

CORVETTE: A French term for a high-speed, three-masted, full-rigged warship equipped with between six and 32 cannon, although usually carrying 18 to 24. This term was also used in the seventeenth century for sailing ships which could also be rowed. In the eighteenth century the name was used for the smallest three-masted ship being in effect a small frigate, with a normal displacement, in

Mediterranean corsair ship

about 1815, of between 500 and 600 tons. They were the equivalent of the English SLOOP (14–18 guns) and sixth rate POST SHIP (20–24 guns). The guns were usually carried on the uppermost flush deck, and because of the lack of quarterdeck and forecastle, this type was termed the flush deck corvette. Corvettes carrying more than 24 cannon were built with light, short upper decks (topgallant forecastle and poop). These short decks accommodated the additional long guns or carronades; the main part of the maindeck, and hence the main battery, was not built over as on the frigate. In the nineteenth century some corvettes were built with one tier of guns below deck and a few uncovered guns on the weather deck, frigate-fashion.

Because of their speed and manoeuvrability corvettes were operated as independent units. They were also used as despatch vessels, fleet scouts and, in battle, as repeating ships (to pass on the comander's signals). The crew strength was between 100 and 130 men.

Sailing corvettes were much used in the French Navy. In Russia, at the end of the nineteenth century, exceptionally fast, slender small warships were termed clippers and clipper corvettes.

The term corvette was resurrected around 1940 for small anti-submarine escort vessels, and has continued to be used for surface warships somewhere in size between a frigate and a patrol boat or strike craft.

COXED FOUR: *see* FOUR.

CURRAGH, *currach, curagh*: A lightweight, wood-framed boat, originally covered with

animal skins, and later with other waterproof materials. The boat was usually rowed, but was equipped for sails when necessary. It was used for fishing, in a similar way to the Welsh coracle, especially on the west coast of Ireland, but also in Scotland and Wales. The boat is 4.5 to 5.5m long, has a beam of around 1m and can carry up to four persons. Curraghs are still in use in the Aran Islands, off the west coast of Ireland.

CUTTER: A fairly small, single-masted, sea-going sailing ship of English origins. The type was developed in England around the mid eighteenth century, at the time when the LUGGER (French: lougre) evolved in France. FH Chapman drew an English naval cutter in 1768. The single-masted vessel carried a large gaff mainsail, plus a rectangular square sail on a yard at the same height as the gaff. Above these two sails were two further square sails set on a topmast. There was a long, almost horizontal jib boom which could be retracted, and which carried a large triangular fore-and-aft sail. This rig must have been difficult to handle, and could only have been operated on warships with a fairly large crew; it was simplified in due course. Gradually, the square sails disappeared, and by about 1900 the tall mast, extended to over 20m by the topmast, only carried the gaff mainsail, above which was a fairly large gaff topsail. The bowsprit was now shorter, and carried three fore-and-aft foresails: the jib, the inner jib and the flying jib.

In comparison with other types of sailing ship, the short, straight-keeled cutter had a low tonnage, and a relatively deep draught. The sections were not full, the stem was straight and nearly vertical, and the stern was of the overhanging transom type. In the navy the cutter served to carry despatches and patrol close inshore, because of its good seagoing and sailing qualities. The cutter was frequently used for smuggling and also by the Customs and Excise authorities.

After the rig had been modified the type became widely popular, because its unusually large sail area was now simple to handle. Its excellent sailing qualities were the product of a deep draught (for stability), and the low-resistance hull form. The relatively short hull length made it very handy when tacking or wearing, and not least amongst the craft's attractions was the relatively low cost of building.

Soon many English sailing fishing vessels — for instance, the Essex SMACKS — were basically cutter-rigged. Cutters became the most

Corvette

1   Corvette under sail
2   Corvette of 1765, front view and main frame section
3   Cathead with stock anchor
4   Hull of a 22-gun corvette on the stocks, 1818
5   Carronade on a swivelling bed
6   Sheer draught plan of corvette
7   Sectional view of the bow of a corvette

Sheer draught plan of a cutter

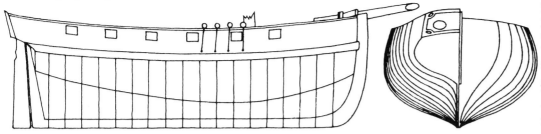

1   *Cutter after Chapman,* ca *1768*
2   *Topsail cutter,* ca *1900*
3   *Cutter,* ca *1900*

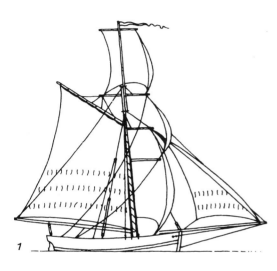

1

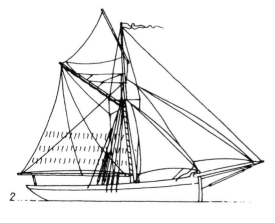

2

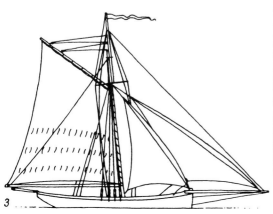

3

common utility vessel amongst other North and Baltic Sea countries, in the form of fishing, pilot, customs and cargo-carrying cutters. Even during the transition period to steam and engine propulsion, it proved possible to modify this type to suit the altered conditions. In a sense, the cutter became the predecessor of the racing yacht. Bermudian-rigged yachts are also sometimes termed cutter yachts, if they carry more than one foresail.

On warships, the term cutter is used for one of the ship's boats, which was equipped for rowing and sailing. They were originally clinker-built and shorter and more seaworthy than the BARGE and PINNACE, as they were usually used as the seaboat. These versions had an auxiliary sail rig which could be set up quickly, were 7 to 10m long and could accommodate 30 to 40 persons.

CUTTY SARK: This is the last surviving ship of those which took part in the tea clipper races in the 1860s and 1870s and it can be viewed at Greenwich to this day. The clipper is of

COMPOSITE construction, and was designed by Hercules Linton. She was launched at Dumbarton in 1869. The ship completed eight voyages in the tea trade, but never managed to beat the times achieved by earlier clippers. One sensational race was run against the *Thermopylae.* The *Cutty Sark* was leading by more than 400 nautical miles when the rudder gave way in a storm, and with an emergency (jury) rudder she took a week longer to complete the course than the *Thermopylae*, which finished in 115 days. From 1883 to 1895 the *Cutty Sark* was used on the Australian wool route, and was then sold to the Portuguese. For a time she was rigged as a barquentine. In 1922, Captain W Dowman bought the ship, had it restored, and refitted with the original clipper rig. After his death in 1936 the *Cutty Sark* was used as a cadet ship until 1949. In 1954, a dry dock for this veteran was built at Greenwich, where the ship is open for viewing as a reminder of the great period of the fast ocean-going sailing ships. The principal dimensions are as follows: length overall 65m, beam 12m, depth 6.50m. The sail area was 2980m^2.

CYMBA, *cumba:* Ship's boat of the Hanseatic cogs.

CZARNOWSKO BOAT: In 1897, the remains of a CLINKER-built rowing boat with a keel were found on the shores of Lake Czarnowsko in Poland. It was 13.76m long and 3.35m wide. The boat could carry six tons and dates from the tenth to eleventh centuries.

Fishing cutter Franz, *1867 (model)*

Bow of the Cutty Sark *in dry dock*

Clipper Cutty Sark, *England, launched 1869; museum ship at Greenwich, London, since 1957 (model)*

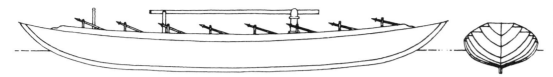

Dark, Indian double-ended boat, nineteenth century

DAGO BOAT, *San Francisco felucca*: A single-masted, lateen-rigged fishing boat of the California coast built by Italian immigrants in the nineteenth century and bearing a close resemblance to many Mediterranean craft. It was a CARVEL-built, sharp sterned boat, with almost vertical stem and stern posts, decked and brightly painted, some 6m in length.

DAHABIYAH: *See* DEHABIYA.

DÂK: A fast mail and despatch boat used in the nineteenth century on the Ganges. The fore and after parts of the boat were of the same shape. The hull was often copper sheathed, and was 16m long. The vessel was decked, and the sails were carried on two folding masts.

DALCA: A boat of limited sea-going qualities used around the Chilean coast. Originally, the dalca was sewn together from pieces of bark, but later then vessels were built primarily from the wood of the Araukarie in the form of a simple planked boat.

DAMLOOPER, *damelopre*: A common ferry and transport ship used on the canals and rivers of Holland in the seventeenth and eighteenth centuries. It was of very full-bodied design, 14 to 18m long, with a deck on which the folding mast with spritsail was set up.

DAR POMORZA: This three-masted, full-rigged ship was launched under its original name *Prinzess Eitel Friedrich* on 12 October 1909 for the German Training Ship Association, to train merchant navy cadets. She was commissioned on 8th April 1910. The specification is as follows: length between perpendiculars 72.6m, beam 12.6m, draught 5.7m. The ship was 1561BRT and had a sail area of 1900m^2. In 1918, the ship was transferred to France and was given the name *Colbert* in 1921, but was not used as a French training ship as had been planned. The Polish state maritime college bought the ship in 1929 as replacement for the barque *Lwow*, which had done long service but was by then obsolete. The funds to allow the purchase were raised by voluntary donations in Pomorze, and for this reason the ship was renamed *Pomorza*, which was subsequently altered to *Dar Pomorza* (gift from the people of

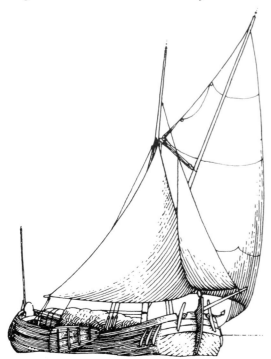

Dutch damlooper, late eighteenth century

Dar Pomorza *under sail*

Dar Pomorza, three-masted full-rigged ship, launched 1909, bow view; the Polish sail training ship.

shapes to the Egyptian papyrus vessels. The Dashur boats probably carried symbolic stem heads similar to the papyrus (rafts) with their characteristic stylized papyrus flowers. The hulls consist of short planks of acacia wood, up to 90mm thick, which are joined by the ancient Egyptian carvel method (interlocking brickwork-like strakes).

Investigations revealed the interesting fact that the boats did not consist exclusively of new timbers; some had been re-used. The edges of the carefully fitted plank components were connected by specially worked double dovetail pieces of wood. This method of butt-joining planks is much more difficult than the method used 1000 years earlier involving simple rectangular dowels, and represents a step forward for Egyptian shipbuilding techniques. To stiffen the hull and to provide a support for loose-fitted deck planks, transverse beams were installed, whose ends were pinned to the side planks with wooden dowels.

DAY DIVING BOAT: A diving boat built by an Englishman, Day, with which diving experiments were carried out in Plymouth harbour. During the tests in 1774 the boat sank complete with crew and inventor. This disaster is thought to be the first total loss in the history of the submersible.

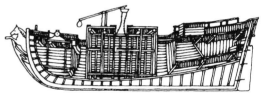

Day diving boat, 1774

Pomorze), after a stormy voyage under tow from St Nazaire to Poland lasting from December 1929 to January 1930. After the fitting of an auxiliary engine regular training voyages began. In 1939, the ship was interned in Stockholm and was transferred back to Poland after the War. After this the ship carried 150 trainees and a regular crew of 30 men for many years. The *Dar Pomorza* is the only large sailing ship to have rounded Cape Horn in recent times (since 1950). She has also taken part in the tall ships races and the sailing ship parades Operation Sail in Kiel, Gdansk and New York.

DASHUR BOAT DISCOVERY: Six boats discovered in Egypt in 1839 during excavations in the region of Dashur near the pyramid of Sesostris III, three of which were in relatively good condition. Two of these boats are at present in Cairo museum. The two are very similar at 9.90m and 10.20m long respectively, and 2.28/2.24m in breadth. The depths amidships are 0.74 and 0.85m. The third boat is now in the Field Museum of Natural History in Chicago. This boat is 9.74m long, 2.45m wide and 1.20 deep. The timber-built boats are of similar dimensions and

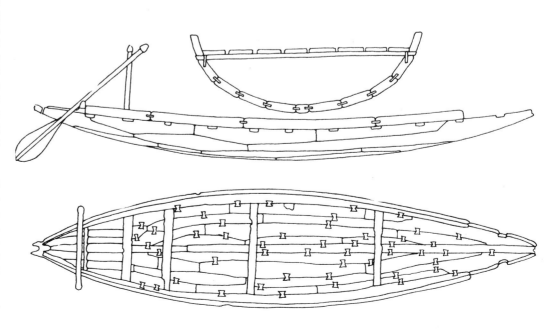

Dashur boat ca *1850 BC; cross-section, side elevation, plank arrangement*

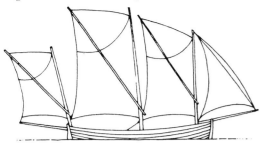

English Deal cutter, mid eighteenth century

DEAL CUTTER: The original term for the CLINKER-built, general purpose ship's boat that replaced the pinnace towards the end of the eighteenth century in the Royal Navy. However, Deal in Kent was also known for larger cutter-rigged vessels (also originally clinker-built) used for fishing, coastal trading, smuggling, and eventually by the revenue service and the navy.

DAHABIYAH: A cargo and passenger sailing ship with mizzen mast which was in constant use on the Nile for passenger trips between 1820 and 1920. It had widely-spaced masts, and could also be rowed if necessary. After Napoleon's unsuccessful campaign in Egypt, interest in this land of ancient civilisations began to grow in Europe. As a result, a ship

Fleute Derfflinger *(model)*

type evolved, expressly to carry the many prosperous Europeans up the Nile to Aswan, in which ancient Egyptian traditions were combined with elements of the European river ships.

The hull of the dehabiyah was flat, to allow for the Nile sandbanks, and was similar to the typically slender European designs. The dehabiyah was up to 15m long and had a beam of around 3.5m. The after part of the ship featured a long, spacious cabin superstructure for 8 to 10 persons, with a light sunshade for those who wished to remain on deck. For sailing upstream, utilizing the prevailing northerly wind, a pole mast standing well forward carried a large lateen sail on a very long, angled yard, which could be up to 1.5 times the hull length. On the mizzen mast was set a smaller, triangular gaffsail, intended to improve manoeuvrability.

DEKERE: A large oared warship from the time of Alexander the Great of Macedonia (356–323 BC). Ten oarsmen were said to propel the ships (hence the name, from the Greek deka, meaning 10), sitting side by side, one man to an oar. This arrangement makes it a single-row oared ship, or **MONER**.

DERFFLINGER: This armed FLEUTE sailed under the Danzig flag with the name of *Wolkensäule* until 1684, when she was acquired by B Raule under commission to the Grand Elector. In 1685, she was renamed *Derfflinger* in honour of the Prussian Marshal Derfflinger (Battle of Fehrbellin). The fleute was 33.5m long, 7m wide, and carried a load of

Large Egyptian dehabiyah, ca *1870 (model)*

340 tons. She was built as a two-decked ship with a large stern opening for the tiller, a typical feature of the fleute. The usual armament included two 6-pounder cannon on the 'tween deck at the stern, and four cannon of medium calibre on the forecastle, as well as a varying number of medium-sized guns on the main deck, depending on the task in hand. Thus the maximum armament would have been a total of 16 guns. The crew strength was between 15 and 20 men.

The *Derfflinger*, like the majority of fleuten, carried two square sails on the foremast and mainmast, and a lateen sail on the mizzen. From 1686 to 1693 she sailed to West Africa and India, was taken by a French pirate in 1693, then recaptured by an English frigate, transferred back to Prussia on payment of salvage dues, and sold to a new owner at Emden in 1694.

DEVELOPMENT CLASS BOAT: *See* CLASS BOAT

DGHAISA: A Maltese water taxi, rowed around the harbour. It has vertical stem and stern posts, each shaped like a scimitar, and a washstrake composed of a number of removable panels. Like many Mediterranean boats, it is brightly decorated.

DHANGI, *dhangiyah*: An Indian DHOW which has been in use since the seventeenth century. It is usually a single-masted vessel, but also existed in a ketch-type form. The hull has

Nurih of 1830 (model), oldest type of the west Arabian dhow, whose origins can be traced back to the thirteenth century

Two-masted Arabian/east African dhow of the nineteenth century; rig and cross-section

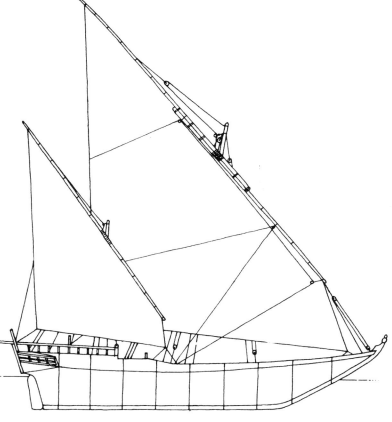

Late medieval dhangi from Oman

a short keel with a long, projecting stem, as on the dhow, and also the typical settee sail set on a mast raked slightly forward. The stem is usually pointed. One dhangi was over 38m long.

DHONI: A primitive form of the Indian/Arabic DHOW group of ship types with sewn-plank strakes, a long, projecting prow and tapered stern. Because of the tall stern, the afterpart tapered to a point, ending in a sternpost which contributed to the good sailing qualities, as well as serving as rudder

post. The original dhoni was uncovered, the hull being stiffened by deck beams which passed through the outer skin. Later variants had a full-length deck. The dhoni initially carried trapezoid lugsails on the main and mizzen masts, but this rig eventually evolved into the later mast arrangement with foremast and mainmast carrying lateen and stay-sails.

DHOW, *dhau*: Generic term for various Arab and Indian sailing ships with similar and characteristic hull forms and mast and sail arrangements. The group includes such types such as the BAGGALA, BATTELA, BÛM, DHANGI, GHANJA, KOTIA, MTEPE, PATTAMAR, SAMBUK and ZARUK.

The origins of these Arab ship types can probably be traced back to the first centuries AD. We do not have definite information on them until the fifteenth and sixteenth centuries, however. The one-or two-masted ships (depending on size — up to 200 tons displacement) featured the typical dhow rig, with settee sails set on long, sloping yards attached to relatively short masts, which were sometimes, sharply raked forward, but were not extended by topmasts. Ships of the dhow type were for many centuries the dominant means of transport over the route along the east coast of Africa to the Red Sea and to the Arabian Gulf and even to the coast of India, a

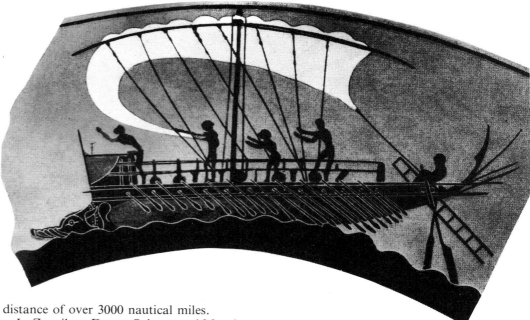

distance of over 3000 nautical miles.

In Zanzibar, Dar es Salaam and Mombasa there were special dhow ports until very recently. On the Kenyan coast, as in many other countries, dhows have been built by the traditional shipbuilding methods for centuries, and are still being built to this day.

DIBAIK: An Indian oared vessel with 30 to 40 oarsmen.

Greek dier under sail, on a sixth-century BC Etruscan vase

DIELEN BOAT, *dielen ship*: A flat-prowed fishing vessel operated mainly on the lower Weser from the eighteenth century to the beginning of the nineteenth century. The sides of this vessel consisted of at least three planks (dielen). The smaller vessels, which were 5 to 6m long, were known as dielen or delen boats. The larger dielen ship had three masts, was around 8m long and 2.5m wide, and featured outward-sloping hull sides.

DIER: A Greek, high-speed oared warship with two rows of oars on each side, which existed around 500 BC. Diers carried up to 100 oarsmen, and for special occasions a mast could be stepped and set. Even bigger warships were built which were known as TRIERS. The Romans built their own versions of the dier, and called them BIREMES.

DINGHI: A rowing boat of around 6m length, used for pleasure trips and trade on Indian coastal waters and on the Ganges in the eighteenth and nineteenth centuries. The after part of the boat was sometimes covered or had a roof over part of the area.

Doni, ca 1900 (model); oldest type of the Indian and Arab dhow, with origins in the early Middle Ages

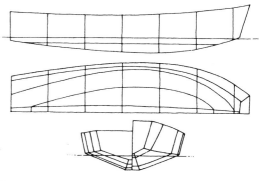

Sheer draught plan of a pram dinghy

DINGHY: Originally, a simple planked boat, without keel, frames or other fittings, which came from East India (Bengal). The planks were originally bound together, then later connected by staples or clamps. At the end of the nineteenth century this term became common in the English and German navies for the smallest ship's boat, built in simple, hard-chine form. It was rowed by one man, and was intended to transport individuals. At the beginning of the twentieth century the dinghy became a popular small racing boat, especially as a rowing or sailing boat for young people. Dinghies are now made using modern materials and construction methods and are used for all sorts of recreational boating.

DIVING APPARATUS, *diving bell*: A bell- or box-like device with an open bottom in which the air is trapped when the vessel is lowered into the water, thus enabling people to stay underwater for short periods. The apparatus has been developed and steadily improved since the sixteenth century. The sides of the diving bell must be airtight, and its own mass must be greater than the mass of water which it displaces. It is placed in the water with the opening downwards and allowed to sink. Because of the air inside the bell, the level of water only rises a short distance in response to the ouside pressure, and the diver is able to undertake tasks around the floor of the bell, or even to leave the bell. The oldest known diving bell dates from 1535, and was designed by the Italian G de Lorena. Another diving apparatus in bell form was built of wood to the design of the English carpenter William Phipps; this was fitted with weights and lowered on a chain.

In order to increase the supply of air, and thus to extend the period that the divers could stay under water, the English mathematician and astronomer E Halley (1656 to 1742) suggested, in 1716, that extra air should be made available in separate barrels, weighted down and connected to the bell by means of hoses. The water pressure acting on the barrels would force the air to flow to the bell as it was displaced by the water. After a method of producing compressed air was invented, this idea was abandoned in favour of pumping air through hoses under pressure. The English waterways engineer John Smeaton built an improved diving bell in 1778, which he called a submerging chamber, the basic design principle of which survived until the nineteenth century. For instance, a chamber with a cast-iron, box-shaped hollow body was still in use in Hamburg for harbour work until the mid nineteenth century. It was 2m high, and had sides 1.75 and 1.25m in length. The inside provided space for two workmen who stood on gratings on the bottom of the box. Air was conducted to the sinking box via hand-operated air pumps and hoses from land or from a diving barge, depending on the depth of diving.

The diving suit came into use at the beginning of the eighteenth century. This was a leather suit with headpiece and eye glasses, and was intended to allow the diver to work over a larger area. In 1797, the German engineer Klingert improved the method of entering the diving suit with the development of a removeable metal helmet. The present-day diving suits, which are supplied with air through a hose, still use this principle. It allows a diver to stay under water at a depth of around 40m for several hours. For greater depths (up to 90m, and in special cases up to 140m for short periods) the hoseless diving-suit, known as the Dräger diving apparatus (developed by the German engineers B and H Dräger) is used, and for even greater depths (up to about 200m) the pressure-proof Gallic diving armour is used. Around the middle of the nineteenth century the caisson was developed from submerging chambers, which permitted quite a large number of workers to operate at shallow depths for construction and salvage work, so was an advance on the diving bell and submerging chamber.

DIVING BARGE, *diving boat*: A barge-like pontoon with low working deck to support diving operations in sheltered waters. As well as the actual diving equipment, such as divng suits and air pumps, the boats carry special winches, lifting apparatus and underwater tools.

DIVING BOAT: The first stage in the development of submarine vessels, propelled principally by muscle power, and which were the predecessors of the engine-driven submarine boats and ships.

DIVING SHAFT, *Hersent diving shaft*: A further development of the diving bell (*see* DIVING APPARATUS). The Frenchman Cave developed the principle of the diving shaft in 1850. A large ship was fitted with either an external shaft-like structure or an internal shaft whose bottom opening was located below the vessel's waterline; the actual submerging chamber, which was manipulated by chains, was raised, lowered, and directed through the shaft. This arrangement made it safer to enter or leave the bell, placed its general handling on a more secure basis, and allowed larger bells to be used.

The French engineer H Hersent designed the first self-contained, floating diving shaft in 1879, for the building of Brest harbour. This consisted of a pontoon-like floating body, which could be sunk by flooding various tanks. Its floor formed a fairly large submarine work space when the side, front and rear walls had been pulled down. The first Hersent diving shaft, which was 10m long and 8m wide, and could be used at a depth of 12m, could accommodate 20 to 25 workers. The work space and open deck were connected by three shafts with air locks for transferring crew and materials.

DJALOR: A two-masted sailing boat which was used in northern Sumatra in the middle of the previous century.

DJERME: A one- or two-masted merchant ship with unusually large lateen sails, which gave the vessel a good turn of speed. They were encountered mainly in the eastern Mediterranean and in the Nile delta from the sixteenth century on. The foremast, which was raked forward strongly, and the very great length of the lateen yard, which could be up to twice the length of the mast were characteristic features.

DOGH BOAT: *dogboat*: A Dutch fishing boat

Diving bell, seventeenth and eighteenth centuries

Diving bell in the nineteenth century

Dogh boat ca 1600, Dutch fishing boat

mentioned in about 1400 and generally well known by 1540. Röding explains the name as follows: 'when this vessel has begun fishing by casting its net, or long-lines to which many baited fishing hooks are attached, then the boat is said to "doggern"'. In addition to the original small boats of this name, the term was also applied to nineteenth-century fishing vessels carrying up to 16 tons, and freight sailing ships carrying up to 60 tons.

DONGHA, *ekath*: A dugout used on the lower reaches of the Ganges and in various regions of eastern India. The basis of the boat is the trunk of the Palmyra palm which grows widely in eastern India. The bottom end of the trunk of this tree grows very thick above the roots. The wood is relatively hard, and for this reason the end of the trunk is not removed. The thickened end forms the bow, giving the dongha a broad, semi-circular cross section forward, tapering towards the stern like the body of a fish. Double donghas were also built on the Ganges, and in Kashmir donghas serve as house boats. The latter are not dugouts,

Double dongha on the Ganges

however, but barges up to about 15m long, with a woven mat sail and propelled by punt pole and oars.

DORY: Originally, a dugout from central America, but now the term is more commonly applied to a planked fishing boat with oars and sails. Dories have existed as flat-bottomed 3.5–5m long work boats since 1760. The vessels had a very broad, flat bottom consisting of three or four planks, with the hull sides sloping outward at around 30 degrees,so that several dories could be piled up on the deck of the fishing craft, one inside the other, if the thwarts were taken out.

Nineteenth-century dory

The Portuguese Bank fishing ships were especially well known; they fished the Newfoundland banks with many dories.

The dories would be rowed or sailed out from the mothership in the best cod-fishing areas in a fan formation, each of them carrying one or two persons, to catch cod using long-lines. The dories were sailed with a triangular sail and a small jib on a removable mast. One oar was then used as an aid to steering.

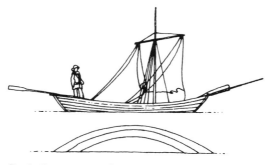

Doshnikes, nineteenth century

DOSHNIKES: A common houseboat on the Black Sea in the nineteenth century, with one mast and a sail.

DOUBLE BOAT: A common form of craft at the beginning of the eighteenth century among the Polynesians, especially on Tahiti, Hawaii and the Tongan and Fijian islands. Two boat hulls lay parallel to each other, permanently connected by transverse rods or platforms. A mast and a roofed-in area or deck-house were often erected on this platform. *See also* ANGULA.

DOUBLE BOAT: A sailing boat designed for confined waters, or for special purposes where manoeuvring is difficult. In contrast to the

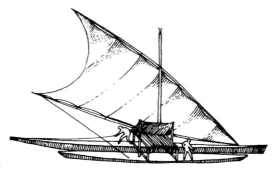

Polynesian double boat

double-ended boat, which had identical bow and stern but a rudder at one end only, the double boat has rudders at both ends of the vessel, to enable it to sail in either direction. Amongst the best-known double boats was one of the fastest of the South Seas outrigger sailing boats from Kiribati (southeast Micronesia). To ensure adequate stability these boats were always sailed with the outrigger on the weather side. The boat hulls were also sometimes built with asymmetrical hull cross-sections, to allow for the fact that the centre of lateral resistance was not in the centre of the vessel.

DOUBLE-ENDER: This term is used for vessels which are built symmetrically fore and aft, or at least are the same shape at bow and stern. In the early stages of ship development double-enders included the Egyptian papyrus vessels and the Viking ships. Smaller vessels with pointed bow and stern were more common. Modern vessels such as river ferries, which travel over short distances in both directions, are usually double-enders with identical bows and sterns.

DOUBLE OUTRIGGER BOAT: A DUGOUT or PIROGUE with an outrigger float on each side of the hull, attached by transverse booms in a variety of ways. Such craft are found in Madagascar, the east coast of Africa, Nissan, Papua, the Torres Strait, North Queensland and Indonesia (except on the Andaman, Nicobar, Nias and Mentawei islands). With the exception of the east African coast, single outrigger boats (craft with an outrigger on one side of the hull only) are also found in these areas. Historically, the distribution of double outrigger boats seems to have been much wider and it is thought that as a type it is older than the single outrigger boat. *See also* OUTRIGGER BOAT and SOUTH SEAS BOATS.

DOUGRE: *See* DOGHBOAT

DRAGON CLASS BOAT: A three-man international one-design keelboat, designed in 1929 by the Norwegian designer J Anker and commissioned by the Royal Yacht Club of Göthenburg. The boat soon became very popular in Scandinavia, Germany and England as the Dragon.

Whilst the shape of the hull has always been kept the same, the rig was improved in 1946. The tall rig of the Dragon is relatively small, and three different headsails may be used plus a spinnaker, in addition to the mainsail (23.6m²). The sail symbol is a large, black 'D'. Measurement is carried out by the International Yacht Racing Union (IYRU). The boat is 8.90m long overall, and 5.70m long on the waterline. The beam is 1.90m, and at full displacement of two tons the draught is 1.20m. The Dragon Gold Cup, instituted in 1936, is competed for annually in England, Norway, Sweden and Denmark. In 1948, France

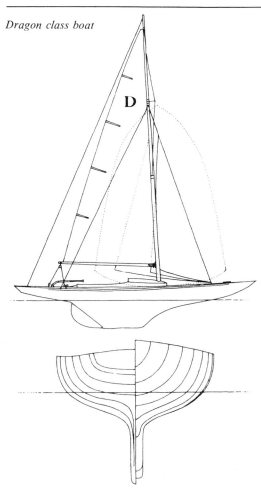

Dragon class boat

Dragon ship stem heads, Norse longboats

founded the Herriot Cup, in 1949 England presented the Edinburgh Cup for competition, and from 1948 to 1972 the Dragon was an Olympic-class boat. Since the 1976 Olympic games the Dragon has been replaced by the SOLING.

DRAGON SHIP: The largest and most imposing of the Nordic longships, the skaiths, were known as dragon ships (ancient nordic drakkar) by the Vikings. The skaiths differed from the other longships mainly in their greater beam and freeboard, and also by the dragon head set on the stem.

The majority of the Viking ships which have been found feature other animal heads on the stems, such as a horse head or a coiled snake (Oseberg ship). These animal sculptures were believed to hold the ship's soul, and were intended to ward off all dangers at sea — symbolic duties later transferred to the figurehead. When the ships headed back towards the homeland the carved heads were removed in order not to frighten or irritate the sympathetic home spirits, known as the landvettir, or guardian spirits of the homeland.

Dragon heads were evidently less common than other animal heads. A removable dragon head was found in the Schelde estuary near Dendermonde. This stem head dates from the eighth or ninth centuries and is now kept in the British Museum in London.

Dragon ships were generally termed kings' ships, because they were maintained by the

crown. It is said that ships with thirty banks of oars or even larger vessels existed. Snorri Sturluson, an Icelandic historian, mentions exceptionally large ships. He describes a ship called the *Ormen Lange* (the long serpent) belonging to Olav Trygvasson, which took part in the sea battle at Svolder (AD 1020); this vessel was 50m long, had 34 pairs of oars, and carried a crew of well over 100 men. Jarl Haakon's ship (AD 1200) is said to have had as many as 40 pairs of oars. Later ships, and especially Hanseatic warships, were often given names in which drake appeared (for

Far-Eastern dragon ship

drachen, or dragon), such as *Mariendrake* or *Jürgendrake*, harking back to the heyday of the Viking ships.

In contrast to the Nordic dragon ships, the Far Eastern dragon ships or dragon boats, such as those built in Hong Kong, were long, narrow vessels, 25 to 30m long, used for ceremonial occasions. These vessels were decorated at the bow with a carved, painted dragon head and with a dragon's tail on the stern. At the bow of these ships sat the stroke, who set the rhythm for the crew's paddles by beating on a small drum. The oarsmen sat in pairs side by side. Similar dragon boats are said to have existed in eastern Indonesia, especially on Banda in the Moluccan region. A picture on an old bronze drum from Salajar near Celebes indicates that these vessels must have been known at least 2000 years ago.

Amsterdam dredger or mud mill with hand wheel, ca 1600

DREBBEL DIVING BOAT: This was a diving apparatus named after the Dutch doctor Cornelis van Drebbel, from Alkmaar. He carried out diving experiments with his leather-covered barrels in England in 1620. A few years later a diving boat made of wood is said to have been built. This had room for 12 oarsmen and several passengers, and was intended to dive to a depth of 4 to 5m. A test dive is said to have taken place before James I. A contemporary report runs as follows: 'the ship was rowed and steered under water from Westminster to Greenwich, a distance of two Dutch miles. Inside the boat the light was so good, without candles, that it would have been possible to read the bible or other book'.

DREDGER: A vessel designed for scouring and deepening channels and anchorages, or for carrying gravel, clay, turf and other dredged materials; it carried machinery powered by men or natural forces to enable it to carry out its tasks. As early as the Middle Ages the fairways of some navigable rivers had to be deepened to counter natural silting. Iron rakes (dredging rakes) pulled by ships, or from the river bank, were adequate for the task at first, provided that the current was sufficiently strong. They were pulled over the river bottom to loosen the material, which would then be swept away by the current, as a picture dating from 1550 shows. Where the bottom was sandy sack dredgers were used — trough-shaped shovels, which were attached to rods of appropriate length in such a way that they could be dragged along by a cable after they had been placed in position.

The oldest report of dredging machines appears in a publication by the Italian Verantius dating from 1617. In 1724, Leupold described in his *Theatrum Machinarium Hydrotechnicarum* a Dutch harbour clearer, known as the modder mole, which can be considered the predecessor of the bucket chain dredger.

The wind-powered wheel dredger and waterwheel driven 'deepening machines' first appeared in the mid eighteenth century. The first dredging machine driven by a Boulton and Watt steam engine was built in 1796. In the second half of the nineteenth century the treadwheel dredger was developed. A rotating treadwheel accommodating two workers was mounted on a barge-like vessel along with a drum and a grab attached to a cable; the contents of the grab were emptied into a second transport barge.

DROMON: The most important Byzantine oared warship in the battle for maritime supremacy in the eastern Mediterranean between Byzantium and Arabia in the ninth and tenth centuries. Certain of this ship's characteristics continued the development of the Greek TRIER and the late Roman LIBURNIAN. These warships displaced about 100 tons, were 36m long, had a beam of 4.40m, and a draught of around 1.10m. The bow ram was often sheathed with metal plates. The upper side of the ram was sometimes located level with the waterline so that it could also serve as a means of boarding. The dromon had two rows of oars one above the other, with 25 one-man oars in each row on each side of the ship, ie a total of 100 oarsmen. The ship had a full-length deck, and the banks of oars were arranged with half of the oar benches under the deck, and half above. In the centre of

Scratcher, hand dredging shovel, first dredging machines

Dromon, ca 850, Byzantine warship, drawing from a Byzantine kodex

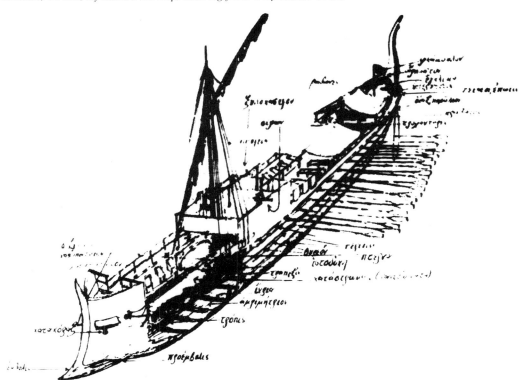

allowing a fire to burn at the bottom of the trunk for a long period. After a section of the log had been split off, the remainder would have been hollowed by the use of glowing timber embers, heated stones and localized fires, then wood, bone and stone tools would be used to deepen the hollow further. Where the dugouts had very thin walls, the walls would be protected with damp earth, moss or leaves during the burning-out process.

In some countries, for example, Bangladesh, man learned to increase the width of the dugouts by filling the inside space with boiling water, and spreading the sides with transverse beams. In Europe, dugouts were usually 4 to 6m long, but in England a dugout about 3000 years old was found at Brigg in Lincolnshire in 1886 which had been cut from a large oak tree, and was 14.80m long with a beam of 1.37m. The dugout was also widely adopted in Russia and Siberia. There the sides were raised by adding side planks, which were bound on with larch roots or osier-like twigs. The joints were sealed with resin.

Dugouts were generally propelled by paddles or by punt poles in shallow or marshy waters, although Chinese writings and drawings indicate that dugouts fitted with mast and sail were known as long ago as 2000 BC.

Nearly all the vessels of the South Sea tribes are based on the dugout principle. In the South Seas, dugouts were fitted with outriggers parallel to the hull to produce a seagoing craft. The Indonesian PIROGUE was in general use for a long period; this was a dugout which was hollowed to a lesser extent, then fitted with side planks. The DRAGON SHIPs used in Indo-China, China and Hong Kong for competition were formerly large dugouts. In India, and Sri Lanka, two dugouts of similar size were

the ship and at the stern were battle towers for 30 to 50 warriors, especially archers and launchers of 'Greek fire', an inflammable mixture of sulphur, tar and other materials which could not be quenched with seawater. Catapults were also carried.

Larger Dromons up to 50m in length were occasionally built up until the twelfth century; they were fitted with supplementary sails, with a large lateen sail on a central mast. But these later Dromons were gradually supplanted by the faster Italian galleys.

DUBAS: A two-masted Russian coastal SHALLOP. It was a cargo vessel of very full-bodied form, and usually made of oak (Russian dub meaning oak), it was used in the mid nineteenth century.

DUBASS: A general term for an oaken trough, but also used to describe a boat or barge used on the Bug (south Ukraine).

DUGOUT: A crude boat made from a single tree trunk and hollowed by hand. Such vessels have been built at some time in virtually all the inhabited areas of the earth which are close to water. It is likely that tribesmen originally adopted naturally occurring hollow tree trunks growing close to water by splitting them and sealing off the ends. At that time man used fire for the first stage of boatbuilding. Trunks uprooted by natural forces had their ends burnt off, and standing trees were felled by

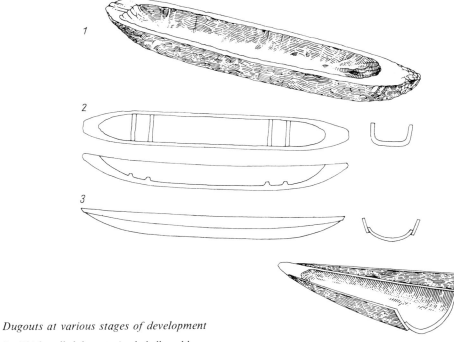

Dubas, Russian sailing freight ship, mid nineteenth century

Dugouts at various stages of development

1. *Thick-walled dugout, simple hollowed log*
2. *Thin-walled dugout with transverse stiffening members left projecting*
3. *Dugout with planks added*

sometimes joined in parallel with a platform on which a mast with sail could be erected, in an attempt to increase the cargo capacity and prevent capsizing. The aboriginal Indian inhabitants of Haiti built dugouts up to a length of 30m to carry 80 persons. The standard term CANOE used for these vessels had been adopted from the inhabitants of the Caribbean islands. The dugout is still in everyday use on tropical jungle rivers today.

DÜMMERSEE DUGOUT: A dugout boat found in the Hunte-Bett on the Dümmersee in Oldenburg in 1937, and one of the oldest remains found in north Germany. The dugout has been reliably dated at around 3000 BC by pollen analysis. The vessel is of softwood, 5.5m long and 0.6m wide, with a side height of 0.25m and of semi-circular outside cross-section. The two ends are spoon-shaped, and a transverse strut 120mm thick was left standing 1.20m from either end. The walls are thin, and the dugout must have been relatively light.

Dümmersee dugout, ca *3000 BC*

Brigantine Wilhelm Pieck *the East German sail training ship, built in 1961; steel hull, length overall 41.0m., beam 7.70mm, draught 3.55m. The total sail area is 433m², which drives the vessel at a maximum speed of 11 knots.*

*Heavy seas with ships. Painting by van de Velde the
Younger (1633 to 1707)*

*Boats in port at evening time. Painting by Caspar
David Friedrich (1744–1840)*

EAST INDIAMAN: Ships built for the East Indies route, also known as East India Company ships, as used by a number of nations for trade with India via privileged East India companies. Among the companies were the Dutch (1602 to 1795), the English (1600 to 1858), the French (1664 to 1770), and the Swedish East India companies (1731 to 1806); there were also Danish, Austrian and Prussian companies. The English concern was known as the Honorable East India Company or 'John Company' more colloquially.

As a type, the East Indiamen were hybrids of the warship and merchantman with one or two decks, and well equipped to defend themselves. The ships displaced up to 1100 to 1200 tons with an average length of around 40m by 1800; they were rigged as full-rigged ships with tall masts and large sail areas, which necessitated a beam of around 10m.

The ships' sterns were richly decorated with carved work, following the pattern of their predecessors, the Dutch and English man-of-war.

ECKERNFÖRDER FISHING BOAT: A nineteenth-century open fishing boat with pointed hull ends; it carried two or three masts and spritsails.

EEL BASKET BOAT: A flat-bottomed, clinker-built boat designed for handling eel baskets, and used in north Germany since since the middle of the nineteenth century. The eel basket boats were up to 7.50m long and 1.60m wide.

EEL JOLLE: A fishing boat with oars and lugsail about 8m long, used for eel fishing. In the nineteenth century it was a well-known boat type on the lower Elbe, especially at Altenwerder, near Hamburg.

EEL SCHOKKER: A single-masted sailing boat specially equipped for eel fishing. The boat carried a trawl net with an oval opening and a tapered, pointed bag, which was 'shot' on a schokker boom (lateral outrigger). The eel schokker operated mainly in the early twentieth century along the Rhine, where fishing was still productive. Fishing took place mostly at night, and one boat could often catch 80 baskets (4 tons) of eel, pike, perch and carp in one night.

EIDER BOIER: A small inland cargo ship employed on the Eider from the end of the eighteenth century. The hull shape was similar to that of the TJALK, while the part of the fore ship was rounded, and the broad stern similar to that of the KUFF. The type was around 12m long with a beam of about 2.70m. The vessel carried leeboards and later a large, flat stern rudder. The folding pole mast carried a gaff sail and a staysail. This ship type has not been built on the Eider since about 1885.

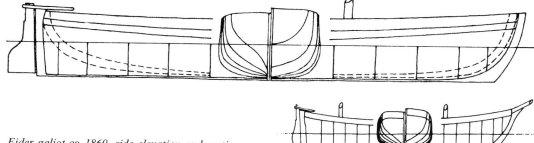

Eider boier ca 1870, side elevation and section

Eider galiot ca 1860, side elevation and section

EIDERBULLE: see EIDER SCHNIGGE.

EIDER GALIOT: A nineteenth-century river and coastal vessel with mizzen mast used in Lower Saxony, and the most important freight sailing ship in the Eider region after the Eider SCHNIGGE. In contrast to the more slender east Friesian and Oldenburg galiots, whose length to beam ratio was more than 4, Eider galiots were beamier and more full-bodied, with a length to beam ratio of about 3:5. Lengths of 16 to 17m and beams around 4.5 to 5m were common. Eider galiots were built on a keel with a rounded stern, considerable sheer, and leeboards. It had fixed masts on which were set fore-and-aft sails, with the occasional addition of a square foresail. The last vessel of this type was built in 1902.

EIDER SCHNIGGE: The most common cargo sailing ship in the Eider region in the

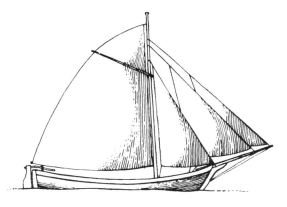

Eider schnigge with fixed topmast, 1875

eighteenth and nineteenth centuries, with the slightly larger two-masted Eider galiot following it in importance.

Schniggen were good shallow water sailing ships, working on the Eider and lower Elbe, but they also sailed as far as England and Russia. In 1864, there were still 120 schniggen, 114 of which were based on the Eider. Around 1900, the total was 75 while by 1913, the number had sunk to 30 vessels in all. The usual size of vessel was between 20 and 40RT with a length of 14 to 16m, a beam of 4.5 to 5m and freeboard of 1.3 to 1.8m. The ships were of broad and beamy design. Usually, the schniggen were single-masted, but there were also versions fitted with mizzen masts, which were termed besanbullen. The single-masters had a fixed mast with gaff sail, gaff topsail and three headsails. They had leeboards and carried a crew of two to four men.

EIGHT: The abbreviation for a racing rowing boat with eight oarsmen and a cox.

EKTHA: see DONGA

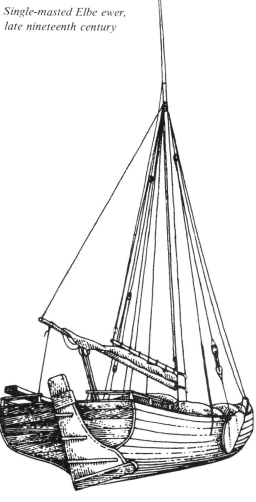

Single-masted Elbe ewer, late nineteenth century

ELBE EWER, *ever*: The most widespread north German ewer on the Elbe. There were two types, differing in size, but both of them were slender inland and coastal ships with relatively low freeboard and a very long, wide main hatch. The Elbe ewers carried grain, wood, peat, building materials and other goods between the mainland and the islands. Lengths of 14 to 20m and beams of around 4 to 6m were most common. The vessels' ancestors were mentioned as early as 1300 as Elbe ships. In the eighteenth century, Elbe ewers carried a removeable mast with yard, sprit or gaff sails and a staysail. Elbe ewers survived throughout the nineteenth century, and some into the twentieth.

ELBE JOLLE: A single-masted, half-decked, round-ended fishing vessel of the nineteenth century. It was around 12m in length and was used in the Elbe estuary for bottom fishing.

ELBE KAHN: The general term used in the seventeenth and eighteenth centuries for single-masted river freight barges. They were fitted with square sails, but were usually towed upstream. The size varied from area to area: on the upper reaches of the Elbe they had up to 50 tons freight capacity, but were twice as big or even more on the lower reaches.

ELBE SCHUTE: A flat, uncovered vessel with no means of propulsion, which was towed on the Elbe for the carriage of freight. At present, Elbe schuten are only used for transferring goods in Hamburg harbour.

EMIGRATION SHIPS: Ocean-going ships used from the beginning of the seventeenth century to carry emigrants, principally to America and Australia. The Portuguese and Spanish carried the first colonists to the newly-discovered territories on their CARAVELS and NAOS, which were their standard vessels at the time.

The emigration ships carrying settlers to North America became especially famous, among them the 100-ton *Halve Maen*, which took the Englishman Hudson to Manhattan in 1610, where he founded New Amsterdam, the present-day New York, and the 180-ton *Mayflower*, on which the English Pilgrim Fathers sailed, landing close to present-day Boston in 1620. Other early emigration ships were of similar size.

Around 1650, the great tide of emigration to

America began. By the mid nineteenth century the French town of Le Havre was the main continental emigration port. The full-rigged ships as built around 1850 could carry about 1200 tons of cargo. Under normal weather conditions such a ship could carry up to 420 emigrants from Le Havre to New York in around 40 days, although the voyage took much longer in unfavourable conditions; in which case conditions on board for the many people squeezed into confined spaces were often appalling. After 1850, the port of Le Havre was overtaken by the ports of Bremen and Hamburg in terms of numbers of emigrants.

By the 1820s regular scheduled services for emigration and postal transport were beginning to evolve from the German and English seaports.

After 1833, steam ships gradually came into use as emigrant carriers, but until about 1875 sailing ships still predominated. From the start of the twentieth century it was almost exclusively steam ships which maintained the emigration routes.

The number of emigrants was often several hundred thousand per year. The following figures for German emigrants give some idea of the strength of the tide: 625,968 from 1871 to 1880; 1,342,423 from 1881 to 1890; 529,875 from 1891 to 1900; 279,875 from 1901 to 1910; 9261 from 1911 to 1920; and 567,293 from 1921 to 1931. During the first decades of steam shipping, conditions on board ship for emigrants were no better than on the sailing ships. It was not until the 1860s that some general improvements were made. Gradually regulations and laws were established concerning the construction and fitting out of the ships; the subdivision of the ship into watertight compartments, a minimum space for each passenger, the inclusion of sleeping berths, ventilation, lighting, sanitary arrangements, medical care, and rescue equipment.

The passengers were divided into classes for the voyage. The third class passengers had the hardest time; these were the 'steerage class'. The 'tween deck was partitioned off for families with children, but unmarried persons were only given a place to lie down in the mass accommodation. Provisions for the emigrants on board consisted mainly of pulse soups with

bacon and salt meat; emigrants often had to look after themselves. Because of the unhygienic conditions and the overcrowding, many deaths occurred on the voyages.

EMS PÜNTE: A single-masted cargo ship, ideally suited to transporting animals, and used on the north German coast, especially in Haren an der Ems and in Leer (pünte, Harener pünte). These vessels displaced up to 120 tons, with lengths varying between 17 and 28m, a beam of 4 to 5m and a freeboard of 1.5 to 2m. The bottom was flat and ended in a projecting prow like a PRAHM, or barge. At the stern, the side planks tapered to a vertical sternpost. The broad, flat bow and the low sheer made the pünte ideal for transporting horses and cattle. In the central part of the vessel there was often a roofed area to accommodate the animals.

The Ems pünte had a folding pole mast which was situated fairly far forward (towing mast), and carried a sail similar to a spritsail. The vessel had two large leeboards, and the crew consisted of two men. Larger spitzpünten were also built on the Ems; these were vessels fitted with mizzen masts, on which the flat bottom tapered in towards the pointed prow, as on the smaller spitzmutten. Around 1900, there were still more than 100 Ems pünten in use; the last one was built in 1936.

ENDEAVOUR: A three-masted barque, on which the English explorer and circumnavigator James Cook (1728–1779) undertook his three-year voyage in the Pacific Ocean to Tahiti and New Zealand. The ship was a cat-built bark, originally built in Whitby in 1764 as a collier, intended to ply between England and Sweden, under her original name of *Earl of Pembroke*. After the Admiralty purchased the ship on 28 March 1768 the vessel was given the name *Endeavour Bark*; the suffix Bark was added as a sloop called *Endeavour* was already in the Admiralty lists. The expression cat-built indicated that the waterlines aft were very full and that the ship lacked the usual naval figurehead.

The quarterdeck was extended and raised slightly prior to the voyage, a square topsail was added on the mizzen mast, and ten 4-pounder guns were fitted. With a deck length of 30m, a beam of 8.9m and a load capacity of 370 tons, the *Endeavour* put to sea on 26 August 1768 with 94 persons on board. After discovering the Society Islands, Cook mapped the entire coast (2400 miles) of New Zealand, then covered the difficult 1000-mile stretch between the northeast of Australia and the Great Barrier Reef which lay off it. After the ship's return on 22 July 1771, three further voyages were made to the Falkland Islands, before the vessel was sold and resumed life as a collier in 1775. In 1790 she was used as a whaler, but ran aground when leaving the port of Newport (Rhode Island), and was severely damaged. So extensive was the damage that it proved impossible to repair the famous ship.

Cutaway model of the emigration ship Theone *(model) ca 1850*

Endeavour, James Cook's three-master, 1768 (model)

woven tubular boats of the Tigris/Euphrates area, which were sealed with ashphalt mixtures or covered with animal hides in a similar fashion to the QUFFA, and remained in use for millennia.

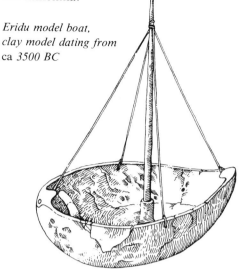

Eridu model boat, clay model dating from ca 3500 BC

ESCORT: A term used from about the seventeeth century for warships which sailed as protection to merchant shipping. *See also* CONVOY SHIP.

ESPINK, *esping*: Originally a dugout made of aspen wood. In the Middle Ages a light boat made of aspen was carried on board sailing ships, or towed behind; eg on the COGs. Later the Brandenburg-Prussian navy called an auxiliary vessel rigged with two spritsails an esping.

ESSEX SMACK: A shallow draught, cutter-rigged boat of around 11m with a flush deck

ENOTAJEWKA: A river sailing ship used in the eighteenth and nineteenth centuries on the lower Volga. These vessels were about 15m long, had a vertical stern and a stem sloping at about 45 degrees. The mainmast was stepped amidships, with the smaller mast or mizzen at the stern. A square sail was set on the mainmast, and a gaff sail on the mizzen.

ERIDU MODEL BOAT: A clay model boat, found in Eridu, about 60km south of the Euphrates-Tigris confluence (in present-day Iraq). The model was found in a grave site near the Eridu temple, which dates from around 4500 BC. The model dates from the time of the Obed civilization (around 3500 BC) and is oval in shape with a slightly pointed bow. The significant feature of this model is the distinct-ive moulded mast base located roughly in the centre of the hull, and the holes for stays at either end and for shrouds on the hull sides. These features make it the oldest known model of a sailing vessel in the world. Tradition has it that date palms were brought from the islands of the Persian Gulf to the mainland even before the Sumerian period. It may be that the vessels used were a larger coastal variant of the

Essex smacks from the fishing port of Maldon

and very low freeboard towards the stern. They dredged for oysters as far afield as Jersey and the Dutch coast, but occasionally also worked as cargo boats.

EWER, *ever*: A ship term based on the Dutch word *envare* meaning one-man vessel; it is probably of Friesian origin, and indicates a ship sailed by a single person. The origins of the vessel can be traced back to the thirteenth century. The oldest documentary evidence comes from a customs tariff dated 1252 from Damme in Flanders, and from purchase contracts from Hamburg dated 1299, in which certain vessels are designated as envar. *See also* BRUGES SHIP.

In the fourteenth century, these were still relatively small, but, nonetheless, sea-going vessels. In the Hanseatic period and in the fifteenth century, the term ewer was applied to a shallow-draught, roomy cargo ship without a keel, carrying about 100 tons. By the eighteenth century, the bow and stern curved up more strongly, but the shallow, strong floor was retained, while the stern featured a more slender, tapering underwater shape, with a keel. Above the waterline there was a transom which sloped aft. The forward part of the ship remained full-bodied.

The nineteenth-century ewer was a multi-purpose ship, built in large numbers. On the lower Elbe it seems that at least 2000 feight ewers were built between 1830 and 1910. Single-masted ewers were known as pfahl ewers — pole-masted ewers — and had a fixed mast and a large square sail or gaff sail. Later, numbers of ewers were built with mizzens — besan ewers (mizzen ewers) with gaff sails on each mast. At this stage we have to differentiate between round-stern or transom-stern ewers. Individual ewer variants were classified according to rig, ie square-rigged or spritsail ewers; and according to purpose, ie ferry ewers, turf ewers, fishing ewers and so on. They were also given regional names, such as Glückstädter, Lägerdorfer, Elbe, or shoal ewers and so on.

EWER KAHN: A small multi-purpose boat used on the lower Elbe, somewhat similar to the ewer in shape.

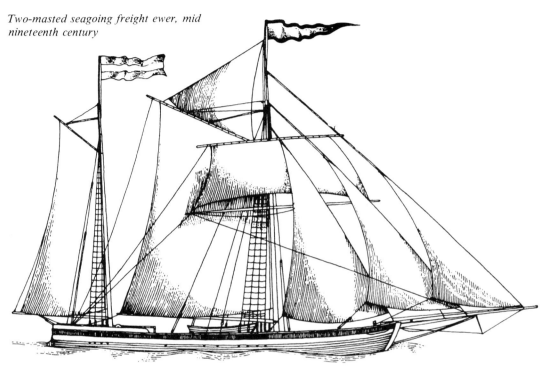

Two-masted seagoing freight ewer, mid nineteenth century

Freight ewer with large loading hatch, second half of nineteenth century, (model)

FALSTERBO PRAMS: Six vessels of varying size discovered near Falsterbo in Sweden in the years 1934 and 1935. They date from around 1300, and are flat, raft or barge-like structures between 13 and 27m long. Around 1300, several castles were built near Falsterbo and Skanør, and we can assume that the vessels found were used for transporting stone for construction work.

The barges have accurately cut bottom planks. A strange feature is the L-shaped cross-section of the transitional side strakes; the effect of this is to eliminate the gap at the chine between the flat bottom and the hull sides. Unfortunately, only small remnants of the sides survived.

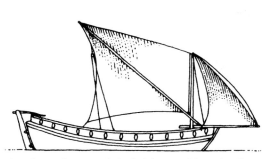

Small, single-masted Arab felucca with spritsail

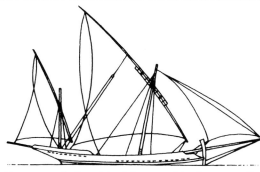

Two-masted Spanish felucca with lateen sails, eighteenth century

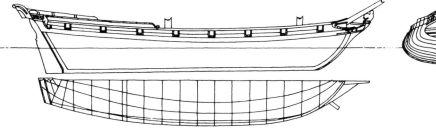

Spanish felucca, sheet draught plan

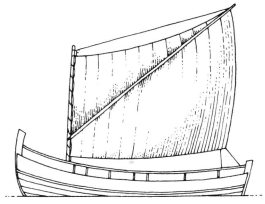

Maltese farella, nineteenth century

FARELLA: A small robustly built, nineteenth-century Maltese sailing boat which was used mainly for fishing, but was also sailed as far as Tunis as a cargo vessel. For such voyages, the freeboard could be increased by means of additional side strakes (washboards). Characteristics of the boat were the stem and stern, which rose very steeply, and the colourful paintwork. The vessels were around 5 to 6m long and 2m wide. They carried a spritsail on a short mast.

FA-TZE RAFT, *Pi-fa-tzû:* An inflated skin raft from western Kansu, China. It consisted of a number of small inflated skin rafts — each using twelve skins — joined together in pairs, so that the raft had between one hundred and two hundred skins and sometimes as many as five hundred. When the raft reached its destination down river, the wooden framework was sold and the skins transported back by camel. The skins were sheep, goat, bullock or yak, stuffed with wool or tobacco leaf and then inflated.

FEHNMUTTE: *See* MUTTE.

FELUCCA: A combined oared and sailing ship, similar to the galley, displacing about 150 tons, and used in the Mediterranean for coastal work. This ship type probably originates in the Berber states of Algeria, Tunis and Tripoli, where feluccas (Arabic: felukah)

were used as early as the sixteenth century by CORSAIRS and slavers.

The ships were about 15m long, with a beam of 4 to 4.5m and 2m freeboard. Feluccas usually sailed fully equipped (oars and sails) with a crew of about 30 men. The two masts were raked forward, and were rigged with one lateen sail on each, with a total sail area of about 100m². This manoeuvrable ship was widely distributed in the western Mediterranean (French: felouque; Italian: feluca), and was one of the lateen-rigged ships which was also encountered further north. The feluccas used in Spain in the nineteenth century as customs ships (Spanish: falua) were built on the same principle, but were up to 20m long, and hence more seaworthy.

FEMBORING: A Norwegian fishing craft with ten oars and a square sail. It was CLINKER-built with almost vertical stem and stern posts, around 12m long with a beam of 2.5m. The fembøring was found in Trøndelag and Nordland. Normally an open boat, some were fitted with a cabin aft, which was used when going to and from Lofoten and Finnmark. When fishing however, the roof was taken ashore, to make room for the nets and catch.

FERRY: A vessel used to transfer persons, goods and vehicles from one bank of a river or inland water to the other. The term ferry derives from the German fahren meaning to travel, and from the Old Norse ferja. The ferryman was also known as the ferje. Dugouts or barges were adequate for carrying people, but vehicles were transported on ferry barges, on which the two ends took the form of flat ramps to allow vehicles to embark and

disembark. In shallow waters ferries were punted. For regular ferry operations, cable or chain ferries were more efficient; here the ferry was pulled to the other side by means of a cable or chain running across the river, hauled either directly by muscle-power or by the use of capstan or windlass.

A different form of cable ferry operated with a single guide cable tensioned above the river surface. The ferry was attached to the guide cable by a central cable and two warp cables. By shortening or extending the warp cables the ferry could be set at the required angle relative to the current to produce the power to crab across the river.

In France, the first permanent ferry line was set up at Commines under Charles VI (1388–1422), and in Germany such ferry lines were set up in the seventeenth century, especially for crossing the Rhine. Larger, free-running ferries with oar or sail power were in use in the Middle Ages.

FERRY EWER: A north German ewer specially equipped for ferry work. This ship type was used for centuries between Hamburg, Harburg, Buxtehude, Stade and Glückstadt. The ferry ewer was an open, tapered-hull vessel, with a square sail, and small deckhouse forward. In the period between 1816 and 1844 the Harburg shipping guild had a total of 17 ferry ewers in operation.

FIFIE: A sharp sterned fishing boat of Scotland's east coast, employed in the herring fishery. Early fifies were open boats and CLINKER-built; later they were decked and, when larger boats were needed, they were CARVEL-built. It normally carried a high dipping lugsail forward and a smaller standing lugsail aft.

FINN DINGHY: A cat-rigged singlehanded round-bilged dinghy, designed by the Swedish yacht builder R Sarby for the 1952 Olympic Games. Since 1956, it has been a standard Olympic Class boat. The boat has to meet standard international design and measurement regulations, and must have a weight of 150kg including rudder, centreboard, mast and sail. The rotating mast has no shrouds and no stays.

The hull is made of wood or fibreglass, and the principal dimensions are as follows: length 4.50m, beam 1.51m, draught less centreboard 0.16m, draught with centreboard around 0.85m. The sail area is 10m² and the sail symbol is two short blue wavy lines.

Finn dinghy

FIRESHIP: Boats and ships of various sizes which were loaded with highly combustible materials, such as oil, pitch or tar, and which were directed towards enemy shipping on a favourable wind or current. The flammable materials and the ship were then set alight, with the aim of destroying the enemy ship's rigging and the vessel itself. Part of the art of a fleet commander was to take up a windward position so that the wind could drive the fireships towards the enemy fleet. They were used, for example, in the naval battle between the French and the Flemish in 1304. The Dutch also used them to defend Antwerp against the Spanish in 1585, and developed them into a form of 'explosion vessel'. The *Fortuna*, for example, gained particular fame

Fireships in The Victory over the Spanish Armada between Dover and Calais, *1588 (etching)*

by destroying a blockship with 18,000 pounds of powder. At the beginning of the battle against the Spanish Armada, the English used fireships with great success against the anchored Spanish fleet off Gravelines on the night before the 28 July 1588. Fireships remained in use in a similar form for as long as warships were built of wood.

FISHING BOAT: A boat designed expressly for catching fish. Collecting shellfish and catching fish were the main sources of food supply in many regions in the early stages of man's development, together with the hunting of animals. In northern Europe the Ice Age lasted until about 10 millennia BC, with the result that it only became possible for fishing and hunting peoples to begin settling the coastal area after this time. The oldest evidence we have of human settlements in connection with fishing in the north date from around 7000 to 4000 BC in Denmark and Sweden (Schonen). At settlement sites dating from the Stone Age, known as kitchen-middens, heaps of mussel shells and seafish bones have been found.

Amongst the oldest vessels employed for catching fish were the wicker woven boats and dugout. The HJORTSPRING BOAT, dating from around 300 BC is one of the oldest surviving northern boat relics. Although only a few artefacts have survived from the first centuries AD it is certain that fishing was carried out in the Baltic and North Seas at that time, using the techniques and facilities

available. Firm evidence exists that fishing was carried out in Flanders in the sixth century. The first documentary evidence dates from the Swedish royal archives for the year 900, which includes information on annual catches; from this data it is possible to deduce the numbers and types of fishing vessels in use.

It is also proven that there was a proper fishing fleet based at the French port of Dieppe by the year 1030. A high-volume herring fishing industry developed very rapidly in Holland around 100 years later, with the result that Dutch herring were exported to almost every country in Europe from the mid twelfth century on. The Hanseatic League also successfully carried out commercial fishing and fish exporting. The first herring company was established in Emden in 1553. A herring fishing company established in Emden in 1769 was granted the privilege to catch fish off the coasts of Prussia. In the course of time this company's fleet increased in size to a total of 41 BUSSES.

Dutch shipbuilding, which held the leading position at this time, developed other types of fishing craft as well as the buss, amongst which the HUKER was particularly important. This vessel was similar to the buss, but larger. The herring LUGGER fleets of Elsfleth on the Weser and Glückstadt also became very well known around this time. The lower Elbe region became one of the important centres of German sea fishing after about 1730. According to contemporary reports the Danish town of Blankenese was home to a fleet

Ketch-rigged Dutch fishing vessel, late nineteenth century (model)

North American fishing schooner Columbia *(model)*

of around 70 sea-going fishing ewers (in 1806 there were 172 ewers). These flat-bottomed, shallow-draught vessels were about 16m long, with a beam of 4.5m. The rig initially consisted of a pole mast with one large square sail. Starting in the eighteenth century the Blankenese ewer carried a foresail as well as the square sail. In the first decades of the nineteenth century the Finkenwärder fishing fleet out-numbered that of the Blankenessers.

FISHING EWER: A EWER with a special type of hold in the hull known as the fish well, whose purpose is to keep the catch alive. The fish well is sealed off from the rest of the vessel, but connects to the sea through holes in the outer skin, so that there is a constant through-flow of sea water to keep the fish in good condition.

FISHING HUKER: *See* HUKER.

FISHING LUGGER, *herring lugger*: This fishing boat was larger than the cutter, and was used for drift-net fishing and trawling. Originally, the lugger was only used for drift-net fishing during the herring season. Drift nets are long, wall-shaped nets which hang at a particular depth below the water's surface, held against the current by the lugger pulling on the net cable. Outside the fishing season the luggers were pulled up on the beach or laid up in harbour. Originally, the vessels were three-masters, rigged with lugsails, but more modern luggers carried gaff sails on two masts. For trawling a triangular sail was set forward, and the net dragged along by two luggers working as a team. In 1930, the last pure sailing luggers disappeared. The modern ship type which was developed from the original lugger, and is similar to it in appearance, has retained the old name.

FISHING SCHOONER: Specialized New-foundland fishing vessels, rigged as two-masted schooners with bowsprit but no jib boom; those with a simplified rig, without even a bowsprit, were also known as knockabouts.

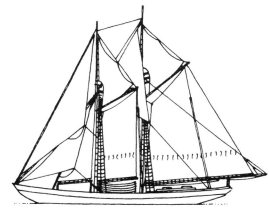

North American fishing schooner without bowsprit

Five-masted full-rigged ship Preussen, *built between 1902 and 1904, length between perpendiculars 121,92m, displacement 11,550 tons, sail area 5560m₂*

FIVE-MASTER, *five-masted ship*: A large sailing ship with five masts, regardless of the type of rig. A five-masted full-rigged ship carried square sails on all five masts, as on the *Preussen* built in 1902, which was the only example.

A five-masted barque set fore-and-aft sails on the aftermost mast, the mizzen, instead of square sails; the forward four masts were fully square-rigged. A five-masted barquentine generally carries square sails on the foremast plus gaff sails on the remaining four masts; however, there were also five-masted schoo-ners with square sails on two masts.

On the five-masted topsail schooner the mainsails on all five masts were gaff sails. On one or more of the forward masts up to three square topsails were set above the gaff mainsails, while the remaining masts carried gaff topsails.

The five-masted gaff-rigged schooner was a popular large cargo carrier in the USA up to the beginning of the twentieth century because of its small crew requirement relative to sail area; all five masts carried gaff mains and topsails.

505: A 16ft, 6in, two-man international class racing dinghy designed by Englishman John Westell. The 505 was the first of the 'modern' planing dinghies but remains highly popular due to its timeless, classic hull shape. The 505 is one of the fastest dinghies in the world with a Portsmouth Yardstick (handicap) of 97. Boats are strictly one design but can be built in either glassfibre or wood. The 505 weighs 280lb and carries a spinnaker and trapeze.

Five master

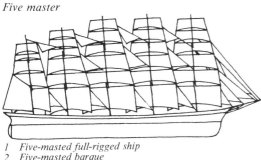

1 Five-masted full-rigged ship
2 Five-masted barque

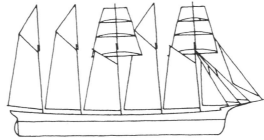

3 Five-masted Vinnen two topsail schooner
4 Five-masted fore-and-aft schooner

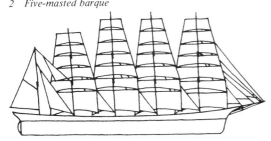

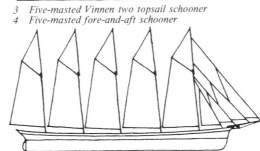

505 racing dinghy

Full-rigged ship Alt Mecklenburg, *473 RT, built by W Zeltz of Rostock in 1856, Museumsheft. Rostock Maritime Museum*

Painting by Hendrik Cornelisz Vroom, 1613. The three-decker Royal Prince *putting into the Dutch port of Vlissingen under foresail and bonaventure lateen sail. On the right is a boat with spritsail and leeboards, with weather-side leeboard raised. In the foreground is a state yacht with spritsail. An interesting vessel is the small boat with the curved mast set well forward, and the tall triangular sail, an uncommon feature at that time. Franz Hals Museum, Haarlem*

The Golden Hind, *Francis Drake's ship, 1577 (reconstruction)*

The destruction of Spanish galleys off the Flemish coast on 3rd October 1602, by Hendrik Cornelisz Vroom. The Dutch galleon Samson *sinks the Spanish galley* La Lucer. *Rijksmuseum, Amsterdam*

Galleys in the battle of Lepanto on 7th October 1571. The fleet of the Holy League, under Don Juan d'Ustria, defeats the Turkish-Egyptian fleet. Painting by a member of the Venetian school National Maritime Museum, Greenwich

FLAGSHIP: The command ship of a fleet, a squadron or other formation, from which the highest ranking officer (flag officer or commodore) exercised his authority. In accordance with its role, the flagship was fitted out to accommodate the fleet or squadron commander and his staff. In the merchant navy this term was adopted for the most important or famous ship belonging to a shipping company. Amongst the most famous historic flagships are the Dutch Admiral De Ruyter's *De Zeven Provincien* and Nelson's *Victory*.

De Zeven Provincien, flagship of the Dutch Admiral de Ruyter, 1666. Detail of a grisaille by Willem van de Velde the Elder

FLAMBARD: An open coastal boat used in Normandy in the eighteenth and nineteenth centuries. The vessel was up to 8m long, and served primarily for fishing, but also as a pilot and supply boat. The boat was usually two-masted and rigged with spritsails, but there were also single-masted flambards which carried square or gaff sails. At the end of the nineteenth century, flambards were also employed as sea-going and river yachts.

FLAT, *flatboat*: A squat, box-shaped vessel with shallow draught of about 1m (hence flat), which was introduced on American rivers around 1750. Also known as a zille, the boat was employed as a ferry. The sides rose vertically from the flat bottom, and were extended upwards to form a covered cabin.

This boat type grew to be a widespred cargo ship on American rivers, and survived until the beginning of the steamship era.

Flambard, French fishing vessel

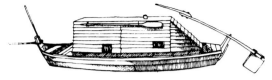

Flat boat, eighteenth and nineteenth centuries

In Britain the term flat was used to describe a species of barge-like vessels used on the rivers and waterways of Lancashire and Cheshire. Flat-bottomed and capacious they were orginally towed by horses or traps on the canals, but sailing versions developed in the nineteenth century. These were either sloop-rigged and were generally confined to the Mersey estuary, or they were the larger ketch-rigged 'jigger flats' which trailed along the northeast coast.

In the eighteenth and nineteenth centuries the term was adopted for flat-bottomed rowing landing boats carried on warships; they could accommodate up to 30 soldiers and also carry light field guns.

FLEUTE, *flute, fluyt, fluite, fliete, vliete*: One of the most important of the Dutch three-masted freight ships. By the beginning of the fifteenth century — and especially after the defeat of the Spanish Armada — Holland had developed into the acknowledged master of European shipping, and thus was the leading shipbuilding country in the world.

The terms fluite or vliete (meaning to flow) first appeared at the end of the sixteenth century, applied to a form of ship which was developed at Hoorn, in Northern Holland. The streamlined flowing form produced an elongated ship with a relatively small draught, in comparison with the more compact vessels which were standard at the time. The fleuten were especially suited to the shallow waters around Holland. The advantages of the type were very quickly recognized, and the ship became widespread in the Netherlands and other northern European countries, where fleuten were soon being built in unusually large numbers. The fleute assumed a leading position in European merchant shipping which it maintained until well into the eighteenth century.

The rapid development of the Dutch fleet and its great freight capacity is made clear by the evident fact that up to 2000 Dutch ships were involved in Baltic sea trading in the year 1607 alone. In 1660, the French statesman JB Colbert estimated the total nmber of Dutch ships to be around 16,000, improbable as it seems.

The fleute raised standards in the transport of freight, and in cargo ships' sailing qualities, to an extent only equalled by the development of the COG in the preceding centuries. Even the cities which had held a leading position with their Hanseatic cogs soon went over to building fleuten; Lübeck built the first ships of this type as early as 1618.

Compared with the usual ships of the time,

De Zeven Provincien in the Dutch-English sea battle of 11–14th June 1666. Painting by Willem van de Velde the Elder.

Dutch fleuten, etching by Wenzel Hollar, 1647

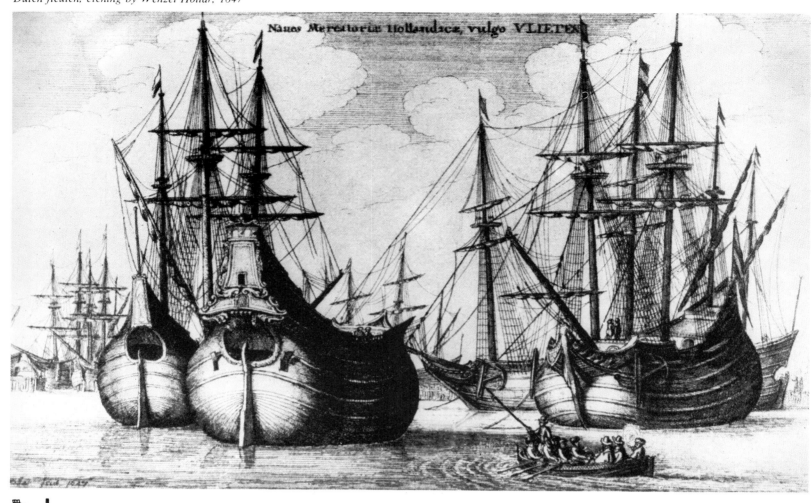

Naues Mercatoria Hollandicae, vulgo VLIETEN

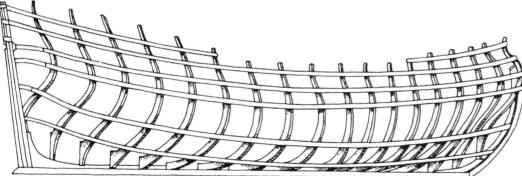

Frame model of a fleute, showing frames narrower towards the top

the fleute's dimensions, shapes and lines were harmonious and well proportioned. From the earliest stages of its development this freight vessel had three masts, and a cargo capacity which was considerably higher than other ships. The greater tonnage was not achieved by increasing all the major dimensions, and thus maintaining the usual length beam ratio of around 3:1. Instead, the designers adopted the unusual expedient (for the time) of increasing the length in comparison with the beam. Undoubtedly the draught limitations dictated by the shallow waters around Holland were a

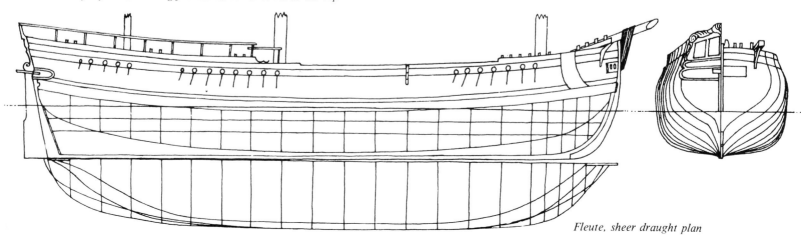

Fleute, sheer draught plan

major influence in this decision. The transition to a ship around 45m long with a relatively shallow draught and a length beam ratio of up to 6:1 was a revolutionary step. The extended, relatively narrow hull with its strongly rounded sections reduced the resistance of the hull substantially. The fundamental changes in the proportions of the ship undoubtedly represented a preliminary stage in the development of the later high-speed sailing ship.

The upper part of the hull was also the subject of further development. The increased hull length was exploited to space out the masts more widely; masts which were now increased in height by means of topmasts, an important Dutch invention dating from 1570, in place of the pole masts universally used up to that time. The total sail area on the extended masts was now subdivided into several narrower, more easily managed trapezoid sails, arranged one above the other. The mainmast and foremast were square-rigged with a mainsail and a topsail, and later a third square sail was added on both masts of larger ships. The mizzen mast carried an easily handled lateen sail, supplemented on the larger ships by a square topsail.

The bowsprit supported a small additional topmast on which a topsail was set, the white below the bowsprit on the spritsail yard there was a further square sail known as the spritsail. Main-, fore- and mizzen masts were thus equipped with a sail complement which proved so successful that it was to survive for several centuries with little alteration right up to the era of the BARQUEs.

The upper hull of the fleute also underwent changes in line with the larger and generally taller sails. The deck sheer, for example, became much more pronounced forward and aft, with the result that the superstructures, which had projected high above deck on other types, were drawn into the arch of the deck; one result of which was improved sail handling. The stern was rounded and featured an oval opening for the tiller, with a flat-faced, tapering superstructure projecting above it. At the waterline the hull was broad and rounded, but above this the frames curved inward strongly to produce pronounced tumblehome, and a reduced deck width compared with the beam of the ship at the waterline. The advantage of this design was the greater rigidity of the curved timbers, although another reason for the feature was probably the taxation structure of the time; for example, the dues levied for passing through certain straits were calculated on the deck area, which was relatively small for the cargo capacity, because of the tumblehome (inward curving) of the hull sides. The vessel could also be sailed by a small crew which made them very economic to operate.

FLIEBOAT, *vlieboat*: A flat-bottomed Dutch coastal sailing boat, which probably developed from the sixteenth-century DOGH BOAT.

Dutch fleute, mid seventeenth century (model)

The term stems from the original region in which it was used, the west Friesian island of Vlieland. Armed flieboats were included in fairly large numbers in the Prince of Orange's mosquito fleet in the war of liberation against Spain around 1588. The cargo capacity of the vessels was between 60 and 140 tons.

FLOATING BRIDGE: A temporary structure similar to a bridge across a river, formed by rafts, boats, pontoons or ships. The vessels would be made fast in the course of the river by means of anchors, placed ashore and in the stream and the vessels were made fast either close together or spaced apart, and covered with suitable materials to form a roadway.

FLOATING CRANE: An unpowered vessel fitted with special lifting equipment which exploited various mechanical principles to raise loads by muscle power. Such vessels have been known at least since the time of Archimedes (210 BC). For instance, special lifting ships have been employed to raise sunken vessels by throwing stone ballast over the side to lighten them and raise the vessel below. Pulleys, blocks and tackles fitted to crane beams, or a sailing ship's masts or booms, were also used for loading and unloading heavy goods. When the first harbour cranes powered by treadwheels had been introduced at important trading ports, they were soon followed by broad vessels with cranes erected on top, driven by treadwheels. For instance, a woodcut of the city of Cologne dating from 1499 shows several such floating cranes.

FLUSH DECK SHIP, *flush deck yacht, flush decker*: A ship on which the upper deck is full-length, without superstructures forward (forecastle), amidships (deckhouse, bridge) or aft (poop). Sailing yachts which have sufficient cabin height below decks without a raised cabin are also termed flush deckers. The deck is only interrupted by skylights and companionways but not changes in deck height.

FLUTE: *see* FLEUTE

FLÛTE: A French term (flûte) for fleute. Open, uncovered inland barges with full-length cargo hold have also been termed flûte since the nineteenth century. The phrase 'armed en flûte' was used in the eighteenth and nineteenth centuries for a warship in which most or all of the guns had been landed or removed into the hold, in order to make space for cargo, or to accommodate toops. *See also* FLEUTE.

FLYING CLOUD: A famous American clipper. Donald McKay (1810–80) was the designer and builder of this fast clipper, the only sailing ship in the world which succeeded in sailing the route New York — Cape Horn — San Francisco in less than 90 days, which feat she achieved twice. With a length of 68.5m, a beam of 12.5m and a displacement of 1728 tons, the *Flying Cloud* was one of the largest ships of her time when she was completed in 1851. The main masthead was 49m above deck, the lower mainmast was 27m long, and the mainyard 25m long. The ship's hull was built entirely of wood, fixed with wooden nails and iron screws (a few were copper). Below the waterline the hull was sheathed with copper plates. Some of the ship's outstanding voyages, which brought her much attention at the time, were as follows: San Francisco to New York in 76 days in 1851, San Francisco to Honolulu in eight days and eight and a half hours in 1852, and New York to Hong Kong via San Francisco in 126 days. From 1857 to 1859 the ship lay idle, and was sold to British owners in 1862. She sank in a storm in 1874.

FLYING DUTCHMAN: A round-hulled dinghy designed by the Dutchman U Van Essen, originally intended for European inland waters, but later sailed and raced on coastal waters. The Flying Dutchman is an International Class centreboard boat, and carries the sail symbol 'FD'. Since 1960, the

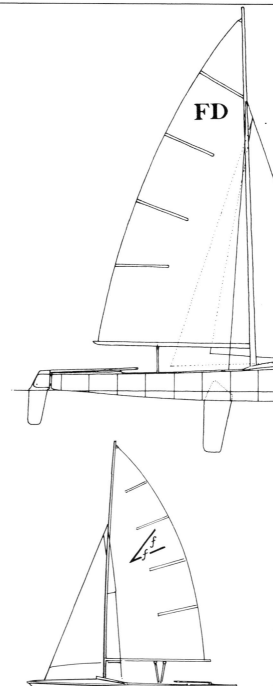

Flying Dutchman

Flying Fifteen

design has been an Olympic Class boat. The prescribed dimensions are as follows: Overall length 6.05m, beam 1.8m, draught including centreboard 1.1m and sail area 15m². A spinnaker of 17.5m² is permitted. The weight of the fully equipped Flying Dutchman must be 170kg, and the racing crew comprises two people.

FLYING FIFTEEN: A two-man, 20ft racing keelboat, originally built in cold-moulded wood but now in glassfibre, designed by Englishman Uffa Fox with a fixed bulb keel that was designed to be unbolted for transport. The class thrives in many countries.

FLYING P LINERS: An internationally recognized term around the turn of the century for the sailing ships of the Hamburg sailing ship company, Laeisz. The Flying P Line ships were four- and five-masted sailing ships whose names always began with the letter P.

In their five-masted ships, the penultimate mast was termed the Laeisz mast. Some of the most famous ships were as follows: *Potosi*, 4026BRT, 1895; *Preussen*, 5081BRT, 1902; *Pamir*, 3103BRT, 1905; *Passat*, 3183BRT, 1911; *Priwall*, 3185BRT, 1920; and *Padua*, 3064BRT, 1926. Among the less well-known ships were : *Pudel, Pangani, Patricia, Posen, Pensylvanie, Pretoria, Parma, Pisaqua, Pinguin* and *Pontos*, and a few others. *See also* PASSAT and PREUSSEN.

FÖHRING EWER: A specialized nineteenth-century variant of the north German EWER, operated around the north Friesian islands and the west coast of Schleswig Holstein. They were built at Wyk on the island of Föhr, and were single-masted ewers of particularly shallow draught, around 14m long and 4.6m wide.

FOLKBOAT: A one-design class CARVEL-, or CLINKER-built or glassfibre keelboat with a sail area of 22m² and a large 'F' as the sail symbol. The length overall is 7.64m, 6m on the waterline and the beam 2.2m. With 1.2m draught, the boat displaced 2.2 tons and has become a popular cruising boat throughout Europe.

FOOCHOW POLE JUNK, *hua-p'i-ku*: A three-masted Chinese junk deriving its Euro-ean name from its function: the carrying of poles (lashed to the sides of the vessel) from Fukien, where most of the junk building wood originated, to the Yangtze estuary. In size, such junks ranged from 37 to 54m and were rigged with characteristic battened lugsails. The foremast raked heavily forward; the mizzen mast was located at the end of the high poop deck, slightly off-centre for convenience in staying. Other distinctive features were the flaring bow and the oval stern elaboratedly decorated with a painting of a yen bird.

It is though that the junk *Keying*, which sailed to London from Hong Kong via New York in 1848, may have been similar to this type.

FORE-AND-AFT RIGGED SHIP: The generic term for all types of sailing ship which are rigged with centreline sails, in contrast to vessels whose sails are set transversely (SQUARE-RIGGED SHIP). Among the best known fore-and-aft ship types are the EWER, the gaff-rigged SCHOONER, the GALIOT, the KETCH, the CUTTER, LUGGER and TJALK. All staysails are fore-and-aft sails as are the jibs, gaff sails, gaff topsails and also the more modern bermudian sails.

FOUR: The abbreviation for a racing rowing boat carrying four oarsmen (each with a single oar). The four-man boat exists with and without cox (thus coxed or coxless four).

FOUR-DECKER: A warship of the line with four tiers of covered battery decks, not including the quarterdeck and forecastle. This type was confined to the famous Spanish *Santissima Trinidad*, which fought against the English fleet at Cape St Vincent in 1797 and was destroyed after Trafalgar in 1805. Most of the great warships of this epoch were three-deckers, and the Spanish vessel began life as such but was reconstructed with a flush upper deck by joining the original quarterdeck and forecastle.

FOURERN: *see* SIXAREEN.

FOUR-MASTED SHIP: The term used for all sailing vessels with four masts. Depending on the type of rig, we can differentiate between the four-masted full-rigged ship, the four-masted barque, the four-masted barquentine, the four-masted square-rigged schooner, the four-masted jackass barque, the four-masted gaff-rigged schooner, and the four-masted schooner. Only the four-masted full-rigged ship has four fully square-rigged masts (foremast, mainmast, mizzenmast and jigger mast); all other four-masters set a combination of square and fore-and-aft sails. During the long period in which four-masted ships built of

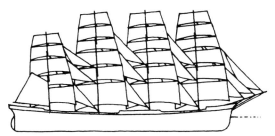

Four-masted full-rigged ship

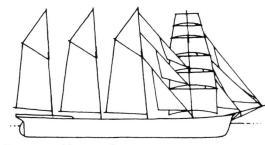

Four-masted barquentine

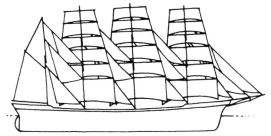

Four-masted barque

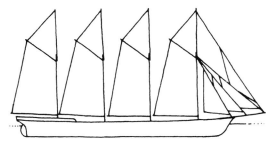

Four-masted gaff-rigged schooner

wood, iron and steel operated, the naming of the masts was not completely uniform from country to country.

470 DINGHY: Designed by Frenchman André Cornu in 1962, the lightweight two-man 470 (4.7m) helped foster the massive explosion in French dinghy sailing in the 1960s and 70s. Olympic status has been a mixed blessing but there are over 30,000 boats world wide with licensed builders in 22 countries. The ideal crew consists of a small helmsman and tall crew on the trapeze. Tactical ability comes second to boatspeed.

470 racing dinghy

Fram. *Fridjob Nansen's research ship, wintering in the ice, 1895*

FRAM: A three-masted topsail schooner, famous for its polar voyages under the Norwegian explorer Fridjof Nansen. The ship was designed and built expressly for polar voyages by Colin Archer, following the ideas of Nansen (1861–1930). The vessel was relatively small at 34.5m waterline length, 11.0m beam (less second outer skin reinforcement) and 4.70m draught. The displacement (fully equipped) was 800 tons, and the cargo capacity 307 tons. The ship had a number of interesting features. The sections were strongly rounded, so that pressure from ice would tend to squeeze the vessel up and out of the ice, instead of crushing the hull. The outer lateral skin timbers were extremely thick at around 750mm, and were reinforced with extra horizontal transverse supports to withstand the pressure of the ice. The ship had electric lighting, powered by a generator which could be driven by a large windmill or by a steam engine. The living quarters were lined with several layers of insulation to protect against

Francis boat, nineteenth century

the cold. The rudder and the screw of the auxiliary engine could be hoisted into a well to protect them from ice.

Originally a gaff schooner, the ship was rigged as a topsail schooner in 1909, with a sail area of 600m². The first voyage lasted from 1893 to 1896, which included nearly three years locked in the ice. The crew numbered 13 men. One aim of the voyage was to drift as close as possible to the North Pole or Franz Josef Land. The second voyage (1898 to 1902) was an expedition to northwest Greenland under Sverdrup. The third voyage, under the command of Roald Amundsen, took the ship to the Antarctic and lasted from 1910 to 1912. The *Fram* had then travelled further north and

further south than any other sailing ship in the world. After the Antarctic voyage the *Fram* was laid up and has been on display as a museum ship at Oslo since 1935.

FRANCIS BOAT: A rowing rescue boat developed during the second half of the nineteenth century for coastal rescue duty, which was adopted by various countries and which proved very effective.

At the end of the eighteenth century, England was the first of the leading seafaring nations to establish coastal rescue stations, one result of which was the development of various types of patented lifeboats, of which the Francis boat, named after its American inventor, and the English Peake boat, were the best known. The Francis boat was made

French Frigate Le Terrible *(model)*

French frigate of 1780, sheer draught plan

Rig of a frigate

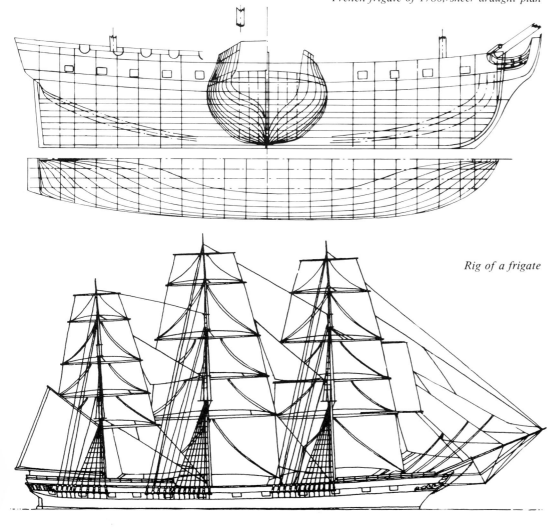

entirely of metal, based on corrugated sheet iron, which allowed the construction of a lightweight boat of adequate strength using relatively thin sheet metal. A number of buoyancy chambers were built into the boat, especially forward and aft, and cork was fixed on the outside, making the boat unsinkable. If the boat turned over in surf, it could be easily righted again. The boat had pronounced sheer and a keel weighing 300kg, these aspects intended to enhance the self-righting and self-draining characteristics. Because of the high bow and stern and the upthrust of the buoyancy chambers the boat would roll onto its side after turning over; at this stage the heavy keel would cause it to rotate further into the normal floating position. The crew strength was usually 10 men.

FREGATA, *see* FRIGATE

FREGATON, *Fregatton:* A seventeenth-century Venetian cargo sailing ship capable of carrying 400 to 500 tons of cargo and which operated in the Adriatic. The ship carried a mizzen mast as well as the mainmast, plus a bowsprit without jib or storm jib. In contrast to similar types the stem had a square transom. In the eighteenth century an oared fishing boat of the Provence region was also termed a frégation; it was around 6m long and 2m wide.

FRIGATE: Originally an Arab-Algerian oared sailing ship around 15m long with two lateen-rigged masts. This vessel was known as a fregata. A manoeuvrable ship, it carried out the duties of a scout and despatch carrier. When the building of warships assumed greater importance in the middle of the seventeenth century, the first fairly large, fast two-decked warships, carrying 40 to 50 cannon in battery, were also termed frigates. Around 1650, the English adopted the term frigate for warships with up to 64 guns (with some of the guns on the upper deck), whose characteristic features were less lofty superstructures and an emphasis on speed. When even larger sailing warships had been developed, the term was transferred to fast warships of medium size and armament. In sea battles the frigates were deployed outside the formal line-of-battle, on the side away from the enemy, in order to engage damaged enemy ships, to tow off prize vessels, to provide support to their own side's damaged ships, to despatch fireships, and to repeat (ie pass on) orders from flagships. They were also used to observe enemy ship movements, to provide convoy escorts and for limited, independent operations aimed at the disruption of merchant shipping and shipping routes.

Until the middle of the eighteenth century, frigates fell into one of two categories; they were either particularly fast ships with 20 or 30 guns in a single main battery, or smaller two-decked warships of around 40 guns. At the time of the great naval wars between England and France, the French navy gained a

Kurbrandenburg frigate Friedrich Wilhelm zu Pferde, *1684; detail from a painting by Lieve Verschuier*

Full-rigged whaler

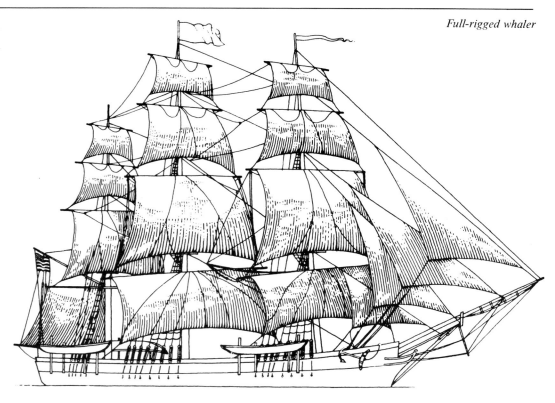

temporary lead in the development of fast, battleworthy warships around 1740, and are usually credited with the introduction of the classic frigate form. These vessels had two decks, but only the upperdeck was armed, the other being placed at, or below, the waterline. This gave a low seaworthy hull which nevertheless carried 13 guns high enough from the water to be used in all weather. Furthermore they were far superior in speed to ships of the line and merchant ships. There were various classes of these ships, varying in displacement from 600 to 1200 tons displacement, mounting from 28 to 44 guns.

In the nineteenth century, even larger frigates were built, with up to 60 guns, a development spurred on by the United States Navy, which built ship like the famous *CONSTITUTION* with 24-pounder guns in the main deck battery. With the introduction of armour plating the displacement of the armoured frigate rose to 4000 tons, and in exceptional cases to as much as 6000 tons. In this case the term frigate implied a single main gundeck like their sailing predecessors, but they were effectively the capital ships of their day.

The sailing frigate was invariably given a three-masted ship rig and so in many languages frigate-rigged became synonymous with the term full-rigged ship, even for merchant ships.

FROMBORK BOAT: This sailing vessel dates from the period between the fourth and fifth centuries, and was found in 1895 on a moor near Frombork, Poland. The boat was 17.4m long, with a beam of 2.8m and a depth of 0.90m and was based on a massive T-section keel. The CLINKER-built outer skin consists of strakes 2.5 to 3m long and 30mm thick, which are connected along the fore-and-aft overlaps by iron rivets with washers, and sealed with tar-soaked cow hair. The hull was stiffened with a total of 15 frames spaced 1.04m apart, the outside edges of which had a saw-toothed pattern to fit the overlapped strakes. The frames extend to the bottom, but are not fixed to the keel. A housing, fitted to the central frame, supported the mast.

FRUIT SCHOONER: Fast, fine-lined nineteenth-century schooners, used to transport fruit from the Mediterranean regions to northern Europe.

FULL-RIGGED SHIP: A sailing ship with at least three masts, all of which are fully square-rigged. The term full-rigged ship arose in the second half of the nineteenth century, applied mostly to three-masted full-rigged merchant

Full-rigged ship Orsono, ca *1900, cargo capacity 3000 tons, built in steel in the Tecklenburg yard*

ships, after the pattern of the earlier FRIGATES which had been developed in the seventeenth century.

In seamen's parlance, the term full-rigger has the same meaning. A full-rigged mast consists of lower mast, topmast, topgallant topmast, perhaps continued with royal mast, and is equipped with a complete set of square sails. Depending on the size of the ship, each mast then carries four to eight square sails.

The three masts of the full-rigged ship are called the foremast (forward mast), mainmast and mizzen mast. The mizzen, stepped aft, carries a gaff sail, called the spanker, as well as square sails.

During the transition to the full-rigged ship, the lateen sail which had formerly occupied the mizzen mast was replaced by a gaff sail, to that additional square sails could be set above the fore-and-aft sail. In place of the small mast on the bowsprit carrying the spritsail topsail came an extension to the bowsprit (the jib boom) and the addition of jibs.

The small square sail known as the spritsail or lower spritsail, set below the bowsprit, was retained for a time after this development. With suitable fore-and-aft sails set between the masts to complement the square sails, the full-rigged ship became one of the most widely used sailing ships in the world.

In addition to the typical three-masted full-rigged ships, a number of four-masted full-rigged ships were built in the golden period of sailing ships, and a single five-masted full-rigged ship, the *PREUSSEN*.

FULTON SUBMERSIBLE: This submersible was designed by Robert Fulton (1765–1815) and built in 1801 at Rouen on the Seine under the name of *Nautilus*. Fulton also worked on steam engines for ships, and soon built a second submersible with the same name. This second diving boat had internal iron frames with wood planking, which was sheathed with copper plates on the outside. The conning tower had glass windows and a mast equipped for a sail for surface running, as did the first *Nautilus*. The boat was intended to approach an enemy ship, then dive and attach a mine to the enemy vessel using a spiral drill. The mine was to be ignited by a clockwork delay fuse. As the inventor failed to find recognition in France, he went to England in 1804 and to America in 1806.

FUNE, *bune, buney*: The general term for Japanese fishing boats (SAMPANs up to 10m in length). The boats have a flat keel, are built without frames and have one or two masts according to size, each of which carries a large square sail. The catch was transported in a fish well (fish hold connected to the sea).

FUSTE, *fusta*: A fast, oared Mediterranean warship of the fifteenth century, often used for reconnaissance purposes. According to a fresco dating from 1470, one special feature of the fuste was that each rowlock served as guide

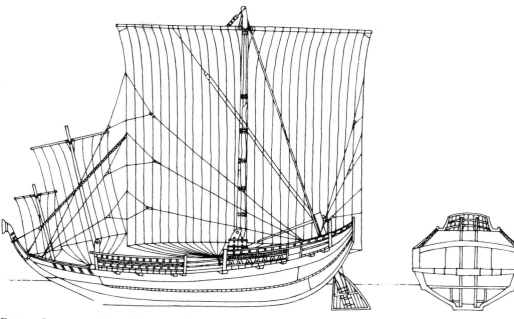

Fune, a Japanese sailing fishing vessel

to two oars, ie the two oars crossed over within the rowlock and in consequence the two oarsmen had to sit close, side by side. This rowing technique was adopted as it allowed more oarsmen to work in a relatively small vessel. It was made possible by the fact that the oars were not pulled in a long stroke at that time, as is standard practice today; instead, they were only in the water for a short period and were pulled in a jerky manner. This technique was known as 'Turkish rowing'.

The term fuste was also applied to small galleys and larger gondolas in seventeenth-century Venice. The fusta-gondolas could accommodate quite a large number of ordinary gondolas.

G

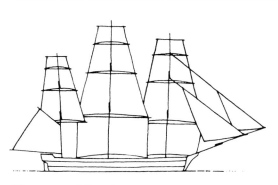

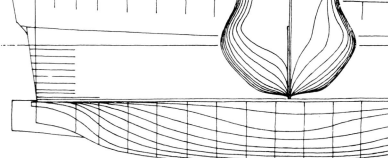

Three-masted French gabarre
Sail rig and sheer draught plan

GABARRE, *gabare*: A broad, shallow-draught rowing boat which was similar to the SCHUYT. It came into use after the seventeenth century, and could be up to 8m long. The same term was also applied to a single- or two-masted sailing ship up to 30m long.

In French ports, the customs guard ship was also termed gabare, and the designation had one further application: in the French navy at the beginning of the nineteenth century it was a three-masted, armed transport ship capable of carrying around 400 tons.

GAFF-RIGGED SCHOONER: A sailing ship with at least two masts, which carried fore-and-aft sails on all masts in the form of gaff sails, topsails and staysails.

With the exception of the brigantine and the barquentine, the original schooners, which sometimes set a square foresail, became obsolete around the mid nineteenth century, supplanted by exclusively gaff-rigged ships, and after this time the gaff-rigged schooners became generally known simply as schooners. On the two-masted gaff-rigged schooner the after mast was taller than the forward mast, but the masts of gaff-rigged schooners with three or more masts were often all the same height and rigged the same. The majority of

Four-masted, gaff-rigged schooner Cordelia E. Hayes, *before launching in Bath, USA, 1901*

Six-masted, gaff-rigged schooner Wyoming, *107m length overall, the largest wooden-hulled ship in the world, built in Bath, USA in 1907*

Five-masted, gaff-rigged schooner, 80.7m length overall, launched 1901

schooners were built as two- or three-masted vessels, the three-masted gaff-rigged schooners developed on the west coast of North America for the China and Japan runs being particularly well known. Sail handling was a simple matter, carried out from the deck, and this made reductions in crew strength possible. As a result, even larger gaff-rigged sailing ships quickly became established in North American merchant shipping circles, right up to the seven-master. Many FIVE-MASTED gaff-rigged schooners in particular were built towards the end of the nineteenth century in the USA, such as the *William C Carnegie* with a displacement of 4500 tons, a length of 88m, a beam of 14m and a crew of only 10 men. An example of the six-masted gaff-rigged schooner was the *Wyoming* with a length of 107m. In 1902, one of the largest sailing ships ever constructed was built in the USA: this was the *Thomas W Lawson*, a seven-masted gaff-rigged schooner with a steel hull 117m long and 12.25m wide displacing 5218 tons.

GALEA, *galee, galeo*: A fairly small oared warship, also known as the moner in some Mediterranean regions. The galea was similar to the fast DROMON, which was common in the Mediterranean in the fifth century, and represented one further step in the development of the fast oared ship. In a report dating from 1189 the galea is described as a long, narrow, low high-speed oared warship with a ram bow on the waterline. The names for a variety of further ship types originated in the term galea or galee, including galley, galiot, galezza, galiette and others.

In the seventeenth century the terms galea, galiotta and galezza were applied to Italian sailing ships, while the galiette was an Italian oared ship. The galeotta (formerly known as the FUSTE) was a warship with 15 to 18 oars a side, which carried a few light guns.

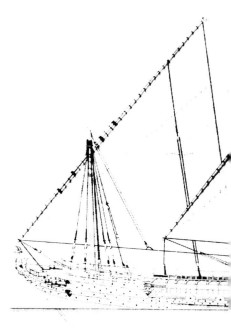

G

Two-masted Mediterranean galeasse (model)

GALEASSE: An attempt to combine the speed and manoeuvrability of the GALLEY — an oar-driven warship with supplementary sail — and the firepower of the large sailing warship. When Venice and other Mediterranean sea powers required warships which could carry a large number of heavy guns, the first solution tried was the construction of larger galleys, known as galea grossa. Eventually, the ships grew so heavy, carrying several hundred oarsmen, that they could no longer be rowed over long distances.

The development of the galeasse from the galea grossa is ascribed to the Venetian shipbuilder Francesco Bressan at the beginning of the sixteenth century. By 1550, the galeasse was a well-known type, its design fully refined, and the largest sailing-oared warship in the Mediterranean in the sixteenth and seventeenth centuries. This three-masted sailing ship with supplementary oar propulsion also represented one of the most significant stages in the transition from the low freeboard, shallow-draught oared ship to the high-sided, fully rigged sailing ship of deep draught. Compared with the galley, the galeasse was a significant improvement in terms of seagoing qualities. The crew was better protected, and the firepower and the range of movement over larger sea areas were greatly increased. The galeasse became the dominant warship of the Mediterranean and formed the core of the main fighting force of the oared warship fleets. The value in battle of a galeasse was usually considered equivalent to that of five galleys.

At the Battle of Lepanto in 1571, one of the greatest galley battles, over 100 ships

French galeasse La Royal

Seventeenth-century Mediterranean galeasse under oars

participated on both sides, and the 26 galeasses played a decisive role in the victory. In the Spanish Armada, in the 1588, there were also four Neapolitan galeasses, which were among the most powerful ships in the fleet. The galeasse flagship carried 18 heavy guns (18- to 60-pounders with barrel diameters of 13.5 to 200mm.) and 26 lighter guns. The Mediterranean galeasses displaced around 600 tons, but they were also built with displacements of up to 1000 tons. They were around 50 to 60m long, with a galley-like, slender hull or relatively small beam. The increase in displacement resulted from the deeper draught. The increased draught, taller hull sides and greater displacement produced vessels which were slower and more ponderous to row, but with considerably improved sailing qualities, with the three larger, lateen-rigged masts. The oars were usually used only in battle. There were 25 to 30 oars on each side, each of them pulled by five to eight men. In addition to the oarsmen, the ships carried a further 200 to 300 sailors, soldiers and officers whose battle stations were on the forecastle and aftercastle and the gangways which ran above the banks of oars-men behind the raised bulwarks of the ships.

As rigging and sailing techniques grew to maturity towards the end of the seventeenth century. This ship, with its extraordinarily large crew, fell out of use since it would then be out-sailed and out-gunned by contemporary ships of the line.

GALEASS, *jacht-galeass, galeass-ship*: This was the name for a two-masted coastal cargo and fishing vessel used around the Pomeranian Baltic coast after the middle of the eighteenth

Two-masted galeasse with square topsail and short mizzen gaff

century. They were mostly based on bilge keels, sometimes with a flat bottom and leeboards, and were around 20m long, with a displacement up to about 200 tons. In contrast to the similar but smaller GALIOT with its pointed stern, which originated in the North Sea area, the nineteenth century galeass had a slightly overhanging yacht-like transom stern, with the result that the type was also known as a 'jacht-galeass'. The yacht-like impression was emphasized by a more fine-lined prow or projecting clipper stem, and a long bowsprit.

The ships were rigged in similar style to the schooner, with gaff mainsail and gaff topsail, but with the difference that the much shorter after mast carried a single small gaff sail on a relatively short gaff.

Larger ships with rounded, projecting sterns were termed galeass-ships and were based on the pattern of the steamship, which was in the ascendant at the time.

GALEASS EWER: A type of EWER with a narrower underwater body, similar to the GALEASS, but with a broader beam at the waterline for improved stability, and a full-bodied form above water, like that of the standard ewer. These ships were rigged like the BESAN EWER, ie with a mizzen mast, and variants existed with and without leeboards. On the version which lacked leeboards the hull was fitted with quite large bilge runners. This hybrid of the galeass and north German ewer evolved in the Baltic in the 1820s. The galeass ewers built on the Elbe up until 1904 were around 16 to 20m long and 5 to 6m in beam, with around 40 to 60 tons cargo capacity, and although they usually sailed the North and Baltic Seas, they also travelled as far afield as the Mediterranean.

GALEONE, *galione, galleon*: Originally, a fairly small oared sailing ship of the ancient Roman era. At the beginning of the sixteenth century in Spain it was a quite small sailing ship which could also be rowed. The dominant Portuguese and Spanish ship types of the time were the NAO and the CARAVEL. However, by the time of the Spanish conquests in America these caravels and naos were no longer adequate for the wide-ranging troop and cargo movements across the Atlantic. During this transitional period, various features of the two types were blended with the galeone to form a new hybrid type, which was suitable for carrying freight over long sea passages. for a long time, galeones were the largest ships in the world, plying across the Atlantic to central and South America. On their return voyages, loaded with plunder, treasure and precious metals, they were a favourite target for pirates. These Spanish galeones generally had four masts, the forward two of which were square-rigged. Three-masted galeones were a rarity.

In comparison with the nao and the caravel the ships were generally larger, but their hull lengths were also disproportionately greater, with a more slender underwater form. The galeones had several full-length decks, but also an oversized, tall aft superstructure with up to seven decks arranged one above the other. As

Baltic galeasse Lucia von Anklam, *1827*

Flemish galleon, 1593 (model)

Spanish (left) and Dutch galleons (right) in the early seventeenth century. Watercolour by Monleon

defence against pirates the ships carried numerous light guns on several decks, on the forward castle and the aft superstructure. Very large galeones displaced up to 2000 tons and drew around 8m. In some cases up to 2000 men were carried on board.

Four-masted galeones were included in the Spanish Armada in 1588 at the naval battle in the channel between Dover and Calais. Compared with the English ships, the large, clumsy galeones were much inferior in sailing and manoeuvring qualities.

In the mid sixteenth century, English shipbuilders began to develop lighter versions of the galeone, based on their experience with the English CARRACK. These vessels were termed galleons. They were considerably smaller, at 500 to 600 tons and a length of around 50 to 60m. Built much lower than the Spanish galeones and better rigged, they could sail faster and were more manoeuvrable. These 'race-built' galleons, as they were known, were subsequently fitted with larger cannon of improved accuracy, which gave them clear superiority in battle. With these advantages the English galleon achieved the ascendancy

English galleon ca *1600 (model)*

and through its development into GREAT SHIP and hence FRIGATE maintained it for a period of around 200 years.

GALEOTE, *galeotta*: A fairly small medieval GALLEY with 16 to 20 oars on each side. In contrast to the large galleys, each oar was generally operated by only one man, and more rarely by 2 or 3 oarsmen. These ships were primarily rowed by freemen, bondsmen and soldiers who were armed with muskets. There were also generally one large and several smaller bow guns.

Galeotes were superior in speed and manoeuvrability to the galleys. For this reason they rapidly found popularity as merchant and pirate ships, especially in Algeria and Tunisia. Later, the Nordic maritime states adopted the term geleote for their small, fast, schooner-rigged sailing ships.

GALIOT: A two-masted ship type which was developed in the Netherlands in the seventeenth century for North Sea and coastal work. The term was probably adopted from one of the Romance languages, as small Italian sailing ships were termed galiotta around this time.

The Dutch galiot's hull form shared certain features with the seagoing BOIER, a type in

Two-masted Dutch galiot, eighteenth century

common use in the North Sea region at the time. The hull was rounded forward, with a steeply rising stern. The underwater body was much finer of line and slimmer. In this respect the galiot represents a transitional type between the boier and the SCHOONER.

The two-masted, eighteenth-century galiot had an average cargo capacity of around 130 tons, with a length between 18 and 30m, and a beam of 4 to 7.5m. The ships were rigged with one gaff sail on the tall mainmast, and one on the much smaller mizzen mast. Up to three square sails could be set above the mainsail, and a large staysail could be carried on the forestay. Up to three were set on the long bowsprit.

Up to the middle of the nineteenth century, the two-masted galiot was one of the most widely built ship types in north Germany, and was particularly popular for use in the North Sea. The galiots were originally designed to be cargo vessels, and as such could carry up to around 240 tons, but they remained relatively

Three-masted, square-rigged galiot, early nineteenth century (model)

Two-masted Dutch galiot, mid nineteenth century (model)

GALLEY *(1):* A long, narrow, low and manoeuvrable oared ship of limited stability and seagoing capacity because of its narrow beam, shallow draught and low freeboard. Although fitted with sails, the oars were the primary means of propulsion. Galleys varied over the centuries in the number of oar banks, the number of oarsmen per oar, the seating arrangements and size. Usually, the oar banks were set on the upper deck at an angle to the centreline, protected only by a light bulwark which left the oarsmen directly exposed to the weather and to enemy fire.

The galley represents the highest stage of development of the fast, large oared warship with supplementary sails, and also necessarily its final stage. Galleys were the most important Mediterranean warships in the Middle Ages, but they were eventually out-distanced by sailing warships, with their smaller crew, greater cargo capacity, more powerful armaments, and improved seaworthiness and speed over long distances.

The galley, as a ship with primary oar propulsion, had many predecessors, some of them very early vessels, including the **DROMON**, the **GALEA** and the later Roman **LIBURNIAN**. In contrast to older Mediterranean vessels, the fourteenth- and fifteenth-century galley had only one row of oarsmen on each side. Thus the 'Galley à la Sensile', for example, featured angled rowing benches accommodating three oarsmen, each of them working his own oar. Other rowing arrangements included that of the 'Galley à la Scaloggio', in which each oar was pulled by five oarsmen. These large oars were up to 12m long and displaced up to 300kg. For the oarsmen to handle them at all, they had to be suspended at their point of balance. The rowing technique employed, with several

small ships for the time. However, they were not restricted to coastal waters and the North Sea. For example, small galiots of around 120 tons sailed across the Atlantic to America, and voyages round the Cape of Good Hope to the East Indies are documented. Regular voyages were undertaken out to Central and South America. Galiots also sailed to the Arctic for whaling and seal hunting. The same hull type was also fitted with heavy mortars for naval service, vessels so equipped being known as 'galiotes à bombes' in France. Schooner-rigged galiots were preferred in the Baltic state navies; these vessels were known as schooner galiots.

In the early nineteenth century, a few three-masted galiots were fully **SQUARE-RIG-GED**, the hull remained basically unchanged. The more modern, faster three-masted galiot which evolved at the same time had a more streamlined underwater hull shape for lower resistance, and a more sophisticated full square rig.

The basic galiot type was combined with other contemporary ship types to produce hybrids such as the **SCHOONER GALIOT** and the **EIDER GALIOT**, to suit local conditions. The galliot was usually built with a flat keel and carried no leeboards, but some ships were built with leeboards or centreboards.

In 1873, the German merchant fleet included 129 galiots, 121 schooner galiots and six kuff galiots. In 1913, 26 galiots, four schooner galiots and seven Eider galiots still existed, four of which were still in use in 1934.

GALIOT EWER: A beamy galiot built on the Elbe around 1890. It featured a flat bottom like a **EWER**, more sharply tapered hull ends and leeboards.

GALIOTTA, *galiote*: *see* **GALEOTE**.

GALLEON: *see* **GALEONE:**

Seventeenth-century Mediterranean galley (model)

oarsmen working on one oar, was markedly different from the modern style where long strokes are used. The great, clumsy oars were pulled using short, jerking strokes, carried out in a strictly maintained rhythm, which varied according to the length of the oar. Because of the precise rowing rate and the short strokes the spacing between the oars could be reduced to a minimum. The oarsmen could then be packed together to cram maximum rowing power into the limited dimensions of the ship. At full speed, a rate of 22 strokes per minute could be attained, with a short-term maximum of 26 strokes per minute. The average speed over a long voyage was around 4.5 knots (2.3m per second); at maximum power, galleys could accelerate to double that speed for short periods. Originally, the ships were rowed by freemen and bondsmen. In the early Middle Ages the powerful city states of Genoa and Venice began to use prisoners and slaves as forced labour. The inhuman treatment of prisoners by almost all the Mediterranean states made the galley probably the most notorious ship type ever.

The Venetian galee bastarde carried 240 oarsmen squeezed in together; some galleys had more than 500 crew, and in some cases up to eight men worked a single oar. It was in Venice that the galley reached its highest state of development in terms of design, maintenance and rowing technique. In the fourteenth century galleys were built using mass-production techniques. A huge construction and maintenance complex called the Arsenale (which gave modern English the word arsenal) was developed, and this included a complete inventory of components, replacement parts and equipment, so that in time of war, 38 galleys could be assembled ready for battle within two days.

By 1571, the number of workers employed in galley building and maintaining the Arsenale reached the enormous figure of 16,000 — a vast number for the conditions of the time — working day and night shifts. In the sixteenth century the larger Venetian galleys with 32 oar banks on each side began to be copied by the major European states. From these large vessels evolved the later GALE-ASSE. There were also various small types of galley, including in particular the Mediterranean BRIGANTINE, the FUSTE, the GALIOT and the SAGITTA. However, the galley itself remained in use into the eighteenth century in the Mediterranean and Baltic regions.

In the power struggles and naval wars of the seventeenth century, galleys were even to be encountered off the Spanish and French coasts and in the Channel. Some of these vessels were borrowed from the Italian cities for war duty for a consideration; others were built in Spain and France as copies of the original. Copies of galleys were also built in Sweden and Russia. France maintained a fleet of galleys at Marseilles up until 1749, which was independent of the general ocean-going fleet, and had its

Two-masted, western Arabian pirate ghanja, early nineteenth century (model)

own officer corps and budget. In 1802 the Marseilles arsenal still included 15 galleys.

Galleys of average size in the seventeenth century displaced around 200 tons with a length of around 50m, a beam of 6m, and a draught of 1.5m. The ship's hull was generally made of light timbers (principally softwoods such as fir) and was of elongated form. A bow ram projecting above the water was designed to destroy the oars of an enemy vessel, and thereby to render it incapable of movement. It was also used for ramming enemy ships, or as a bridge for boarding. The original large side rudder was replaced by a powerful stern rudder in the fourteenth century. The slim hull was fitted with a rather clumsy, box-shaped, rectangular superstructure, which was known as the 'talar'. In the fifteenth century the superstructure was reshaped with greater sheer, and was thus better integrated into the ship's hull. The hull forward supported a platform fitted with slings and catapults; later, when guns were available, the most powerful bow cannon was set up on the centreline, with three smaller cannon set at either side of it. Light swivel guns were arranged to fire through spaces between the oars on the ship's sides.

The forecastle platform was connected to the after deck by a gangway (Italian and Spanish: corsia, French: coursie), running above the oars. To supplement the efforts of the oarsmen, and for long voyages in general, the galleys normally carried two and later three masts, rigged with lateen sails. The largest of these supplementary sails was known as the artemon, as on the vessel's Roman ancestor, while the smaller sail was termed the terzaruolo.

The Prussian navy of the eighteenth century included a completely different ship type which was also known as a galley. This was a covered bay-fishing barge or ZEESEN with two masts and square sails, converted for war service.

GALLEY (2): A seventeenth-century oar-driven personnel transport boat fitted with a stern cabin, and used on the Thames. In the eighteenth and nineteenth centuries an open rowing boat with six to eight oars was known as a galley. The term was also applied to boats with two lateen or lugsails, mostly used as captains' boats. The term has survived in the Scilly Islands for the large clinker-built rowing boats which are raced by means of watermen from the islands.

GALTABÄCK BOAT: The remains of a boat

found near Traaker in the Swedish district of Halland in 1928. The boat was 13.10m long, 3.60m wide, had a depth of 1.16m, and dated from the twelfth or thirteenth centuries. The find is now on show in Göthenburg museum. The vessel's steeply raked, elongated stem and stern, of virtually identical form, are similar to the picture on the Dunwich seal dating from about 1200. The stamp of a mast indicates that this was a sail-driven vessel, and four deck beams projecting through the outer skin are evidence that the boat was at least partially covered.

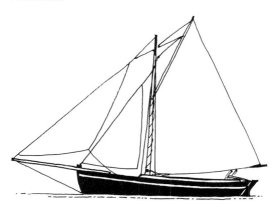

A Galway hooker

GALWAY HOOKER: A heavily built cargo carrier from Ireland's west coast, occasionally used for setting long lines. It was single-masted and gaff-rigged with headsails. Around 13m in length, it was partially decked with a very pronounced sheer, considerble tumble-home, a sharply rising floor and a raked transom stern. Boats of the same general design but around 10m were known as gleotogs. Still smaller was the poucan or pookhaun, which was an undecked fishing vessel, carrying a dipping lugsail and a jib.

GARVEY: A type of American SCOW, of the New Jersey and Delaware coasts. Both rowing and sailing garveys were built between 4 and 10m in length. The sailing boats were fitted with centreboards, the larger usually being one-masted with a gaff mainsail, jib and short bowsprit. The smaller sailing garveys had one or two masts setting spritsails.

GAULOS: An ancient Greek term for a cargo ship, adopted from the Phoenicians.

GDANSK-ORUNIA BOATS: The remains of three Slav rowing boats from the tenth to eleventh centuries, which were found in a moor near Gdansk-Orunia in 1933. In design the salvaged boats were similar to Viking vessels, the site of discovery being close to the sea route used for trading by the Baltic Vikings at that time. The shallow hulls indicate that the boats were used mainly within bay waters. The boat lengths are 11.0, 12.3 and 12.8m, with respective beams of 2.2, 2.4 and 2.4m. Two of the boats were fast, fully-crewed vessels with seats for 20 oarsmen each. One boat only had six oarmen's seats, and may have been used to transport freight.

GHANJA: A two- or three-masted, fast, sea-going west Arabian trading dhow, similar to the Indian KOTIA.

On the three-masted ghanja, the foremast was raked forward, the mainmast was vertical and the mizzen raked aft. All three masts were rigged with the typical settee sail on an angled yard set high on the mast. On the two-masted ghanjas, which were mostly built later the middle of the eighteenth century, the two masts were both raked forward at about seven degrees from the vertical. The sail area was around 300m².

The vessel had pleasing lines, the slimness of the hull emphasized by the long projecting stem and the unusual projecting stern ending in a transom. With a usual keel length of 15.5m the waterline length was 20.5m, and the length overall around 30m. The beam was usually around 5m. Because of the relatively light construction combined with the low freeboard, the draught was shallow for sailing ships of this size at about 2 to 2.5m.

GHEBÂU, *gaïbao*: A coastal fishing vessel used in the South China seas in the nineteenth century; it was about 10m long and had its own peculiar rig with sliding gunter sails. There were usually three masts with the forward two masts much shorter than the third. The larger vessels of this type had virtually circular sections. The smaller ships were slimmer, with very strongly raked stem and stern, and were excellent sailing craft.

GHE YOU: A South Vietnamese sailing junk, with one or more masts. As in the case of the Chinese junk, high topsides rise almost vertically from the flat, keel-less hull floor. Cross beams project through the outer planking, stiffening the side walls and hull. On the single-masted ships the mast is stepped in the middle, while on the two-masted vessels both masts are set up in the forward half. Both masts carry a large, rectangular sail similar to a lugsail. Originally, the vessel had a peculiar feature which showed the influence of Malay immigrants for a supplementary outrigger was fitted, weighted with a movable, heavy stone, to improve lateral stability, the position of the stone could be altered to suite the wind strength. The vessels were around 15 to 20m long, and remained in use until recently, primarily for fishing.

GIEK EWER: A EWER with a special rig; basically, a gaff-rigged ewer fitted with a giek boom, attached to the mast with an articulated joint, by means of which the sail clew was hauled out. This form of rig grew popular in the nineteeth century until eventually it became standard. Originally, the ewer had carried only a spritsail, then after the beginning of the nienteenth century a gaff sail without a boom, known as the sheet sail.

GIG: A light, slim, clinker-built rowing ship's boat with tapered hull ends and auxiliary sail, used in the era of the sailing ship. With an average length of 8 to 9m, the boats were around 1.6m wide. Because of the small beam, the thwarts, usually six in number, were occupied by one oarsman each. The gig's oars

Gunter-rigged German naval gig

were longer than those of other ships' boats, hence the boat could achieve higher speeds over short distances when rowed by a hand-picked crew. In contrast to other ships' boats (LAUNCHes, PINNACEs, SLOOPs, and JOLLY BOATs) carried on board warships and merchant ships, the gig was usually intended for the commander or captain (captain's gig). On medium-sized sailing ships the gig was carried suspended from the stern davits, so that it could be lowered rapidly when necessary.

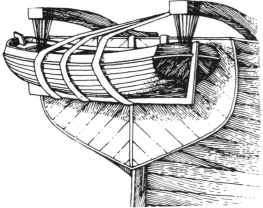

Captain's gig in stern davits

GLEOTOG: *see* GALWAY HOOKER.

GLOUCESTER SCHOONER: A mid nineteenth-century type of North American fishing schooner, specially designed for cod fishing on the Newfoundland Banks. Gloucester schooners were fast sailing ships with a slender hull of yacht-like form, but more strongly built, so that the catch could be landed without delay even in poor weather. The schooners carried a large number of DORIES, stacked up on deck. Each dory could carry one or two fishermen to the fishing

areas, where the fishing was carried out using long-lines.

The two- or three-masted ships were rigged like a schooner with gaff sails. At the bow the jib boom carried foresail, jib and flying jib. Additional topsails could be set above the gaff mainsail on topmasts.

GOBELETTE: A line fishing boat about 7m long and 2m wide, with a square sail on a stayed mast, and used mainly in the Somme estuary in the eighteenth century.

GOELETTE: French term for schooner.

GOKSTAD SHIP: A typical Viking longship, discovered in 1880 in a family burial site belonging to King Olaf Geirstada-Alf on the Oslo fjord near Sandelfjord, and dating from the second half of the ninth century. It was fitted with a mast to carry a sail area of around 70m². The mast itself was about 13m high, removable and made of oak, as was the yard. In calm conditions the ship could be rowed by means of the 16 oars on each side. The oars were passed through holes in the hull sides. If the ship was sailed, shields were set up to provide some protection.

Gokstad ship – view of hull section from the bow

As on the NYDAM BOAT, the underwater portion of the hull was much more strongly built than the upper part. The ship was 23.80m long, 5.10m in breadth, had a depth of 1.75m and a draught of 0.92m. On each side were 11 strakes, bound to the 17 natural-grown curved frames, spaced about 900mm apart, by means of cleats cut into the timbers. The strakes were rivetted to each other, and the joints sealed with ox hair. Transverse beams were lashed across the top of the frames, and short boards

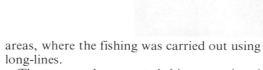

Two-masted goelette, sail plan

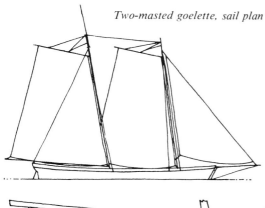

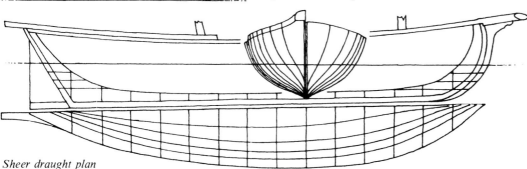

Sheer draught plan

Gokstad ship – ribs and thwarts

The restored Gokstad ship, view of the starboard quarter

Gokstad ship, mast socket and deck planks

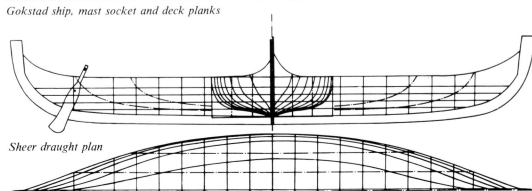

Sheer draught plan

were fitted from one transverse beam to the next to act as a covering.

The upper hull consisted of five strakes per side, joined to the transverse beams by means of timber knees, and to the underwater body by means of short supplementary ribs. The upper strakes were nailed to the short upper ribs with treenails. In the third strake from the top were 16 rounded, recessed holes to accept the oars. The mast was stepped just forward of the centrepoint of the hull, in a heavy mast housing on the keel. At deck beam level a broad, thick, tapered, fishtail-shaped plank provided support. A T-shaped carling was provided for the removable mast and yard. As on all Viking ships steering was by means of an oar fitted on the starboard side.

The Gokstad ship was found in relatively good condition, and is now on view in the Bygdøy Museum near Oslo. Two copies of the ship were built to demonstrate the seagoing qualities of the vessel, and sailed from Norway to America as an experiment. The first copy sailed to the World Exhibition at Chicago in 1893. The second version, named *The Viking*, was fitted with an auxiliary engine and propeller as a precaution, and completed the voyage from Bergen to New York in 22 days.

GOLDEN HIND, ex PELICAN: This small English galleon from the time of Elizabeth I (1558–1603) has become famous the world over as a result of the voyage and circumnavigation of the globe by Francis Drake. Drake (*ca* 1543–1596) set off on his voyage on 13 December 1577 with a squadron of five small, armed merchant ships and 164 crew, on a voyage promoted by the Queen and other influential people. The declared purpose of the voyage was trade in the Mediterranean and at Alexandria. The actual plan was not explained by Drake to the hand-picked crew until the ships were at sea. It was, in spite of the peace treaty between England and Spain, to reconnoitre the shipping routes used by the Spanish-Portuguese fleets for world-wide trade, to destroy those countries' world trade monopoly, and to plunder ports and ships in the New World. Drake even had the appearance and paintwork of his ships altered, so that they looked like Spanish galleys, and his ship renamed *Golden Hind*. The *Marigold* (around 30 tons, with 16 cannon), the supply ship *Swan* (around 50 tons, with five cannon) and the pinnace *Benedict* (around 15 tons, with one cannon) did not survive the Straits of Magellan and perished.

The fourth accompanying ship, the *Elizabeth* (around 80 tons, with 16 cannon), returned to England under Captain John Winter, after it had lost contact with the leading ship. Only the *Golden Hind*, commanded by Drake, succeeded in continuing the voyage to the American west coast after passing the Straits of Magellan.

Although no precise information or pictures of the ship are extant, many models of the ship have been built, based mainly on information which was gathered during the period of more than a century when the *Golden Hind* lay in a brick-built drydock in Deptford as a display piece. Eventually, the ship disintegrated through lack of maintenance.

Amongst the most reliable data is Drake's own concerning the ship's draught. On his trip to the American west coast, from Cape Horn roughly to the site of present-day San Francisco, he captured so much treasure that the ship's draught increased to 13 feet (around 3.97m) from the normal figure of 9 feet (around 2.75m). The daring freebooter attempted to find a direct return route around North America, during which he reached the latitude of present-day Vancouver (roughly 43 degrees north), when he was forced to turn back. After the ship had been repaired in a bay near San Francisco, Drake decided to return to England by crossing the Pacific Ocean. Stopping points on this return voyage, begun in June 1579, were the Palau Islands, Bali, Java, the Cape of Good Hope in June 1850 and then Sierra Leone.

On 3 November 1580 the *Golden Hind* put into Plymouth after a voyage lasting almost three years, with the remainder of its crew (54 men) and booty stated to be worth 2,225,000 gold pounds.

About six months later the ship was laid up in dock at Deptford for public viewing. Information on the ship's dimensions varies. The length could have been between 23 and 25m. The most likely dimensions are those suggested by the Science Museum in London, which state an overall length of 75 feet (22.88m), length between stem and stern of 60 feet (18.30m) and a beam of 19 feet (5.80m). This corresponds to a tonnage between 100 and 150 tons. The three-masted galleon was rigged with a foresail and mainsail on the fore and mainmasts, plus topgallants, and carried a lateen sail on the mizzen mast, and a spritsail on the bowsprit. It was armed with 18 cannon.

In 1973, a reconstruction of the *Golden Hind* was built in Appledore, Devon.

GOLETA: Spanish term for schooner.

GÖLLE: A flat, nineteenth-century river vessel employed primarily for transporting timber. About 25m long and 3 to 5.5m wide, it featured a small covered area on the fore part of the ship and a cabin at the stern.

GONDOLA, *gondolo, gondole*: A light, narrow rowing boat which is a special feature of Venice. Up to 10m in length and primarily intended for transporting passengers, the gondola is propelled by the gondolier using a

Golden Hind, *Francis Drake's galleon, 1577 (model)*

special one-sided rowing technique. To balance the non-symmetrical populsion, the hull is built asymmetrically about its centreline, so that on normal-sized boats there is about 0.25m less on the starboard side than on the port side. There are seats for two to four persons under the covered midship area.

A further peculiarity of the Venetian gondola is its black paintwork. The noble and patrician families used to vie with each other to decorate their gondolas ever more lavishly and fit them out more luxuriously, until eventually the Venetian Senate forbad the contest by decree, and prescribed an overall black paint scheme.

GOUDEN LEEUW, The Golden Lion: The painting by Van de Velde the younger (1666–1707) shows the *Gouden Leeuw* in the port of Amsterdam in 1680. The ship was built at the Admiralty yard as an 80-gun ship of the line commissioned by the Amsterdam Admiralty during the second Anglo-Dutch War (1665–1667). The *Gouden Leeuw* was a three-master with topmasts and topgallants on the foremast and mainmast. Both fore- and main-masts were square-rigged, the foremast carrying foresail, fore topsail and fore topgallant sail, while the mainmast carried mainsail, main topsail and main topgallant. The mizzen mast carried a lateen sail and a square sail (crossjack) above it, while two spritsails were set on the bowsprit.

The *Gouden Leeuw* was the flagship of the famous Dutch Admiral, Cornelius Tromp (1629–1691), at the Battle of the Texel in 1673. In the battle the ship was severely damaged, but was nevertheless repaired. *De Gouden Leeuw* was taken out of service in 1686, by which time she was obsolete.

GOURD RAFT, *Calabash raft*: A raft consisting of a large number of hollowed-out, dried gourds, lashed to a rod framework. Such rafts were known in the Sudan, around Lake Chad and also in Egypt and Central America.

Gourd raft

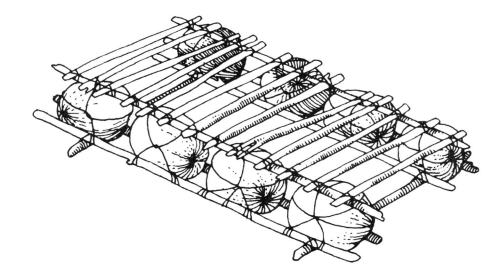

Venetian gondolas

GRAVENEY BOAT: The remains of an Anglo-Saxon ship, found in a Kent marsh in 1971. Although the upper part of the oak vessel had rotted away over the centuries, it proved possible to reconstruct the boat, which was roughly 12m long. The vessel dates from the mid tenth century.

GREAT HARRY or HENRY GRACE À DIEU: The construction of this warship was begun on 3 October 1512 under the supervision of the master shipwright W Bond, and the vessel was launched at Woolwich in June 1514. The ship was built by order of Henry VIII, and was very large for its time. The ship, officially named *Henry Grace à Dieu* but known as *Great Harry*, was a four-masted CARRACK with eight decks. *Great Harry* was rigged with three square sails on each of the two forward masts, lateen sails on the two after masts and a spritsail on the bowsprit.

The original armament consisted of 184 cannon, 43 of which were of heavy calibre. The keel length is said to have been about 38m and the deck length around 50m, with a beam of around 12.5m. With no more accurate data surviving, the probable displacement has been estimated at around 1500 tons. By the standards of the time, these dimensions corresponded to Henry VIII's demand 'to build a ship the like of which England has never seen'. The crew numbered 700 men, of whom 301 were sailors, 349 soldiers and 50 gun crew. A notable feature is said to have been the external decoration, with the ship's sides and stern richly painted and flying a full complement of flags. Contemporary reports state that the ship's sails even had gold threads woven into them. In 1535 and 1536 the ship was refitted, and the armament reduced to 122 cannon. The carrack was only once used belligerently, off Spithead in 1545. The ship carried the following hand weapons: 500 yew longbows, 10 dozen bowstrings, 200 pikes, 200 boarding axes and a large number of arrows and spears. One hundred and twenty pots of unslaked lime were carried on board, with which to blind the enemy, should there be a favourable wind in time of battle.

The *Great Harry* was destroyed by fire at

Great Harry, *or* Henry Grace à Dieu, *built between 1512 and 1514, copper engraving by PC Canot 1736, after the painting by Holbein*

Woolwich in August 1553. A contemporary painting, which shows the ship after its refit, survives among the pictures known as the 'Anthony Anthony Roll'.

GREAT REPUBLIC: This clipper was launched in Boston in October 1853, and was designed by probably the most famous shipbuilder of his time, Donald McKay (1810–80). The *Great Republic* was the largest merchant ship in the world at the time: 102m long, 16m beam and had a depth of 11.50m with a tonnage of 4555RT. To prevent this large wooden ship from sagging, diagonal iron bands were incorporated. Originally designed as a four-masted barque, the ship suffered a serious fire even before she sailed. The severely damaged ship was later rebuilt, almost completely, although she now had three instead of her former four decks, a somewhat reduced sail area and 3357RT. Nevertheless, she was still the largest ship of her time, and a very fast one too. After being used as a troop transport in the Crimean war, she was

employed to carry grain from USA to England. In 1869, the ship was re-rigged as a three-masted full-rigged ship, then sold to England under the new name of the *Denmark*. In 1872, she was abandoned at sea and sank.

GREAT SHIP: Late sixteenth and early seventeenth century English term for the large warships developed from the GALLEONE. They were gradually replaced by FRIGATE-built ships from 1650 and the term came to denote the largest rates of ships of the line.

GREENLAND SHIP: A sailing ship specially equipped for the northern voyage to Greenland for seal hunting and whaling. The earliest evidence of whaling dates from the twelfth and thirteenth centuries in the Basque country. Documentary evidence of voyages from the German coastal area to Arctic waters and to Greenland for hunting has survived from 1611. In 1674, a German whaling enterprise under the name of the Greenland Company was set up in Bremen. The strongly built full-

bodied FLEUTEs, GALIOTs and HUKERs proved suitable for the northern route, as they were strong enough to survive the high stresses encountered in areas of drift-ice, and could even withstand the pressure of the ice reasonably well when frozen in. Greenland whalers were readily recognizable by their ships' boats, which were suspended in davits on the ships' sides, ready for work. The whales were hunted from these small vessels and speared with hand-thrown harpoons. The captured creatures were cut up close to the whaler or hauled onto deck in one piece or in sections. The liquid whale-oil, produced by boiling the blubber on board, was poured into barrels, which were either carried on board assembled, or in knocked-down form for assembly on site.

This perilous method of hunting cost the lives and the health of many members of a whaler's crew. The fact that it was expected that equipment would also be lost is indicated by the inventory of a Greenland ship dating from the year 1827. As whaling equipment this

Painting by Vittore Carpaccio (ca *1465–1522). Detail from the Ursula cycle, 1459, Venice. Three-masted Mediterranean carrack with crow's nest and small topmast,* Gallerie dell' Accademia, Venice

*Bow of an English warship, late seventeenth century
(model)*

*Cog, model based on the cogs shown on the city seals
of Stralsund (1329) and Elbing (1350)*

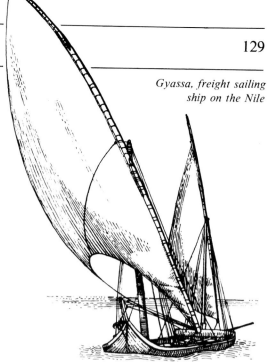

*Gyassa, freight sailing
ship on the Nile*

ship carried the following items: 60 harpoons, 39 whale spears, five walrus spears, 10 seal harpoons and 50 seal clubs. Modern whaling began in 1868 with the invention by the Norwegian Sven Foyn of the grenade harpoon and the harpoon gun. Legislation has now had to be passed to protect these great mammals.

Smaller ships were employed specifically for seal hunting. A successful seal hunter which sailed several times in, say, 1850, would kill up to 5000 seals in one year with a single crew. Here again protective measures were soon urgently required to preserve the species.

GRIPPA: An oared sailing ship about 17m long and 3 to 4m in breadth, used in the northern Mediterranean region in the fifteenth and sixteenth centuries, and similar to the Mediterranean BRIGANTINE. The ships were employed for cargo transport and fishing, were equipped with 8 to 14 oars per side, and were sometimes armed.

GRUNDEL: An eighteenth- and nineteenth-century Dutch yacht type designed for fishing (and featuring a fish well). It was also used for transport on inland waters, and is still encountered today in modified form as a pleasure yacht. In this case it is usually fitted with a small cabin. The boats were 6 to 10m long, 2.5 to 3.5m wide had a draught of only 0.30m, and a sail area of up to 20m².

GUARD BOAT, *guard cutter, guard ship*: Vessels employed for guard duty by harbour police, customs and other authorities. Converted fishing cutters displacing around 70 tons were often used as guard cutters for coastal defence. For example, Prussia's customs guard ships in 1812 were the *Schwalbe* (swallow), a square-rigged schooner 16.3m long and 5m in breadth, lightly armed with three- and four-pounder cannon, and the three-masted lugger *Adler* (eagle).

In 1831, when there was a threat that cholera might be introduced into Prussia from the sea, the government hired ships to act as guard vessels, including the sloop *Der Junge Carl*, the sloop-galeasse *Lena*, and the brig *Fanny*. These ships' task was to stop vessels as they arrived, and take them to the quarantine anchorages.

A naval guardship was a vessel designated to protect a naval dockyard, harbour or anchorage, and to regulate and control the affairs of the port. Specific duties would include the setting of guard boat patrols at night, looking after ships out of commission or laid up, and receiving press-ganged seamen before they were allocated to individual ships.

GUNBOAT: The term used from the eighteenth century to the mid nineteenth century for open, shallow-draught, relatively broad rowing boats, which were fitted with one or two light guns and pressed into service to defend coasts, bays and harbours. They were particularly popular with Mediterranean and Baltic navies. From 1840 to 1848 the Prussian navy possessed gun boats about 15m long with a beam of around 3.2m, propelled by 20 oars and carrying one 60-pounder cannon. For longer voyages the boats carried two removable masts rigged with lugsails. Around 1810, Swedish gunboats carried two 24-pounders, and had a length of around 20m with a beam of 4.5m. They were propelled by 12 oars.

The Prussian gunboats used in 1848 and 1849 were mostly CARVEL-built, but some were already of iron construction. They displaced around 40 tons with a length of 19.2m and a beam of 3.4m. Propulsion was by 26 oars, each of them pulled by two men, and a lugger rig was carried, with three removable masts setting a total sail area of around 120m². Armaments consisted of one 24-pounder and one 25-pounder carronade.

Gunboats were only usable in wind strengths up to about Force 4, and were not equipped for the crew to spend the night on board. The term gunboat was later applied to steam-driven vessels; at first they were hardly more powerful than their oared predecessors, but gradually they grew in size and firepower to become the kind of small cruising ship that was synonymous with imperial policing duties.

GUNDELOW: An eighteenth-century warship similar to the SHALLOP, built in North America in particular. In the American Wars of Independence the English and the Americans fought a sea battle on Lake Champlain to the North of New York. The American fleet included three SCHOONERs, one shallop, five GALLEYs and eight gundelows.

The English used four FRIGATEs, two schooners, 20 gunboats, four LONG-BOATs and one gundelow.

In the 1930s one of the sunken gundelows was salvaged from Champlain Lake from 18.5m of water, and subsequently restored for the Smithsonian Institute

This ship is 17.4m long and 5.2m wide. It carried one gun on each side and a swivel gun. The tall single mast, extended by a topmast, carried two relatively large square sails one above the other, plus a staysail. There were also gundelows which carried a lateen mainsail with a long upper lateen yard, and a balanced, shorter lower section.

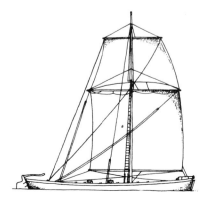

Gundelo, North American sailing gunboat

GUNTER-RIGGED BOAT: A boat or yacht with a triangular mainsail, which is hoisted on a near vertical gaff fixed to the masthead. this gaff has the same effect as an extended mast. The rig was influenced by the Huari sails commonly used on Indian sailing canoes and dinghies and was known as the sliding gunter, or simply the gunter rig. The name refers to the mathematician E Gunter (1581 to 1626), to whom is ascribed the invention of the slide rule, and the rig which bears his name uses a similar sliding principle. A long, vertical gaff is set on a relatively short mast, by means of which the bermudian shaped mainsail fixed to it can be raised.

GUNWALE EWER: A transitional form of the north German EWER halfway between an open and a covered vessel. The top edges of the side planks of the open ewer were reinforced by massive timbers, known as gunwales, which were fitted along the whole length of the hull. These stringers formed the ledge which later supported the deck. They contributed to the great strength of the boat, provided a secure attachment point for the shrouds, and also served to protect the upper side planks from damage during landing or fishing.

GYASSA, *gaiassa, ayassa*: From the end of the eighteenth century to the twentieth century, the gyassa was an important large cargo ship on the Nile, in the southwestern Mediterranean and on the Red Sea. Like the Egyptian bulk-carrying river ships, the broad, flat-bottomed hull was CARVEL-built, and featured a pronounced sheer forward. The vessels had one to three masts.

On the most common type, the two-masted gyassa, the mainmast was stepped very far forward, with the mizzen mast set at roughly one third of the ship's length. Both masts had slight aft rake. A typical feature was the exceptionally long yards, made up of several spars, and rigged with lateen sails. The mainyard could be up to 1.7 times the length of the ship.

H

HAFF KAHN: A full-bodied cargo ship of the nineteenth and early twentieth century based in the estuary of the Oser. The vessel had a large foresail and three massive poles masts, each of them carrying a large spritsail. As early as the thirteenth and fourteenth centuries the Oderhaff fishing vessels were known as Rahne, while cargo barges which operated further abroad than the haff were termed simply kahne.

Around 1800, the haff barges were around 23 to 30m long; by the twentieth century the typical length had risen to about 40m with a beam of about 4.5m and 2.0m freeboard.

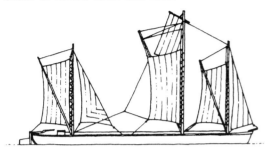

Three-masted haff kahn with spritsails

HAITHABU SHIP: The wrecked remains of a longship from the late Viking period. The vessel was about 16m long, and was found in the harbour of Haithabu on the river Schlei in Haddebyer Moor in 1953.

HALF CLIPPER: A very general term for a North American cargo ship of the mid nineteenth century, built and rigged like a clipper, but smaller, and used on secondary trade routes.

HALE: A boat similar to a PIROGUE, varying in length from 10 to 16m, and of virtually rectangular cross-section. It was based on the southern French Atlantic coast, and used primarily for grain transport.

HALSNÖY BOAT: The remains of a boat dating from the first or second century, found in Sunnfjordland in Norway in 1896. The frames are fixed to projecting cleats on the outer skin strakes, as on the Nydam boat.

HALVE MAEN: This Dutch vessel became famous as a result of Henry Hudson's voyage of discovery aimed at finding a Northwest Passage. The *Halve Maen* (*Half Moon* was one of the smaller three-masted Dutch sailing ships, which carried two square sails one above the other on the foremast and mainmast, and a lateen sail on the mizzen, and were known as jachts. As the original plans of the *Halve Maen* have not survived, the only means of reconstructing the ship with reasonable accuracy has been to refer to reports and to study detailed pictures of similar Dutch ships. The cargo capacity would have been around 80 tons. The main armament consisted of four

Hale, a French longboat

Halve Maen (Half Moon) 1609, Henry Hudson's ship, from a model of the full-size reconstruction

fairly small guns, which were set up in pairs on the broadside, on the upper deck between the mainmast and the forecastle. The rudder was operated via the whipstaff from a quarterdeck which was slightly raised (0.4–0.5m), from where the helmsman had an unobstructed view forwards and out to sea.

Hudson (1575–1611) put to sea in the *Halve Maen* on 6 April 1606, hoping to find a northern passage to the Pacific ocean, under contract to the United East India Company. He reached the North Cape in a heavy storm, snow and ice. Past the great Newfoundland

Bank he followed the coast from Cape Sable to Delaware, and in July he sailed round Manhattan and up the river later named after him, along Long Island to Albany, to make certain that there was no possibility of a passage there.

At the end of the voyage and after the return to Holland the ship sailed from Amsterdam to the East Indies in 1611, and was burnt out and sunk off Java in 1611 after a battle with English ships.

A reconstruction of the *Halve Maen* based on contemporary pictures of similar ships was built in Holland in 1909 to celebrate the 300th anniversary of Hudson's voyage. The new version was shipped from Amsterdam to New York as deck cargo. After going on display, the *Halve Maen II* sailed on the Hudson river under its own sails, manned by a crew of 18 men.

HAMPTON BOAT: A small two-masted fishing vessel developed in New Hampshire, USA, in the early nineteenth century. It was sharp-sterned with a long sharp bow. Later in the nineteenth century a centreboard was added and a square stern adopted. Two spritsails, and on some of the larger boats (up to 9m) a jib on a short bowsprit, was set.

HARD CHINE BOAT: A boat whose hull cross-section is composed of straight lines, in contrast to the round bilge boat which consists entirely of curved surfaces. In its simplest form a hard-chine boat has a flat bottom to which sides and ends are fitted at a sharp angle. However, if an extra angle is added at the keel, a more efficient compound V-shaped cross-section is formed. The STAR class keel boat and OK DINGHY are examples of racing boats with hard-chine hulls.

HASTINGS LUGGER: A CLINKER-built, decked fishing boat from the south coast of England. Now mechanized, earlier sailing luggers carried two masts, with a dipping

Heck boat, late seventeenth century

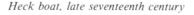

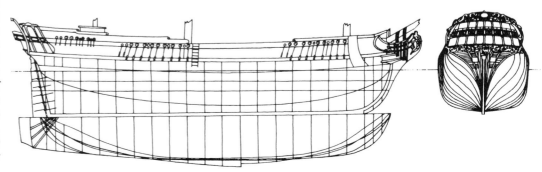

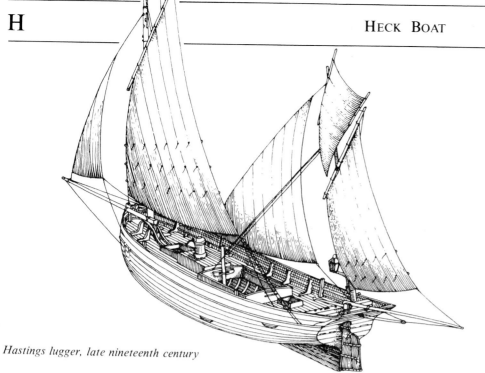

Hastings lugger, late nineteenth century

deck beams which project through the upper side strakes, providing lateral rigidity to the ship's hull. This style of reinforcement allowed the designers to omit the girdle of cable wrapped round the ship's hull. The tensioning hawser (hogging truss) above the deck, which provided longitudinal rigidity, was still in use, and is shown in the relief pictures.

HAVEL KAHN, *Havel zille*: see KAHN, ZILLE.

HECK BOAT: The usual term (literally meaning stern) in northern Europe at the end of the seventeenth century for a type of three-masted cargo ship, which evolved as a hybrid form of the FLEUTE and the PINNACE. The heck boat was somewhat flatter of bottom than a FRIGATE, but was more streamlined than a BARQUE and featured an aperture in the stern through which the tiller passed, like the HECK TJALK or heck yacht. The

lugsail on the main and a standing lugsail on the mizzen. It could also set a jib, a main topsail, a mizzen topsail and a mizzen staysail. The sailing lugger was unique amongst British fishing boats in being fitted with an iron centreboard. The most distinctive feature of these boats is the stern shape. Originally, the lugger ended in a vertical transom, but in the second half of the nineteenth century an overhanging projection was built in, the lute stern. At the beginning of the twentieth century a new form developed — the strakes were brought up and round, forming an elliptical stern. Both the lute and the elliptical stern still exist. Luggers are between 9 and 10m, but smaller verisons, known as bogs and punts, are also built.

HATSHEPSUT SHIP RELIEF: A series of relief pictures on the terraced rock temple of Deir el-Bahari in the ancient Egyptian city of Thebes. They provide detailed information in pictures and words of a successful sea voyage to the land of Punt, undertaken in the reign of Queen Hatshepsut around 1480 BC. The land of Punt was probably part of the Somalian coast near Cape Guardafui in the Gulf of Aden. From ancient Egyptian history it is known that an even earlier Punt expedition had been undertaken in the eleventh Dynasty under Pharaoh Mentuhotep II (*ca* 2040 BC), with the high official Heneau commanding 3000 men. Dismantled ships were transported from Koptos on the Nile through the Wadi Hammanat to the coastal city of Kosser, from where the actual sea expedition to the land of Punt began.

The reliefs of Deir el-Bahari include five very carefully portrayed ships some of them under sail, before a background of beach scenes and columnar structures typical of the Hamite people. The boats are shown setting off, returning and loading. The ships shown are unambiguously Egyptian vessels, of framed construction. They feature transverse

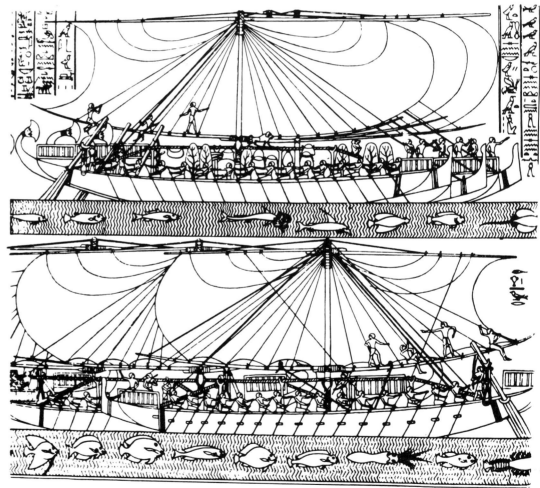

Relief picture of Egyptian seagoing ship ca *1480 BC, from the time of Queen Hatshepsut*

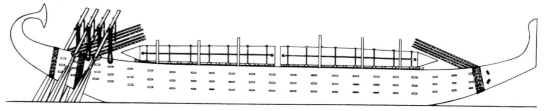

Egyptian obelisk transport ship, from the time of Queen Hatshepsut

foremast and mainmast set square sails, while the mizzen mast carried a lateen or gaff sail. A spritsail was carried on the bowsprit. The usual length of the ship was around 32m with a beam of 9m. At a later period the boat suspended in davits at the stern of a ship was also termed a heck boat (stern boat).

HECK TJALK, *heck yacht:* A fairly large TJALK or tjalk yacht, on which the tiller passed through a stern opening known as the helm port instead of being routed above the stern, as was usual on the tjalk. This design feature provided more shelter for the helmsman. The helm port was formed in a tall stern in which the upper strakes curved upwards at a sharp angle.

HELGOLAND SCHNIGGE: A freight SCHNIGGE with a mizzen mast introduced around the end of the eighteenth century. The vessel featured leeboards and a low keel, pronounced deck sheer and a cabin deck, and was sailed mainly between the German mainland and Helgoland.

HEMMEMA: A cross between the GALLEY and the FRIGATE, designed by the Swedish shipbuilding engineer Frederik Hendrik Af Chapman, and built in Sweden around 1770. It was an attempt to combine the qualities of the galley with those of the sailing frigate, but only three ships of the type were built. They were

Hengst, with gaff mainsail, ca 1800 *(model)*

Heck yacht, late seventeenth century (model)

Heck tjalk, 1714 (model)

Mecklenburg heuer, sheer draught plan

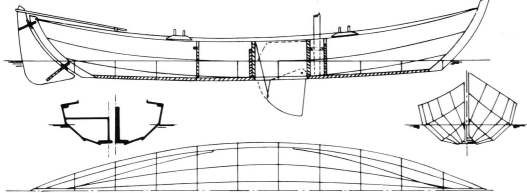

equipped with long guns, were 43m long, and carried 20 pairs of oars.

HENGST: A flat-bottomed Dutch fishing vessel, which also proved suitable for cargo transport and ferring. The earlier types were open vessels rigged with spritsails. One characteristic feature of the type is the stem, which is strongly raked forward. The partially covered single-masted version has been in use since the eighteenth century on Dutch inland waters and around the North Sea coast, in this case rigged with gaff mainsail and foresails. By the end of the nineteenth century the vessels were around 10 to 12m in length and 3 to 4m in breadth, and were covered in from the forecastle back to the mast, while the rig consisted of gaff mainsail, staysail and jib.

HENRY GRACE À DIEU see GREAT HENRY

HEPTER: A very large oared Mediterranean ship from the ancient period. The word hept is supposed to indicate seven oarsmen, and the suffix, the number of rowing decks, but whether such ships ever existed is very doubtful. Even on the more modest ancient ships, as built, for example, under the direction of Archimedes, the oars must have been almost imposible to handle even when deck heights were kept very low. Nevertheless, various methods of squeezing in a great number of tiers of oarsmen are possible, with short, narrow rowing seats staggered in height and fore and aft, some suitable for seated rowers, some standing, all based on the standard short-stroke rowing technique of the time. In contrast to the long strokes used in rowing today, a brief, jerky oar movement was standard from ancient times to the age of the galleys, with the oars remaining in the water for only a short period. As a result, the oarsmen required only a little space for movement, which in turn allowed more oarsmen to be fitted into a given size of ship to maximize power and speed.

HERMAPHRODITE BRIG, *true brigantine*: Also known in Europe as a brig-schooner. A two-masted sailing ship, with brig-like square sails on the foremast, but only fore-and-aft sails on the main. The true brigantine differs in having a square topsail on the mainmast, while the after mast on brigs was fully square-rigged as well as having a fore-and-aft spanker. The term brigantine eventually superseded hermaphrodite or brig-schooner in common usage for this rig.

HERRING LUGGER: A specialized fishing lugger designed for catching herring using drift nets. The length of the herring lugger was between 19 and 24m and the beam around 6m. A typical feature was the slender underwater hull combined with a more full-bodied upper portion, flat stern and high bulwark. The two-masted vessels cast drift nets which were several kilometres long and around 15m deep, consisting of individual net sections known as fleets. Depending on the direction of the current and the wind, the drift net remained attached to the lugger at one end, and could either be held by the ship anchored at the weather end, or could drift with the lugger, the ship being made fast on the lee side. The last wooden vessels were built around 1910, and after this time all sailing luggers were built of steel. The herring lugger was still being built in large numbers during the transition to trawling and rig-netting.

HEUER: A single-masted Mecklenburg fishing boat also used in the Oder estuary, and which was still in service in the twentieth century. The vessels with their narrow flat keel, slightly rockered, and raked, rounded stem and stern, were CLINKER-built with a small number of broad bottom and side strakes, resulting in a cross-section similar to that of a hard chine hull. Other characteristic features were the relatively large forward and aft sheer, the arched forward deck, and the centreboard, which could be extended by about 0.5m. With centreboard retracted, a heuer drew about 0.5m, and were up to 10m long and around 2 to 2.5m wide. A fish well was fitted, divided into sections, to keep the catch alive. The boats were usually rigged with a main spritsail of 10 to 15m^2 and a foresail of about 5m^2.

HEXER: One of the ancient oared ships, with a claimed length of around 50m. The oarsmen were said to sit side by side in six rows.

HJØRTSPRING BOAT, *Als boat*: A boat dating from 300 BC, found on the Danish island of Als at Hjørtspring 1921, and one of the oldest maritime finds in northern Europe. In view of the state of technical development at the time, the Hjørtspring boat is powerful

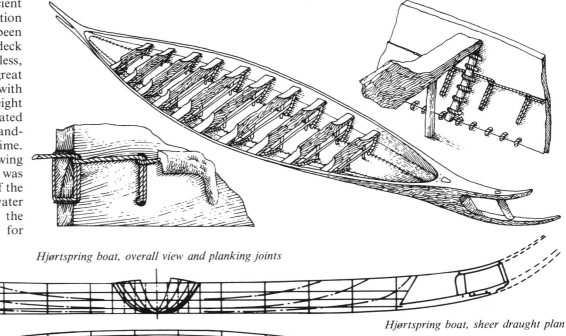

Hjørtspring boat, overall view and planking joints

Hjørtspring boat, sheer draught plan

evidence of the sophistication of Scandinavian boatbuilding, with its streamlined form, double stem/stern, and workmanlike construction. The boat was 13.28m long and 2m in breadth. The floor of the boat consisted of a virtually straight, hollowed-out, trough-shaped floor timber, without a projecting keel. At the bow and stern the floor timber curved up to form identically shaped lower stem and stern timbers, the shape being reminiscent of an ice-skate. The stem and stern proper projected past the actual hull ends by about 2m.

This double-ended design is typical of the vessels shown on extant Nordic pictures and rock drawings dating from the first and second millennia BC. This form of paddled boat, devoid of oars or a fixed rudder, made for simpler construction and increased the vessel's manoeuvrability, as it never needed to turn around. The long, projecting ends served to protect the thick keel timber and the hull itself when voyages had to be undertaken in waters where drift ice or a shallow, rocky bottom were likely to be encountered. The skid-like form and the vertical bridge piece which stiffened and linked the lower stem/stern with the upper stem/stern timbers also eased the task of manhandling the boat on land. It also allowed several people to pull on the extended boat ends simultaneously.

Two broad side strakes of lime wood were fixed to the edges of the keel timber on each side. They overlapped in clinker fashion, and were sewn to the floor timber and to each other with vast fibres. Holes were bored through the wood about 20 to 25mm from the plank edges and around 70mm apart. The planks were arranged with the bottom edge of the upper strake aligned with the line of holes drilled in the lower plank, ie overlapped by about 20 to 25mm. The holes, bound areas and the joints were carefully sealed with resins. To stiffen the hull, a total of ten bound-in ribs made of 35mm-thick, natural-grown hazelnut branches were fitted at a spacing of about one metre. The method of joining the side strakes to the ribs involved cleats which were left (projecting) when the planks were hewn, similar to those found on the later NYDAM, OSEBERG, and GOKSTAD ships. The outside edge of the upper strake was left slightly thicker to form a gunwale. The boat had the relatively small sheer of about 90mm. Ten transverse stiffening timbers, similar to deck beams, were also fitted, located at and above the rib positions. They were cut away to form thwarts at the sides of the boat.

Towards the bottom of the boat the transverse timbers were supported by vertical struts.

The boat was propelled by paddles, of which 16 were found. They varied from 1 to 1.5m in length and had rectangular blades. The vessel was steered by means of a loose side rudder, the blade of which was 50mm thick, flat on one side, and convex on the other.

HOOGAARS: A Dutch flat-bottomed cargo and fishing ship with leeboards, which was

House boat in one of Hongkong's floating colonies

built using particularly broad planks, in similar fashion to the SCHOKKER. The term was in use by the sixteenth century, applied to an open cargo ship of 30 to 40 tons which sailed on the River Maas. Because of the shallow draught (which was greater forward than aft) and the large amount of useful space resulting from the flat hull bottom, yachts of similar design are still built today. An average size for these vessels would be about 13m long and 4.20m in breadth while the sail area can be up to 80m^2, consisting of a gaff mainsail and staysail.

HOOKER: see HUKER

HOUARI, *huari, herry*: The original term for a FERRY BOAT, sometimes also applied to a covered vessel which was used for fishing. On racing boats of recent vintage the gunter rig was also originally known as the Huari rig. *See also* GIG *and* WHERRY.

HOUSEBOAT: A boat, pontoon or raft with accommodation, used as temporary or perm-

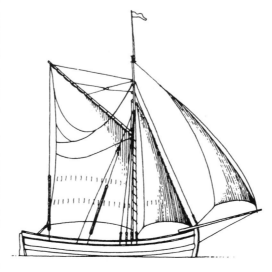

Hoy, Dutch coastal cargo vessel

anent living quarters. In various densely populated regions of East Asia the houseboat is still encountered to this day on rivers, lakes, harbours and sheltered bays. Simpler structures are also used, such as rafts with a deckhouse, dugouts with side planks added or planked vessels with more or less temporary roofed areas. In the west modern houseboats are used for holidays as well as for more permanent accommodation.

HOY, *heu, heude*: A Dutch sixteenth-century coastal freight ship which originally carried one mast and a spritsail and operated in the North Sea and the English Channel. Later on some versions were built with two masts and leeboards. The tonnage could be up to 40 tons. In the seventeenth century, hoys were also adapted for personnel transport, in which case a cabin was erected behind the mast to provide shelter for the travellers. Cargo carrying versions were used to re-supply warships at sea (for example during English blockades of French ports) and were used to help loading or off-loading larger cargo vessels.

HUA CH'UAN: *see* CANTON FLOWER BOAT.

HUA-P'I-KU: *see* FOOCHOW POLE JUNK.

HUISSIER, *usciere*: Early medieval French and Italian horse transport ships of particular importance in the Mediterranean at the time of the Crusades. The term has been traced back to the French term huis for door or door ship, and also to usciere, meaning horse transport ship.

The vessels were broad of beam, and had a door-like lateral loading port above the lowest deck which was used for loading horses, cattle and sheep. The port also made it possible to transport long timbers. The bottom deck was loaded first, and the port closed with a heavy external cover and sealed, as it was partially under water when the ship was fully laden and

Dutch fishing huker, mid nineteenth century (model)

Dutch fishing huker, mid eighteenth century (after Chapman)

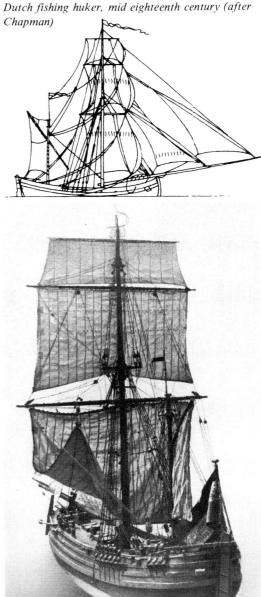

Single-masted merchant huker from the second half of the eighteenth century (model)

at sea. The Sicilian versions carried a landing bridge on board, and were large enough to carry 40 riders with horses, weapons and servants. *See also* USCIERE.

HUKER, *hukker, hoeker, hooker*: This was the second most important fishing type on the Dutch and Friesian coasts in the seventeenth and eighteenth centuries, second only to the BUSS. The word huk or hoek means a projecting tongue or spit of land, and so the huker was a ship which sailed beyond the spits, ie a sea-going vessel.

The broad, full-bodied huker was an excellent vessel, whose qualities made it popular in German sea ports, along with other similar ship types of Dutch origin, until the mid nineteenth century. The ship also proved to be well suited for voyages to Greenland and the Arctic for seal hunting. In the second half of the nineteenth century, the more stream-lined, high-speed sailing ships with keels supplanted the more beamy ship types in those northern waters. The principal use of the huker, however, was for herring fishing in the North Sea. A contemporary report reads as follows: 'Fishing usually extends from 20 June to 1 November. Each year 90 to 100 huker set out, nearly 60 of them from Flushing alone. In favourable conditions each ship returns with

Huker galeasse Greiff, *from Greifswald, 1782*

Three-masted armed huker

900,000 to 1 million herring.'

The huker was a two-masted ship with a cargo capacity of 100 to 200 tons. The forward mainmast carried three square sails and the smaller mizzen a gaff sail. The bowsprit carried one or more foresails. On larger ships a brig-like rig was usual. The rounded hull resulted in bulbous fore and aft sections, with reinforcements in the anchor hawse region (hawse cheeks).

HUKER-GALEASSE: *see* GALEASSE, HUKER.

HULK: The hull of a sailing ship stripped of its mast and rigging. Warships which were no longer seaworthy were often used as customs or guard ships, anchored at the entrance to rivers and ports, or at customs stations on rivers. In times of war hulks armed with guns were also used as floating batteries to protect and block the mouths of rivers and ports, or were sunk, less armaments, to form port barricades. Hulks were also used as coal and provisions stores, floating magazines or arsenals, barracks, hospital ships or as ships' churches and at times as floating prisons. A sheer hulk was a specially equipped cut-down hull, fitted with sheer legs (a primitive form of crane) used to fit or remove the heavy lower masts of sailing ships.

HULK, *holk*: A medieval northern European sailing ship with full lines, flat bottom and no keel. This ship type had a long history of development undergoing many variations in size, construction, propulsion and intended purpose, finally evolving into a three-masted CARVEL-built ship. The origin of the term hulk can be traced back to the words hulec, hoele, holcas and holk, which were probably brought to northern Europe during the Roman occupation and referred to a ship towed from the land. Dugouts in southern Scandinavia in the early Germanic period were also known as holker.

The Utrecht hulk, which was a Dutch vessel dating from around 800, featured a mast step located very far forward, in the typical position for a towing mast. This is certain evidence of a towed ship, pulled from the land by people or draught animals. Roman frescoes show similar mast arrangements on Roman ships. *See also* OSTIA FRESCO.

In the succeeding centuries the type designation spread to vessels other than river ships. For example, English lists of port duties dating from around 1000 make it clear that medium-sized, sea-going ships were termed hulk by this time. The fees were set at four pence for hulks and keels, ie the two ships types were roughly the same. At that time the fee for very small craft was a halfpenny, and for small ships a penny.

Around the year 1200, a hulk in the Lothringian-Lower Rhenish region was a small river ship carrying about 20 tons of cargo. Good representations of the hulk have survived from the end of the twelve century in stone reliefs on the baptismal altar at Zeedelgen near Bruges and in Winchester Cathedral.

An interesting insight into the hulk's importance in the thirteenth century is provided by a seal of 1295 of the medieval English town of Hulkesmouth. The ship depicted is specifically named as a hulk.

By the thirteenth century the hulk had increased its cargo capacity to about 100 to 120 tons. By the end of the fourteenth century the type was similar in size to the contemporary COG, but after this time the hulk overtook its competitor, and by the fifteenth century its cargo capacity had reached about 300 tons.

Originally, the hulk always had a flat bottom with no keel and rounded hull sections. The bow was usually bluff while the stern was flat and curved up steeply. This stern shape was the result of continuing the flat hull bottom aft, and arching it upward above the waterline.

The three most important large ship types in the North Sea and Baltic regions, the French NEF, the Hanseatic COG and the Flemish HULK, developed relatively independently of each other until the fourteenth century.

Thus the single-masted hulk of around 1400 can be considered as a mixture of hulk and cog, which was then further developed to produce a considerably larger and more seaworthy ship, with cargo capacites above 200 tons.

Many of the pictures on thirteenth- to seventeenth-century seals portray a full-bodied ship with one or more masts, and without fore and after castles. In contrast to the framework-like castles on the early cogs, the hulk's superstructure was formed by curving the side strakes up fore and aft, so that the raised ends were integrated into the hull. Although the flat bottom was a typical feature of the hulk, and the clinker-built hull with keel typical of the cog, hybrid types were also built, such as the three-masted, clinker-built ship, similar in shape to the hulk, shown on the Danzig seal of 1400. The terminology used at the time is even less standardized, very similar

Lübeck hulk, sixteenth century (model). Overall length about 30m, beam around 8m, draught up to 3m, 150 to 200 tons cargo capacity, approx. 300m² sail area

ships being named as cog and hulk in pictures completed at the same time but in different places.

In its later hybrid form, a result of the marriage of the original hulk and the cog, the hulk combined the best features of both types. From the earlier version it retained the flat, broad bottom with rounded bilges and the resultant full-bodied hull section, which gave excellent stability and cargo-carrying capability. From the later version of the cog it adopted the structured keel, the extended stem, the centreline stern rudder, super-structures, and good sailing qualities. Both types were still clinker-built. The main distinguishing feature of the two ships, which were very similar in their final stages of development, is the formation of the forward and after superstructures, and the manner in which they are integrated into the hull structure, with side strakes curving upward.

In terms of size, the hulk represents the limit for a clinker-built hull. The problems lay in the increased complexity of construction, the frames having to be notched to fit the overlapped strakes, the strength of the joints between planks and frames needed in order to absorb racking and twisting loads, and the method of sealing the seams between the planking. These difficulties were overcome by the adoption of carvel planking, and the transition to this style of construction, which had always been the norm in the Mediter-ranean, was completed in the North Sea and Baltic regions quite quickly, roughly between 1460 and the turn of the century. This move was accelerated by the sea links between Brittany and the Mediterranean.

There remained one further barrier to the successful development of larger ships: the rig. The increased sail area required for the larger ships brought the dimensions of the single sail on the single natural grown mast to a size where they were difficult to handle. The solution was the transition from a single-masted to a multi-masted ship, with three-masted ships being the most popular.

The three-masted carvel-built ships, which had evolved from the single-masted hulk, were termed three-masted hulks or simply hulks. The full, beamy shape, in which the ratio of ship's length to beam remained around 3:1, was a common feature of the northern cargo ship, the cog and the hulk.

HUMBER KEEL: The last large British craft to employ a square sail, the Humber keel was a flat-bottomed, wall-sided cargo vessel with bluff bows and a rounded stern, equipped with leeboards. They were generally single-masted, setting a topsail and occasionally a topgallant sail above the mainsail. Some of those working on the River Trent, which were the largest, 25m, also set a lugsail on a mizzen mast.

HUMBER SLOOP: A barge similar in construction to the Humber keel but with a finer run aft and, instead of the distinctive

A Humber Keel (model)

square sail, setting a gaff mainsail and foresail. The larger sloops set a full cutter rig; others set a jib on a short bowsprit and a yard topsail. On average they were around 22m in length with a beam of 5m. A similar vessel, with cutter or ketch rig and square topsails and top gallants, was known as the BILLY BOY. They ranged much further than the sloops.

HUNLEY DIVING BOAT: During the American Civil War (1861–1865), Captain HL Hunley of the Southern States, supported by the naval engineers JR McClintock and B Watson, built diving boats driven by human muscle power. The vessels succeeded in sinking enemy ships in a few instances, but their fame rested much more on the fact that 32 men lost their lives in them. Explosive mines were towed behind the boats on long lines, and they also carried what were known as spar torpedoes, fixed to poles on the front of the diving boat. Amongst others, the Hunley diving boat *H L Hunley* sank the 1400-ton *Housatonic* on 17 February 1864 with a spar torpedo, although the diving boat itself was also destroyed with the loss of the entire crew.

These submarine boats consisted of converted iron boilers about 11m long, with a diameter of about 1.8m. Depth control involved the use of ballast tanks and external ballast which could be jettisoned so that the vessels could be held just under the surface of the water. A dome with a glass window was fitted, which was not submerged, and through which the vessel's Commander could see. The diving boat was propelled by the power of eight men turning a crankshaft oriented fore-and-aft, ending in a propeller shaft fitted with a large propeller appropriate to the low speed of

rotation. The boat could achieve a speed of around 4 knots, and could stay submerged for half an hour without rising for air.

HURKE, *Hooker*: A Spanish-Portuguese cargo ship of fairly small size. The type was also built in the Netherlands, while the military version was built in large numbers in Holland, Zeeland and Brabant around 1520 for use as a transport ship. *See also* HULK.

I

ICE BOAT: A lightweight boat with sled-like reinforcements on the bottom. Ice boats are used on waters which are part iced up and can be pulled or sailed over the ice.

ICE YACHT: A sail-driven sledge running on three skids (two at the front), the rear one of which is moveable and is used to steer the machines. Speeds of up to 100 kph are achieved using a single sail.

ICELAND SCHOONER: A nineteenth-century boat rigged in similar fashion to a

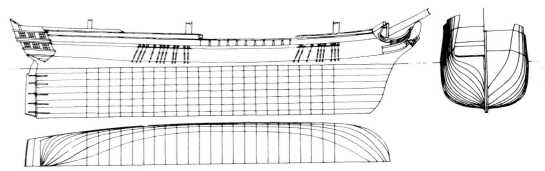

East Indiaman, sheer draught plan

Iceland schooner, sail plan and sheer draught plan

French Iceland schooner, mid nineteenth century (model)

schooner, used by the English, French, German and, to a lesser extent, Icelandic high-seas fishing fleets in Icelandic waters and in the North Sea. In contrast to the larger NEWFOUNDLAND SCHOONERS, which were often three-masted, these smaller ships were usually two-masted and carried square sails on the foremast instead of gaff topsails. A sheer plan of an Iceland schooner from Brittany, drawn by E Paris in 1868, had a length overall of 20.4m, a design waterline length of 18.5m, a beam of 6.5m, a forward draught of 1.5m, aft draught of 2.0m and a cargo hold 9.8m long. The foremast and mainmast of the two-masted ship each carried topmasts, and were rigged with gaff sail, foresail, fore topsail, fore topgallant, main topsail and topmast staysails. The headsails were set on a fixed bowsprit and jib boom. The total sail area was between 300 and 390m², and the crew strength was eight. After 1890, a few two-masted Iceland schooners were built in England for foreign customers; they were 15 to 20m long and 4.0 to 5.5m wide.

ILMENAU EWER: A special type of sailing EWER used on the Elbe until the end of the nineteenth century, especially on the upper Elbe. The vessel was of CLINKER-built with a flat bottom and a pointed bow and stern. It was an open cargo sailing ship with an overall length of around 24m, a beam of 4.5m and a freeboard of 1.30m.

INDIAMAN, *East Indiaman*: In the era of the sailing ship this term was applied generally to the armed merchant ships which sailed regularly between northwest Europe and India. In fact, the expression originated from the English East India Company, which assumed and maintained the leading position in East Indian trade between 1660 and 1858 because the State had bestowed trading privileges upon it. While the term Indiaman implied vessels sailing to the East Indies, there were also much smaller West Indiaman trading with the Caribbean. *See also* EAST INDIAMAN.

INFLATED SKIN RAFT: Rafts made of inflated and sealed animal skins. Such vessels were in general use in an area stretching from

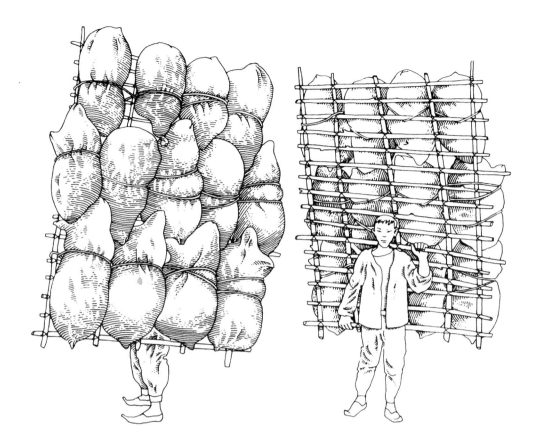

Animal skin raft from Tibet

the Near East to China thousands of years ago. The animals were skinned, the hides then being turned inside out and rendered waterproof with salt and grease. They would then either be stuffed with a lightweight filling material or inflated after sealing the skin openings by tying. Inflated sheep and goat skin rafts (kelek) were still in general use on various tributaries of the Euphrates and the Tigris until fairly recently, exactly as depicted on the Khorsabad relief from the Assyrian Empire dating from about 800 BC. On the Upper Tigris, large animal skin rafts were also used for transporting goods and cattle, in this case consisting of many (up to several hundred) animal skins stuffed with reeds or straw, and held together with rod frameworks. *See also* Pi-fa-Tzû

INTERNATIONAL CLASS BOAT: International CLASS BOATS of the one-design classes are subject to the mandatory rules laid down by the International Yacht Racing Union (IYRU), in contrast to National class boats. *See also* RACING BOATS.

INTERNATIONAL 14: A 14ft dinghy whose ancestry can be traced back as far as 1890, the International 14 class was formed after a suggestion from Leslie Lewis in 1923 and became the first dinghy class to be conceived on a national scale. The class attained international status in 1927 and has evolved over the years from a relatively heavy, non-planing CLINKER-built boat into a lightweight modern dinghy with two trapezes.

International 14

IRON SHIP: The general term used for vessels built of iron (rather than the later shipbuilding material steel, which consists of iron and carbon) instead of timber. The first vessels were built as isolated examples towards the end of the eighteenth century, but iron increasingly displaced wood in the course of the nineteenth century.

English East Indiaman, ca 1640 (model)

JACHT, JAGD, *jaghd, jaegd*: This term originated in Holland around the turn of the seventeenth century, and referred to a new type of three-masted Dutch ship which was rigged in similar style to the BARQUE (with square sails on the two forward masts and fore-and-aft sails on the after mast). Amongst the most famous jagden of this period were *DE HALVE MAEN* of 1607, and the *MAYFLOWER* (*ca* 1620).

Other types of small, single-masted sailing vessels evolved in Holland in the seventeenth century, suited to that country's narrow canals and rivers and coastal waters. The development of these manoeuvrable vessels was based in part on types which were already common, eg the BOIER yacht. These jagden were usually rigged with gaff or bermudian mainsails, large foresail and a fairly small square topsail.

Around 1660, King Charles II was presented with two Dutch state jagden, the *Bezan* of 35 tons and the *Mary* of 92 tons. Both jagden had bluff bows, leeboards and a few small cannon which could be fired through gunports decorated with gilded carvings. The bow, stern and elegant, glazed stern cabins typical of all Dutch

jagden were also richly decorated with painted carved work.

The *Mary* was rigged with a boomless mainsail and a long, steep gaff known as the 'half sprit'. In contrast to this, the *Bezan*

Single-masted Dutch jacht, late seventeenth century (model)

J-class yacht Endeavour II

Dutch tall-rigged jacht, mid eighteenth century (model)

carried the BESAN rig, with a boomless mainsail and a very short gaff. From these vessels the term acquired its reference to pleasure craft, and the English spelling of yacht has become accepted for all vessels sailed for sport or leisure.

J-CLASS YACHT: Large racing sailing yachts of the International class, carrying the sail symbol 'J'. They are particularly well known for their participation in the America's Cup competition.

Among the best-known J-class which sailed for the America's Cup were the American *Enterprise*, *Rainbow* and *Ranger*, and the English *Shamrock V*, *Endeavour* and *Endeavour II*. The large American yacht *Ranger* won the cup in the last such race before the Second World War. She had an overall length of 41.54m, and a waterline length of 26.51m. The beam was 6.36m and the draught was 4.57m. The 50m-tall, light alloy mast carried a total sail area of 701m². The main boom, also constructed of light alloy, was of triangular cross-section, its upper surface broad enough to walk upon, and to allow the foot of the mainsail to be set in a curve, to gain aerodynamic advantage. A further innovation was the quadrilateral jib, with two clews and hence two sheets to flatten it. Due to the cost of building and of upkeep, these great racing machines never reappeared after the Second World War. Since 1957, new regulations for the America's Cup have been in force, aimed at restricting the size of the yachts taking part in these races to sensible dimensions. The result is that the yachts have to meet the requirements of the 12-METRE class of racing yacht. The rules for the 12-metre stipulate a length of

about 21m and a sail area of 180 to 200m². 1958 saw the first race for the America's Cup in which 12-Metres took part.

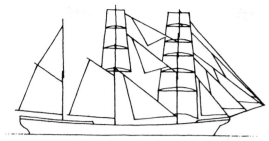

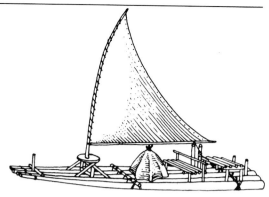

Jackass barque or polka barque with gaff mainsail on mainmast

South American jaganda raft

JACKASS BARQUE: A three-masted sailing ship related to the BARQUENTINE, but which carried fore-and-aft sails on the lower mainmast and square sails on the topmasts. Four-masted versions of such ships also sailed round Cape Horn in the later nineteenth century. In these cases the two forward masts were square-rigged, while the two after masts carried fore-and-aft sails. In general usage the term was applied to any unconventional rig that did not quite fit a normal category.

JANGADA, *jangade*: A South American raft with a triangular sail, and also a raft without sail used on the Portuguese coast. These vessels

consisted of a single layer of shaped logs pegged together.

JOLLY BOAT: A standard-class two-man sailing dinghy, especially popular in England and the USA, developed by the designer Uffa Fox, and carrying the sail symbol 'J'. The boat is 5.49m long, 1.57m in beam, has a hull draught of 0.20m and a draught of 1.42m with centreboard extended.

In naval usage, a small ship's boat used for taking men ashore or other light duties.

JUNK: The European name for the wide range of one- to three-masted Chinese sailing cargo

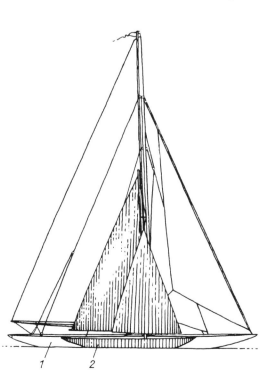

Size comparison between the J-class (1) and the 12-metre (2)

Two-masted junk

Three-masted Chinese seagoing junk between Hongkong and Macao

vessels employed on river and sea, and also in specialized form as warships, pirate and fishing vessels. They are widespread in Korea, Japan and the Philippines, as well as in China. The basic features of this ship type evolved thousands of years ago in Asia. In the southern part of China inland shipping on the great rivers and tributaries was highly developed very much earlier than in Europe. The first canals passable by ships were built in China about 1000 BC, among the early channels being the Imperial canal, which was built under Emperor Yang-ti (605 to 618 BC).

The junks built specifically for river travel were usually rather narrower, and were fitted with a single, tall mast, because of the sloping banks which obstructed the wind. The difficult sailing conditions in the coastal waters off the long, convoluted coasts of China, with the many offshore islands and the East Asian monsoons, are reflected in the utilitarian design and rig of those junks designed for the estuary regions of the great rivers and the most

important sea regions. There are clear differences in detail between the junks developed in the widely-spaced regions, but although the variety of types and sizes is great, the basic principles have remained unaltered for many centuries. Thus the northern vessels differ from the southern ones in the bluffer, somewhat squatter shape, the blunt, spoon-shaped bow, the addition of a transom stern, and the straight lines and reduced belly of the sail. Centuries earlier than in Europe, the ship's hull was stiffened and subdivided by transverse bulkheads to form watertight compartments. The CLINKER style of planking of the junk also has a special peculiarity. The European method of clinker planking was carried out by fitting the bottom planks first, and overlapping towards the top, whereas on a junk the planking starts from the upper side plank and ends at the bottom. With this sequence of construction the rib framework, or at least some form of temporary framework, has to be erected

before planking can commence. The larger vessels were built with a deck. The method of constructing this was also different from that used in Europe, in that the deck beams were generally fitted above the deck planking, resulting in a somewhat awkward-looking structure.

While there is no evidence of the existence of the centreline stern rudder in northern Europe until the beginning of the thirteenth century, Chinese junks were fitted with stern rudders as early as the forth century BC.

The mast arrangement and the sail design form other characteristic features. The short pole masts were not usually extended by means of topmasts, nor supported by shrouds or stays, and hence the sail could, if necessary, be rotated right round the mast. This was a clear advantage compared with square sails, as the sail could be swung into the wind more easily, and the ship could sail more close-hauled. The typical sail was the Chinese lugsail, either rectangular or trapezoid, with the after edge varying from straight to strongly curved. Originally, the sails were made from a woven, mat-like material, which was stiffened by a large number of light bamboo battens. The bottom batten was straight or only slightly curved, and the front edge of the sail was usually somewhat longer than the top edge, while the upper boom was set at an angle, so that the sail outline was that of an irregular quadrilateral. The almost straight (northern type) or strongly rounded (southern type) leech, or after edge of the sail, featured a full-length seam, or had a line attached, by means of which the sail could be hauled up for rapid manoeuvring, as on modern yachts.

Each of the light, divided (wishbone) sail battens was fixed to the mast with a separate truss, and belayed at the ends with sheets, so that the entire sail could easily be hoisted, reefed or lowered from the deck. This arrangement also resulted in the sail forces being transmitted directly to the mast at the level of each transverse batten, and then via the sheets to the deck. By comparison with the concentrated loads resulting with a single square yard, this arrangement resulted in a favourable load distribution, smaller bending moments and hence a greater safety margin against failure of the mast. The advantages of this combination of square and fore-and-aft sails were recognized very early on in the Far East, at a time when the square sail was used exclusively in the Mediterranean and northern Europe.

It is possible that the Chinese lugsail was the pattern for the early dhow types built by Arab seafarers, which gradually evolved into the settee dhow sail, and thereafter into the triangular lateen sail of the Mediterranean.

In spite of their clumsy appearance, junks were good sailing craft. In their three-masted, ocean-going form (in some cases with more than three masts), they sailed from South China to India, East Africa, the Persian Gulf and the Red Sea. The ships' size varied according to the purpose for which they were built. There were many vessels which could carry 400 tons, with a length of 60m and a beam of about 9m, and others up to 500 tons, with rare examples carrying up to 800 tons.

K

Dutch kaag with spritsail, ca 1760 (model)

River ship with pointed kaffe

Pictures on seals dating from the Middle Ages show river freight ships whose kaffen were bound with extra ropework to hold the planks together at the hull ends, and to damp down waves caused by the vessel's movement. The kaffen was still common in the nineteenth century for simple cargo vessels used on inland waterways, and the last kaffen barges were built around 1900 on the Uecker.

KAHN: A generic term applied to open, flat-bottomed rowing barges used on inland water, rivers and in harbours, but also referring to open, flat-bottomed inland and coastal ships carrying up to several hundred tons of freight, sometimes fitted with sails. The words kahn, kane, cane and similar terms are among the oldest boat names and have been in use on the German Baltic coast since earliest times. The boom kahn, for example, was a dug-out type of boat, while the hafcan, according to the Anklam customs roll of 1302 was a grain transport ship for the haff (coastal) waters. The cane was a type of lighter of the Hanseatic period. Sailing cargo barges, known as steven kähne, were still in widespread use in the Baltic

Two-masted cargo kahn, nineteenth century (model)

KAAG: A flat-bottomed, single-masted ship type with an aggressive-looking stem, rectangular cross-section and leeboards. The type was known in the early Middle Ages, at that time sailing off the North Sea coasts. The vessels were roughly 15m long, and were still in use in the seventeenth century for cargo transport and river fishing. Originally, they carried spritsails, but these were superseded by gaff sails in the eighteenth century. A larger type of Kaag of 80 to 100 tons cargo capacity survived in Denmark in a somewhat more modern form up to the middle of the present century.

KAFFEN RIVER CARGO SHIP: A small to medium-sized cargo vessel designed for work on rivers, inland waters and shallow waters generally. The ships had a flat-bottomed or slightly rounded hull, devoid of keel, stem and stern. The hull curved inward and up at the ends to form simple tapered shapes known as kaffen. The form and width of the hull ends varied, hence the vessels were variously known as spitz (pointed) and rund (bluff) kaffen vessels.

Favoured for its simple construction, the kaffen was widespread by the twelfth century.

Seals of the cities of Lübeck, Wismar, Rostock and Stralsund on a document dated 19th May 1361

Large cog seal from the town of Stralsund, print from the original stamp, dating from 1329

Second Wismar city seal, ca 1350, on a document dated 19th May 1361

Stern of the Dutch flagship Zeelandia, *1662 (model)*

Painting by Wilhelm van de Velde the Younger (1633–1707). Ships on a calm sea (1653), Museum de Bildenden Künste, Budapest

The Kalmar boat at the site of excavation   *Reconstructed Kalmar boat*

until the beginning of the twentieth century. The large haff kahn had up to three tall pole masts, without shrouds, rigged with large rectangular or gaff sails, and carried swivelling leeboards. Haff or steven kahns were also used in Mecklenburg and Pomerania for fishing. The zees kahn, which was first mentioned around 1450, is still used today in the Stralsund/Rügen area for trawling, and the tucker kahn has also survived to the present day.

Various types of kahn were employed on the rivers which flowed into the North Sea. Of particular importance were the Weser kahns used on that river as lighters to cater for the intense traffic between Bremerhaven, Vegesack and Bremen. A smaller type of freight barge which was known as the Stecknitz kahn operated between Hamburg and Lübeck; this vessel's cargo capacity, around 1820, was around 12 tons. Significantly larger (able to carry up to 240 tons of cargo) were the rhine kahns, which were also known as kahn aak in Holland. Even larger Rhenish vessels (eg 265 tons cargo capacity) were generally known as kahn ship. The long, narrow shallow-draught Rhenish cargo kahns and kahn ships were two-masted vessels. The usual dimensions were: length around 42m, beam around 6m, freeboard 1.6m and draught about 1m. The flat, CARVEL-built floor curved upward gently at the hull ends, and ran to a point, while the topsides were clinker-planked.

Another type of kahn of similar construction, but of smaller size, was the Maas kahn, used on the river of that name. In Europe, the term triedel kahn (towed bridge) was the general term for vessels which were pulled upstream by draught animals or people where the current was strong, or when there was no wind. *See also* AAK.

KALMAR BOATS: The remains of several boats and ships which were discovered near Kalmar castle on the southeast Swedish coast. They provided sufficient information for the reconstruction of a mid thirteenth-century open sailing boat. It is 11.2m long and has a beam of 4.6m.

The discovery confirms what was already known from other sources about the construction of such boats in the Middle Ages. For instance, the transverse deck beams on the Kalmar boat project through the topsides, a feature shown in many pictures of ships from the same period (Dunwich *ca* 1200, Danzig *ca* 1300, Hythe thirteenth century, Rye *ca* 1400, Southampton *ca* 1400). The deck beams are also fixed to the hull sides with shaped timbers. A peculiarity of this vessel is the forked tabernacle at the bow to accept the mast when folded. The Kalmar sailing boat has a CLINKER-built hull, as all northern boats had at the time, and is made almost entirely of oak. The frames are cut saw-tooth style to fit the overlapping strakes, and rivetted to the planks.

KAN-CH'UAN: A Chinese river boat from Kiangsu carrying 30 to 40 tons, designed for travelling on rivers with strong currents, whirlpools and rapids. The boats were narrow, with bulbous hull sections, the hull ends tapered sharply and the whole had considerable sheer in a fashion reminiscent of the large Canadian canoes. They were rigged as two-masted vessels, with the smaller mast stepped far astern. The entire length between the two masts was usually occupied by a covered deckhouse.

KARBATZ: A northern Russian rowing boat for around 10 persons. The boat could also be fitted with a mast and sail.

KARFE: A Nordic ship type from the early Middle Ages. The Karfe was smaller and

Single- and two-masted Russian karbatz

lighter than the Nordic longships, had up to 16 rowing benches, and a folding mast. The ancient Nordic term karfafötr indicates that these were narrow-built ships. The OSEBERG SHIP (15 oars per side), the GOKSTAD SHIP (16 oars per side) and the TUNE SHIP (12 oars per side) could be examples of this type.

KARLSTAD SHIP: The remains of a Viking ship found near the Swedish town of Karlstad on the Vänersee. The significance of this find is equivalent to that of the OSEBERG SHIP.

KATORGA: Russian term for a galley.

KATZE: A small, ancient Byzantine oared ship for reconnaissance and despatch duties.

KAYAK: A hunting boat of the polar regions of America and Greenland, extending to the Aleutians and the Chukchee off northeast Siberia. In its original form the kayak was a boat with a framework made of driftwood, whale, seal or fish bones, and a waterproof covering of seal or walrus leather. The covering of the boat was sewn up with leather thongs, leaving a round opening only just large enough for the body girth of the hunter. The Eskimo sitting in the boat wore anorak-like outer clothing, made of skins and pelts. It was possible to obtain a virtually watertight seal by tying the funnel-like extension of the cockpit opening tightly round the body. The boat's

Greenland eskimo kayak

equipment comprised a double paddle and hunting gear, such as harpoon, spear and floating bladder tied to the boat with leather belts and within reach of the hunter. The rounded or U-shaped cross-section of the kayak and the watertight seal made it possible to develop a special technique for righting the boat when it had turned over, without the hunter having to quit the boat: the Eskimo roll.

The usual length of the Eskimo kayak was about 5m. In some areas of the Aleutians and in south Alaska, kayaks were built to carry two or three persons. Even today the Eskimos' kayaks retain the original kayak principle, although modern materials are now used for the framework and outer skin.

In the mid nineteenth century the Eskimo kayak was the pattern for the development of the racing kayak. This branch of watersport has developed over many decades to embrace various disciplines, including all those boats in which the sportsman stands, sits, or kneels facing the direction of travel, and propels the boat with single-bladed or double paddles. In 1934, kayak sport was recognized by the Olympic committee as an olympic discipline, and the first kayak slalom was held on the Danube in Austria in the same year. Canoe racing slalom was held on the Danube in Austria in the same year. Canoe racing and wild water canoeing have also become particularly popular. The standard sport kayak is produced as a collapsible boat using shells of GRP construction, but folding kayaks are not permitted to take part in official sport competitions. *See also* CANADIAN CANOE.

KEEL, *keelman, kiel*: Originally, this was a

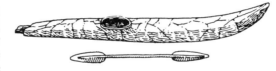

Kayak from the Aleutians

small, animal-skin covered boat, called by the northern Europeans chiule, cyule or ceol. The term keel which derived from these words was probably transferred to small cargo carrying sailing ships by the eighth or ninth centuries. The song of Beowulf, an English heroic poem written in the eighth century, contains references to the keel or kiel. Around the year 1000, the ship term ceol appears in the London customs tarrif. These must have been fairly large ships, as they were charged at four times the fee for the usual small sailing ships, and were thus equivalent to a HULK.

The term kiel or keel is also mentioned in the Völuspa song of the Edda, a thirteenth- or fourteenth-century Nordic poem. In the twelfth century, a keel was a ship with a cargo capacity of around 20 tons. On the rivers of northern England, the keel was a single-masted river cargo ship with a flat bottom and full-bodied hull, mainly used for carrying coal. It was rigged with simple square sails and survived from the fourteenth to the eighteenth century. On the rivers Tyne and Humber, the keel was about the same size, but continued in use until the nineteenth century. The cargo capacity of these vessels became a standard unit for coal transport: one keel being about 20 tons of coal. The largest version was the Humber keel with a length of 17 to 19m, a beam of about 4.5m and carrying up to 100

tons of freight. The smaller Tyne keel of about 13m length and up to 6m beam carried about 20 tons, and was originally rowed by three men. Later, it was sailed with a square sail and staysails. After the mid nineteenth century the square sail and replaced by a spritsail. *See also* HUMBER KEEL.

KEEL BOAT: General term for any sailing boat with a fixed keel or ballasted lifting keel whose weight rather than that of the crew, as in a dinghy, is chiefly responsible for providing stability. Keel configurations range from the single, efficient deep fin found on racing yachts to the shallower twin bilge keels on which a yacht can dry out fitted to cruising boats.

The traditional long keel, which is an extension of the yacht's underbody incorporating ballast, has been largely superseded by keels which bolt onto the hull.

KEEL EWER: A flat-bottomed EWER with the addition of a beam-type keel. The first keel ewer was produced in 1876 by fitting a keel to the otherwise flat bottom of the standard ewer. This resulted in significantly increased lateral resistance, which, in conjunction with a retractable centreboard, provided better manoeuvring characteristics. These improvements allowed an increase in the area of sail to more than 180m². The reason behind the construction of this keel ewer was that the large English smacks which had originally been intended to transfer fish catches at sea had too deep a draught for the northwest German coast and the river Elbe, and also lacked a fish well (a water-filled hold for keeping fish alive).

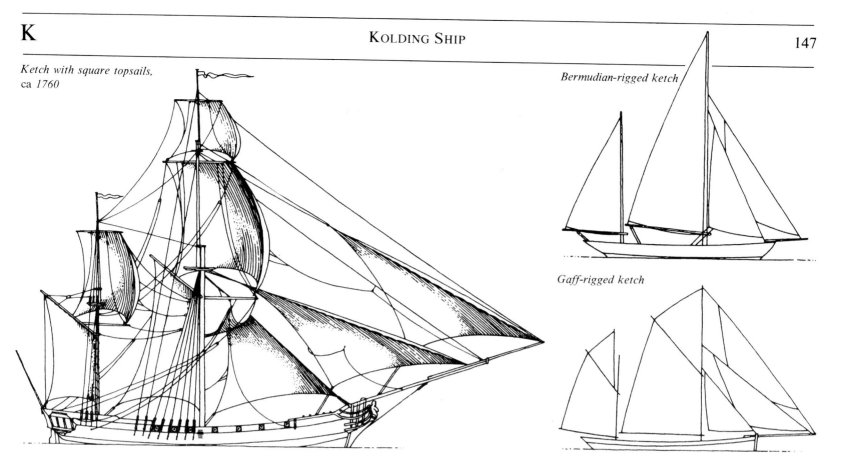

Ketch with square topsails, ca 1760

Bermudian-rigged ketch

Gaff-rigged ketch

KEITELKAHN: A flat-sided, CARVEL-built fishing boat of the eighteenth and nineteenth centuries. The hull was rectangular in cross-section, 9 to 13m long, and 2.5 to 3m in breadth. The keitelkahn was employed in bays to tow a ground trawl net, which was held open by a boom spreader known as the keitel. The mainmast carried gaff or lateen sails, while a small mast stepped forward carried spritsails. A typical feature was the open fireplace in the aftership.

KELEK, See INFLATED SKIN RAFT.

KETCH: A two-masted ship carrying up to 50 tons, which was developed in England and North America in the mid seventeenth century for fishing and coastal freight transport. The type is distinguished by its special mast arrangement, known as the ketch rig, in which the taller mast is stepped in the forward half of the ship, and the smaller mast — the mizzen — fairly far aft, but forward of the rudder post. The ketch rig can be sub-divided into the earlier gaff-rigged form, and the modern bermudian rig which has been generally adopted on yachts since about 1920. The staysail ketch and WISHBONE ketch are less common variants.

KEYING: *see* FOOCHOW POLE JUNK.

KHORSABAD RELIEF: Representations of Assyrian and Phoenician transport ships carved on bas reliefs in the ruins of the palace of the Assyrian King Sargon II (721–705 BC), discovered in 1843. The relief illustrates the loading or tree trunks into cargo holds. Today the reliefs are in the Louvre.

KIANGSU TRADER: *see* PECHILI TRADER.

KIRJIME: A decked trading and fishing boat on the southwest coast of the Caspian Sea, with a single square sail, between 5 and 10m long.

KNARR, *knorre*: A Scandinavian cargo sailing ship first mentioned in 872 in epic verses describing the battle of Hafrsfjord. Certain of the ship's design features, including pointed hull ends, and carved animals heads at stem and stern, are similar to those of the Norse long-ships — the slender DRAGON ships of the Vikings. In contrast, however, to the longships, the knarren were much broader, shorter, more full-bodied, had a greater draught and higher freeboard. The length of a medium size ship was around 15m and the beam around 5m; in the Biskupa søgar [Bishop's saga], a knarr's length is stated to be about 21m. The BRÖSEN SHIP is of similar dimensions. The strongly rounded, bulbous shape of the ships, and the stem and stern curling up and back, resulted in the type earning the nickname 'knarrarbringa', which meant something akin to 'full bosoms'. By the ninth century, knarren accounted for a considerable part of the Viking fleets. Because they were better sea-going ships, the knarren were also the preferred means of transport for the emigration voyages to Iceland, and several Icelandic settlements have names such as Knarrarnes and Knarrarsund, illustrating the connection.

Knarrs were sailing vessels, and only rowed on rare occasions. The usual crew is said to have been 15 to 30 persons, but for exceptional cases crews of 50 to 60 men were claimed. A particular type of knarr, which was somewhat smaller, and was used primarily for voyages to the East (especially to Russia) was known as the 'east-faring knarr'. The Danzig seal dating from 1299 probably represents a development of the knarr in the direction of the COG.

KNIEP EWER: A low-German EWER of the late eighteenth and nineteenth centuries, rigged with an old form of sail known as the kniep sail. This was a small lugsail of around 10m^2, set on a small mast (3 to 4m tall) close to the rudder, and designed to supplement the rudder. The Kniep ewer was supplanted by the BESAN EWER which was introduced around 1820.

KNOTS: A full-bodied Belgian shrimper of the nineteenth and early twentieth centuries. At around 10 to 12m long and about 3.5m broad, it was smaller than the OTTER, which was an otherwise similar Belgian fishing vessel.

KOJER, *koyer, koier*: A nineteenth-century wet well fishing boat, whose central area contained a hold partitioned off front and rear. Holes in the hull sides kept the hold flooded and allowed the caught fish to remain alive until being landed.

KOLDING SHIP: Parts of a wrecked ship dating from the thirteenth or fourteenth centuries, found in the Koldingfjord in Denmark in 1943. The ship was about 18m long and 6m in breadth, and had a flat, CARVEL-built bottom and CLINKER-built side walls. The size and construction, especially the straight keel and stem, are typical features of an early COG.

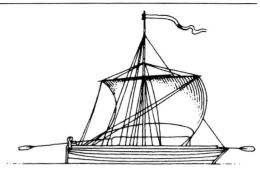

Korennaja, single-masted Russian river cargo ship

KREYER, *kraier, crayer*: A sea-going cargo vessel, used primarily in the Baltic region, but also on the Friesian coast and for voyages to Bergen and Flanders, between the fourteenth and sixteenth centuries. The cargo capacity could be up to 120 tons, and the three-masted ships carried square sails and a crew of 12 men.

KUFF GALIOT: GALIOTS with a kuff-like aftership and projecting foreship, built in east Friesian yards in the mid nineteenth century.

KUFF, *koff*: An eighteenth- and nineteenth-century two-masted coastal cargo ship employed on the Dutch and Belgian coasts, and also on northwest German coasts from the early nineteenth century. The hull was full-bodied, based on a KEEL and featured a broad, flat bottom. The hull ends were strongly rounded, but the bow and stern had fairly pronounced sheer, with the result that the ship, in spite of its compact form, had good sea-going qualities for coastal work. The usual size was between 40 and 90BRT.

Only a few smaller kuffs carried leeboards. The two-masted version carried a gaff mainsail

KORA-KORA, *caracora, caracore, corocora, corocore*: A slender, combined sailing oared boat of the Moluccan region. These boats varied in size, the largest being up to 35m long, with a beam of 4 to 5m, and a draught of 1.7m. As late as the nineteenth century they were being used as warships, carrying about 90 persons. On each side of the ship there were three rows of 12 oarsmen, one behind the other. The oarsmen sat on external frame-works, similar to outriggers. The large ships carried two sails on a short mast or on trestle-like spars. The smaller kora-koras had two rows of oarsmen on each side and carried a single sail on a short mast.

KORBUIS: A seventeenth- and eighteenth-century Japanese rowing vessel with up to 30 oars.

KOTIA, *khotia, kutiyah*: A two-masted Indian dhow, similar to the GHANJA.

KORENNAJA: The term used for a single-masted, crudely-built cargo vessel employed on the Oka and the Volga in the nineteenth century.

KRAGENJOLLE: A Danish boat with pointed stern and laterally projecting hull sides, designed to prevent water breaking on the deck.

Kora-kora with double outrigger, first half of nineteenth century

Kuff, late nineteenth century (model)

Kuff with square topsails, ca 1790

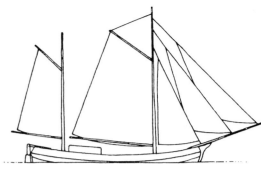

Gaff-rigged kuff

on the mainmast, and one or two further square sails above it on a topmast, depending on the size of the ship. Up to three foresails were set on the bowsprit. The mizzen mast, stepped well aft, had no topmast extension and carried a single gaffsail. The smaller vessels were rigged as pole-mast kuffs or topsail kuffs. There were also a few larger vessels which were rigged as schooners, and were known as schooner kuffs. Occasionally, a three-masted ship with barque rig was built and was known as a barque kuff. Other hybrid types with modified hull forms also evolved, including the KUFF TJALK and the KUFF GALIOT.

Kuffs were most widely used in the east Friesian region, where the type was superseded by the galiot in the second half of the nineteenth century because of the latter's better sailing qualities. Nevertheless, the kuff had lasted an entire century. In 1805, there were 138 kuffs at Emden alone, along with 16 galiots and 70 tjalks. In 1873, a total of 201 kuffs were still in use in northwest Germany. The last kuffs were built on the Weser in 1895, and by 1913 no working kuffs remained in the ships' registers.

Kuff, mid nineteenth century (model)

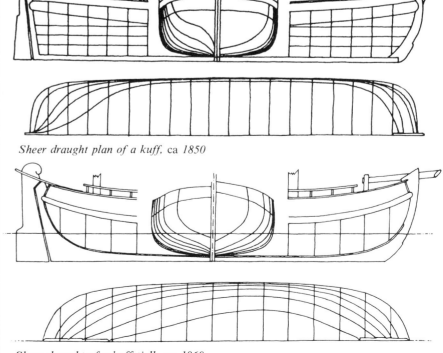

Sheer draught plan of a kuff, ca 1850

Sheer draught of a kuff tjalk, ca 1860

Sheer draught of the Kvalsund ship

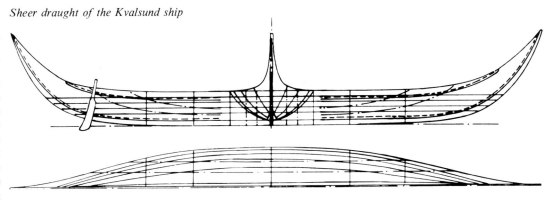

KUFF TJALK: A hybrid ship which evolved around the early to mid nineteenth century, combining the typical features of the KUFF and TJALK. The fore-part was similar to that of the kuff, but the hull was slimmer while the spoon-shaped after-part was adopted from the tjalk. This hybrid type evolved in the Netherlands, and was later copied in large numbers in Lower Saxony. The kuff tjalk was also built without a keel, but usually with two large leeboards. Smaller vessels carried a tjalk rig, while the larger ships were rigged like topmast kuffs. The cargo capacity of this type was between 30 and 75 tons, with hull length between 15 and 23m, a beam of 4 to 5.5m, and a freeboard between 1.5 and 2m. The crew consisted of two to four men. The last German kuff tjalks disappeared at the beginning of the twentieth century.

KUJUNDSHIK RELIEF: Assyrian river boats, involved in hunting and battle scenes, are depicted on the temple ruins of Kujundschik on the banks of the Tigris near ancient Niniveh. The temple ruins date from the eighth century BC.

KURREN KAHN, *kurkahn*: A barge about 10 to 12m long and 3m in breadth, used for trawl fishing. Originally, a boom trawl net was employed, but this was later replaced by the type using otter boards.

KVALSUND SHIP: The much decayed remains of two wrecked ships of different size, found near the Norwegian Schäen island of Nerlandsoy in 1920. The larger ship was 18m long, 3.2m in breadth, and had a depth of 0.80m, and would have drawn about 0.35m. It was a 20-oar ship, and dates from around the seventh century. The hull was CLINKER-built, and had tall, upward-curving stem and stern. The floor planking had the beginnings of a keel in the form of a thickened portion running the full length of the hull. The strakes were hewn from oak, with cleats cut into them as an attachment point for binding the frames. The upper gunwale strake was made of spruce and rivetted in place.

The ship is of particular interest as it included all the methods of fixing which were known at that time in northern Europe, including binding with natural fibres and osiers, pegs (treenails), iron round-head rivets with washers, and iron nails with proud heads. The oak planks were an average of 28mm thick and 250 to 300mm wide. The oaken keel also featured worked cleats as on the side strakes, but in this case they served only to support the ribs nailed to it. In addition to the usual transverse beams, the ship was subdivided fore and aft by bulkhead timbers. The aft bulkhead was specially reinforced to accept a fixed side rudder. The oars were made of spruce. The rowlocks were fixed to the gunwale with wood nails, and were similar to those on the NYDAM SHIP.

The second, smaller, boat also dates from the seventh century. It was 9.56m long, 1.50m in breadth and had a depth of 0.62m. It was a rowing boat for four persons. The T-section keel was of oak, and was connected to curved oak stem and stern timbers. Four oak strakes were fitted to either side of the keel. A fifth strake, this time of spruce, featured a thickened gunwale edge. It ended about 1m short of the stem and stern, where it has joined to specially shaped short planks forward and aft. The butt joints of the individual planks were connected with iron rivets and washers, and were overlapped clinker fashion. The rowlocks have not survived, although the nail holes are still visible. All planks had low, projecting cleats to which a total of five spruce frames were fixed with wooden nails. The forward and aft ribs were reinforced to form bulkheads. The aft bulkhead had a further reinforcement on the starboard side for the rudder, which was fitted on the outside. Only fragments of the spruce oars survived, but they indicated an unusually narrow blade.

KYRENIA SHIP: A Greek cargo ship about 15m long dating from the fourth century BC, found near Kyrenia in Cyprus in 1967. Parts of the inner and outer planking have survived, along with some other components. The remains of the cargo, found near the wreck, made it possible to determine the vessel's age. The ship was carrying a cargo of wine in amphorae and almonds and it is an astonishing fact that the almond shells of the cargo survived intact for more than 2000 years. The 400 wine-filled amphorae, stowed on the port side, were virtually undamaged and were discovered arranged as originally loaded. They were of various types, and study of the amphorae made it possible to estimate the ship's route. A cooking area, as found on some other ships of the same period, was not found. This suggests that the ship travelled by day, keeping close to the coast, and anchored by the shore in the evening, as was common at the time.

LADBY SHIP: A Viking ship grave dating from around 900–950, which included the remains of a merchant ship 22m long and about 3m wide. It was found under a grave mound on the Kertenminder Moor near Ladby on the island of Fyn in 1934. The CLINKER-built hull had been built of oak, but was only recognizeable by its impression in the ground. It was a narrow, shallow-draught ship, which could be sailed as well as rowed. There were four heavy iron rings on the outside of the midship ribs, which probably served as the attachment for the shrouds. There were also oar holes in the forward and after parts of the hull. The planks were not bound to the ribs, as on older ships. Instead, the ribs were notched to accept the clinker-built outer planking, and the planking was nailed to the ribs and floor planks. The stem was specially reinforced.

The ship's equipment included a large iron anchor next to the bow, with about 9m of chain. The ship was accompanied by the bones of 11 horses and a few dogs, lying in the front end section of the ship, and — in spite of earlier plundering — a few utilitarian items and jewellery made of silver, bronze and iron were found, among them 12 iron spirals and an axe.

LAKANA: A dugout without outrigger from the east coast of Madagascar.

LAKATOI: A sailing vessel in the coastal waters of Papua, New Guinea, consisting of

Two-masted lakatoi with crab's claw sails, New Guinea, early twentieth century

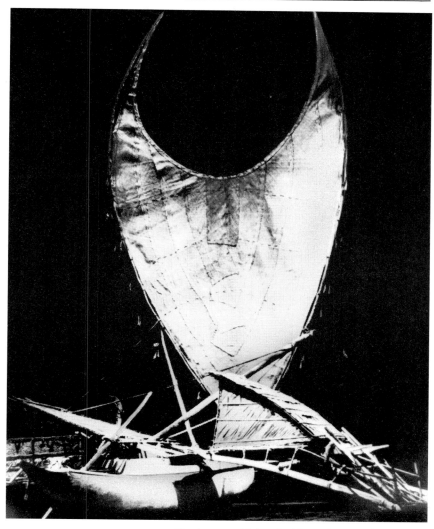

Single-masted lakatoi with outrigger and crab's claw sail

three or four dugouts linked together. The hulls lie parallel to each other, and are connected by transverse beams and a lattice platform of bamboo stems, which is used to carry goods during the annual trading voyages. A characteristic feature is the sail, shaped like a crab's claw and made of woven matting and the leaves of the sago tree (although sails of rectangular and elliptical form are also common). Lakatoi with five or six such mat sails are also built, the sails being set between spars similar to gaffs.

LAKE NEMI SHIPS: Elaborate ships which the Roman Emperor Caligula, the successor to Emperor Tiberius, had built between AD 37 and 41 for his personal use as houseboats on Lake Nemi, a crater lake in the Albani Hills, not far from Rome.

Similar large houseboats, known as thalamegi, had been built before Caligula's time. They were built like palaces with columned halls, temples, dining rooms, sleeping quarters, artificial gardens and ponds. The Emperor Caligula suffered from a persecution mania, and chose his floating

Salvage of the Lake Nemi ship belonging to the Roman Emperor Caligula, built between AD 37 and 41

palace as his refuge. A second, less richly ornamented ship served to accommodate his retinue and servants. Despite these safety measures, the Emperor was murdered after only four years in office.

Leaden stamps bearing the name of Caligula indicated that the ships must have been of remarkable size and complexity. Nevertheless, they probably sprang leaks shortly after his death, due to lack of maintenance, and sank. The ships were subsequently rediscovered, and divers established that unsuccessful attempts had already been made to drag the larger ship onto land.

The first attempts to salvage the ships were made around the mid fifteenth century. Cardinal Prospero Colonna wanted to have the ships raised and restored. He commissioned the Florentine architect Leon Battista Alberti to undertake this task. Alberti brought divers from Genoa, and built a large raft, based on empty barrels, on which he erected raising apparatus. Several parts were recovered, but when an attempt was made to raise the main body of the ship, the hull broke, and the attempt had to be abandoned.

A century later, the fortification engineer Francesco de Marchi made a renewed attempt, which was carefully worked out and which he described in detail. He too, only succeeded in tearing pieces out of the hull with his winches, without raising the ship. A third unsuccessful attempt was made in 1828 by the engineer Annesio Fusconi. The Italian Count Orsini subsequently had a few pieces of bronze decoration raised in 1895. Amongst them were a Medusa head, several lions' and wolves' heads, which once had decorated the ends of massive hull beams. He also recovered a decorative bronze beam plate from the second ship, carrying an outstretched hand, which was intended to ward off the evil eye. A bronze grating, marble items and inlay work were also salvaged. These finds are now in the National Museum in Rome. It was not until 1928 that another salvage operation was undertaken.

Some years earlier, the former Director General of Arts, Corrado Ricci, had worked out a plan to lower the water level of Nemi to a depth of 22m by draining the water through an ancient 2km long drainage tunnel into a nearby lake, which was 31m lower. On 20 October 1928, electric pumps began to work. Each day the water level of Nemi sank by 50mm. After 170 days the remains of the imperial ship came into view. The second ship lay a further 6m down in the mud.

With elaborate safety measures completed, the imperial ship was dismantled, preserved and reassembled in a museum near Nemi, built specially for it. The Emperor's ship was 70m long and 17.5m in breadth. Both hulls are CARVEL planked, with the planks joined by wooden dowels. Where necessary, the ribs were fitted after the planking had been completed. The outer skin was covered with tarred woollen fabric and sheathed with lead plates which were nailed in place. The deck supports for the upper deck took the form of fired clay pipes. The Imperial ship was richly decorated externally with bronze figures, rare hard-woods and carvings in honour of the goddess Diana. Inside the hull, several rooms were luxuriously fitted out with marble. Only a few fragments remained of the mosaic decoration which had once existed. They showed the holy colours of the goddess Diana: green, white and red.

The ships' equipment and fittings included a 1400kg anchor, iron transverse beams, a movable platform on rollers, lead and bronze plates, tiles, clay pipes, doors with bronze hinges, gratings, nails, coins and various other artefacts such as clay lamps and vessels and fishing equipment. There were also the remains of a wooden water container with a bronze tap which was in good condition, plus parts of a well apparatus and a wooden pump. Amongst the great bronzes of artistic merit were several lions' heads, a wolf's head and the head of a panther. The panther skin is an impressive weaving in various metals. The

ships themselves and most of the finds were destroyed in the war.

LAMPEDUSE: An Italian fishing boat originating on the island of Lampedusa, south of Sicily. The boats became well-known after they were used in the Italo-Turkish War (1911) as troop transports, and as landing boats on the Libyan coast.

LANCHA, *lanchia launch*: A large, Brazilian nineteenth- and twentieth-century sailing craft with two or three masts. The foremast was vertical and stepped relatively far forward, while the after mast had a very marked aft rake. The main and mizzen masts set gaff sails, the foremast a square sail. The vessels were used principally for transporting cocoa beans, and featured a deck-house or awning aft to accommodate passengers, or to provide shelter for the crew.

In Spain and Portugal the term lancha is also applied to a variety of small fishing boats.

LANDFJÄRDEN SHIPS: Wrecks of three Viking ships discovered and photographed by Swedish divers in Landfjärden Bay, 35km from Stockholm in 1959. It has not been possible to salvage the vessels to date.

LANDING CRAFT: A nineteenth- and twentieth-century term applied generally to boats carried on warships, which were used for putting ashore soldiers or marines. Originally rowing boats, in the nineteenth century they were often towed by launches. Modern landing

Dalmatian liburne with two rows of oars

craft with engine propulsion have featured in the naval fleets since the Second World War, although rather primitive designs were tried out in the First World War.

LASER: Designed by Canadian Bruce Kirby in the late 1960s, this 13ft, $10\frac{1}{2}$in single-handed, glassfibre dinghy numbers hundreds of thousands and is sailed throughout the world. The Laser is a strict one design class. All boats are identical and the sails can only be bought from licensed sailmakers. One of the most fiercely competitive of all the classes, top Laser sailors often graduate to Olympic FINN dinghies, but the class itself has resisted Olympic selection.

LAUNCH: A very broad ship's boat which was the main workboat of a warship, and was a replacement for the LONGBOAT. The launch was usually stowed on the upper deck between foremast and mainmast with the PINNACE, and was used for carrying out heavy anchors, for sailing around coasts and into ports, and for transporting supplies of drinking water. It began life as a dockyard utility boat, but was taken up by sea officers who found the longboat inadequate. A frigate's launch was around 12m long, was rowed by 14 to 16 oarsmen and carried two masts. Launches could also be fitted with small guns (80mm cannon), and they doubled as gun transporters and landing boats, in which role they could carry up to 100 men. Launches were sometimes purely rowing boats and sometimes combined oared sailing boats. The special

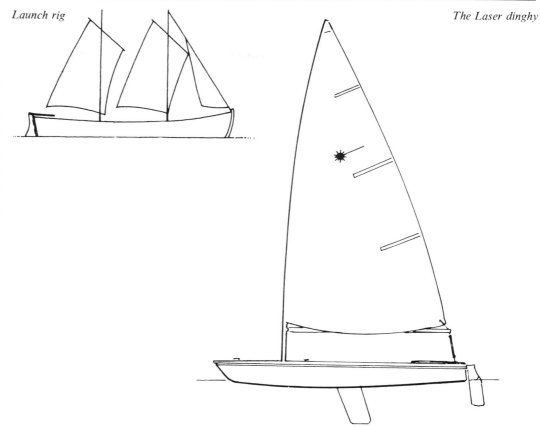

Launch rig

The Laser dinghy

launch rig consisted of two small masts with lugsails and a small staysail running to the stem which did not have a bowsprit. The oarsmen worked two men to each oar. The sides of a launch were not usually reinforced with wales, but were fitted with extra strakes instead. The launch was further developed into steam- and motor-driven versions. General-purpose boats found around ports are still termed harbour launches today.

LANTA, *lantea*: A large Chinese oared cargo ship with a cargo capacity of up to 800 tons and eight banks of oars on each side. Lantas were used by the Portuguese, who traded with Canton from their base in Macao. The vessels had to be fitted out as houseboats during the market period, as foreigners were not allowed to stay on land overnight.

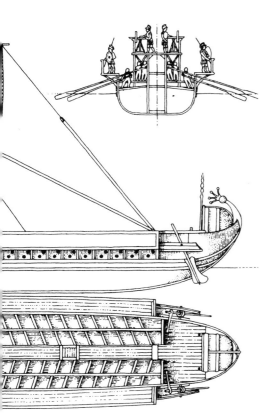

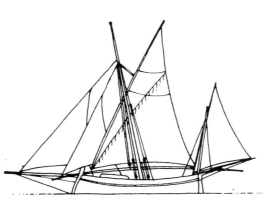

Sicilian laoutello

LAOUTELLO: A widely-used Sicilian fishing boat which survived until the end of the nineteenth century. It was two-masted, with a lateen mainsail, lateen-mizzen and topsails. A characteristic feature was the stem, with its reverse rake. The largest vessels were up to 20m long and carried a crew of six men.

LEDING SHIP: In the Scandinavian countries 'leding' was the duty of all towns and districts to supply men for the fleet in time of war. Leding ships attained special importance in the tenth century, when the Norwegian King Haakon (931–951) created a huge leding fleet, which was said to have numbered 30,000 to 40,000 men. The Norwegian leding ships were rowing warships, usually with 20 or 25 per side oars, and less frequently 30. The ships carried up to 100 men each.

LIBURNIAN: A Dalmatian warship and pirate ship, which evolved in Liburnia, the region between Istria and Dalmatia on the Adriatic coast. At the time of the Punic Wars (around 240 BC) the Illyrian liburnian was the type on which the light, fast Roman oared warships were based.

The Roman Liburnian usually had a single bank of oars though it was sometimes built as a two-banked BIREME. This arrangement allowed higher speeds to be developed than other warships of the time. The Liburnian was further developed to produce the DROMON and finally the GALLEY.

LIFEBOAT: Traditionally, the main method of rescue on board ships. Up until the eighteenth century, the most seaworthy of the ship's boats was usually pressed into service as lifeboats during emergencies at sea. The first specialized lifeboat, fitted with buoyancy chambers and cork inserts was built by the Englishman L Lukin in 1786 for the Tyne estuary. In 1810, the Frenchman Rouan claimed the patent in Paris for a lifeboat which could not capsize. The development of self-righting, self-draining lifeboats, the apparatus for lowering the boats in an emergency, and regulations designed to ensure that ships are equipped with an adequate number of life-saving devices, ready for use, to save crew, passengers and the shipwrecked, have been steadily improved over the years. *See also* COASTAL LIFEBOAT.

LIFTING SHIP: A vessel specially designed for salvaging sunken ships, but also used for

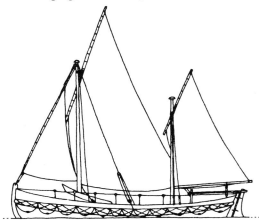

English lifeboat, ca 1900

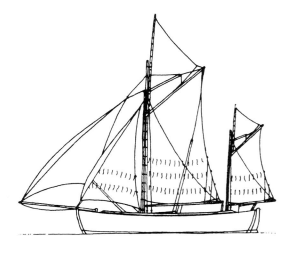

Norwegian lifeboat, 1893

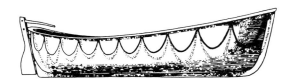

Ship's lifeboat, ca 1940

transporting cargoes and ships which have to be raised to allow them to be moved. The oldest lifting ships known are the Egyptian obelisk transport ships dating from around 1500 BC, which were loaded with as much stone ballast as could be carried, then floated along specially dug channels until they were underneath the heavy obelisks. When the stone ballast was removed, the buoyancy of these ships was sufficient to raise the obelisks.

In his work *Historia de Gentibus Septentrionalibus*, written in Rome in 1555, Olaus Magnus described how a wreck could be raised using four ships and cables. His recommendations were as follows. Two or four particularly stout ships are set on both sides of the wreck. The ships are filled with water and connected by means of beams. Skilled divers then place powerful cables under the ship to be raised, and the ends are fixed to the beams. The water is then pumped out of the ships, with the result that they rise gradually, and the sunken ship rises to the surface at the same time.

The Dutch CAMELs worked in a similar fashion. They were buoyancy hulls similar to a dock, which were fixed to both sides of a ship to be lightened, in order to allow it to pass through shallows.

In 1698, the Italian master builder Petrini succeeded in raising a ship sunk in the Trave, using raising ships and winches. The first patents for the use of compressed air in submerged raising balloons were taken out by the Englishman Edward Austin in 1837. Wilhelm Bauer patented his idea for using barrels emptied by air in 1861, and Professor Wilhelm Raydt from Hannover claimed a patent in 1879 for using the vaporization of liquid carbon dioxide to raise ships.

LIGHTER: A generic term covering a variety of open or covered vessels with or without sail or other propulsion. They evolved in order to fulfill three tasks: to permit larger, deep-draught ships to put into river estuaries or ports (by off-loading their cargo beforehand), to load ships lying in the roads with a full cargo, and to free ships which had run aground. After the fifteenth century there was a substantial increase in the size of sailing ships, but the facilities for creating and maintaining navigable channels of sufficient depth were very limited. With the exception of pontoons such as the Dutch CAMEL, which was used to raise ships sufficiently to enable them to pass through the shallow waters of river estuaries, lighters became the standard method of transporting cargo to and from the larger ships. They were simply small, flat-bottomed vessels.

LIGHT VESSEL: A stationary anchored ship which served as a warning to mariners in difficult and dangerous seas, where it was not possible to set up a permanent light-house. There were LIGHT VESSELS as well as beacons on land in the Mediterranean in

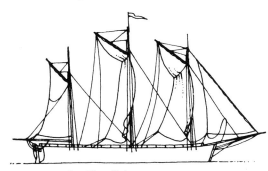

Decked kahn lighter

Three-masted sailing lighter

ancient times, equipped with open fires or torches. Later the fires consisted of candles, lanterns, oil and petrol lamps.

In 1807, Robert Stevenson combined several lamps and concave mirrors to form an optical device which surrounded a column. The French physicists AJ Fresnel (1788–1827) and DF Arago (1786–1853) invented the Fresnel lens which was fitted to navigation lights on ships. Even today several separate methods of lighting are required in the interests of safety. The light signals are transmitted from the highest possible point on the LIGHT VESSEL, in clearly recognizable pulses, utilizing a fixed code. Locations and codes for light vessels and lighthouses are shown on marine charts, which enables the ship to pinpoint its exact position by means of bearings taken on the light.

Light vessels have to contend with the special problem of sea swell, and the resultant movements of the ship. To ensure that the light always shines out horizontally, or at the correct angle to the horizontal, the light sources are suspended on gimbals, or stabilized by other means. Bearing in mind the curvature of the earth, it is possible to recognize a light signal placed 16m above the sea's surface from a distance of 28 nautical miles (52km), provided that weather conditions are favourable.

As light vessels are constantly subjected to every extreme of sea and weather, their design has to be especially strong and seaworthy. In the sailing ship period, two-masted ships about 45 to 50m in length, 8m wide and with a free-board of 6m were usually employed. These ships were as slender as possible, with clipper bows and pointed sterns, and were intended to offer as little resistance as possible in the fore-and-aft direction to the action of the sea, and to allow the sea to flow away freely behind the ship. To reduce the rolling movements, the ship's hull was fitted with bilge keels.

Light vessels are secured using long anchor chains with a length roughly ten times the depth of the water. Nevertheless, the ship's position has to be verified after severe storms, and the security of the anchorage checked. Wherever possible, the crews of the light vessels carry out additional signal, pilot or rescue duties. It has been possible to reduce the number of light vessels, which are expensive in terms of building and maintenance, thanks to improved techniques in building fixed installations, and the use of modern navigation aids.

LIGGER: This was a wooden hull similar to a pontoon which was used to store live eels, the hull walls being perforated in order to supply fresh water to the creatures. The vessel remained in use on rivers and Baltic river estuaries, especially in Pomerania, until the first decades of the present century. Liggers were made fast in running water or attached to locks, and could accommodate several hundred hundredweight of eels during the winter months.

LINER: A cargo or passenger-carrying ship which regularly travels a particular route. Regular lines for short sea routes have existed for several centuries, but the use of liner proper did not begin until PACKET shipping began in 1836, whereby ships were employed expressly to carry post between Europe and North America. Until the mid nineteenth century the liners were almost exclusively sailing ships, but the first steam liners to travel from Britain to New York were the *Sirius* and *Great Western* in 1878. In effect, these ships raced one another, foreshadowing the competition between engine-driven liners to provide ever faster crossings, which was to last almost a century. Passenger liners are now almost exitinct, but cargo is carried on regular liner services, particularly by container ships.

LJUBLJANA RIVER SHIP: The remains of a CARVEL-built river cargo ship dating from around 800 BC, found on a moor near Ljubljana, Yugoslavia. The vessel had a full-bodied, flat-bottomed hull. The sides were only 0.50m high, and were sealed with lime bast. The most remarkable feature of the vessel was its overall length of 40m, and its narrow beam of 4.5m. The cargo capacity would have been between 30 and 40 tons. The bottom planks of fir were 300 to 350mm wide, and were held together by 40 transverse elm beams and hawthorn nails. The sides were joined to the bottom by several naturally curved oak ribs set between the transverse beams and fixed with wood nails, although iron nails were also found at vital joints.

LJUNGSTRÖM YACHT: A sailing boat with rotating mast and no stays or shrouds, developed by the Swedish designer Ljungström at the end of the nineteenth century. The sail was in two parts, and could be rolled up around the mast by rotating the mast. With fully extended sail area on both sides, for sailing downwind, the sail rig had the appearance of a pair of spread butterfly wings, which led to the nickname, butterfly sailing boat. The principle of the rotating mast has been adopted experimentally by several designers, but to date the problems have not been satisfactorily solved.

LODJA: A sailing river ship of the eastern Baltic region dating from the Hanseatic period, smaller than the COG, and crewed by three or four men. The vessels were single-masted or two-masted, and some of them were also suitable for coastal sailing. The principle task of the lodja was to off-load cargo from the cogs, which were unable to negotiate some estuaries and rivers because of their draught, and to carry the cargo further upstream. The wreck of a ship found on the bank of the Aa near Treyden in Livland was probably a Lodja, and it exhibits one interesting peculiarity of design. The deck consisted of

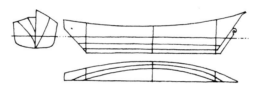

Russian lodja

double planking, between which was laid a thick woven woollen material, in order to prevent any leaking.

In Russian, lodja is the general term for a boat or barge, and is thus used to denote a large and diverse group of river and coastal utility vessels, employed for transporting goods and people and for fishing. For example, the type existed at the river estuaries of the Black Sea and the Caspian Sea.

LODKA: A flat-bottomed Siberian rowing boat, up to 7m in length.

LOG CANOE: A sailing boat used in Chesapeake Bay (USA). It was 8 to 11m long and 1.6 to 2.7m in breadth, and was made of a number of logs shaped and bolted together. The vessels were often fitted with two small masts and sails, and were used mainly for collecting oysters and for fishing.

LOMME: A flounder fishing or general fishing boat on the Fischen Bay (Wislahaff). The boats were 5 to 7m long and rigged with two spritsails, with the forward mast raked very sharply forward. Some coastal cargo sailing ships used in the bay also shared this name. These were very broad, full-bodied vessels of robust construction, with a transom stern, usually supporting stern davits to carry a ship's boat.

The vessels, known as lommen yachts, usually had only one mast, but by the middle of the nineteenth century the larger lommen had a mainmast and mizzen mast, gaff rigged with a light square sail on the mainmast. One or two jibs were set on the bowsprit. The vessels had leeboards and were good sailing ships in spite of the bulbous design.

LONDRA, *londrus, londre*: A small, galley-like oared sailing ship used in the Mediterranean between the thirteenth and fifteenth centuries. In the seventeeth century the term applied to a rather clumsy oared sailing ship of low freeboard, with lateen sails and 25 oars on each side. The vessels were fitted with light cannon.

LONGBOAT: Originally, the main working boat of a warship and intended to be rowed and sailed, it was replaced from about 1760 with the LAUNCH. The longboat was probably more handy under sail, the launch was more capacious and better under oars, so in general more useful.

LONGSHIP: The general term for the long, narrow Viking ships. The larger Viking longships (up to 30 oars on each side), which were built in the ninth century, were known as skaiths. Like the smaller SNEKKJAs, they were of narrow design. At the stem and stern they were taller, but were not usually embellished with symbolic heads on the stem and stern. Similar to the skaiths, but longer and broader, were the dreki, the Vikings' DRAGON ships, on which the stem and stern supported horse and dragon heads.

LOWESTOFT SAILING DRIFTER: A two-masted fishing boat from England's east coast, used principally for driftnet fishing but also occasionally trawling. Approximately 20m in length, they developed from lug-rigged smacks, first adopting a boomless gaff mainsail and later a gaff mizzen. They ceased to be built at the beginning of the twentieth century.

LUGGER, *logger, lougre*: A type which originated in France and is called a lougre in that country. In the eighteenth century it was a small, fast sailing despatch vessel, warship or privateer, as well as a versatile coastal cargo carrier varying in size between 40 and 140 tons capacity. The vessels were fine lined keel boats.

The lougre featured a special mast arrangement and sail rig to which its name alludes. The original lougre carried three rather short masts, the two forward ones of equal height and capable of being folded down, while the smaller mizzenmast was stepped relatively far aft. All three masts carried a lugsail. The lugsail was trapezoid in shape, and set on an angled yard which was attached to the mast one third of its length by means of a ring.

French three-masted lugger, ca 1775

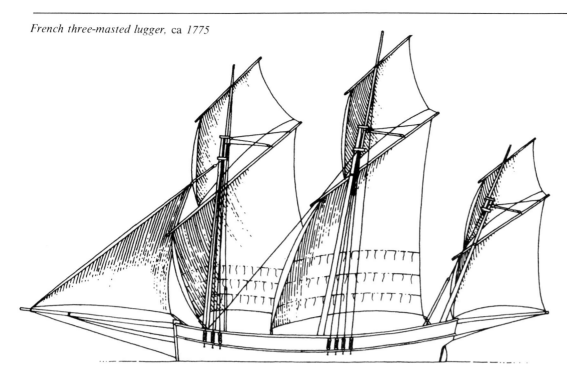

Sheer draught plan of a French armed lugger, ca mid nineteenth century

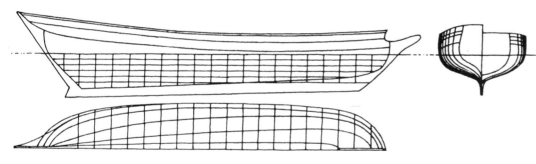

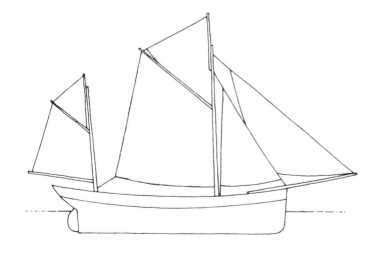

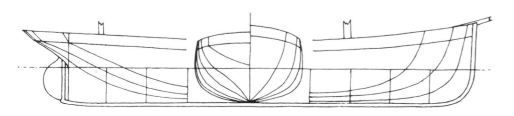

Ketch-rigged steel fishing boat, early twentieth century, 24m long, 6.5m in breadth, and 3.5m in depth

The type was adopted in England, where it was known as the lugger. The English version was a two- or three-masted fast sailing vessel which retained the trapezoid sail, and was used for postal service as well as for fishing.

By about 1865, the type had become one of the standard coastal vessels around Holland and north Germany for fishing, pilot services and general work. As driftnet fishing became widespread in the nineteenth century, the two-masted sailing fishing lugger evolved, based on the three-masted sailing lugger, which had proved so versatile a vessel.

Lugsails

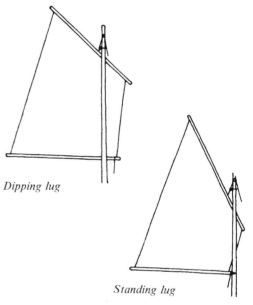

Dipping lug

Standing lug

LÜHE EWER: A nineteenth-century north German EWER, designed mainly for carrying fruit. This peculiarity was proclaimed externally by a brightly painted bow, depicting branches of fruit trees and the fruit itself. Most Lühe ewers were built on the River Lühe — a tributary of the Elbe near Hamburg — in the towns of Grünendeich, Mittelkirchen, Höhen and Borstel.

LÜHE JOLLE: A type of boat used on the lower Elbe until the early twentieth century, mainly for fruit transport, and also known as the altenlander jolle or kirschen (cherry) jolle. The boat was very broad in relation to its length, carried no leeboards, and was built on a relatively high keel. The Lühe jolle was around 9 to 12.5m long and 3.2 to 4.2m broad. The hold depth of 1.3 to 1.8m allowed 7 to 17RT of cargo to be carried. A folding pole-mast carried a gaff sail and a staysail, and the vessel could be operated by two men. Larger jolle, known as see jollen (seagoing jolle) carried an extra jib on the bowsprit.

MAHAILA: A small, single-masted coastal sailing ship of the Arab DHOW group. The hull has a short foredeck, and a covered deckhouse aft. Around midships there is a forward-raked pole mast, carrying the trapezoid shaped dhow sail on an angled yard. This type of sailing ship is still in use today, although rarely, in the Red Sea and on the east coast of Africa.

MANCHE: An early type of Arab DHOW; a two-masted fast sailing vessel used in Arabian waters and the Indian Ocean. The hull strakes were still connected by binding or sewing, but the open hull was stiffened by ribs or frames. The vessel had a short keel in relation to the overall length, with a strongly raked stem and a somewhat steeper, pointed stern. The mainmast and mizzen mast were pole masts with a parallel forward rake of about 20 to 23 degrees. After the sixteenth century, both masts carried the typical trapezoid dhow sails on angled yards. By the end of the eighteenth century a bowsprit and staysail had been added.

MAONA: A rare, large Turkish cargo ship of the sixteenth and seventeenth centuries, similar to the GALEASSE, with oars and sails. Five or six oarsmen operated each oar. In contrast to the triangular lateen sails commonly used in the Middle Ages these vessels carried rectangular sails.

Manche with sewn plank seams

Mahaila from the Lamu coast (model)

MARKETENDER BOAT, *bumboat*: A nineteenth-century term for boats which carried provisions, fruit and other food to ships anchored in the roads.

MASHHUF, *mash-hûf*: An Iraqi planked boat with a high, beak-shaped prow. This tall bow was especially suitable for travelling through reedy waters. The boat was based on a broad bottom plank, with one side strake added on each side, and it was stiffened inside with ribs and strong transverse timbers.

MASHUWA, *mashwa*: A general term for fairly small Arab and Indian coastal boats; they were partly-covered rowing and sailing vessels 5 to 9m long, with transom sterns and strongly raked fore stems. Two or three pairs of oars propelled the craft, while the mast, which was angled sharply forward, carried a settee sail on an angled yard.

In the Bombay region the same term was used for fairly large, two-masted vessels of 18m length and up to 35 tons cargo capacity, which were also used with settee sails for coastal work and fishing. These vessels were well known as high-speed sailing ships. They had a strongly raked stem, were narrow up forward and relatively full-bodied aft, with a rounded stern.

MAST SHIP: A special-purpose ship designed for transporting tree trunks for the manufacture of masts and topmasts. These vessels had rectangular ports at bow and stern, which allowed the long timbers to be shipped and stowed under deck. In the seventeenth and eighteenth centuries, mast timber was transported to England, France and Spain from the forested states on the Baltic sea. In the nineteenth century, the material was brought to Europe from North America.

MASULA: The European name for the frameless sewn boat of the Coromandel coast. Before the development of harbours on India's coast, the masula was employed in transporting cargo and passengers between the shore and ships anchored in the open roadsteads, rowing across very heavy surf. Such boats were between 9 and 12m, with beams between 3 and 4m. Today, similar craft, known as PADAGU or PADUWA, are employed in beach seine fishing on this coast. They are also rowed, although a smaller version (around 7m) has been developed in Andhra Pradesh which hoists a boomed lugsail, and is used principally for setting gill nets.

MATOR, *mataur*: A small planked boat of southeast Iraq for two to three persons with a tall, beak-shaped bow, similar to the MASHHUF. Two side planks were fitted to the bottom plank, and the structure was stiffened by ribs.

MA-YANG-TZU: A three-masted river junk of the Upper Yangtze. Such boats could be

Mayflower, *three-masted jacht*, ca 1620 (model)

Western Arabian mashuwa (model)

more than 30m in length, plying below Chungking with cargoes of 100 tons down river, for which a crew of more than fifty was needed, and 80 tons up river, which required a crew of more than sixty. However, as many as four hundred men might be required to haul the boat over the rapids at Hsint'an.

The hull was turret-built with a narrow deck superimposed upon it. Some 14 bulkheads, several projecting cross-beams and long heavy wales running the length of the vessel combine to make it a boat of considerable rigidity.

MAYFLOWER: The famous three-masted sailing vessel in which the Pilgrim Fathers — 105 Puritans — and a crew of about 25 men left England in 1620, with the aim of settling in the New England states. The ship was similar to a barque, but rigged after the fashion of a three-masted Dutch JACHT. The *Mayflower* was an English trader with a cargo capacity of about 180 tons, and was not so squat as the contemporary Spanish galleons, so Dutch influence is quite possible.

The ship reached the North American coast under Captain Christopher Jones after a crossing lasting 67 days. The Pilgrim Fathers founded the first permanent colony in the USA in the region of present-day Plymouth, Massachusetts, after arriving at Provincetown Harbour on 11 November 1620.

On the initiative of the Plymouth Plantation society based in Plymouth, a reconstruction was built in that city in 1955, and was intended to serve as a museum ship. In spite of the lack of original drawings, efforts were made to construct an accurate copy by using contemporary information as far as possible, but some modifications had to be made. This applied in particular to deck heights, which had to be raised in order to accommodate present-day human statures, and thus to allow the ship to function as a museum. The reconstruction was built with the following dimensions: overall length around 40.0m, waterline length 24.2m, maximum beam 7.8m, depth 5.5m, sail area in all, 470m². The fore and mainmasts were square-rigged with main and topsails on each. The mizzen mast was fitted with a lateen sail, and there was also a spritsail on the bowsprit. For the crossing from England to New York in 1957, the 5420 nautical miles took 53 days to complete. Since 1958, the *Mayflower II*'s final resting place has been Plymouth (Mass) in the USA.

MERCHANT SHIP: The generic term for the wide variety of utility vessels, often designed for specific purposes, which in constrast to warships, fishing ships, auxiliary and research ships, are used to transport goods or people. In the era of the sailing ship the term included such important types as the COG, HULK, BARQUE, BRIG and SCHOONER.

MESHEJMOK: A nineteenth-century freight barge used on the Volga, and driven by a large square sail.

MIRROR DINGHY: Designed by Jack Holt and Barry Bucknell, the pram-bowed Mirror dinghy was the pioneer of the DIY 'stitch and glue' building technique whereby plywood panels are joined to form the basic hull shape. This 10ft 10in dinghy is the largest class in the UK.

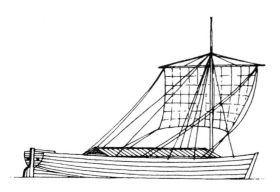

Russian meshejmok

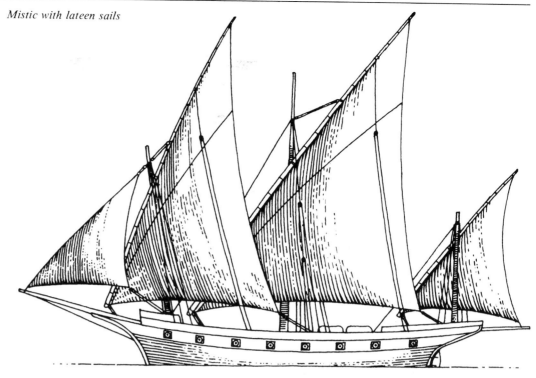

Mistic with lateen sails

Mirror dinghy

MISTIC, *mistique*: A two- and three-masted Mediterranean coastal cargo vessel of the eighteenth and nineteenth centuries, especially widespread on the Catalonian and Tunisian coasts. The ships were often armed, and frequently used by pirates. They were generally fitted only with lateen sails, but some versions carried square sails or a hybrid rig, in which case two staysails were always carried. The after part of the ship often featured a raised half deck with a bulwark, and the hull sides had apertures for oars and sometimes gunports. The term was also used in the Mediterranean for a variety of similar vessels, which differed widely in design and sail rig.

MOKSCHANA: A common nineteenth-century boat on the River Mokscha (tributary of the Oka, in Russia).

Russian mokschana

MOLICEIRO: A single-masted boat of the Aveiro lagoon, Portugal, used to collect and transport seaweed which is used as fertiliser. It carries a standing lugsail. The bow, which curves upwards greatly, and stern are decorated with colourful paintings and the boats are around 15m in length with a beam of around 2.5m.

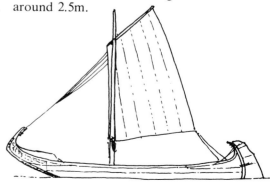

A Portuguese moliciero

MON: A boat made in the Solomon Islands featuring a planked hull and no outrigger, with tall bow and stern parts. The boats could carry up to 90 men in wartime.

Greek moner on a red-figure vase dating from the fifth century BC, showing Odysseus' ship and the sirens

MONER: The general term in ancient Greece and Rome for a ship which featured one row of oars on each side.

MORECAMBE BAY PRAWNER: A CARVEL-built, decked, cutter-rigged vessel with a slightly curved keel, cutaway forefoot and counter stern — rather yacht-like in appearance. Such boats were used for trawling for shrimps and ranged between 8 and 12m in length.

Burmese mor-pankhee

MOR-PANKHEE: A paddled pleasure vessel from Burma with a superstructure in the form of a temple, and an upward-curving stern from which the boat was steered with a large steering oar.

MOSES BOAT: In seamen's parlance, the smallest ship's boat carried on board ships or yachts in the sailing ship era, the name alluding to the nickname of the youngest ship's boy,

Moses. The name refers back to the biblical story of the infant Moses and his floating cradle.

In the eighteenth century, it also applied to a flat bottomed barge used in the West Indies for bringing off hogsheads of sugar from beaches for loading aboard cargo vessels.

MOSES BOAT: A West Indian rowing boat with very marked sheer which was used in transfering molasses from ship to shore. There were two types: the single moses, which had a transom stern, and the double moses, which was sharp-sterned. CLINKER-built, they were propelled by two pairs of oars and were between 4.5 and 5.5m in length.

MTEPE: A type of DHOW with a short keel, a long, projecting stem, a narrow after body and a pointed stern.

The hull was formed of strakes sewn together. The rudder was suspended on rope loops, and was set on the centreline. The mast was raked forward slightly and was secured at the foot with a rope lashing. Though it was characteristic of other dhow types, it carried a square coconut mat sail on a transverse yard rather than the typical dhow settee. On the east African coast around the island of Lamu a single-masted mtepe up to 20m long and 30 tons cargo capacity was still in use until the mid twentieth century, carrying a crew of up to 20 men. The plank strakes of this vessel's narrow hull were still sewn together, with sewn-in ribs. A square mat sail was still carried on the mast, and there was a bamboo-covered deckhouse aft of the mast.

MUD SLEDGE: A small sliding box (about 2m long and 0.6m wide), which is used to cross marshes and muddy terrain. Shoal fishermen, and cultivators and gatherers of mussels, use mud sledges at low tide, for gliding across soft mud to the best areas for fishing and collecting, and to where mussel cultivating areas are located. The owner stands or kneels on the device with one leg, and pushes himself along with the other foot.

The mud sledge has been in use for thousands of years, and is considered to be one of the earliest devices invented by man for the collecting of food on beaches. It is said that the plenteous supply of mussels on French coasts

Mtepe, early form of dhow

led to the establishment of mussel cultivation in the early Middle Ages.

MUFFERDEI BRIG: *see* SCHOONER BRIG.

MULETA:
A Portuguese, lateen-rigged fishing boat with an exceptionally bluff bow and only slightly less rounded stern. Characteristic features of the vessel were the bowsprit, which projected far beyond the stem, and a boom or angled mast extending equally far beyond the boat's stern. The resultant sail area was very large for a boat of this size. For example, a muleta of 1888 had a sail area of 170m².

Portuguese muleta with long sprit booms at bow and stern

MULTI-HULL:
A modern expression used to describe CATAMARANs and TRIMARANs.

MUTTE, *east Friesian mutte*:
A very small, single-masted river and canal boat based in Ostfriesland and Oldenburg, employed for carrying freight and peat. It was a flat-bottomed relatively narrow craft with leeboards. The mutte was rigged with a folding mast carrying a gaff mainsail, topsail and staysail. The crew was one or two persons. We can differentiate between two types, according to design and purpose: the rounded, TJALK-like peat carriers, and the spitz-mutten (pointed mutte), with pointed stem and stern, used for carrying personnel and freight. In the seventeenth century the vessels were 11 to 14m long and 2.5 and 3.5m wide, with a cargo capaicty of 8 to 16RT. By the second half of the nineteenth century they had increased in size to 15 to 18m long, and 4 to 4.5m wide, and carried 20 to 40RT of cargo.

East Friesian mutte

Portuguese muleta from the Tagus delta, sailing in front of the extended trawl net

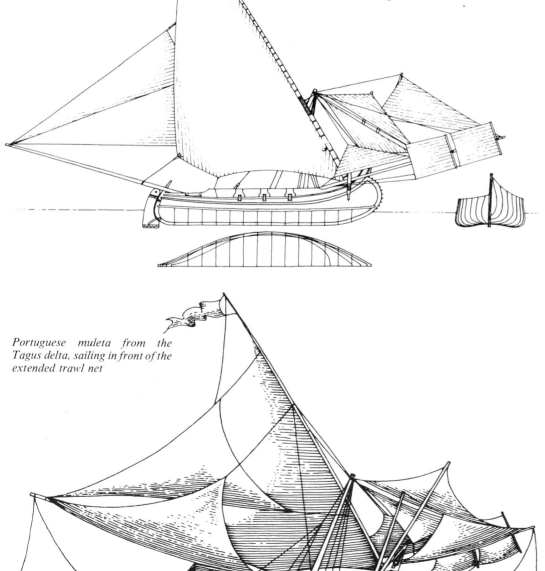

N

Catalonian nao, ca 1450 (model)

NACHEN: A small, flat-bottomed barge, propelled by punt pole or oars. In old High German nacho meant a small, trough-shaped boat. The term might originally have applied to small dugouts.

NÄHE: A fifteenth-century ferry based on the Rhine and Neckar, and used for carrying persons and animals; it was large, flat-bottomed and shallow of draught.

NAO, *nave, nau:* A type of Portuguese-Spanish sailing ship with a long history of development. The NEF, which had its origins in the north and west of France, was the vessel preferred by the crusaders during the Crusades of the eleventh and twelfth centuries, and in consequence the type had a strong influence on ship design. The Crusades also provided the opportunity to draw comparisons with Italian ship types, with the result that the words nef, nao, nave and nau came to be used as terms thereafter covering any large, full-bodied, multi-masted ship. In the fourteenth century, the nao existed as a two-masted ship, but thereafter was usually built as a three-master. One of the oldest ship models surviving from this period of oceanic Portuguese voyages dates from the fifteenth century, and shows a Catalan nao. The original model is now in the Prins Hendrik Maritime Museum in Rotterdam.

The model is important in that it shows various design features which otherwise have only come down to us in terms of written descriptions and illustrations. In the fifteenth century, the nao was built in Spain in large numbers, and was rather heavier and larger than the CARAVEL. In his diary, Columbus always referred to the *Santa Maria* as a nao, while he called the two other ships, the *Nina* and *Pinta*, caravels.

NATIONAL CLASS DINGHIES: Dinghies recognized by the official sailing organizations in their country of origin as opposed to international class dinghies which are recognized throughout the world. The forerunner of all national dinghies was perhaps the National 12 class which remains indigenous to Britain. The dinghy has its counterparts throughout the world.

NAU, *naue, nauen:* A generic term, with its origins in the Latin navis, for a fairly large vessel, which was brought to the north by the Romans; it has also been used for a variety of boats in Western Europe. For example, the naue was a small fishing boat in Switzerland; in the fifteenth and sixteenth centuries a small barge was known as a naffe in the Bavarian-Swabian region, and naf, nawe or naue in Alsace. In the Danube region this was the name for a small ferry boat. In that area nau travelling meant journeying downstream through a valley on a boat without means of propulsion. On Lake Lucerne, nauen was the term used for a large, wooden barge, originally driven by oars and sail, and in the twentieth century by propeller.

NAUTILUS: *see* FULTON SUBMERSIBLE

NAVE: Another term with its origins in the Latin navis; this one referred to large sailing ships which sailed in the Mediterranean region in the Middle Ages. From the eleventh to the thirteenth centuries, for example, a Crusader ship was considered large if it could carry about 90 persons. In 1227, Heinrich von Lettland wrote a chronicle in which he described journeys and ships in the Baltic region from his own observations. Although the term was not generally adopted in northern European languages, naves or naviculas denoted ships which could also travel upstream, ie could be sailed.

NAVIS: A general latin term for large ships and boats. Appropriate suffixes indicated other characteristics or types of vessels, such as NAVIS LONGA or navis constrata (covered ship).

NAVIS LONGA: A Latin term used from ancient times to the Middle Ages for warships characterized by a relatively long, narrow design. The Greek and Roman oared warships (MONERS, DIERS and TRIERS), the Nordic Viking warships and the GALLEYS were all long and relatively narrow. The length to beam ratio of an Attic trier was 10:1 and that of a Venetian galley more than 8:1.

NAVIS ONERARIA: This Latin term survived right into the Middle Ages, and referred to a short, rounded, full-bodied cargo ship. With the transition from oars to the sailing ship, and the greater lateral stability then required, ships came to be built broader and shorter. Typical were the Roman grain transport ships.

Representation of a nef on the oldest city seal from the southern English port of Winchelsea, thirteenth century

NEF: The French term for ships in general and the single-masted freight vessels in particular which evolved through various stages from the eleventh to the sixteenth century. Ships similar to the COG, based on the western French coast from the eleventh to the thirteenth centuries, were known as nef. They evolved as a hybrid between the northern ships and the more full-bodied types from the Mediterranean countries.

During the Crusades, nefs were often used as Crusader ships, with the results that they came into contact with other Mediterranean ship types, as well as the original cogs encountered on the northern French coasts. That this was a widespread type is indicated by the pictorial representations on the city seals of La Rochelle of 1308, Lübeck of 1230, Sandwich of 1238, Dunwich of 1269, Dover of 1281, and Poole of 1315, as well as on miniatures from Biscay, Portugal and Spain and even from thirteenth-century Iceland.

Although the ships varied over the years, and according to region, the nef remained as a CLINKER-built, broad, bulbous ship, built up from a keel. In comparison with the Nordic cog the nef's stem and stern shapes were usually more rounded. The top strake ran almost the whole length of the hull with virtually no sheer, but then curved upward sharply at the ends of the hull.

After the eleventh century, the nef was fitted with large framework structures fore and aft (castles), which were subsequently planked, then eventually blended into the hull to form an integral part of the vessel. The single-masted ships were rigged with one square sail. By the end of the thirteenth century a bowsprit had been added. As with the cog, the single or twin side rudders originally fitted were superseded by a centreline stern rudder around the same time. Although the nef had developed into a very similar ship to the cog by the end of the fifteenth century, the terms nef, nao, nave and nau remained in general use for large, full-bodied ships. Typical dimensions were around 18 to 20m length, 6 to 7m beam and 2.5 to 3m freeboard.

During her heyday Venice also contributed to the development of the nef into a large ship. The nefs built in Venice reached a cargo capacity of 200 tons, a considerable figure for the time, with a length of up to 42m, a beam of 13m and a depth of 7.5m. In the sixteenth century the nefs were superseded by the galeasse.

NEWFOUNDLAND SCHOONER, *Grand Banks schooner*:

A two- or three-masted, ocean-going fishing schooner. As the majority of these schooners were built and based in Gloucester (Mass), USA, they were also known as Gloucester schooners. Other sections of the schooner fleet were based in Halifax (Nova Scotia) and St John's (Newfoundland). From these ports the fast Newfoundland schooners sailed to the Newfoundland banks or the Grand Banks, carrying their fishing boats (DORY). For centuries, rich catches of cod, herring and mackerel had been made in the cold waters of the Labrador stream between April and October. European fishing ships had travelled to Newfoundland to fish for many years. For example, the Bretons sailed from northern France to the Newfoundland banks every year. The Grand Banks were also a traditional fishing ground for the Portuguese.

Statue of Nike from Samothrace, ca 300 BC, showing the hull and outrigger of a Greek bireme.

NEW GUY'S HOUSE BOAT: Fragments of a Romano-British river boat dating from the Roman occupation of England in the second century, found near London Bridge close to Guy's Hospital. Coins found at the same site enabled the boat to be dated accurately. It was a CARVEL-built, flat-bottomed oak boat of around 12m length and 4.20m beam. The depth was around 1.20m amidships. Very broad oak planks were used, 25mm thick, which were joined to each other with hazelnut branches and the joints then sealed. The boat was painted with pitch externally for protection. There are many structural similarities to the BLACKFRIARS SHIP.

NIKE DIER STATUE: A statue found on the Greek island of Samothrace, depicting the goddess of victory, Nike, as messenger of Zeus, standing on the forward part of a DIER. The statue is important in terms of shipbuilding history, as it shows the form of the forepart of a dier, including the lateral outriggers for the oars. The statue has been in the Louvre since 1879. As it was a memorial to a victory, it is supposed that the sculpture was commissioned by Demetrius Poliorcetes (336–283 BC), who was known as The Beseiger of Cities, to commemorate his victory over Meneleus in Cyprus in 306 BC.

Three-masted French Newfoundland barquentine, ca 1930, with several square sails on the foremast

Assyrian round boat, ca eighth century BC, on the Nimrud relief plate

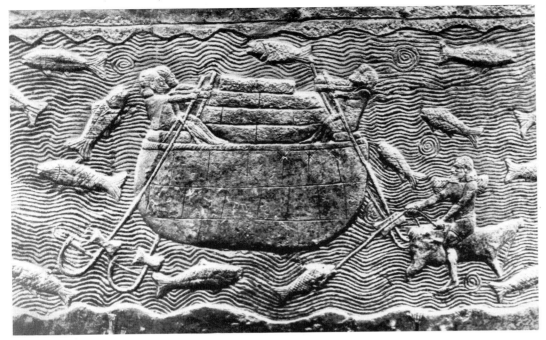

NIMRUD RELIEF: A relief dating from around the eighth century BC, respresenting the Phoenician-Assyrian fleet. It was discovered on the site of the old Assyrian city of Kalach, roughly 40km south of King Sennecherio's (705–681 BC) former capital, Nineveh. *See also* NINEVEH RELIEF *and* PHOENICIAN SHIPS.

NINEVEH RELIEF: A fragment of an eighth-century BC relief showing the bow of a Phoenician warship in Assyrian service. It is an oared vessel with two banks of oars. At the time that the relief was sculpted, the Phoenician peoples living on the Mediterranean were

ruled by the Assyrians. Niniveh, the capital of the Assyrians under King Sennacherib (705–681 BC), was on the eastern bank of the Tigris, opposite present-day Mosul, and was totally destroyed by the Babylonians in 612 BC. Excavations in the ruins began in 1820, and the relief was found in 1843.

NORFOLK WHERRY: A cargo carrier developed for use on the narrow, shallow inland waterways of the Norfolk Broads. It was a CLINKER boat, with a pointed stern, curved floors and considerable sheer. One large hatch took up most of the length of the vessel. The Norfolk wherry had a single mast

the heel of which was fitted into a heavy tabernacle and it was supported only by a forestay. The mast was pivoted, for passing under bridges. A large, boomless gaff mainsail, black in colour, was the only sail employed.

The Norfolk wherry developed during the eighteenth century, replacing the Norfolk keel, which was similar to the wherry but had a transom stern and hoisted a square sail. Some wherries were as little as 12m, but more usually they were around 19m. They survived well into the twentieth century.

NORMAN SHIP: An intermediate stage between the slim, open, oared sailing Viking ships and the decked, more full-bodied cargo ships. Though the hull form was more bulbous, it still had similarities to the Viking ship, with its tall, curving ends. The beam, however, was much greater, the importance of the sail had increased, and the oars were now the secondary means of propulsion.

The Norman ship became especially famous in the reign of William the Conqueror (1027–1087). Prior to invading and conquering England in 1066 he had a large fleet of these ships built, capable of carrying his army, its horses and the apparatus of war across the Channel. An impressive representation of the fleet during the crossing is included in the famous Bayeux tapestry. The Norman ship represented an early intermediate stage towards the later types used in the Crusades, especially the NEF.

NORTH FERRIBY BOATS: The remains of boats which were discovered and examined in the Humber estuary in 1938, 1940 and 1963. The boat found in 1940 dates from around 1500 BC. It was a river vessel, 15m long and 2.6m broad, with a flat bottom consisting of three planks, of which the longer central plank was curved upwards at the ends. The side walls each consisted of three strakes, the planks being joined on their short edges by the CARVEL method, ie butt-jointed. All the planks were held together under tension with closely-spaced bands of flexible but strong yew wood, and strips of ash wood were bound in on the inside of the joints. Extra ropework was wound round the hull ends, as shown on various medieval pictures on city seals. The ropework at the stern was situated very far aft, and to prevent it slipping off the half-round hull a cleat was fitted underneath the stern.

NORTH CAROLINA SHAD BOAT: a single-masted seine net fishing boat with a spritsail, jib and — uniquely among North American small craft — a topsail. It was between 6 and 10m in length, CARVEL-built with a raked stem post and transom and with only washboards round the sides as a deck. A centreboard was fitted.

NYDAM BOAT: The remains of two boats which were found in a moor near Nydam in Schleswig-Holstein, on the west bank of the

Phoenician-Assyrian bireme, dating from the eighth century BC, on the Niniveh relief plate

Norman ships based on the city seals of Dam (1226) and Dover (1281)

Alsensund, in 1863. The larger boat was dated as a third-century vessel from the bronze dress needles which were found. The smaller boat was evidently made of fir, and had a double stem/stern, similar to the HJORTSPRING boat. The remains of the larger boat were destroyed during the Prussian-Austrian-Danish War of 1864.

The surviving boat is made of oak, is 22.84m long, 3.26m broad and has a depth of 1.06m. The outside skin consists of 10 full-length oak planks, each 350 to 450mm wide and 22 to 25mm thick. The planks are rivetted to each other CLINKER-style, with iron round-head nails and rectangular roves on the inside, spaced about 140 to 180mm apart. The joints were sealed with resin-soaked moss.

The keel plank is shorter, at 14.32m, and at each end the gently curving stem and stern timbers, 5.40m long, are affixed with 50mm wooden nails. The boat has no keel timber, nor a mast socket, hence it was propelled exclusively by oars. The hull is stiffened by 19 transverse ribs made of natural-grown curved oak, spaced about 1m apart. The ribs are joined to the bottom and the side planks not with nails, but with bast cords. The planks were cut leaving projecting spigots or cleats, to facilitate joining them. The cleats are 400mm long and about 70 to 80mm high, and are drilled through close to the ribs. The bast cords used for binding were pulled through these cleat holes and corresponding holes in the ribs. The uppermost strakes feature a reinforced gunwale edge on each side of the hull, on which the rowlocks were bound in place with leather thongs. The boat was propelled by 14 oars, each 3.5m long, and a total of 28 oarsmen. The oarsmen sat on boards placed loosely on the individual transverse ribs. The side rudder is 3.20m long, and the rudder blade has a streamlined shape. At the top end of the rudder shaft is a square spigot, on which a specially shaped timber is fixed, with transverse and fore-and-aft grips. This is the tiller. The Nydam boat is stored in Gottorp Castle in Schleswig. A copy of the boat was made in 1934 at the yacht yard of Abbeking and Rasmussen.

Reconstructed Nydam boat

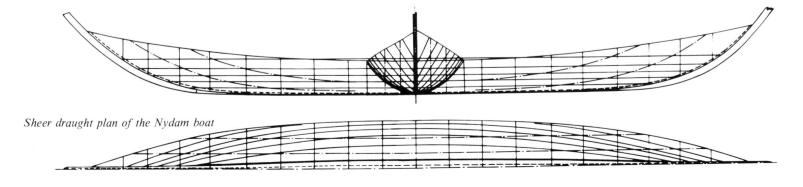

Sheer draught plan of the Nydam boat

O

OBELISK TRANSPORT SHIP: *see* ANCIENT LARGE SHIPS

OBLAS: A cargoboat used on the Dvina in the nineteenth century.

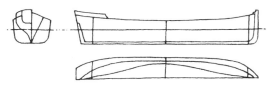

Oblas from the river Dvina

An ocean racer setting bermudian mainsail, spinnaker and blooper

OCEAN RACER: Term used to describe offshore racing boats, in particular those which take part in Royal Ocean Racing Club events and international series like the Admiral's Cup and the Southern Ocean Racing Conference. Ocean racers do not restrict their activities to offshore events as many of the international ocean racing events include inshore or 'round-the-buoys' races. There is virtually no distinction now between racing boats which sail offshore and those which restrict their activities to sheltered waters.

The classic ocean racers of the postwar period were fast cruisers, but today ocean racers are a breed apart, specially designed and with stripped out interiors that make them virtually useless for cruising.

Almost all ocean racers are designed to a rule, the most common of which is the International Offshore Rule (IOR) which measures hull shape, sail area and a host of other factors to arrive at a rating figure from which results are calculated according to a Time Multiplying Factor (TMF).

OK DINGHY: A one-design, single-sail racing boat designed by the Danish yacht designer K Olsen. It gained general recognition in 1966. The OK is 4m long and 1.42m broad, has a retractable centreboard and a mast stepped fairly far forward. It has a sail area of $5.0m^2$ or $8.5m^2$, the smaller one being used for youth training.

OLYMPIC CLASS BOAT: A generic term for sailing boats chosen by the IYRU (International Yacht Racing Union) for Olympic sailing competitions. Amongst the newer Olympic centreboard types are the FINN, the

FLYING DUTCHMAN and the 470.

Finns first sailed in the 1952 Olympic Games in Finland as singlehanded dinghies, and thereafter superseded the Olympic dinghy, which had been raced up to that time.

The Flying Dutchman replaced the previous $12m^2$ Sharpie after the Rome Olympic Games in 1960. The IYRU decided in 1969 that the TEMPEST class should be added to the list for the Olympics of 1972 and 1976, making it the sixth Olympic class boat.

The STAR class and the SOLING class are among the approved keelboats. The Star class is the oldest Olympic boat class, having been raced at the Olympics from 1932 to 1972 and again since 1980. When this boat class was omitted from the 1976 Olympiad, the TORNADO catamaran was introduced as an Olympic boat, but when the IYRU cancelled the Tempest class after the 1976 Olympics, the Star class was re-introduced for 1980 and 1984.

From 1948 to 1972 the DRAGON was an Olympic keelboat class, supplanting the 6 metre as an Olympic class, which had been raced since 1936. For 1976, a further dinghy, the 470, was introduced.

The Soling class replaced the 5.5 metre keelboat, which had been recognized as an Olympic class from 1948 to 1968. The 5.5 had superseded the 8 metre, which had Olympic status until 1936.

In 1980, windsurfing (board sailing) was approved as an Olympic discipline for the 1984 Olympiad. The IYRU selected the Windglider designed by Fred Ostermann (BRD).

ONE-DESIGN BOAT: *See* CLASSBOAT.

ONE TONNER: Slightly anachronistic term which has no relation to actual weight used to

describe ocean racers of about 40ft in length which rate exactly the same under the International Offshore Rule, thus allowing them to race boat for boat without any time allowance (Level Rating).

Other 'Ton classes' include Half Tonner, Three Quarter Tonner, Two Tonner which cover the IOR spectrum from about 20ft in length up to 44ft. All have their own world Championships as well as taking part in racing against other IOR boats.

The One Tonner has been the focus of design recently and has inevitably grown in popularity as against other Ton classes. Its size makes it big enough for offshore racing series like the Admiral's Cup and due to recent development it is fast enough to hold its own with larger IOR yachts, often beating them boat for boat on the water.

OPIUM CLIPPER: A relatively small fast-sailing vessel (often a schooner, brig or brigantine) used in the Chinese opium trade in the middle of the nineteenth century. Speed was essential since the trade was frowned upon by the Chinese authorities and at various times was actually illegal.

OPTIMIST DINGHY: A small single-chine dinghy for a crew of one young person. The Optimist is only 2.3m long and 1.3m broad, and draws 0.77m with centreboard down. The Optimist carries the sail symbol 'O' on the spritsail. The boat can be made of plywood or glassfibre-reinforced polyester resin, and weighs 32kg. It is reported that the Danish naval architect A Damgard was struck with the idea of a minimum-sized sailing boat for children of six years or more when he watched the street racing which was popular in

Olympic sailing classes

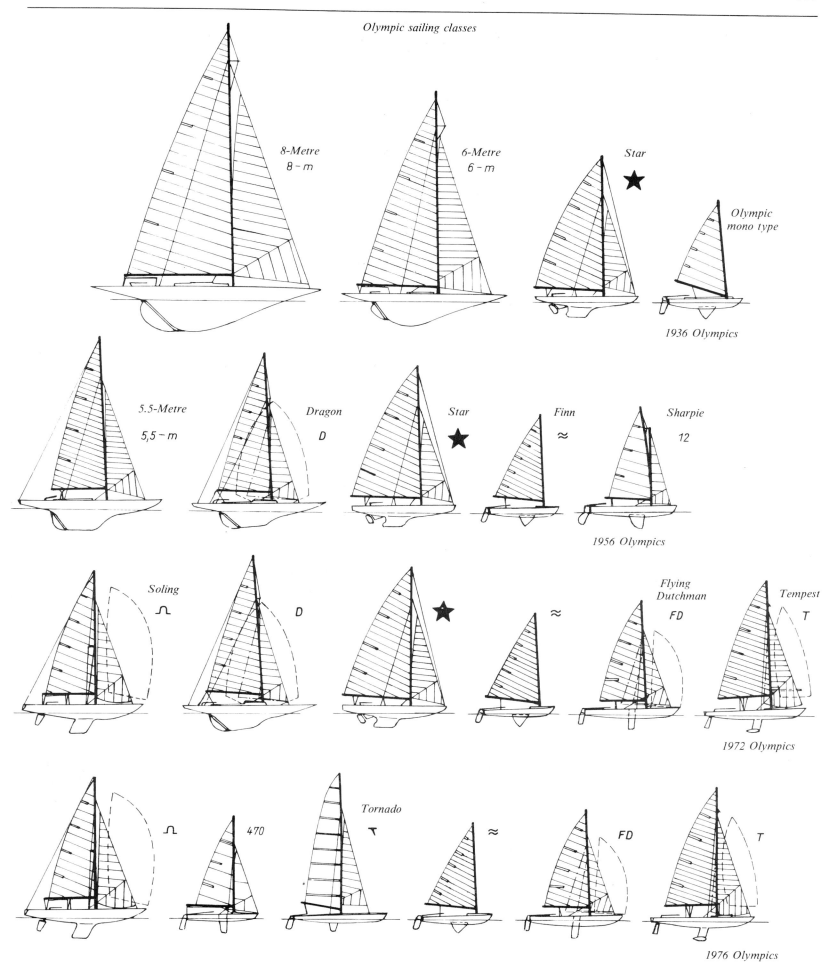

8-Metre
8 - m

6-Metre
6 - m

Star

Olympic
mono type

1936 Olympics

5.5-Metre
5,5 - m

Dragon
D

Star

Finn
≈

Sharpie
12

1956 Olympics

Soling
⊓

D

≈

Flying
Dutchman
FD

Tempest
T

1972 Olympics

⊓

470

Tornado
⊤

≈

FD

T

1976 Olympics

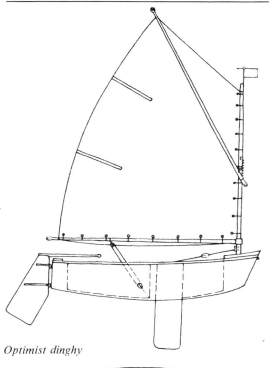

Optimist dinghy

Clearwater (Florida), using boxes fitted with small sails, and he took the idea back to Denmark.

OREMBAI: A vessel fitted with a tripod mast and square-sail, but usually paddled, and still in common use today in the Moluccas for passenger transport. The planks of the hull are fitted with cleats to which the ribs are attached; the ribs are bound in place afterwards, using palm bast. Notable features are the decorated stem and stern, which curve strongly upwards. European influence is evident in the rig, especially the gaff mainsail with its boom, and the staysail and the jib on the bowsprit. Smaller vessels can accommodate about 10 passengers, and larger ones up to 30 passengers.

ORKNEY YOLE, *jol*: A broad, sharp-sterned sailing boat of the Orkney Islands used for long-lining and seining. Such boats were around 8m in length with a beam of 2.5m. They carried two masts, the mizzen raking aft. On the Northern Isles two standing lugsails and a jib were set; on the Southern Isles spritsails and a jib were used. The yole was eventually replaced by the FIFIE.

ÖRUSUND BOAT: A fishing boat employed for net and driftnet fishing in Sweden. Originally, it was an open vessel, but covered versions were in use by the end of the nineteenth century. The single-masted vessels were rigged with a rectangular spritsail,

triangular topsail, a staysail and a jib on a looose jib boom. The boats were around 9m in length and 3.5m broad, had rounded stem and stern, were CLINKER-built and had a fish well.

ORUWA: A range of outrigger boats from Sri Lanka, used for a variety of fishing operations. They are between 1.5 and 10m in length. The smaller are simply dugouts; the majority, however, have a vertical washstrake sewn onto the top edge of this. Regardless of size, the dugout is always of the same form: slightly flat-bottomed with considerable tumble-home, with almost punt-like ends. The outrigger has two cleats carved on its top surface, and to these the outrigger booms — naturally curved branches — are tied. Except for very small oru (plural) and those engaged in shooting beach seines, all are equipped with sail. The most common form of sail is rectangular, set from a double mast (oeanic spritsail), but settee and square sails are employed in some areas.

OSEBERG SHIP: In 1903, a large, oared sailing Viking ship was found in a burial mound on the western bank of the Oslo fjord. The ship was 21.4m long overall, had a keel length of 17.7m, a beam of 51m and a depth of 1.3m. Inside one ship was buried the corpse of Queen Asa, daughter of King Harald Redbeard, who died around the .year 850. According to the custom relating to ship burials, the keel was oriented north to south with the bow facing south. The ship was tied to a great stone with a thick rope, as if made fast.

The peat soil had provided a virtually airtight seal, and the ship, its equipment and other artefacts had survived in good condition for more than a millennium. Although the grave had collapsed over the years, and its contents compressed, it proved possible to reconstruct the original parts by dint of careful, painstaking work. The Oseberg ship is proof of the shipbuilding skills of the Vikings, and also of their general manual skills. The principal components of the ship are of oak,

Sternpost of the Oseberg ship

Oseberg ship at the excavation site

with the exception of the mast, which is of fir. The design is similar to that of the GOKSTAD ship. Twelve planks are fitted on either side of the T-section keel, which is hewn from a single oak trunk. The keel is not straight, but curves gently to produce an increase in draught of 0.30m amidships. Whether this shape was intentional or arose by accident, cannot be deduced, but its effect would have been to confer good manoeuvring characteristics on the vessel.

The top planks on both sides each have 12 oar holes with slots for the oar blades. The planks are overlapped CLINKER-fashion, are rivetted together, and bound to 17 naturally curved grown ribs. To facilitate the binding, cleats were left projecting when the planks were hewn, as on the Nydam boat and other Nordic ships. The joints were caulked with spun sheep wool.

Transverse beams are attached to the top ends of the ribs, to provide lateral rigidity to the hull, and to provide support to the short deck planks, some of them loose, and some nailed in place. The angles between ribs and transverse beams are reinforced with timber knees, each of which extends across two outer skin planks. The knees are fixed in place using oak nails.

The ship was steered by means of a side rudder 3.18m long, swivelling around its vertical axis on a pivot. The rudder shaft was bound to the hull with osiers, and also attached to a special cleat low down on the sternpost.

The forward part of the ship contained equipment and tools, including a 1.2m long stockless iron anchor weighing 9.8kg. As well as the mooring rope by which the ship was symbolically made fast, there was a further 100m of rope which had survived. A 6.9m long grooved fir plank served as a bridge between the ship and the 'mooring' point. Other items in the ship included a wooden well tub with handle for drawing water, adzes, knives, gouges, chisels and an awl.

Slightly aft of amidships was the covered burial chamber itself, with the accompanying sepulchral items, amongst them several oak trunks. For her last voyage the dead queen was also provided with a two-axled waggon, four richly decorated sledges, and 15 sacrificed horses and several dogs.

In view of the cultural, historical and ship-building importance of the find, a ship museum was built on the Bygdøy peninsula near Oslo, in which the Oseberg ship is now displayed, together with the Gokstad and Tune ships and other significant historical objects.

The individual components were systematically photographed and scale drawings prepared, before the work of reconstruction began. Plaster casts or copies were also made. The ship was re-assembled using the original wooden and iron parts and fittings as far as possible. A variety of different preservation techniques proved necessary, because of the condition of the timber, and the different types of wood which had been used. The oak parts mostly required no more than steam cleaning followed by treatment with creosote, but the beech, fir, spruce and limewood parts were found to require 12 to 16 hours' boiling in alum, after which they were dried and preserved with linseed oil and matt varnish.

OSTIA FRESCO: A tomb fresco made around the time of Christ which depicts a Roman merchant ship bearing the name *Isis Giminiana*. The fresco was discovered in the vicinity of Ostia, the second port of ancient Rome, which was completed in 335 BC on the former Tiber estuary for importing grain and for troop embarkations. When the Tiber estuary silted up in the fifth century it fell out of use and decayed.

The permanence of the fresco pictures is due to the fact that the painting was done on fresh lime plaster, using paints mixed with lime-

The partly reconstructed Oseberg ship

water, with the result that the paint penetrated deep into the plaster and formed an indelible compound with it. Various fresco paintings using this durable technique have survived to the present day from the Egyptian and Roman epochs. This ship shown on the Ostia fresco is probably a vessel which was destined to be used for grain transport from Ostia up the Tiber to Rome. The ship's mast is fairly tall and stepped far forward, an indication that it was equipped for towing, ie to be pulled along by draught animals or people from the towpath. The tow rope was fixed fairly high up on the mast so that it did not get caught on vegetation on the banks.

The fresco illustrates grain being loaded and suggests that Arascantus, who is shown on the picture and in whose honour the grave fresco was painted, was the owner of the ship. The captain of the ship is called Farnacas, and a porter is just saying to him: '*Feci*' – 'I have done my work'.

OTTER: A Belgian inland freight ship similar to a PLEIT or TJALK, displacing around 100 tons, with a length of about 18m and a beam of 5m. The Otter existed in a single-masted form, and also as a two-masted vessel with gaff sails.

The term was in use as early as the beginning of the seventeenth century, and at the beginning of the twentieth century several hundred timber-built otters were still working.

OUTRIGGER: This term refers to boats, used primarily in the island region of Southeast Asia and in the Pacific, fitted with a lateral outrigger float to lessen the danger of capsizing. The float usually consists of a tree-trunk sharpened at both ends, and slightly shorter than the boat. It lies parallel to the main hull, and is connected to it by transverse booms.

The shallow draught is an advantage for landing on shelving coasts. The float and booms are bound together with rope. The increased lateral stability due to the outrigger permits the use of larger sails; the mast is fixed to the forward transverse beam and held in place by shrouds. In early times the sails were made from the leaves of the sago tree, or strips of leaves from the Pandanus palm. Outrigger boats are usually DOUBLE-ENDED, enabling the outrigger float to be kept to windward. *See also* DOUBLE OUTRIGGER BOAT *and* SOUTH SEAS BOATS.

The term has another, quite different application. Before the 1920s the standard rowing boat had rowlocks fixed to the hull sides. During the transitional period which followed, when racing rowing boats were built with ever more slender hulls, and thus had to have lateral frameworks built out to support the rowlocks (the outriggers), the boats became known as outrigger boats until their design became the norm.

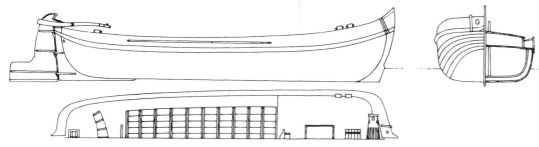

Otter, outboard profile, body plan and midship section and half breadth plan

Schelde otter, nineteenth century (model)

Outrigger boat from Bora-Bora (Society islands)

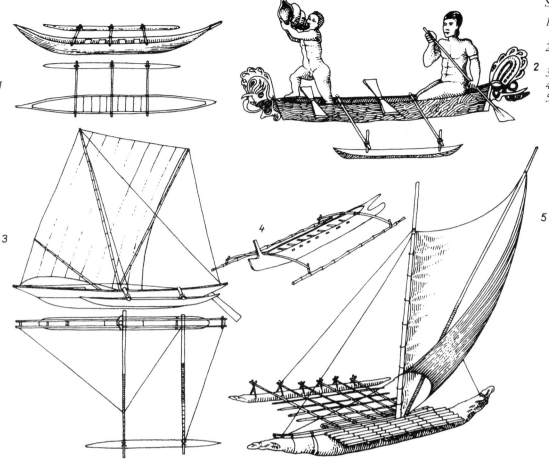

South Seas outrigger boats

1 *Boopaa, small South Seas pirogue with single outrigger*
2 *Outrigger boat without sail, from picture by A Tasman*
3 *Modern outrigger boat of the Philippines*
4 *Small pirogue with double outriggers, from Java*
5 *Outrigger sailing canoe from New Guinea*

Philippino double-outrigger boat

P

PACKET BOAT, *packet ship*: A boat or ship used specifically to carry mail, since packet was the usual eighteenth century term for a piece of mail. At first these were mainly fast dispatch vessels, operated by the state or by private companies, to carry post to and from warships or on other government business, but eventually was applied to an early form of LINER service. Transatlantic packet shipping started up in 1818 when the Black Ball line was set up to carry mail, passengers and cargo between Liverpool and New York.

The regular postal service from Germany across the Atlantic was organized by RM Sloman, and began in 1837 with four ships. The number of sailing ships used by the Sloman shipping company for packet shipping (and termed packet boats or packet ships) had risen to seven by 1845. Although the steamships *Sirius* and *Great Western* first ran from Britain to New York in 1838, sailing ships remained in use for packet shipping for several decades, sailing to New York and other American ports, and even Australia, when the emigrant trade developed. The first North Atlantic packets were only about 450 tons but the *Roscius* of 1838 reached 1000 tons, while vessels of 1400 tons were being built by 1850. They were usually strongly built since they had to sail the Atlantic in all seasons, but also carried lofty spars, with skysails and studding-sails so they could be driven hard when necessary.

PADAGU, *paduwa*: see MASULA.

PADUA: One of the last great sailing ships and the last four-masted barque built for the sailing ship company, F Laeisz's Flying P Line. Designed for bulk freight she was launched on 24 June 1926. After the Soviet Union acquired the ship, she was named after the Russian Admiral and Hydrographer I F Krusenstern (1770–1846), who carried out the first Russian circumnavigation of the globe between 1803 and 1806, a voyage which was very successful in scientific terms. The ship now serves as a training ship. The dimensions of the *Krusenstern*, which is maintained at its home port of Riga by the Ministry of Fisheries, are as follows: length overall 114.5m, beam 14.0m. The height of the mainmast above deck is 55m.; the main yard is 29m long. She is the largest Soviet sailing ship.

The ship is what is termed a 'three-island ship', ie the forecastle, bridge deck and poop are separate superstructures, all interconnected by gangways. The crew consists of 50 men and 200 trainees. The total sail area of $3427m^2$ is divided up between foremast $(845m^2)$, mainmast $(874m^2)$ and mizzen mast $(144m^2)$, the remainder of the area comprising staysails. Two auxiliary diesel engines rated at 588kw have been fitted so that the vessel can still proceed in a dead calm, or manoeuvre in

Heyerdahl's papyrus raft RA I *in the port of Safi*

confined spaces. Under sail alone the ship has achieved good and remarkably uniform times between Europe and America and Europe and Australia. In 1933 and 1934 the ship covered the distance from Hamburg to Port Lincoln (Australia) in the record time of 67 days.

PADUAKAN, *Padoucann*: A two or three-masted Indonesian sailing ship of the eighteenth and nineteenth centuries. The two-masted vessels were usually 15m long and could carry up to 50 tons of cargo, while the three-masted variety, with a length of around 23m, could carry up to 100 tons. The ships, which sailed in the Moluccan region, had two cannon fore and aft to ward off pirates.

PAIR: The abbreviation for a racing rowing boat for two oarsmen. Coxed and coxless pairs are classes of rowing boat, and sculled pairs and double pairs also exist.

PALME: A two-masted merchant ship employed on the East Indies run until the early nineteenth century. It had a low freeboard and carried guns for self-defence. The rig consisted of gaff mainsail and topsail on the mainmast, and a very small mizzen aft. She also carried a staysail and jib.

PAMBAN-MANCHÉ: A very light boat built on the Indian west coast. It was up to 20m long, and made of tree bark. The light weight, slender hull and complement of 30 to 40 paddlers permitted speeds of 10 to 12 knots to be attained for short periods.

PAMPHILE: A ninth-century Byzantine warship with one row of oarsmen on each side. The pamphile represents a successor to the

LIBURNIAN. At around 20m in length, it was somewhat smaller than the DROMON, which was the more common vessel at the time.

PAPYRUS RAFT: Bundles of papyrus bound together to form a buoyant raft. Boat-shaped papyrus rafts which were operated on the Nile were among the first vessels to be used by man, and remained in constant use for thousands of years.

The papyrus shrub (*Cyperus papyrus*), which grew wild on the Nile in great quantities in ancient times, is a sedge similar to the rush, growing more than 3m tall. The triangular base of the stem can be up to 150mm thick. The Egyptians used the papyrus shrub to construct huts and rafts, but also extracted the pith and compressed it to form papyrus sheets which could be used as a writing material. Wild papyrus plants scarcely exist today.

Papyrus vessels were easy to build, requiring few tools. Depending on the thickness of the stems and the size of the vessel to be built, a number of plants (10, 20 or more) were bound together tightly at their tips. More stems were pushed into the first bundle before further binding was carried out. Thus the length and girth of the bundle increased until an adequate thickness was obtained, after which the procedure was reversed to form an equally tapered, spindle-shaped second end. The buoyant body thus formed was of elliptical cross-section, and further bundles could then be joined on, either on the side, to produce a useful area similar to a deck, or on top, to increase the freeboard and thus afford shelter to the deck.

The ends of the raft were drawn up high, the projecting sections being supported by ropes on the larger vessels, the tension of which

Papyrus raft

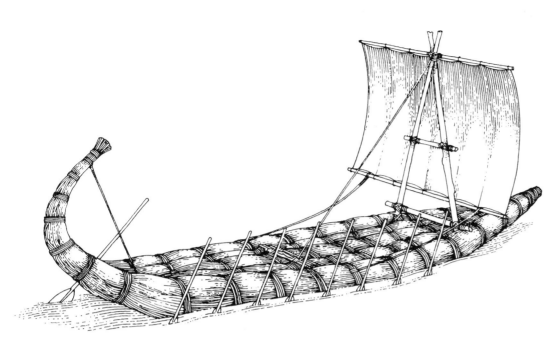

Italian paredgia

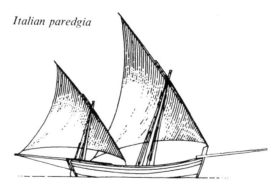

could be adjusted. The raised ends increased buoyancy, made it easier to pull the raft onto land and over marshy terrain, and also improved the vessel's steering characteristics.

The vessels were propelled by paddles, punt holes or by a sail on a bipod mast.

In recent times, the Norwegian explorer Thor Heyerdahl decided to investigate whether it would have been possible to cross the Atlantic and complete other long sea voyages using the vessels which ancient man had at his disposal. To this end he had two boat-like papyrus rafts built with the help of Aymara indians from Lake Titicaca in Peru, where reed vessels are still made and used to this day.

The vessels were named *Ra I* and *Ra II* after an ancient Egyptian sun deity. Each of the vessels weighed around 15 tons, had a bipod mast with a sail, and consisted of around 200,000 papyrus stems, which were bound together by hemp ropes. *Ra I* was 15m long and 5m wide. The voyage had to be broken off early on when the vessel sustained damage. However, with the 12m long and 5m wide *Ra II*, Heyerdahl, with the crew of seven, succeeded in completing the voyage from Morocco to Barbados in the Caribbean.

The distance covered was 6300 miles, and the voyage lasted 57 days, from May to July 1970.

PARANZELLA, *paranza*: A single-masted Italian fishing vessel of the eighteenth and nineteenth centuries. It was about 12m long, had a rounded stern and a strikingly tall bow. These vessels were often decorated with paintings on stem, stern and sail, and were rigged with a lateen sail.

PAREDGIA: A two-masted Italian ship with a lateen sail, used at the end of the nineteenth century.

PARICIL: *see* CORACLE.

PASSAT: A four-masted barque belonging to the Hamburg sailing ship company F Laeisz, and one of the famous Flying P liners. This steel-hulled, four-masted barque was laid down on 2 March 1911 and was ready for sea on 28 November 1911. The specifications were as follows: length overall 115.0m, length between perpendiculars 98.0m, beam 14.4m, internal depth 8.1m, draught around 6.7m, cargo capacity 4750 tons. She could spread a total sail area of 4100m². The main mast is 52.0m above deck. Originally, the *Passat* had no auxiliary engine, and speeds of up to 16.4 knots were achieved under sail. The ship was designed for the nitrate trade, and made six voyages up to August 1914. The homeward run from the sixth voyages did not take place until 1921, when the vessel was transferred to French ownership.

After being brought back in December 1921 and repaired, the *Passat* was again engaged in the nitrate trade until 1927. In that year a further refit was carried out, to convert the vessel into a freight-carrying training ship. After collisions and repairs the Finnish shipping company Gustaf Eriksen acquired the vessel and used it until 1939 for voyages to Australia. From 1939 to 1944 she was laid up , and from 1944 to 1946 was used as a stationary grain store in Stockholm. In 1951, the *Passat* was due to be scrapped, but she was then purchased by the Schliewen shipping company, and thoroughly overhauled and modernized. An auxiliary engine of 660kw output and watertight bulkheads were fitted. After this conversion the crew consisted of 80 to 90 men, about 50 of whom were trainees. Since 1957, the *Passat* has been anchored as an accommodation and museum ship in Travemünde.

PATACHE: A guard-vessel revenue cutter, or armed tender used by the French in coastal and harbour waters. It usually took the form of a large sloop or armed cutter. The term was also applied to an early seventeenth-century Turkish warship, and a small ship of around 60 tons in the Spanish Armada in the later sixteenth century.

PATELÁ: An Indian transport ship used on the Ganges river from the nineteenth century to the start of the twentieth century.

PATTAMAR: A sailing ship of the DHOW group made of the teak found on the west coast of India. Smaller pattamars without deck or with a half-deck were much valued for coastal sailing and fishing because of their good sailing qualities. Medium-sized and large pattamars could carry up to 200 or 300 tons, and were built with full-length deck and sometimes with a supplementary after deck. These were ocean-going ships with excellent sailing characteristics, although they were primarily sailed close to the coast. Only rarely did they threaten the trade monopoly which the Arabs had achieved by dint of longer voyages in their BAGGA-LAs and SAMBUKs.

As with all types of dhow, the hull and sail rig had certain characteristic features. In relation to the overall length and the keel length, the ship's sloping bow was exceptionally long, and ran down below the waterline to the keel. The keel curved upwards towards the bow, with the result that the forward part of the ship had a slender, tapering profile, which bestowed exceptionally good directional stability on the craft. Aft of the midship region the keel line continued to descend to meet the straight, less severely raked and very slender stern. Above the waterline the stern was quite rounded and full-bodied.

The smaller and medium-sized versions were rigged as two-masted vessels, but there were also larger three-masted ships. The masts were raked forward equally by about 20

Large Indian patamar (model)

degrees or more, and the typical settee sails were set on long, angled yards, which sometimes consisted of several spars bound together. The length of the mizzen yard was usually around two thirds of the mainyard length.

Because of its outstanding sailing qualities the type is still in use today on the coasts of India, and the pattamar hull shape and rig are still employed on some types of specialized sailing yachts.

PEACE SHIP, *peace cog*: A COG or HULK used to combat pirates. In the fifteenth century, the lack of security at sea meant that the Hanseatic merchant ships needed some from of escort. The 20 to 30 merchant cogs constituting a convoy would elect a small number of ships' masters to form a commanding committee, whose ships were known, literally, as peace ships. The city federation of the Hanseatic league did not maintain such peace ships, nor any other warships; the cost of providing the escort was met by the individual city, the freight carrier or the ship's master.

PEAKE BOAT: A heavy, timber-built coastal lifeboat developed by the Englishman Peake specifically for life-saving around the English coast. In the second half of the nineteenth century, this heavy boat was virtually the only type used for life-saving. Because of their great weight of 1500 to 2000kg the boats required special launching rails at the lifeboat stations to run them down to the water, or, failing that, plenty of people and muscle power. The lighter FRANCIS BOAT was preferred for the shallower German coasts. *See also* LIFEBOAT.

PEAPOD: A boat developed in Maine in the latter part of the nineteenth century for lobster fishing. Sharp-ended and usually 5m in length, they were originally built CLINKER or CARVEL, but the latter method eventually prevailed. When rowed, the oarsmen stood facing forward. When sailed, a spritsail was set on a short mast.

PECHILI TRADER, *kangsu trader, shantung trader:* One of the two basic types of northern Chinese junk, the other being the ANTUNG TRADER. The hull was turret-built, with a bluff bow, a broad flat stern and an overhanging counter. It carried five masts, none of which were stepped vertically and only the fore- and the mainmast were located on the centreline of the vessel. The bow mast was stepped on the port side and canted well forward. The fore- and the mainmast were also raked forward. The quarter mast was housed against the port fore side of the rudder well and was canted both forwards and outboard. The mizzen was stepped against the inboard face of the counter, slightly to port of the centreline and raked aft. The sails were near-rectangular and a topsail could be set from the mainmast.

Crewed by 20 to 30 men, the normal cargo

was oil and disks of compressed soya bean. A muzzle-loading cannon was always carried. Approximately 41m in length, the pechili trader survived into the twentieth century and was thought to be the oldest type of ocean-going Chinese junk.

PEHENUKA RELIEF: A relief from the grave of Pehenuka (ancient Egyptian Empire, fifth Dynasty, 2770–2270 BC), showing a large Egyptian ship. It must have been around 80 Egyptian Ells long (about 42m). It is a planked ship built of wood with flat bottom and straight stem and stern, similar to the hull shown on the SAKKARA RELIEF. The ship also features a deckhouse to accommodate the officials or merchants. The 30 oarsmen and five helmsemen on each side, and the bipod mast with its tall, narrow sail, are typical features of the fast oared sailing ship of the old Empire. The relief is now stored in the Berlin museum of the Middle East.

PELOTA: A South American vessel which can be categorized as a skin boat. The boats are made of osiers or other branches and covered with cow hide, and are used on the waters of the Pampas down as far as the Matto Grosso. The larger pelotas are rowed or paddled, but smaller versions are sometimes pulled or pushed along by the owner as he swims.

PENTEKOR: A Greek, oared warship from the Trojan period, around 100 BC. The vessel was flat-bottomed like a raft, tapered forward and aft, and was propelled by 50 oarsmen. Homer defined the pentecor as a 'long, unsinkable ship'. It is supposed to have been subdivided into a large number of compartments by watertight bulkheads, and thereby stiffened. The length might have been around seven times the beam.

PENTEKONTER: An oared ship built by the Greeks following the pattern of the Phoenician ships of around 500 BC. These ships had 50 oarsmen, ie 25 oars on each side. Ancient writers such as Herodotus, Thucydides, Diodorus and others mention this type.

PENTER: A ship probably built first by Dionysius I of Syracuse at the beginning of the fourth century BC, with five banks of oars, or five groups of oarsmen. In the Punic wars (240 BC) Syracuse achieved superiority over the enemy's three-banked TRIERs. The Romans copied these penters and added boarding bridges, to enable them to exploit their experience and superiority in land warfare in sea battles.

PEOTTA, *peota*: A fast sailing despatch vessel employed by the Italian marine cities up until the seveneenth century. The peotta was a small, light SHALLOP with a small crew.

The term also referred to a flat-bottomed vessel used for wine transport, with a virtually circular bow and stern and a small sail.

Finally, the escort vessels to the Venetian

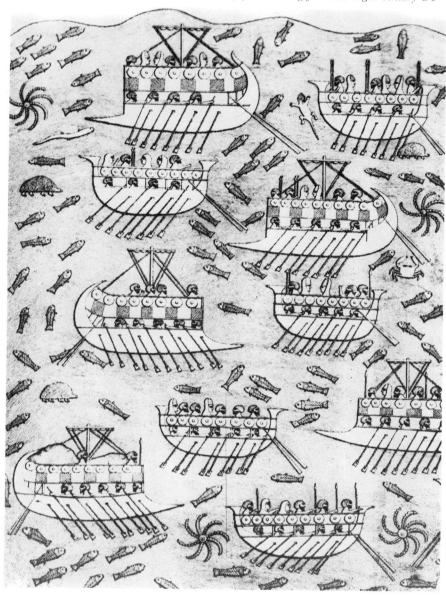

Phoenician-Assyrian fleet on the Nimrud relief plate, dating from the eight century BC

inefficient method of using space, so by 1877 the first experiments were undertaken using permanent, built-in tanks, leading eventually to the development of the sailing tanker.

PHOENICIAN SHIPS: Sea-going oared sailing ships built by the Phoenicians. The people now known as the Phoenicians called themselves Caananites or Sidonites after their places of origin but they were called Phoinike by the Greeks, and Poeni (Punic) by the Romans, particularly those who had settled Carthage on the northern coast of Africa. The Phoenicians were a Semitic farming and trading people, who settled the coastal regions of present-day Lebanon, Northern Israel and part of Syria around 2000 BC. Little direct information concerning the Phoenicians' ships has survived in the form of archaeological finds and pictures, and most of our knowledge about the Phoenician ships comes from Egyptian Assyrian and Greek sources.

These vessels were probably the first ships in the world to undertake extended voyages lasting several years. Herodotus (484–425 BC) describes how Phoenician ships travelled right round Africa in less than three years, under the orders of the Egyptian King Necho (609–595 BC). Egyptian pictures provide conclusive evidence that wood — especially cedar — suitable for shipbuilding grew plentifully in the areas settled by the Phoenicians. The Egyptians required this desirable timber for shipbuilding and other enterprises, and brought it to Egypt by sea. The Phoenicans, therefore, became familiar with their ships early on, and eventually overtook the Egyptians in the construction of sea-going ships and in sea travel.

It seems likely that the Phoenicians differentiated between various types of ship at an early stage, building merchant ships with full-bodied hulls as well as slimmer warships featuring a bow ram. The average length of the transport ships may have been around 30 to 33m, as most of the cedar trunks which are known to have been transported in ships, and were used in surviving Egyptian ships, are about 20m long. These transport ships had a beam of around 10m and drew about 2m, and would have displaced between 200 and 300 tons.

The ships were presumably built in shell form, ie the hull was CARVEL-planked, with ribs fitted later. In view of the extensive trade relations and sea connections which existed, it appears quite possible that sufficient quantities of naturally grown curved timbers could have been obtained, for example, from mangroves, which produce prolific curved branches, and other types of timber.The widely-held view is that the Egyptians knew about neither ribs nor keel, but this is not proven and now seems unlikely. For example, the Greek historian Herodotus reported that he was familiar with 'ships' ribs' (ie hull frames). The Egyptian ships were designed primarily for travelling on the Nile, and

Doge's BUCENTAUR also shared this name; they were like gondolas, but were larger and broader.

PERAMO: A small sailing vessel which was restricted to the Aegean, serving as a personnel and goods vessel in the ports, and for general work and fishing around the coasts. They remained in use until the beginning of the nineteenth century.

PETROLEUM CLIPPER: Around 1860, the first, small cargoes of petroleum barrels were transported to Europe from the North American ports of Philadelphia, New York and Baltimore, by the sailing ships plying the North Atlantic route. The first petroleum to reach Germany was imported via Bremen in 1862. The European demand for the commodity increased rapidly, especially for lighting, and by the 1870s petroleum had become an important freight cargo, with a large number of sailing ships dedicated exclusively to the transport of petroleum

barrels. These ships could carry an average cargo of more than 1000 barrels of petroleum, and nothing else. The smell of the substance was so penetrating that the vessels were rendered unfit for most other cargoes, apart from timber, coal or coke. For this reason newly-built ships were seldom used. Instead, old freight or emigration ships — one or two decades old — were brought as cheaply as possible, and pressed into service. Many different types of sailing ship were used for the petroleum route, but all sailing ships carrying petroleum in barrels came to be termed petroleum clippers by the seamen, regardless of the design and rig.

A good example of a genuine petroleum clipper was the American-built ship *Donald McKay*, which was bought by the Bartling shipping company of Bremen. In May 1879, this vessel set sail carrying the greatest load of its time: 14,450 barrels, a total of 728,365 American gallons (1 American gallon = 3.785 litres). Transporting cargo in barrels was expensive in time and labour and was an

Syrian-Roman cargo ship from Roman-occupied Lebanon on a Sidon sarcophagus, second and third century

therefore a keel and strengthening timbers were only required for special-purpose vessels. In contrast, the Phoenician ships were intended for coastal work, and had to be seaworthy. Although there is no clear evidence of this, we can assume that the Phoenicians took the state of Egyptian shipbuilding as their starting point, and continued development by adopting the keel and stiffening ribs occasionally used on Egyptian cargo ships and other vessels. They then refined the techniques to produce a standard method of construction based on keel and frames.

In spite of their large size, the Phoenician sea-going ships remained oared sailing ships, fitted with a mast and a large square sail. On each side of the stern there was a steering oar. According to Greek pictures, the Phoenician ships could be divided into cargo ships (cauloi) and battle or warships (hippoi: horse, warhorse). The rotund vessels depicted on the Assyrian KHORSABAD and NIMRUD reliefs are probably Phoenician merchant ships, while those with bow rams are probably Phoenician warships. At the time of the reliefs the Phoenicians were ruled by the Assyrians, hence we can assume that the picture of this combined Phoenician-Assyrian fleet was intended to celebrate a successful mutual undertaking. After suffering continued subjection at the hands of the Assyrians, the Phoenicians established a number of new settlements on the Mediterranean coasts, specially in Carthage, which was settled in 814 BC. (Phoenician, carthada: new city).

PIAHIAP: A light, two-masted pirate boat used in the Moluccan region. The vessels were 6 to 12m long, and carried a crew of between 25 and 75 men. They escorted the larger BALOUR on pirate raids. The hull was slender, and in consequence the boat was a fast sail in calm conditions, with the two sails rigged as on a chasse-marée. The foremast was raked slightly forward and the main mast slightly aft.

PIELSTEERT GALIOT: A seaman's term for a schooner-rigged GALIOT, usually built in lower Saxony, dating from around 1860, when the steam ship was in the ascendant. It was built in similar style to the larger brigs, barques and full-rigged ships, and featured a conspicuously projecting stern (pielsteert: low German for a tail high in the air).

PILOT BOAT, *pilot launch, pilot cutter*: Vessels specially engaged in the pilot service. Their purpose is to transport the pilot between the pilot station or pilot ship and the vessels requiring assistance.

The smaller pilot boats were rowing boats, which were fitted with cork or watertight buoyancy chambers to render them unsinkable, as they had to be capable of operating in stormy weather and heavy seas. A wide variety of vessels have been used as pilot boats, but in the sailing ship era oared sailing launches, sailing cutters and smaller schooners (pilot schooners) were particularly common.

The cutter rig was generally preferred, because it was easy to handle. Pilot boats had to be able to render pilot service to bring help to ships under all circumstances, and for this reason the vessel's sea-going qualities, steadiness and steering characteristics were of great importance. Pilot boats also had to be easy to turn, and easy to handle close to land. The majority of these manoeuvrable and seaworthy vessels were between 10 and 15m in length.

PILOT SCHOONER: A fast, sea-going schooner originally developed on the American east coast for pilot duty, and which remained in service until the 1930s. They were equipped to permit several pilots to remain on board for a considerable period. When a ship requiring a pilot arrived at port, the pilot would be transferred to it on a small rowing boat. The American pilot schooner eventually became a forerunner of the modern schooner yacht. The easily-managed schooner rig had clear advantages over other types, and by the end of the sailing ship era most northern European pilot vessels were fast, two-masted schooners.

Dutch pilot schooner, ca 1890

Ships and boats in the late seventeenth century on the Maas off Rotterdam. In the centre of the picture is an English yacht similar to the Dutch state yachts. On the left a three-masted Dutch warship under the state flag

Ships and boats in the late seventeenth century off Amsterdam. Behind the rowing yacht is an admiralty state yacht and a warship. Painting by A Stork

The jacht Heinrich, *40 tons, built in 1862, home port Barth*

Full-rigged ship Ennerdale, *built by W H Potter & Co, Liverpool, 1874,* Museumsheft, Rostock Maritime Museum

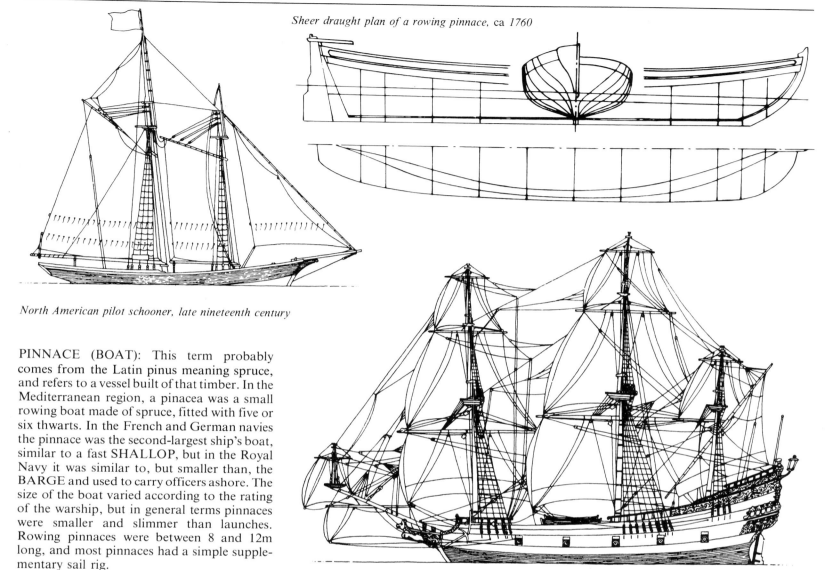

Sheer draught plan of a rowing pinnace, ca 1760

North American pilot schooner, late nineteenth century

PINNACE (BOAT): This term probably comes from the Latin pinus meaning spruce, and refers to a vessel built of that timber. In the Mediterranean region, a pinacea was a small rowing boat made of spruce, fitted with five or six thwarts. In the French and German navies the pinnace was the second-largest ship's boat, similar to a fast SHALLOP, but in the Royal Navy it was similar to, but smaller than, the BARGE and used to carry officers ashore. The size of the boat varied according to the rating of the warship, but in general terms pinnaces were smaller and slimmer than launches. Rowing pinnaces were between 8 and 12m long, and most pinnaces had a simple supplementary sail rig.

In India, the term referred to a medium-sized sailing ship of the mid nineteenth century, but this was probably an abbreviation for pinnace ship.

PINNACE (SHIP): In the sixteenth and seventeenth centuries, this term was used generically in Holland, France and England for small, armed, three-masted ships of around 35m length. Originally, they were equipped with about 18 guns, and later about 30 and were employed much like the later FRIGATE. The Dutch East Indies vessels were for the most part large pinnaces, of around 45m length. The hull was similar to that of the unarmed FLEUTE, but was slimmer, and had a square tuck (a transom stern which continued down below the waterline). The stern gallery usually extended upward to form a rather high but imposing structure. The ships had two full-length decks, a forecastle and a half-deck aft. The two forward masts were each rigged with two square sails, while the mizzen mast had a square topsail above the lateen sail. The bowsprit supported a small lower spritsail and an upper spritsail. There was also a small square sail set on a short, vertical mast on the peak of the bowsprit.

Seventeenth-century pinnace ship with square sails on the fore and main masts

Dutch pinnace ship at anchor in port, painting by Bonaventura Peeters, 1636

Pinke from Genoa, ca *1800*

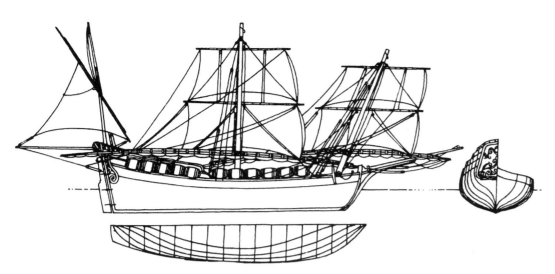

PINKE, *pinke, chitiha*: A three-masted 200- to 300-ton coastal sailing vessel used in the western Mediterranean in the fifteenth century, and thus a contemporary of the CARAVEL. The type survived until the end of the nineteenth century. The fore part of the deck tapered sharply, while the after part of the ship featured a tall, narrow, extended superstructure which included the deckhouse and an enclosed cabin. The foremast was raked forward and the after mast raked aft. For long voyages the lateen sails which were usually set would be replaced with square sails, the long lateen spars being stowed on deck.

PIRAGUA: *see* PIROGUE.

PIROGUE, *piragua, pirogua, piroge*: A dugout fitted with additional plank strakes to increase the freeboard. This simple method of boatbuilding evolved independently in various parts of the world including Europe, Mexico, the American northwest coast, the Santa Barbara islands, the lesser Antilles, Asia and the South Seas.

The extra side planks were fixed by a variety of methods. Quite frequently they were sewn onto the dugout or in some cases cleats were left projecting when the planks were cut, as on the Nordic boats. Holes were then drilled through the cleats, and the ribs and planks were bound together. On the Tongan Islands it was normal to link one smaller and one larger

pirogue together in parallel, spaced a fixed distance apart by a platform, to form a double-boat.

War pirogues of the South Sea islanders were sometimes decorated with carved wooden human heads and had rich decorations on the sides. They were propelled by 30 to 40 persons, their shovel-shaped paddles operated in a strict rhythm.

PLATT BOAT: Literally a flat-bottomed boat; a mid eighteenth-century northern French military vessel employed as a transport for infantry and cavalry units. The vessel was around 30m long and 8m broad and had a flat bottom. The freeboard was around 25m.

PLATTE: A mid nineteenth-century two-masted fishing vessel of northern France. It

was a full-bodied, shallow-draught vessel, rigged with lugsail and foresail. The platte was 9.3m long and 3.1m wide, and displaced about 10 tons. Such vessels were still in use in the twentieth century on the French Atlantic coast for oyster and mussel fishing.

PLÄTTE: A simple flat-bottomed vessel for transporting rock salt on mountain rivers in the high-altitude mining districts in the Salzburg region of Germany. The plätte was similar to the PRAHM, with tapered bow and stern, and was steered downstream in the manner of a raft, with the boatman wielding long poles similar to oars. When the vessel reached its destination its structural timber was sold as well as its cargo. The boats fell out of use at the end of the nineteenth century.

PLEIT, *pleyt*: A coastal merchant sailing ship of the Hanseatic period, and the fifteenth century in particular, carrying up to about 160 tons. The Flemish and Brabant pleiten of the Netherlands and Belgium were probably even older. The large pleiten were sea-going ships, employed mainly around the coasts, while the smaller vessels, which were mentioned in documents as early as the thirteenth century, were inland vessels. In the late 1930s, a pleit was measured at 23.5m long before it was scrapped. The pleit was similar to the Dutch TJALK, but somewhat smaller, and larger than the Belgian OTTER.

PLUTT: A variant of the small Dutch SCHOKKER or PUNT boat, it had an overall length of 8 to 10m . Examples of the type existed amongst Dutch yachts until quite recently.

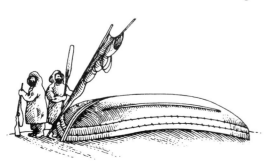

Northern Siberian pirogue

Three-masted polacre, ca *1650*

POJAMA: A Swedish rowing gunboat built in the 1770s by FH of Chapman armed with two traversing 24-pounders at each end of the flush deck and twelve swivel guns. It was propelled by 16 pairs of wars or a ketch rig with square main topsail.

POLACCA, *polacre, pollacca, polacka, polacker*: An Italian sailing ship of medium size, used in the Mediterranean in the sixteenth and seventeenth centuries. The vessel's main mast was a pole mast (polacca mast: pole mast without topmasts), and was square-rigged. Lateen sails were retained on the other masts until the nineteenth century. Eventually, the square sails common in northern Europe were adopted in the Mediterranean, but the transition from the exclusive use of lateen sails to a hybrid rig including square sails only took place gradually. During this transitional period the square-rigged pole mast was preferred, as the smooth mast permitted the crew to lower the upper yard down almost to the level of the lower yard from the deck, in similar fashion to a lateen rig.

Three-masted ships whose lower masts were made in one piece, but which were in other respects rigged like a barque, were known as polacca BARQUEs. Similarly, ships with two pole masts, rigged like a brig, were termed polacca BRIGs. In more recent times one-piece pole masts made of metal have also been termed polacca masts.

POLE EWER, *pole galeasse, pole kuff*: A single-masted EWER with a pole mast, which could not be extended by means of topmasts. Up to the end of the nineteenth century the pole ewers carried a simple rig consisting of a large square sail. Other ships types, such as the GALEASSE and the KUFF, were also given the prefix pole when their masts were of this simple design.

POLKA BARQUE: A German sailor's term for a three-masted schooner with square sails on the foremast, square and gaff sails on the middle mast, and gaff sails only on the aft mizzenmast. This type of combined rig evolved around 1840, under the influence of the American schooner, and was aimed at simplifying sail handling. *See also* SCHOONER-BARQUE.

POLT, *pult*; A simple, hardchine boat varying in length between 3 and 6m, built on the island of Rügen. The boat is flat-bottomed, has virtually no sheer, and features either a transom stern raked gently aft, or a pointed stern. The boats can be rowed or sculled.

POLYER: Generic term for those ancient Greek ships which had multiple rows of oars, in contrast to the MONER, the Greek ship with a single bank of oars.

POMOR BOAT: *pomor ship*: This term arose in the nineteenth century with the develop-

Russian pomor ship in the port of Hammerfest, ca 1890

ment of a particular form of trade between Russian sailing ships, to which the name refers, and fishermen of northern Norway. The pomor trade was an exchange of goods, with Russian agricultural products being exchanged for dried and salt fish in the north Norwegian port of Hammerfest.

POMPEII GRAFFITO: A representation of a cargo vessel with a towed ship's boat, shown on a graffito decoration on the wall of a Roman merchant's house. Pompeii, close by Vesuvius, was buried in AD79 when the volcano erupted. Excavations were begun in 1748, but not until 1806 did the work begin in earnest. The uncovered city gives us an unusually profound insight into the ways of

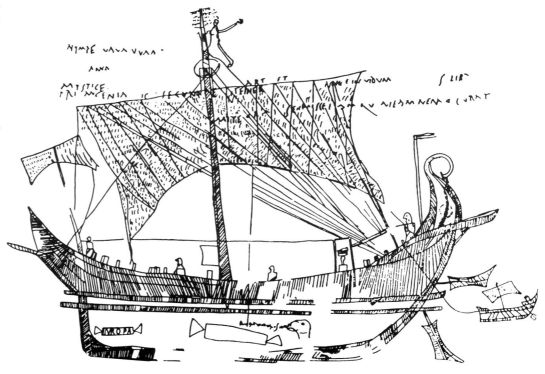

Pompeian graffito, Roman freight ship, ca 50 BC

Paviljoen poon with gaff mainsail, nineteenth century (model)

life and the culture of the Roman Imperial period.

Amongst the most significant finds relating to ships is the graffito decoration, which dates from around 50 BC. A graffito is a wall plaster decoration, in which layers of plaster of different colours are applied on top of each other, so that multi-coloured pictures emerge when the surface is scratched to varying depths.

The Roman cargo sailing ship depicted is probably a CORBITA, and the scratched inscription *Europa* could have been the name of the ship. The rig is of the type common at the time with a rectangular mainsail on the mainmast and a rectangular foresail set on a small forward-raked mast, called the artemon.

PONTO: An early medieval gallic ship, of heavy construction, with a high freeboard.

PONTOON, *floating pontoon*: A square vessel, with flat bottom, vertical sides and flat, vertical or raked bow and stern. Pontoons are moored utility vessels used for carrying stationary structures such as piers or pontoon bridges. They are also used for raising and lifting. Because of their role their handling characteristics are relatively unimportant.

POON: A generic term for TJALK-like southern Dutch inland freight sailing ships such as the Zeeuwsche poon from Zeeland, the Paviljoen poon and other poon types. They had a full-bodied flat-bottomed hull, virtually no keel, and leeboards. In comparison with the tjalk, the vessels had a more pronounced sheer and featured large loading hatches. They were single-masted, originally rigged with a spritsail

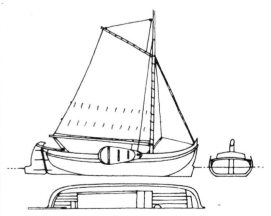

Gaff-rigged poon without bowsprit

and later with a large gaff mainsail and one or two foresails. Early ships had no bowsprit.

According to a report by Lecomte (1831), these ships were built in sizes from 16 to 60 tons cargo capacity in Alblasserdam, Boskoop, Dortrecht, Ijsselmonde, Willemstad and various small towns on the Ijssel. A medium-sized poon was about 15m long with a beam of 4.5m.

POST SHIP: In the later eighteenth century, Royal Navy 28-gun ships were the smallest

Poon with bowsprit and spritsail, late eighteenth century (model)

vessels described as FRIGATES. However, smaller Sixth Raters of 20 and 24 guns were also commanded by full, or post, captains (unlike sloops, brigs and other 'unrated' ships in the charge of a commander or lieutenant) so these vessels came to be called post ships to differentiate them from the larger frigate and smaller sloop. They were the equivalent of the French Navy's CORVETTE.

POUCAN: *see* GALWAY HOOKER.

POTBOAT *see* TIGARI

PRAENESTE SHIP RELIEF: A bas-relief dating from about 30 BC, which survived in the ruins of the Temple Pimigenia near Praeneste not far from Rome. The reliefs depict an oared ship, which is presumably the flagship of the Roman general and statesman Marcus Antonius (82–30 BC). The ship is shown carrying Roman legionaries prepared for battle, short swords at the ready. Until recently the relief was thought to show a Roman BIREME, but recent research indicates that it is a TRIREME. This proposition is based on the fact that two warriors are shown

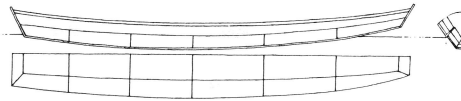

Small Swedish clinker-built prahm, ca 1760

standing on the lateral outrigger (parodos); the blades of the third bank of oars could be shipped here. As a flagship was generally large and particularly powerful and the Romans were very familiar with Greek warships, this assumption could well be true. At the bow of the ship there is a crocodile. This could be the emblem of an Egyptian legion, as Egypt was then under Roman rule.

PRAHI: A two-hulled Tahitian vessel consisting of two plank-built, keeled hulls set parallel to each other, linked by a platform with a deckhouse built on top. The prahi was decorated with wooden carvings at the bow and sometimes at the stern, like the New Zealand pirogues.

PRAHM, *pram*: A vessel similar to a PONTOON, and usually open. The remains of pontoon-like vessels have been discovered in several different regions, proving that the relatively simple prahm form developed independently in various centres of settlement, some of the vessels being quite large. For example, the remains of an oak hull prahm were found on Falsterbo in Denmark, the hull of which was about 13.5m long and 3.5m broad. *See* FALSTERBO PRAHMS.

In the Hanseatic period, prahms were often used as lighters. The terms präm and praam feature in the Stralsund port order of 1278 and other port documents, referring to shallow-draught, low-sided vessels. The term and the type were widespread in the entire Baltic region and the North Sea coasts of Holland and France. In Holland the term applied to a single-masted freight ship with flat bottom,

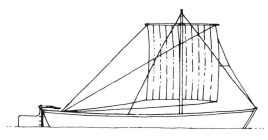

Rostock prahm with square sail

which was particularly full-bodied at the hull ends. It was designed for shallows and shoal waters, and carried leeboards.

Later prahms had no sail and were simply general-purpose auxiliary vessels similar to a pontoon. They were full-bodied, broad and low, with no bulwarks, hull ends of simple form, and without means of propulsion. The term pram has come to refer to a flat upturned bow, whatever type of vessel it is applied to.

PRAM, *pram dinghy*: A round-bottomed, open, planked boat with a raked transom at each end. It is not however double-ended — the bow is narrower than the stern. There is no keel, although some prams are fitted with a skeg. The pram originated in Scandinavia as a fishing vessel, sailed as well as rowed — in Norway for example it was rigged with a lugsail — but the basic design has been adopted throughout northern Europe.

PRAU, *prahu, proa*: A general term applied to a variety of Indonesian and Malayan sailing craft, both those of strictly traditional build

Dutch sailing prahm, ca 1800 (model)

and those influenced by European designs. Such boats may have traditional Oceanic lateen or tilted rectangular sails, but some are gaff rigged in the European fashion. Many retain quarter rudders, but some have stern rudders. A few are DOUBLE OUTRIGGER BOATS. The term proa is sometimes applied more generally to incorporate SOUTH SEAS boats.

PREUSSEN: The only five-masted ship in the world to be built as a five-masted full-rigged ship (square sails on all masts). The *Preussen* was built between 1902 and 1904 in Geestemünde at the Tecklenborg yard for the Laeisz sailing ship company. The specifications of this large sailing ship were as follows: length overall 133.19m, length between perpendiculars 121.92m, beam 16.40m, draught 8.23m, freeboard 9.909m, total sail area 5560m^2, crew 48 men, weight of empty ship 3550 tons, total load 8000 tons, height of the mainmast (from mast base to masthead) 68m, displacement 4765NRT and 5081BRT. The ship could achieve speeds up to 18 knots with a relatively small crew. The sail area of 5560m^2 consisted of 46 sails, which were hoisted by hand winches alone; the running rigging included 1200 blocks, 17km of rope, 24km of wire cable, and 700m of chain. In a

storm, up to eight men were required to handle the wheel.

The ship proved uneconomical to run, as the full cargo capacity was never fully exploited. There was not sufficient cargo for the outward voyages and the full tonnage was only used on the return voyage. The *Preussen* only twice carried a full load on its outward runs, one of them being her fourteenth voyage on 6 November 1910, destination Valparaiso. During this voyage she was rammed by the English passenger ship *Brighton* in hazy conditions in the English channel; the forward rigging and part of the foremast were badly damaged in the accident. This greatly reduced the ship's manoeuvring ability. Shortly before reaching Dover a storm blew up, the tug's tow cable failed, and the ship drove past the jetties off Dover and beached below the cliffs. Fortunately, not one life was lost, but the steel-hulled sailing ship was a total loss. *See also* FIVE-MASTED SHIP.

PRISON SHIP, *hulk*: A ship withdrawn from active service, and employed as a prison. They were used in France, Great Britain and Spain from the eighteenth to the twentieth century.

PRIVATEERS: Officially sanctioned private warships carrying commissions which allowed

them to attack the commerce of the enemy. They were often converted merchant ships but at various times specially constructed ships were employed. Some powerfully armed merchantmen on ordinary trading voyages would carry the necessary 'letter of marque' which would allow them to attack targets if the opportunities arose, and the term eventually become synonymous with privateer.

PRIZE, *prize ship*: A ship and its cargo captured in wartime and claimed as booty. The victorious ship would then place a detachment on the prize, which would be used as best befitted the capturer (supply of provisions etc). Ships of a neutral state were also commandeered if they were carrying contraband.

PUNT: A small, flat-bottomed paddled, rowed or poled boat with a simple hull shape used for duck and wild fowl shooting. The

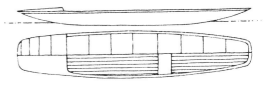

A punt

The Preussen *beached below the cliffs of Dover*

waterline is almost rectangular, only tapering at the extreme ends of the boat. The bottom is straight for half the hull length, rising for the last quarter at each and over the whole width of the hull, resulting in a shallow-draught shape.

PUNT KAHN: A barge used for fishing and inland cargo transport, propelled by punt pole. For small boats and shallow waters the pole needs to be no more than a simple thin rod. The punter usually stands in a fixed place in the barge. Heavy cargo barges, on the other hand, require long, strong poles, called quants, fitted with a crossbar at the top end, against which the punter can rest his shoulder for extra leverage. To ensure that the barge is propelled forward as far as possible by each stroke of the quant, running planks are fitted on both sides of the vessel, extending almost the entire length of the barge, for the punter to walk along. The bottom end of the pole is fitted with points and saucer-like plates, rather like the fittings on a ski stick, which are designed to ensure that the punt pole finds a secure hold on any type of river bottom.

PÜNTE: A relatively shallow-draught ship employed as a coastal or river transport. It was almost rectangular in shape, and was rigged with square sails on one or two masts. The ship's ends were either rounded (rundpünte) or pointed (spitzpünte). The latter type were built on a keel, and were used for coastal work, while the rounded-hull types were river vessels. The ships could displace up to 150 tons, and were sailed in the North and Baltic Seas with a cutter rig.

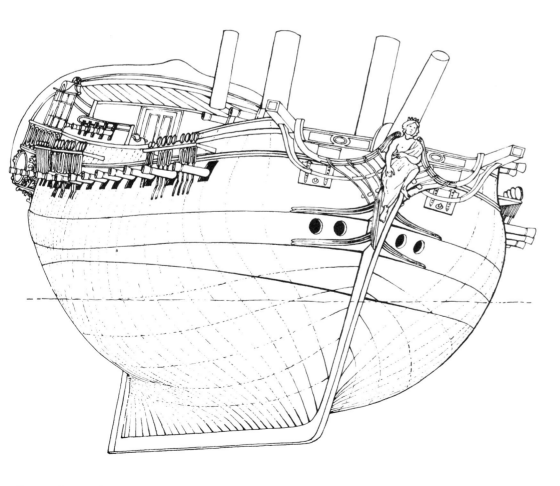

Foreward view of a three-masted privateer, ca 1700–50

Q

Quffa, Mesopotamian-Indian round framework boat

QUADERGHA, *Quadirgha kadirga*: Turkish term for the GALLEY.

QUADRIREME: An ancient Roman oared warship whose name is based on the Latin quadri meaning four, and remus meaning oar. It could mean a ship with four men operating each oar, or a ship with four rowing banks stepped above each other in a similar fashion to the BIREME and TRIREME. *See also* QUINQUEREME.

QUFFA, *guffa*: A circular boat made from coiled basketry and made watertight by a coat of bitumen, found in Iraq. Historically there was a circular, Mesopotamian boat consisting of a skin-covered framework, in use around 5000 years ago. Its homes were on the Euphrates and Tigris. Pictures of these boats from the seventh century BC have survived on a relief plate found in the Assyrian capital of Niniveh. *See also* SKIN BOAT.

The historian Herodotus of Halicarnassos (484–420 BC) reported seeing circular boats on the Euphrates during a journey to Babylon. He describes how the Armenian boats travelling upstream to Babylon were woven from wicker-work like baskets. The vessels had no clearly defined bow or stern, were covered with animal skins, and carried straw or some other animal foodstuff spread on the floor. Where possible, the skin covering was omitted, and replaced with a sealing layer of natural bitumen. The quffa was built in various sizes to serve as a cargo and personnel-carrying vessel on rivers, but was also used by fishermen on the coast. Because of the simple construction, vessels for one or two persons were the norm, but quffas were also built to carry up to 10 persons and several horses. The practice of binding several circular boats together to form a platform was also known, the platforms being used as floating bridges.

These lightweight vessels were very unlikely to capsize even in rapids, provided that they were deeply enough laden.

QUARTER BOAT: Usually a light ship's boat, carried on davits over the ship's quarters. On sailing ships it was often the captain's gig. *See also* GIG.

QUASE: A two- or three-masted fishing vessel, 9 to 10m in length and about 3m wide, usually rigged with spritsails, but occasionally with gaff sails, and especially common in the bays of Kiel and Flensburg until the end of the nineteenth century.

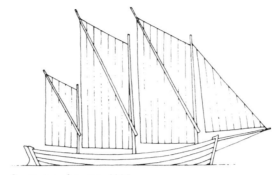

Sprit-rigged quase, 1885

QUATZE, *quatz, sea quatze:* A broad sailing vessel which was used to store live fish, and transport them at sea and along the coasts. They could be open, half- or fully decked boats, and were employed at Rügen and on the Pomeranian coast until the beginning of the present century.

The ships had a CLINKER-built outer skin. The fish well, the compartment in which the fish were kept alive, was 5 to 8m long, and was partitioned off from the rest of the vessel by means of transverse bulkheads. Holes were bored through the outer planking, to allow an adequate through-flow of fresh seawater in the fish well. This method of keeping fish had been in use since the beginning of the seventeenth century, although the transport of living fish from the island of Rügen is only documented since 1860. The quatze also carried freshwater fish such as roach, perch and pike to the main inland markets of Stralsund, Greifswald, Wolgast and Barth. The boats also travelled to Denmark and Sweden and even Norway and Finland, where fish were bought and then transported home.

The quatzen were around 12 to 17m in length, and were built in Wolgast, Ueckermünde, Neuwarp and Wollin. The rig consisted of a thick pole mast and a loose footed gaff mainsail. The small quatze *Colberg*, ex *Speculant*, became particularly well known after she had been bought and armed to act as guard ship for Kolberg (Kolobrzeg) in July 1812. The *Colberg* was 12m long and 4m in breadth, with a hold depth of only 0.78m. This single-masted vessel was fitted with two six-pounder guns in 1812 and two three-pounder swivels in 1813. Although a few quatzen were built after 1918 they were fitted with auxiliary engines and the last examples disappeared in the 1930s.

QUINQUEREME: A Roman ship with five slaves to each oar, or with oar banks arranged in fives. The literal translation of five-oar ship, indicates a rowing ship with five banks of oars, but they would have to have been staggered in height, in a similar fashion to the BIREME, TRIREME, and possibly the QUADRIREME. Such five-deckers could only have been rowed with the very short, jerky rowing technique which was standard at the time, and if the oar banks were displaced in height by no more than half the height of a man's body.

Quatze from the Oder Haff, early twentieth century

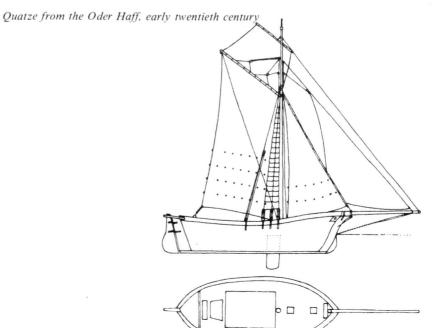

R

RABELO, *barco rabelo*: A specialized craft of the River Duoro, Portugal, used to transport barrels of wine down river to Oporto. Such craft have been in existence since at least the ninth century. Rabelos were about 20m in length with a beam of 5m, capable of carrying about 50 barrels (22,750 litres). Characteristic of this boat was a large square sail, and a tall platform upon which the steersman stood. The steering oar was up to 10m in length (hence the name of the craft: literally 'boat with a tail'), counter weighted at the loom so that the blade would float in the water at about the same draught as the vessel. By this design tremendous leverage and great manoeverability was obtained, as well as giving the steersman an advantageous view of the river ahead. Because of recently constructed dams, rabelos are no longer in use, although some are preserved for regattas by wine companies in Oporto.

RACING BOATS: General term for craft, both dinghies and keelboats, designed specifically for competition, as opposed to cruising boats, which seldom take part in anything other than local racing, and cruiser racers which are highbrid craft based on racing boats but often heavier and with more or less fully-fitted accommodations. See the table OLYMPIC boats and the individual class entries, which are arranged in alphabetical order.

RACING ROWING BOAT: A type of boat whose racing history can be traced back to ancient times. Originally, the races took place during festivals and other community occasions. Gondola races were held in Venice from about 1300 to 1500 and were very popular. Modern competitive rowing developed from the rowing skills of sailors, fishermen and ferrymen, and was promoted in England in particular.

The English universities had a decisive influence on the development of rowing as a team sport; the first eight-man racing took place at Eton in 1811. The now world-famous eight-man races between the universities of Oxford and Cambridge have taken place on a regular basis since 1823.

The international union, of which the national rowing clubs are members, is the Fédération Internationale des Sociétés d'Aviron (FISA). The annual European and world championships are organized by FISA, and the body also carries out preparatory work relating to the Olympic rowing events.

Over a period of slightly more than a century great efforts have been made to develop types and shapes of racing boat which combine minimum resistance, high directional stability and best possible rowing characteristics for racing. The result has been two basic groups of boat types: the gig and the racing shell proper.

The gig represents the preferred training and

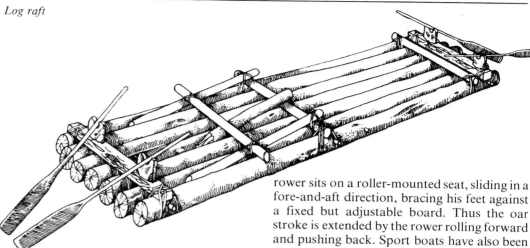

Log raft

practice boat for rowing races. It is CLINKER-built with a structural keel, and continues the design principles of the Viking boats in respect of construction and shape. The boat hulls are usually built from light timbers such as spruce, cedar or larch.

The boats are categorized according to whether they are rowed or sculled, whether they have a cox or not, and according to the number of oarsmen. They include two-man boats, four-man boats and eight-man boats, all with cox.

The sculled boats include the coxless and coxed scull, the coxed and coxless pairs and the coxed fours and eights.

The differences between oar and scull lie in the method of operating them as well as their respective dimensions and mass. An oar provides propulsion on one side of the boat only, with both the oarsman's hands working the oar. In a sculled boat two sculls are operated by one man, so that propulsion is equally divided between the two sides.

The boats are sometimes fitted with double rowlocks suitable for oars or sculls, depending on the type of practice required, so that one vessel can be used for training in both disciplines. The average size for an oar is 3.75m long, 140 to 160mm blade width, and weighing 4kg. Sculls, in contrast, are 2.95m long with a blade width of 150m and a mass of 2kg.

Amongst the best known rowing boats are the following: coxed and coxless pair, coxed and coxless four, and coxed eight; the most popular sculled boats include the one-man (Scandinavian term: skiff), the double, and the coxed and coxless four.

The hull of a racing shell is built very light (using plywood or high technology man-made materials like kevlar), and is very narrow and slender. Because of the boat's small beam and high centre of gravity, it is only stable when occupied, the occupants providing, in effect, trimmable ballast. Considerable demands are made on the hull in terms of structural rigidity and external surface quality, as the outer skin is only a few millimetres thick. The rowlocks are mounted on light outrigger struts, and the

rower sits on a roller-mounted seat, sliding in a fore-and-aft direction, bracing his feet against a fixed but adjustable board. Thus the oar stroke is extended by the rower rolling forward and pushing back. Sport boats have also been developed with a fixed seat, and outriggers which slide forward and back. The oarsmen sit with their back to the direction of travel, while the cox, who is as light as possible, usually sits aft, looking forward.

Usual striking rates are between 32 and 36 strokes per minute, but the rate can be increased up to 44 per minute. The following table indicates the relationships between boat types, striking rates and speeds.

Boat type	Striking rate per min	Speed in km h
One-man (6–7m length)	25–30	13.5
Two-man (around 10m length)	28–32	15
Four-man (around 12–13m length)	30–40	16
Eight-man (around 16–18m length)	35–40	17.5

RAFT: A buoyant structure which floats because the density of the raft material is less than that of water. In forested regions with wide rivers, the timber-built raft was often of greater importance to the settlement areas and ports than were cargo or passenger vessels. Gigantic wooden rafts up to 200m long were floated downstream on European, American and Siberian rivers, especially in the spring, when the ice had melted. This practice continued into the nineteenth century. The rafts were formed by lashing tree trunks together — the number depending on the conditions obtaining on the river — using transverse logs or hawsers, sometimes arranged in several layers. The raftsmen built the vessels as well as navigating them, and often lived for days on end on the raft, where they even had a cooking area

Among the most famous of raft vessels made of materials other than wood are the ambatche rafts, the papyrus rafts of the Nile, and the Chinese and South Seas rafts made of bamboo. Those made of papyrus, bamboo or bush material were sometimes constructed in a shape similar to a boat, with upward-curving ends. On the Arabian coasts, especially in Oman, the fishing tribes constructed sea-going rafts with 10 to 12 trunks, and fitted them with masts and sails.

The original inhabitants of northern Japan, the Ainu, built a special type of lightweight log raft, with the joints well sealed, and a layer of planks fitted on top. The result was a hybrid form of vessel, whose buoyancy was a combination of the material's low density and its displacement.

RAFT BAG: A bag made of waterproof sailcloth, which was employed by the cavalry around 1900 for the purpose of crossing rivers or other waters. The raft bag was packed out with straw, reeds, foliage or similar materials.

RAFT PIROGUE: A log raft of boat-like appearance built by the inhabitants of the Caroline island of Yap. The core of the craft was a single, large tree trunk with tapered ends. One each side of this trunk a further, thinner log was fitted, its ends also tapered. The result was a platform which was shaped like a boat. The vessel was fitted with a raised framework made of bamboo stems and four masts with mat sails.

RAOUL DIVING BOAT: A diving boat designed for sponge fishing on the Mediterranean coast, developed by the Frenchman Abbé Raoul around 1910. It was 5m long and 1.6m wide. Driven by hand, it was intended to travel along the seabed on wheels.

The boat was designed to carry a crew of two, who could operate mechanical gripping devices from inside the boat to collect the sponges and deposit them in containers.

RAISING JACK: A pontoon-shaped hull fitted with a capstan or winch and a trestle framework, for lifting heavy loads.

RASEYL: A term applied to the three-masted Hanseatic ships of the fifteenth and sixteenth centuries, usually rigged with square sails. The term was applied to the HULK in particular. This ship was about 23m long and 7 to 8m wide and could carry around 200 to 250 tons. These vessels were larger than the COG, and also differed in their build and in the shape of the stern. They were CARVEL-built and had a transom stern, while the cog was CLINKER-built and had a rounded or pointed stern.

REED RAFT, *reed boat*: A boat-shaped raft comprising many individual bundles of reeds bound side by side and on top of each other, with tapered, upward-curving ends and a trough-shaped central section.

Reed rafts were developed because of their simple construction, and they remain in use in regions where timber is scarce, including east Africa, the Persian Gulf, the Ganges and other Indian waters.

Among the best known boat-shaped reed rafts are the Egyptian PAPYRUS RAFTS the TOTORAs of Lake Titicaca, and the ancient

RA I, reconstruction of a large papyrus reed raft, used to cross the Atlantic by Thor Heyerdahl in 1969

Peruvian CABALLITOS. The oldest Far Eastern pictures of this type of reed raft were discovered in Mohenjo Daro, on the lower Indus river. They were found on a seal, an amulet, and a shard from a pot dating from 3000 to 2500 BC. One of the reed rafts depicted already shows a small deckhouse, and the other even has a mast with two yards. The load-carrying capacity and durability of reed rafts are not good, because of the tendency of the material to soak up water and rot. Various boat-shaped reed rafts have been covered with animal skins in an effort to overcome these disadvantages. For these vessels the term reed boat is more accurate, as the covering transforms them into displacement vessels. The historian Herodotus mentions that some Egyptian papyrus boats were sheathed in hide.

RESEARCH SHIP: A ship built, equipped and employed specifically for the discovery of shipping routes, or to investigate areas of the sea and coasts with the aim of gaining hydrological, meterological and biological knowledge. The tasks of the original research ships were the discovery of new sea passages and the search for unknown lands, usually with a strong commercial motive. Since these voyages were almost indistinguishable from normal trading ventures, the ships used for this purpose were mostly proven small or medium-sized types, with excellent sea-going qualities and the best possible manoeuvring characteristics, equipped with the supplies and equipment required for long voyages. Among the earliest known ship voyages whose purpose was discovery were the voyages of Egyptian sailing ships to the land of Punt between the seventeenth and fourteenth centuries BC(see Hatshepsut ship relief), the

Greek and Phoenician voyages in the Mediterranean, the probable rounding of Africa by the Phoenicians, and the voyages to the North and Atlantic crossings of the Vikings. The first of the great mediaeval voyages of discovery were the long disputed voyages to the Far East by the Venetian Marco Polo in the thirteenth century, and the Portuguese voyages of discovery, especially to the north-west coast of Africa, under the aegis of Prince Henry the Navigator.

Further voyages of discovery followed in the fifteenth and sixteenth centuries, with the aim of finding the eastern and western routes to India: Bartolomeo Diaz (Cape of Good Hope, 1488), Vasco da Gama (sailed round Africa and to Goa in India, 1498), Christopher Columbus (West Indian islands, Bahama, Cuba, 1492; Honduras, 1502), and the voyage of Ferdinand de Magellan (voyage through the Magellan Straits into the Pacific Ocean, Marian Islands, Philippines, 1515). At the beginning of the seventeenth century came the famous voyages of Henry Hudson (Spitzbergen, 1607; Hudson Bay, 1609) and of Abel Tasman (circumnavigation of Australia, Tasmania, New Zealand, 1642).

In the year 1400 only about 10 per cent of the world's surface was known to Western Europe. By the end of the sixteenth century the figure had risen to 30 per cent, much of the increase being due to the many voyages of discovery undertaken in the two intervening centuries. By 1700 virtually two thirds of the Earth's surface was documented, although there were still many 'blank spots'. After 1700 the ships, now better equipped for research work, were used primarily for further exploration of the sea and coastal regions. Cartographers, botanists, meteorologists, draughtsmen and artists were all included on these voyages, to provide more expert judgments and records of the research efforts. Examples are the voyages of James Cook (1768 in *Endeavour*), George Nares (1872 in *Challenger*), F Nansen (1893 in *Fram*), Charles Darwin (1831 in *Beagle*). Amongst the developments of a general type which faciliated this kind of research voyage were: exact determination of time by means of chronometer (Hugghens 1660, Harrison 1737), and navigational aids such as wind and current charts, sailing instructions and log books (M F Maury, 1806–1873).

The last third of the eighteenth century was a fruitful period for sea expeditions equipped specifically for purposes of scientific research, voyages supported by far-sighted individuals such as Benjamin Franklin, Conde Massighi and later Alexander von Humboldt. This period saw the beginnings of scientifically-based marine geographical research. The decades which followed produced wealthy proponents of particular areas of research, such as Duke Albert I of Monaco (1848–1922). He promoted research into deep sea areas out of personal interest, and founded in Monaco an important institute and museum relating to the plants and animals of the deep sea.

Among the best known historical ships concerned with deep sea research were the English *Challenger* (1872–1876), and the German *Gazelle* (1874–1876). In the nineteenth century research voyages continued unabated, now attempting to find northern sea passages, and the North Polar sea. Important groundwork, on which later research voyages were based, was carried out by Captain M F Maury in the 1850s. He introduced the modern form of logbook, now standard on all sea-going ships, in which he recorded the essential details of sea and weather conditions. General knowledge of ocean navigation could then be extended by exchanging and examining these ships' diaries. For instance, the logbooks of German sailing ships, which are archived in the marine weather centre at Hamburg, contain about 20 million items of information regarding weather conditions on all the world's oceans, including air pressure, wind speed and direction, air and water temperature, cloud, weather and swell, and visibility. Later on, weather observation ships were stationed in particular sea regions. The great era of the research ship did not begin until the end of the sailing ship epoch. There are now a great number of research ships in use for a wide variety of research duties.

REVENUE CUTTER: A vessel used by the revenue service (as forerunner of Customs and Excise) to combat smuggling. At first these craft tended to be CUTTER-rigged, but the term was eventually extended to cover any vessel employed in this service.

RHIN EWER: A north German ewer of the eighteenth and early nineteenth centuries, employed for transporting vegetables, and built on the Hershorner and Kremper Rhin, at Elmshorn and in Glückstadt on the lower Elbe. It was a shallow-draught vessel, and relatively low, narrow and fast. The average dimensions were 12.5 to 15m length and 3.5 to 4m width. The rhin or vegetable ewers often featured painted bow decorations, depicting flowers or twigs.

RIDDARSHOLMEN SHIP: The remains of a ship dating from about 1375, found at Nordberg in Sweden during dredging operations. It was a CLINKER-built vessel 15m long and 4.5m wide, built with oak planks and ribs. The 7m long keelson (a fore-and-aft beam set on top of the keel inside the boat) was of pine.

ROMAN SHIPS: The classical Roman seagoing ship of ancient times. The Roman Empire grew to be a dominant maritime power, controlling the mediterranean region, and this position is mirrored in the Roman term 'mare internum' (internal sea), which signified the Mediterranean. Rome's rise was preceded by the decline of the Athenians' dominance in the eastern and central part of the Mediterranean after their military defeats on land at the hands of the Macedonians.

In the mid third century BC Rome began to extend the sea connections which had been controlled by the Phoenicians, Greeks and Carthaginians until then. Although Rome possessed no significant maritime power before the outbreak of the first Punic War against Carthage in 264 BC (the last Punic War took place between 148 and 146 BC), it was only four years later, in 260 BC, that a Roman war fleet consisting of 100 PENTERS and 20 TRIREMES was able to claim an important victory against the Carthaginians, sinking or defeating 50 enemy ships. The battle took place off Mylae, present-day Milazzo (Sicily), and was described by the Greek historian Polybius (210–127 BC).

Thus within a few years the land-based Roman army had achieved the amazing feat of

Roman cargo vessel from the Imperial period, on the Ostia torlonia relief

creating a powerful war fleet without any prior experience. All the ships available in the region ruled by Rome were commandeered, and foreign sailors were pressed into Roman service, to be employed mainly to transport troops. The Greek ship types, with centuries of development behind them, were adopted as the model for the Roman warships, especially the manoeuvrable TRIERS, which were known as triremes in the Roman fleet. We can assume that the 20 triremes mentioned by Polybius were not newly-built vessels, but ships belonging to the Greek-influenced southern Italian cities, and already in existence.

A decisive factor in the naval victory at Mylae was the battle tactic employed, which the Romans adopted from their methods of fighting on land. There they concentrated their warriors in small areas at any one time, and in order to exploit this proven strategy in naval battles, they required ships with greater carrying capacity than the triremes, for carrying more foot soldiers.

The pattern for this larger ship type was the Carthaginian penter. The Romans noted the dimensions and methods of construction of an enemy ship stranded on the mainland opposite Messina, and the penter (renamed the QUINQUEREME by the Romans) was copied in quite large numbers in a short space of time. Thus the Romans made up for their lack of experience by copying proven foreign ship types. Rome was rapidly able to overcome the lack of indigenous, experienced shipwrights by two methods: with the help of the Greeks and Etruscans who had become resident in southern Italy, and by transferring their own bridge-building and general carpenters.

Another remarkable aspect of the Roman transformation was the arrangements made for preliminary rowing training on land. Polybius reports that the oarsmen sat on static rowing frames set up on land, with a seat arrangement identical to the actual ships. The rowing tutor would stand in their midst, and make the oarsmen practice rowing simultaneously, with the tutor keeping them in strict rhythm.

One of the most important technical innovations introduced by the Romans was the heavy, swivelling boarding bridge fitted to the quinqueremes. This was called the corvus (Latin raven, presumably because of its beak) and was about 9m long and 1.20m wide. The invention is ascribed to the Roman consul and fleet commander Gaius Duilius, who gained a naval victory over the Carthaginians with his fleet. The boarding bridge could be rotated around a post standing on the fore deck of the ship; its forward end was fitted with a spike, and could be pulled up high by a tackle. If a Roman quinquereme ran close enough to an enemy ship, or if an enemy ship tried to ram, then the boarding bridge was dropped onto the deck of the enemy, and the pointed spike would stick fast. The Roman foot soldiers would then storm over this bridge onto the the

enemy ship, and then usually proved superior to the enemy in hand-to-hand fighting, to which they were accustomed.

After the Punic Wars, Roman merchant shipping expanded at a rapid rate, and required protection from the piracy which had become prevalent in the Mediterranean. This situation led, in the first century BC, to the construction of copies of the LIBURNIAN, which had one bank of oarsmen on a full-length enclosed deck. This was the vessel which had become notorious as a fast pirate ship of the Illyrian Liburnian peoples.

Later the two-bank DIER was developed from the Liburnian; in Roman hands the vessels were called BIREMES.

Roman warships were then built with deckhouses or towers, probably copied from Hellenistic prototypes. The precise date of particular modifications to Roman warship types is uncertain, as Rome only rarely maintained a permanent war fleet for a period of several decades, in contrast to the land-based armies, on which the power of the mighty Empire rested. However, it is certain that Octavian's fleet, which defeated that of Mark Antony in the naval battle of Actium, consisted principally of liburnians.

The Roman warship types (liburnian, bireme, trireme, quinquereme) were oared ships with supplementary sails, and were relatively narrow-hulled vessels with low freeboard and shallow draught, in contrast to the more full-bodied cargo ships which were primarily sailing vessels. As such, the warships were classified as naves longae, or long ships.

When the Imperial power had spread to the entire Mediterranean region, Roman merchant shipping necessarily expanded. The port of Ostia was built, and an entire fleet of ships assembled, just to ensure adequate supplies to Rome of corn, meat, wine, fruit, fine hardwoods and slaves, as the city grew ever larger. Because the freight ships were heavily built, and constructed in such numbers, much more evidence of them has survived than of the lightly-built warships. Various sources, among them J Huasen, list more than 40 authenticated finds of Roman cargo vessels, most of them dated, and including information on ship's size, dimensions and cargo.

According to this information Roman cargo ships varied in carrying capacity between 60 and 300 tons, with ships of 200 to 300 tons taking preference. A ship of this size would be about 20m long, with a beam of 6m and a draught of 3m. The full-bodied cargo ships were known as naves onerariae (Latin onerarius, cargo-carrying). The design of the ships is typical of the eastern Mediterranean region. The hull was basically CARVEL-planked, built with frames on a keel and with projecting deck beams. Whether the frames were installed before or after the outer skin planking is not known for certain. For example, a gravestone from Ravenna shows a carpenter cutting a section of frame for a ship

which is already planked. Loading hatches were fitted in the full-length deck, which was carefully sealed to protect the cargo of grain. On the foredeck was a projecting beam from which the anchor was handled; it could also be used for taking soundings, on some ships there was also a small framework at the stem. On the aftership there was a deckhouse, sometimes with a gallery for the ship's commander, travelling merchants or passengers, and also quite often a curving swan's neck with a gilded swan's head, in honour of the gods. Bulwarks provided some protection to the steering rudders on both sides, which could be hoisted up in heavy seas to prevent damage.

When circumstances permitted, Roman sea routes hugged the coast, to allow the crew to spend the night on land. Transportable fire hearths were used for cooking. The apostle Paul described a voyage in a Roman ship, providing details of conditions on board, and the duration of a typical voyage. His was a problematic voyage from Phoenicia (roughly present-day Lebanon) to Rome, which lasted five months. The size of the ship and the cramped conditions can be judged from the fact that a total of 276 passengers with their belongings and domestic animals travelled on the ship.

In addition to the discoveries of actual ships, information on the rig of the Roman merchant ships is provided by various items of pictorial evidence: including the mosaic pictures in a house near Ostia, dating from the first century. The high-sided, full-bodied ships, known as CORBITAe, were already pure sailing ships which could only use oars as an aid to manoeuvring. A stayed pole mast carried a large, rectangular square sail, and above the main course a small triangular sail. A short raked mast forward carried a further, smaller square sail termed the artemon. Roman ships carried leather-covered wickerwork boats on deck, known as the carabi. Further evidence of the shipbuilding skills of the Romans is provided by the LAKE NEMI SHIPS.

ROSKILDE SHIPS: Ships discovered in the Roskilde fjord near Skuldelev close to the historic town of Roskilde on the Danish island of Zeeland. It consisted of the wrecked remains of a ship barricade comprising five Viking ships which had been sunk in the period around 1000 to 1100. Roskilde, with its royal court and cathedral, was an important centre and, to prevent enemy ships entering the narrow channel, the inhabitants loaded down their own ships with stones and sank them close together.

The Danish National Museum began archaeological investigations in 1957. Strong currents made salvage by diving impossible, and a cafferdam wall was built around the site of the discovery, which was an area of around 1600m². In 1962, the site was pumped dry. Under the direction of O Olsen and O Crumlin-Pedersen, around 20 archaeologists painstakingly examined and salvaged some

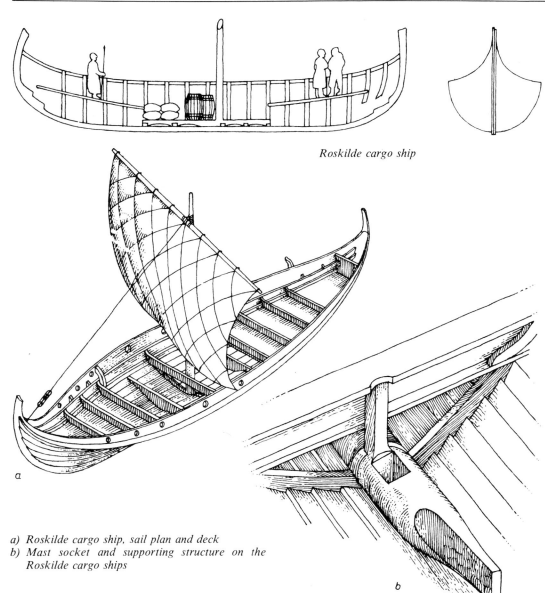

Roskilde cargo ship

Russian rybniza

feature is also present on the LADBY SHIP (Fyn, Denmark, ninth- or tenth centuries), the BAUMGARTH BOAT (formerly west Prussia, tenth or eleventh centuries) and on the KALMAR BOAT (southern Sweden, mid thirteenth century).

The mast arrangement is also an improvement. The mast no longer stands free in a large mast socket, but is supported at its bottom end by a transverse beam, connected securely to the ship's main timbers. The transverse beams are fixed to the upper plank strakes by fore-and-aft timbers instead of knees.

RYBNIZA: A Russian term for a small fishing craft which sometimes set a lugsail on a short mast.

a) Roskilde cargo ship, sail plan and deck
b) Mast socket and supporting structure on the Roskilde cargo ships

50,000 individual items, mainly oak artefacts. In order to preserve the parts, they were first kept moist, then sprayed with a formalin solution, packed in plastic bags and finally stored in polyethylene glycol preserving baths for six months to two years, depending on size. A modern museum was built on the Roskilde fjord to display the reconstructed ships.

The largest of the wrecks was a 30-bank longship (warship) for 50 to 60 warriors, with a length of about 28m. It is typical of the vessels which the Vikings used for their long voyages of discovery and pillage. It features oar holes along the entire ship's length, and is thus primarily a rowing ship, although it is also equipped to carry supplementary sails.

Among the finds was a smaller warship, also of slender build, of the type more often used for coastal voyages in the Baltic and North Seas. It is 18m long and around 4.0m in breadth. It has oar holes for a total of 24 oarsmen.

Two cargo ships were also among the wrecks. The larger of the two is 15.5m long and 4.5m in breadth with sides 1.9m high. Both

ends of the hull are reinforced with an additional strake which extends for about one third of the ship's length. This vessel is a KNARR (predecessor of the COG), whose design made it suitable for transporting a large number of persons with household effects and domestic animals over quite long sea voyages, for example to Iceland and Greenland.

The second cargo ship is smaller, at 13.3m long, 3.3m wide and 1.6m deep, but there are no major constructional differences. It also could be sailed, and might have been used as a coastal sailing ship in the Baltic region. The fifth wreck was probably a fishing or ferry boat, 12m long, 2.5m broad with a depth of hold of 1.2m. It is also equipped for sailing, but there are no traces of oar guides or thole pins.

Some design improvements are evident when the vessels are compared with Viking ships known to be about 100 years older. The strakes of the CLINKER-built ships are rivetted together, in similar fashion to the earlier Viking vessels, but the ribs on the later ships were notched to fit the overlapping planks and rivetted firmly in place. This

Two-masted sakoleva

Board sailing

SACOLEVA: A slender sailing ship of medium size used in the eastern Mediterranean. This ship type had two or three masts, and was built by the Greeks, Egyptians, Turks and the Syrians until the end of the era of sailing ships, with many variations in construction and rig. A common feature of all variants was the marked sheer and the pole masts. On the three-masted ship the tallest mast was stepped amidships, raked forward, and carried topsails and topgallants on yards. The two other masts (both masts on the two-masted variety) carried lateen or gaff sails.

SADKA: The term for a large nineteenth-century Russian vessel (Russian *sadok* meaning container) used for transporting wood to St Petersburg (Leningrad). The clumsy, crudely-built vessels carried a large square sail.

SAETTA, *saettia*: An Arabian-Algerian oared sailing boat of about 15m length with a lateen-rigged mast.

SAGITTA, *sagittia*: A fast twelfth- and thirteenth-century ship, smaller than the GALLEY, which could be rowed or sailed. the Genoese and Sicilian fleets employed the type as a despatch and scouting craft, but it was more generally used as a merchant or fishing vessel. Contemporary reports state that the ships were rowed by up to 58 oarsmen, but no special characteristics are mentioned which differentiate it from the galley.

SAHU-RE RELIEF: In 1907–8, members of the German Orient Society discovered pictorial and inscribed reliefs at the sepulchral temple of Pharaoh Sahu-re at Abussir. Sahu-re was of the fifth Dynasty (*ca* 2500 BC), and the reliefs show detailed representations of contemporary sea-going Egyptian ships. Parts of the reliefs are now museums in Berlin and Hamburg.

The inscriptions state that the ships were about 18m long, 4m wide and 1.2m in draught, and were thus relatively small compared with ships from other evidence dating from the same era, such as the HATSHEPSUT SHIPS

or the 42m long PEHENUKA ship. The inscriptions relate that these ships were used in the thirteenth year of the reign of Sahu-re for a successful voyage to the land of Punt, whence they returned with 80,000 measures of myrrh, 6,000 measures of electrum (gold alloy) and 2,600 trunks of a rare type of timber. Possibly this destination explains the small size of the vessels. Other sources indicate that ships were

dismantled and carried overland from the Nile to the coast of the Red Sea.

In contrast to the slender, tapered ends of the Nile vessels, which were similar in form to the boat-shaped PAPYRUS rafts, the stem and stern of the Sahu-re ships rise vertically, thus reducing the ship's length and the resultant stresses on the hull ends in rough seas. A powerful rope ran from the bow to the stern,

Egyptian Mediterranean ships, ca 2500 BC, relief from the pyramid grave of Pharaoh Sahu-Re

supported on two forked struts, and could be tensioned by a rotating rod. This truss supported the hull ends and prevented the ship from hogging. A double belt of rope, with the thinner one laid zig-zag fashion to act as a spacer, was wrapped round the ship's hull; this feature is known to have been fitted on earlier Egyptian ships. The usual bipod mast (A-frame) is folded down flat, as the ships are shown at the time of departure and after the return home.

Sailboard

SAILBOARD: A form of surf board, usually manufactured in glassfibre with a rotating, unstayed mast fixed to the deck by a universal joint. The sport of board sailing is comparatively new and has its origins in surfing. The board is sailed by one person standing up who steers the board by adjusting the tilt of the mast, and by moving his body weight. It has no rudder. The sailboard became an Olympic Class in 1984.

SAILING BOAT: Generic term for all types of sailing boat up to a certain size (around 12m length), of open, fully-covered or partly-covered construction. The design construction and fittings of the individual vessels are subject to international regulations, or tailored to match the conditions of the region in which the boat is sailed or simply the owner's tastes. The ideal hull design would be light weight, using steel, timber, plastic or composite materials; have adequate strength; a hydro-dynamically efficient shape for minimum resistance; high directional stability; adequate lateral stability; good control characteristics, and efficient use of the energy of the wind in all conditions, without undue strain on the sailor. The modern sailing boat comes close to fullfilling these criteria.

The centres of lateral resistance of the sail area and of the hull must be correctly positioned relative to each other. The centre of lateral resistance of the sail area, for instance,

must not be so high that lateral stability suffers, but on the other hand, tall sails offer more thrust. In terms of directional stability, boats tend to turn into the wind if the sails' centre of lateral resistance is located aft of the hull's centre of lateral resistance. The boat will fall off the wind if it is positioned forward. Lateral stability (the boat's ability to right itself when heeled over) can be achieved by making the hull broad, as in some dinghies, or by adding mass low down (as on keelboats). The tendency of a boat to make leeway is contained either by a centreboard, a keel or leeboards.

Early sailing boats generally employed the cutter rig, with a gaff mainsail, topsail, staysail and jib, but this arrangement is only rarely encountered today, and the BERMUDIAN

rig, in a variety of forms, now predominates. Because the areas of sail are well balanced, and form a smoother area with fewer interruptions, the airstream over the sails is less disturbed, and this promotes higher pressure on the weather side of the sails, and lower pressure on the leeward side. In aerodynamic terms a sail is usually more efficient if bellied, and to aid the formation of effecient shapes, modern sails feature curved trailing edges (leeches) instead of straight ones.

If the boat is sailing with the wind astern it is said to be sailing downwind and modern vessels set an additional balloon-shaped sail in these conditions, called the spinnaker. The first experiments using a downwind sail were carried out on the English sailing yacht *Sphinx* in 1866. From this broad, short downwind sail

A typical modern, bermudian-rigged sailing boat

evolved the tall spinnaker which is commonly used today

When a boat turns close towards the wind, it is said to luff and when pointing too close to the wind, forward motion will cease. Depending on the type of the boat and rig, sailing boats can sail on a course up to 30 degrees or less against the wind. In this case a zig-zag course has to be sailed against the wind, with turns at either end; this technique is known as tacking.

SAILING GIG: *see* GIG.

SAILING SHIP: A generic term applicable to most types of waterborne vessels whose principal means of propulsion is the power of the wind converted into thrust by sails, and which, by dint of size and design, are not covered by the term sailing boat, which usually applies to smaller vessels.

Sailing ships can be divided into two main groups according to the type of sails fitted: square-rigged ships and fore-and-aft rigged ships. Square sails are carried on yards set at right-angles or at an angle to the mast, and are swung round to the required position by means of braces. Fore-and-aft sails, on the other hand, are set along the centreline of the ship. They are carried on masts, gaffs, or stays and are controlled by means of sheets. On FULL-RIGGED SHIPs, ie fully square-rigged ships and large sailing ships in general, both basic types of sail are encountered, combined with each other in such a way that the best possible use is made of the available wind power commensurate with easy sail handling in varied wind conditions.

One of the oldest surviving pictorial representations of a sail is a rock drawing found in the south of the Nubian desert, dating from around 6000 BC, in which a bull's body forms the hull of a vessel, and on which a mast and sail are fitted.

It is clear from discoveries dating from the ancient Egyptian civilization (CHEOPS ships and others) that the favourable conditions prevailing there made possible the development of such primitive craft into the sailing ship proper, via the PAPYRUS RAFT, shaped in boat-like form and equipped with sail, and the later built-up, bound or sewn planked boat and planked ship.

In the Nordic region, the terms for types of rowing boat and ship are significantly older than the expressions for mast and sail. The first written evidence of a sail amongst Germanic tribes is provided by Tacitus (55–120) in AD 70, when the Batavians, living at the estuary of the Rhine, revolted. Tacitus reports that the barbarians sewed their brightly coloured woollen war coats into sails. At about the same time the Roman sage Pliny described how German women wove sailcloth. In the north, the old Norse mast, and mazdo, and the Russian maĉta came into use to mean mast. They were adopted from the Roman, while the terms sigla (Roman) and segl (old Norse) are

Detail from the Sakkara relief from the grave of the official Ti, showing the construction of Egyptian wooden vessels ca *2500 BC*

among the oldest terms for sail. From the evidence of Nordic boat finds, especially those in Scandinavia, the first firm evidence of the sail dates from the period when long sea voyages were first being undertaken, roughly from AD 400 onwards.

Until well into the sixteenth century the ability to build wooden sailing ships was one of the most highly prized skills which an experienced master carpenter could have. Experience in shipbuilding was passed down from generation to generation, trade secrets being strictly guarded. It was only when drawings of ship forms came to be made, covering keel, stem and stern and deck lines, and including some dimensions and details, that the knowledge became more widespread, and the possibility of comparison and development arose. Until the early nineteenth century the drawings contained little more than the principal dimensions, shapes and basic structural design of the ships' hulls.

In certain cases, such as Venetian ships and warships, which were built in large numbers under state control, more accurate drawings of the timber components, joints, fittings and rigging were prepared much earlier. Up to 20 types of timber were used in one ship, for the hull, masts and spars, depending on requirements. The durability of hulls built of oak was only exceeded by those made of Italian teak. Such ships, which were very resistant to rotting, could remain in service for between 30 and 50 years if well maintained, while the use of beech or lighter softwoods resulted in failure of the joints, and hence the failure of the vessel's watertight integrity after as little as 15 years. Resinous pine woods were ideal for the upper deck, such as the wood of the North American pitch pine. As timber-built sailing ships grew in size, the greater stresses on the hull and the main timbers could only be absorbed by the wholesale adoption of CARVEL construction (replacing CLINKER planking), and by the replacement of grown curved timbers by formed, constructed frames and corner reinforcements. The result was a sophisticated, highly developed method of timber construction.

When COMPOSITE construction was introduced in England in the nineteenth century, the requirements made on the timber craftsman were much reduced, even on larger

sailing ships, as the timber frames and deck beams were replaced with iron components, planked with a wooden skin. The composite ships were also stronger and more watertight, with the result that a well-built composite ship could have a useful life of about 40 years.

The adoption of iron and later of steel even for the external skin, which began around the middle of the nineteenth century, had profound effects on methods of construction and shipbuilding techniques and with the move away from wood towards steel, a large number of leading shipyards, which had specialized in wood construciton were doomed.

SAILING TANKER: The first type of oil tanker, also known as a tank sailing ship. In contrast to the PETROLEUM CLIPPERs, which carried the petroleum in barrels, tank sailing ships were vessels fitted with large, permanent metal containers, linked to each other by pipework. One of the first sailing tankers was the American ship *Charles*, which sailed between North America and Europe from 1869 to 1872.

SAKKARA RELIEF: Detailed pictures of ships under construction on a stone relief tablet found at the grave of the high official Ti from the fifth Dynasty (2480–2350 BC), discovered near the ancient Egyptian city of Memphis. The reliefs depict various sizes and types of ship, some with flat bottoms and simple end forms, others slimmer and more rounded. The representations also show various shipbuilding tasks being carried out, such as sawing beams to size, cutting dowel holes, fitting planks and smoothing a finished hull with tools similar to an axe. Various details of construction methods can be made out on the relief, including a plank fitted with seven dowels supported on a rope, in the process of being fitted to the vessel by two workers and an overseer.

SALAMBA: A raft from Malaysia made of bamboo stems with a bipod framework erected on top. This structure projects at an angle, and is used by the fishermen to haul up the net, which is suspended on long bamboo poles.

SALERNO RELIEF: A bas relief in the Cathedral of Salerno near Venice, which

Fune, a Japanese sailing fishing vessel

American whaler in the process of tacking. Her whale boats are in the foreground, and on the right a frigate is sailing with wind abeam, National Maritime Museum, Greenwich

Arrival of state yachts at Rotterdam, painting by L Verschuier (1630–86)

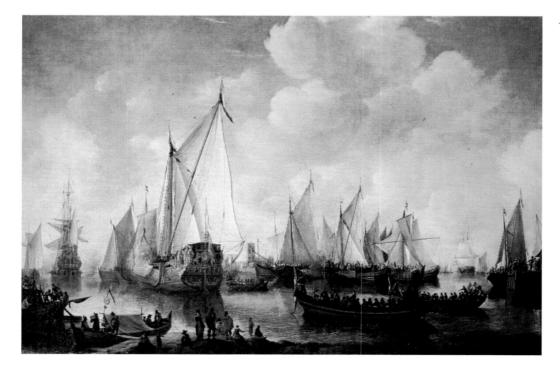

Salerno corbita relief

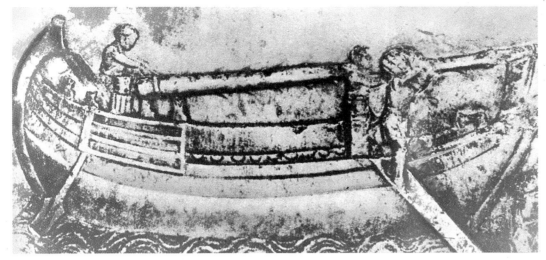

depicts a cargo of sacks being discharged from CORBITA. The mast is folded down, and is shown to be fitted with wood cleats on both sides in order to make it easier to climb.

SAMBUK, *sambug*: A fast, two-masted sailing ship of the Arab DHOW type. Together with the BAGGALA and BUM the sambuk remains one of the best-known types of dhow on the Arabian, east African and Indian coasts to this day. It is an ocean-going sailing ship with a narrow, low hull, the overall length of which is usually at least four times the beam, and it can carry between 15 to 50 tons.

The afterpart of the underwater body ends in a pointed stern, opening out above the waterline to a flat transom. The full-length deck stretches as far as the short poop deckhouse standing aft, the floor of which is set deeper than the deck. The mainmast is stepped at the level of the main frame, is raked forward by about 10 degrees, and carries the settee mainsail on an angled main yard, made up of two or three spars. The much smaller mizzen mast, with the smaller mizzen settee, has little or no forward rake.

There are a number of unmistakable similarities between the sambuk and the Portuguese CARVEL of the fifteenth century. Until the mid fifteenth century the larger western European sailing ships were exceptionally short, broad and full-bodied, with tall fore and aft castles; typical vessels of this type were the NAO and the CARRACK. In contrast, the CARAVEL represented a completely different type of design for western Europe; lighter, more manoeuvrable and faster, and thus well suited to voyages of discovery. As the Iberian peninsula was ruled for many centuries by Moorish Arabs, only being displaced by Christians in the fifteenth century, the Arab sambuk can be considered in some respects to be the predecessor of the caravel.

Pottery model sampan of the first century AD, found at Canton

SAMPAN: This term originates in the Malayan region, but is based on the Chinese expression 'shan pan', which means something like three planks. The term thus sums up the basic construction of these simple vessels which are so widely used on Chinese rivers, as well as in Bangladesh, Burma, Malaya and Japan. The boats are flat-bottomed, often with a pointed bow formed by drawing the side planks inward. The boats are 3 to 10m in length and simply constructed. The upper side planks are generally left longer, projecting over the broad, uncovered stern, and this overhanging part is used to support the long yuloh, by means of which the vessel is steered as well as propelled. To sailors, the term sampan has become a general and slightly perjorative term which is applied to all types of simple vessel.

Larger sampans of similar design have also been built, intended as houseboats and transport vessels. These usually have an

Sambuk, a fairly recent, fast sailing dhow (model)

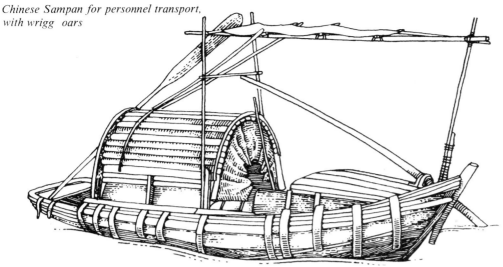

Chinese Sampan for personnel transport, with wrigg oars

enclosed deck with deckhouses, and are propelled by oars and sails set on one or two masts, or towed by rowing boats, or people or draught animals on towpaths alongside the rivers. The sails are of matting or cotton fabric, and are supported by bamboo rods as well as booms top and bottom. The mast is free-standing without shrouds or stays. The upper, slightly angled boom, the bamboo rods and the lower boom are attached to the pole mast with a fitting similar to a truss, and can be rotated and reefed to suit the strength and direction of the wind.

A few of these vessels were equipped with paddle wheels driven by people operating an apparatus similar to a treadmill and were influenced by the European and North American paddle steamers.

SANDALE: A one- or two-masted Arab fishing and freight vessel rigged with lateen sails, and used in the nineteenth and twentieth centuries. The length was around 12m and beam 3m.

SANDBAGGER: A mid nineteenth-century sailing yacht with over-large sails. It carried sacks containing 25kg of sand, which were used as movable ballast to reduce the tendency of the boat to capsize. When going about the sandbags were moved to the windward side of

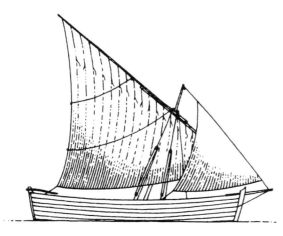

Single-masted Arabian sandale

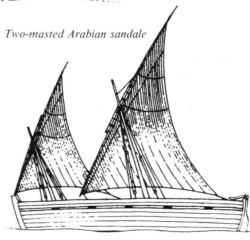

Two-masted Arabian sandale

the boat by the crew. In consequence, the yachts came to be known as sand boats, or sandbaggers. There were frequent accidents with boats capsizing when the wind direction altered suddenly, and after 1885 it was forbidden to carry movable ballast on yachts.

On the Mecklenburg coast the same term signified boats which were used to glean gravel and sand from the sea. These vessels varied widely in design, and could carry anything from two to 25 tons. The boats were usually sailed by two persons, and were originally rigged with a spritsail, which was later replaced by a loose-footed gaff sail.

SANGARA: A vessel made of tree trunks, and used on the Red Sea coast into the nineteenth century for carrying personnel and cargo.

SANTORINI SHIP, *see* THERA FRESCO.

SAYKE, *sayken: see* TSCHAIKE.

SCAFFIE, *scaffa, scaith*: A one-, or two- or even three-masted fishing boat of Scotland's northeast coast with a fine, raking stern and cutaway forefoot. An average length for a two-master would have been around 20m. Most were CLINKER-built and originally they were open boats, a development from the shorter craft of the area, such as the ORKNEY YOLE. They in turn were gradually replaced by the

ZULU toward the end of the nineteenth century.

SCAMPARIA: The Italian term for a small, uncovered nineteenth-century packet boat, which was equipped with a gun as a defence against pirates.

SCAPHA: A latin term, adopted from the Greek, for a barge or boat. Essentially, it was a small vessel which could be rowed or paddled.

SCHACHTUR: A simple, box-shaped boat made of flat boards, with a flat bottom and straight sides, front and back. It is 7 to 10m long and is commonly used on the Euphrates.

SCHEIK: Originally, a seventeenth-century single-masted oared sailing ship about 15m long with a beam of 3.5m, used as a troop transport in the Black Sea. The vessel carried a square sail on a pole mast, and could accommodate up to 70 people. At the beginning of the nineteenth century the term applied to a short, full-bodied boat with a spritsail and staysail, which was used for fishing and oyster collecting.

SCHELCH: A flat-bottomed, open cargo barge for transport of goods on the river Main in the seventeenth and eighteenth centuries. There were two sizes: one about 28m long and another half that length.

SCHIFAZZO: A two- or three-masted nineteenth-century Italian sailing ship with almost vertical stem and stern. The type was lateen-rigged, sometimes with an additional staysail. It was mainly used for transporting grain and wine, but was also used for fishing. The ships were 10 to 15m long, 3.5 to 5m in beam, and could carry up to 35 tons of cargo.

SCHITIK: A Russian cargo vessel used on the rivers Volga and Don in the nineteenth century. Roughly 15m long and fitted with one mast, the vessel carried a large square sail and featured a roofed area over the cargo hold similar to a deckhouse. Originally, these were sewn boats (Russian shitj meaning to sew).

Schitik, Volga cargo kahn, nineteenth century

On the Scandinavian coasts the snekkja was usually a fast, slim rowed ship with 40 oarsmen amongst its 90-man crew. It could set supplementary sails. In the Middle Ages the term schnigge generally referred to a small rowing and sailing boat, while the Hanseatic schnigge was a fairly small, fast-sailing despatch vessel and warship capable of carrying around 60 to 100 tons.

The type survived into the eighteenth and nineteenth centuries as a small sailing freight vessel, often with supplementary regional names, such as Eider schnigge, Helgoländer schnigge and others. On the German North Sea coast, schniggen also operated as single-masted fishing vessels, less often with two masts.

SCHOKKER: A Dutch sailing fishing ship which passed through various stages of development from the thirteenth to the nineteenth century. The schokker was originally designed for fishing in the Zuidersee and the name may refer to the island of Schokland, which lies in that sea. A typical feature of later versions was the schokker boom, a spar which could be swung out over the ship's side for catching fish with trawl nets. Our knowledge of the original schokker comes mainly from pictures on seals dating from the thirteenth and fourteenth centuries. Pictorial representations of a schokker, together with some other ship types, were found on a bier at Workum in Friesland dating from 1600.

A schokker is mentioned in the Groningen

Schnigge, ca 1800 (model)

Two-masted schmack with square foresail and spritsail ca 1676 (model)

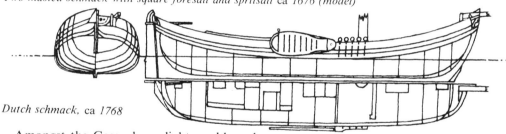

Dutch schmack, ca 1768

Amongst the Cossacks, a light washboard boat, similar to the PIROGUE, was also termed a schitik. This vessel remained in use up to about 1930. The bottom of the hull consisted of a poplar trunk hollowed out like a trough. To increase the freeboard, plank strakes were added on the sides, and connected to each other and the floor with leather thongs.

SCHLUP: *see* SLOOP GALEASSE

SCHMACK, *schmack ship, smak*: A single-masted, flat-bottomed Dutch coastal sailing ship which existed between the sixteenth and nineteenth centuries. The schmack had a jib boom, and was rigged with gaff mainsail and staysail and jib and flying jib on the jib boom. In a few cases a small mizzen mast was stepped aft, carrying a small gaff sail; this type can thus be considered as a transitional type leading to the KUFF TJALK.

SCHNIGGE, *schnikke, snigge*: A fast oared sailing ship which was built in northern Europe between the tenth and the nineteenth centuries in a variety of forms. The type was particularly widespread between the tenth and twelfth centuries. The term in German means snail but it did not indicate the speed of the snail, but rather the manner of forward movement, ie, gliding. Thus the name of the ships, which glided over the water.

Schokker from Vollenhoven, late nineteenth century (model)

Lines of a single-masted schokker

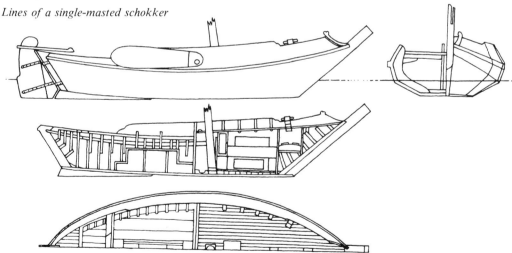

archives in 1789. In the 1940s a flat-bottomed schokker from Vollenhove, then about 70 years old, was measured and drawn by the Dutchman Sopers. While the earlier schokkers were generally sprit-rigged, this particular vessel was a single-masted gaff-rigged version with a slightly aft-raked mast. The mast height was 10m above deck, the boom 5.16m long and the gaff 2.15m. The length of the hull was 10.75m overall, and 8.5m at the waterline, with a beam of 3.6m. The massive stempost was cut away on the starboard side to form a housing for a pulley for the anchor rope.

It is not possible to draw definite conclusions about the size of preceding versions of the schokker from the dimensions of the measured vessel.

SCHOONER: A group of sailing ship types rigged predominantly with fore-and-aft sails, whose origins go back to at least 1700. Around 1760, schooners were fitted with square topsails on both masts, and the long jib boom supported up to four foresails. Later on, gaff topsails made their appearance and some 'topsail schooners' had crossed yards on the foremast alone.

In the 1830s, the shipbuilders of Chesapeake Bay developed the BALTIMORE SCHOONER, and it achieved world-wide fame. Further development in schooner hull design in particular had a revolutionary influence on shipbuilding, and represented an outstanding step forward at the time. The long projecting stem and stern increased the usable deck length significantly. The keel sloped down towards the stern, producing greater draught aft, and consequently the centre of lateral resistance moved further aft, which provided a better balance to the centre of sail pressure. In the midship region the hull section was V-shaped rather than rounded or U-shaped, as was the case on more orthodox vessels. These design features were also adopted for the schooner yachts, which were developed later.

With its all-round improvements and smaller crew requirement, the schooner soon became a popular fast sailing ship all over the world where valuable or perishable cargoes had to be carried. The schooner also proved ideal for passenger transport on the high seas as well as around the coasts, because it could be rapidly prepared for departure and was easily trimmed to cope with changing weather conditions. The schooner also served as a deep sea fishing vessel for many decades. Schooners became notorious for smuggling opium, carrying slaves and other dubious activities like privateering.

Many variants of the basic rig were developed. In some regions the two square topsails were supplemented by a large square foresail which extended from the yard down to the deck. Gaff-rigged schooners required an even smaller crew than the topsail or main topsail schooner.

The final state was the development of the staysail schooner in which only the mainsail was carried on a gaff and boom.

Because of their very small crews schooners were economical cargo carriers and grew to large sizes in the late nineteenth century.

The number of masts ranged from the basic two-masted schoner, through three- to five-masted schooners, up to six-masted and even one seven-masted gaff-rigged vessel.

SCHOONER BARQUE, *barquentine*: This was the usual German term for what would be called a barquentine in English. That is to say a vessel fully square rigged on the foremast, but fore-and-aft rigged on the main and mizzen. An occasional variant was a three-masted schooner, rigged as a topmast schooner on the fourmast. Yet another, a POLKA BARQUE, was square rigged on the fore, fore-and-aft on main and mizzen, but had square topsails on the main. Jackass was a term applied to anything that was somewhat out of the ordinary. Thus we have four-masted JACKASS BARQUE, square-rigged on fore and main, with the two after masts fore-and-aft rigged.

SCHOONER BRIG, *brig schooner, brigantine*: Invariably a two-masted sailing ship, like the BRIG, but not fully square-rigged on the two masts. Because of the hybrid rig the term HERMAPHRODITE BRIG was also used. The most common rig for the schooner brig was a fully square-rigged foremast devoid of gaff sails, and a gaff-rigged mainmast. Topsail schooners (lower mast and topmast) and topgallant schooners (lower mast, topmast and topgallant) can also be considered as further brig-schooner variants, varying in fore-mast construction and type of rig. However, the Mediterranean term brigantine is the more usual description if the vessel sets a square fore course. Schooner brigs, which were relatively full-bodied cargo ships, were built in Holland as early as the seventeenth century. By the mid nineteenth century schooner brigs of 100 to 300BRT were being built in large numbers in Europe and North America.

SCHOONER GALIOT: A GALIOT with a fine-lined hull, sloping bow form and schooner rig. This ship type was developed in Holland around 1830 and was also built in Ostfriesland and Oldenburg. The ships were two-masted and rigged either as topsail schooners or schooner brigs. In contrast to the standard galiot, the schooner galiot's after mast was taller than the forward mast, as on the schooner. According to Szymanski, the German merchant fleet of 1873 included a total of 121 schooner galiots, but by 1913 there were only four remaining ships of this type in service.

SCHOONER YACHT: A further development of the North American Baltimore SCHOONER, which evolved in the 1830s. At the time, the original schooners were still partially square-rigged, but schooner yachts carried only fore-and-aft sails. With the introduction of the BERMUDIAN sail the standard gaff main and topsails were superseded by a bermudian mainsail. The usual schooner yacht had two masts, carrying a total sail area of about 1000m², but three-masted schooner yachts were also built, such as the *Atlantic* with a sail area of 1720m². The North American two-masted schooner yacht *America* gained world-wide fame for its outstanding sailing qualities, and in 1861 won the 100 Guineas Cup now known as the America's Cup.

SCHOONER KUFF: A typical two-masted KUFF, with full-bodied hull, but rigged as a SCHOONER with the after mast taller than the forward one. The type was developed in the Dutch town of Groningen in the 1820s, and was usualy rigged as a topsail schooner. In Germany, Szymanski reported that schooner kuffs were last built in Papenburg, Leer and Emden in 1868.

SCHUYT, *schuite, schute*: A simple vessel similar to a barge, usually uncovered, and with no means of propulsion. It was used primarily to transport bulk cargoes and store them temporarily, and for carrying loads from ship to ship within ports, inland harbours and sheltered roads. The term harbour schute is also common.

At different periods the term schuyt has referred to a variety of boat and ship types.

Dutch 'water schute' for transporting fresh water to breweries, and brine to saltworks

Schuyt, mid nineteenth century (model)

Originally, the expression arose in northern Europe around 900, based on the old Norse skuta meaning a rowing boat. In the later Middle Ages it came to be used as a generic term covering fast sailing despatch, reconnaissance, supply and escort vessels serving the naval fleets. This use of the term is related to schott (bulkhead) and schutt (rubbish).

The schuyt which were common in the Hanseatic period on the German and Dutch coasts, known as schyte, schuite or scheute to the Dutch, were CLINKER-built, flat-bottomed, uncovered vessels, like most early types. In the nineteenth century, schüte was a standard term in northern Europe for the freight barges used for inland shipping. They were mostly without means of propulsion, although some were fitted with a mast and a simple square sail. In the Baltic region, schüte meant a broad, three-masted vessel, with pointed hull forward and aft.

Scow, centreboard schooner, nineteenth century

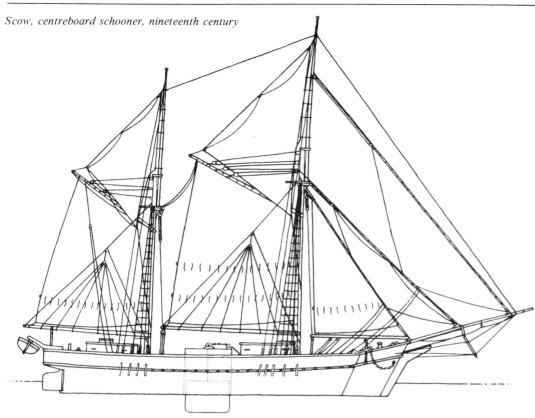

SCOW: An English form of lighter. The vessels were flat-bottomed, with vertical sides, and were used in the nineteenth century as LIGHTERS for sea-going ships. They also operated as ferries and for personnel transport close to the coast, in which case they would be towed or rowed.

The term has also been applied to a broad, flat-bottomed boat, with flat bow and stern and bilge keels, which originated in North America. The shallow hull, of similar form to a planing boat, facilitates fast downwind speeds. An interesting feature is the deck line, which has a reverse sheer.

SCULLER, *scull boat*: A racing rowing boat, in which the oarsman operates a pair of short, light oars called sculls, as opposed to oars proper, which are moved by one man with both arms. There are single sculls (one man) and doubles (two men).

SEA EWER: A north German EWER. The type evolved in the early nineteenth century, and was rigged with two masts. Like the inland and coastal ewers, the sea ewer carried leeboards, but the hull was more stoutly built.

SEA SCHLUP, *sea sloop: See* SLOOP.

SELANDER, *schlander*: Originally, a ninth-century hybrid Byzantine vessel, combining elements of the DROMON and the PAMPHILE, which were the successors of the liburnian. Like most ancient warships the selander types, although combined oared and sailing vessels, were primarily rowing ships, the lateen sail only being used with a favourable wind and for long sea voyages.

During the crusades, many Italian coastal towns built selanders as transports and warships.

SEVEN-MASTED GAFF-RIGGED SCHOONER: The only seven-masted ship, built in the USA in 1902 and named *Thomas W Lawson*. The ship was 117m long, had a beam of 15m and displaced 5218BRT. The vessel was of steel construction and sailed with a crew of 16 men.

SEVERN TROW: A flat-bottomed cargo vessel used on the River Severn and its estuary. It was around 23m in length with a beam of 6m and a draft of 2m. The bow was bluff and the stern terminated in a broad, deep, almost vertical transom. Some were equipped with a removable keel, held in place by chains, for estuary work. The hold was open. Originally, the trow had a single square sail, but this was later replaced first by a sloop rig and then by a ketch rig. A few trows survived into the twentieth century.

SEWN BOAT: A generic term for boats whose outer skin planks are joined by means of sewing or binding. Weaving, tying and sewing are among the oldest methods of joining ship's components, and evolved in many regions of the world. In a sense the sewn, CLINKER-

built boat had many ancestors, including the Egyptian boat-like rafts made of bundled papyrus; the woven, skin-covered Assyrian river boats; the sewn animal-skin boats and BARK boats; the Egyptian CARVEL-planked boats and ships with sewn seams; and the dugouts with bound-on side planks. However, all these various types of vessel and methods of joining probably evolved quite independently of each other in the different cultures.

In northern Europe, the HJORTSPRING BOAT, dating from around 300 BC, is among the oldest evidence of a boat with sewn planks. On this boat two limewood planks were bound or sewn on either side of a trough-like, hollowed-out keel plank, with their long edges overlapping. The leather straps, thongs, bast fibres, roots or osiers used for binding were sealed with resins, as were the holes and joints.

The English NORTH FERRIBY BOAT, dating from around 150 BC, is different from the Hjørtspring boat in that it was carvel-planked, and used a different method of sewing. The planks were butt-jointed along their long edges, and holes (for the binding cords) were bored opposite each other, equally spaced from the edges of the planks. As on the ancient Egyptian timber boats, ash strips were fitted over the carvel joint on the inside of the planks, to form an additional seal.

This method of construction was not restricted to Scandinavia and western Europe. For instance, the *Essa*, written by the Icelander Snoori Sturluson (1179 to 1241), states that deacon Sigurd Slembi from Lappen had two schuyts built, incorporating natural grown curved timbers, osiers as ribs, clad with timber planks, which were bound together with animals tendons, without using a single nail. The vessels were said to be large enough to accommodate 12 oarsmen on each side. Sewn boats were also built in fourteenth- and fifteenth-century Flanders.

In Lapland and northern Russia, ultra-lightweight planked boats with flexible sewn seams still existed at the beginning of the twentieth century. According to a description by G Hallström, boats were built in certain regions of Lapland and Finland, where lakes and rivers abounded, by overlapping very thin planks clinker style, drilling through them and sewing them together zig-zag fashion, using reindeer tendons or thin roots. The tendons, once pulled tight through the holes, were wedged into the holes with wooden plugs, then treated with wax, resin or pitch to seal the joints and make the craft durable. These boats were so light that a man could carry one over a considerable distance. In Africa also (on Lake Chad in particular), and elsewhere, boats

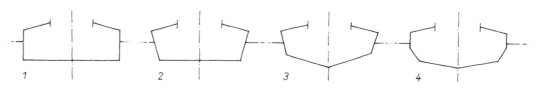

Sharpie hard-chine hull forms: –1 Box form –2 Trapezoid form –3 Single chine form –4 Double chine form.

Shallop. The illustrations indicate how difficult it is to give an exact definition of shallop, sloop, chaloupe and other related vessels.

1   Gunboat
2   Austro-Hungarian shallop, seventeenth century
3   Shallop with divided square sail, 1880
4   Pilot shallop or cutter
5   French pilot shallop

5   Small shallop with double oars, 1880
7   Small shallop with single oars
8   Plan and side view of a shallop, after Paris
9   Spritsail-rigged shallop, 1768
10   Rowlocks and thole pins on shallops used as ships' boats

11   Rib construction of a shallop
12   Lowering and raising a shallop using stay loading tackle
13   Stropped viol block, part of the lowering tackle

made of planks sewn together are still used as fishing vessels although ocean-going sewn boats have existed. *See also* MASULA.

SHALLOP: A term for the largest or second largest rowing or sailing boat (the latter with one or two short masts) carried on board ship, but in English usage they were replaced by the LONGBOAT from the seventeenth century. The term was used by European navies until the nineteenth century. On merchant ships the shallop served for loading water and supplies, and for lowering the anchor. Greenland ships had six to seven shallops on board, and continental warships also carried several, depending on the ship's size. Where more than one shallop was carried on board, one would be the captain's shallop, reserved for the captain and officers, the remainder being working shallops for general duties and crew transport.

In shape and design these were quite small, broad boats, CARVEL- or CLINKER-built, with round bilges. The stem was vertical or raked slightly forward, while the aftership tapered to a pointed, rounded or flat stern.

In the late seventeenth century the type grew from a mere open boat into a small coastal trading vessel, used particularly in the New England colonies. They had a single-masted fore and aft rig or a simple two-masted square rig of the large mainsail and small foresail. This latter rig was used for fishing shallops which developed in sea-going vessels. They were also used as coastal traders and the name survived into the nineteenth century.

Single-masted shallops were also built in Europe. They were used for North Sea fishing, with a displacement of up to about 40 tons, and as traders in the Baltic, carrying up to 50 tons. The ships were of cruder construction, and carried simpler equipment and rig than the cutter. Whereas the cutter had two or three headsails, the single-masted shallop usually set only one foresail. The mast was raked aft and fitted with a topmast.

In the first half of the nineteenth century more modern cargo-carrying shallops were developed, and the type then became confused with the SLOOP.

Ships-of-the-line in the battle of Aboukir, 1798. Painting by Nicholas Pocock (1741–1821)

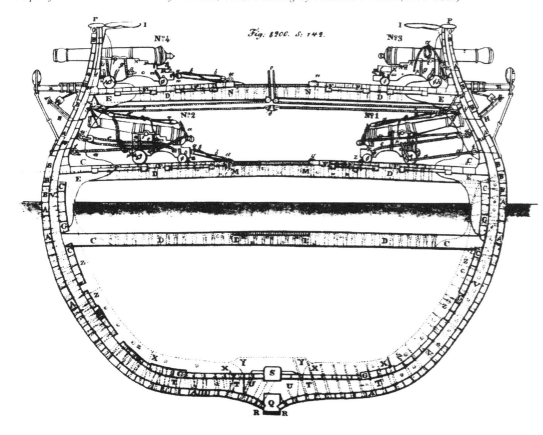

Cannon arrangement on a two-deck ship-of-the-line

SHANTUNG TRADER: *see* PECHILI TRADER.

SHARPIE: A long, flat-bottomed boat of the North American east coast. It developed in the nineteenth century as a fishing and pleasure boat and was up to 22m or more in length. The stem was near-vertical and the stern rounded. A centreboard was carried and the boat was decked at bow and stern. The rig usually consisted of two leg-of-mutton sails with sprit booms.

SHIKHARA, *shikar*: A Kashmiri water taxi, also used as a floating shop stand for traders, or a floating workshop.

SHIP-OF-THE-LINE: This term evolved in the mid seventeenth century when the tactic of fighting in line ahead was developed, to exploit the broadside fire-power of warships. This technique was first adopted by the English Admiral Blake and the Dutch Admiral De Ruyter, and was known as the line-of-battle, and ships of the line were also known as line-of-battleships. From the eighteenth to the middle of the nineteenth century, ships-of-the-line were usually warships displacing around 1200 tons, although ships of 2000 to 3000 tons displacement were preferred later. Their distinguishing feature was the arrangement and distribution of the batteries. Depending on whether the muzzle-loading cannon were set up on two or three complete decks one above the other, the ships were known as two- or three-decker ships-of-the-line. The crew strength could be up to 1300 men. At the end of the eighteenth century the 74-gun ship was the most common ship-of-the-line, but thereafter the number of rose to 80 or 90.

Among the first English ships-of-the-line to be fitted with three full-length gun decks were the *Prince Royal* (built in 1610, displacing around 1200 tons and fitted with 64 guns) and the *Sovereign of the Seas* (built in 1657, displacing around 1630 tons, with 100 guns).

The last occasion on which the heavy ships-of-the-line faced each other in large numbers was at the battle off Cape Trafalgar in 1805, when 15 Spanish and 18 French vessels faced 27 English ships. The English fleet achieved its famous victory over the united Spanish and French war fleet, and one ship has survived from the battle. This is the *Victory*, the flagship of Nelson, Admiral and Commander of the English fleet. This famous vessel has been converted into a museum, and now rests in dry dock at Portsmouth for public viewing. The last actual battle in which sailing ships-of-the-

line participated took place at Navarino in 1827, with three English, four French and four Russian ships ranged against seven Turkish ships.

Around the turn of the nineteenth century the Royal Navy differentiated between three rates of ship-of-the-line.

First Rate ships included vessels of 2000 tons and more displacement, with 100 to 130 guns and a crew of 850 to 900 men.

The Second Rate included ships displacing 1650 to 1950 tons, carrying 84 to 90 guns and 750 to 850 men.

The Third Rate included smaller ships-of-the-line with displacements between 1200 and 1600 tons. Sixty-four to 80 guns were carried, and the crew was between 520 and 750 men.

All guns were still muzzle-loaders, the heaviest ones being 32-pounders, which, because of their great mass, were mounted as low as possible on the bottom gun deck, with the result that the gunports were situated only a few feet above the ship's waterline. After a salvo it took a couple of minutes with a well trained crew before the heavy guns could be reloaded and made ready again. Up to 10 men were required to operate each gun. Maximum range was about one kilometre. The second battery of medium calibre guns was on the deck above, while on three-deckers there was a further battery of lighter guns. Most ships of the line also had guns on the forecastle, quarterdeck (and sometimes the poop) and these were often the short-ranged but powerful carronades.

In the mid nineteenth century, steam-driven ships-of-the-line became important, but it was not until the latter half of the nineteenth century that auxiliary sails were given up completely for long voyages. With the invention of explosive shells, breech-loading guns, external hull armour and rotating gun turrets, the ship-of-the-line was subjected to major alterations, the term line-of-battleship was eventually shortened to battleship.

English ship-of-the-line Nelson, *1814 (model)*

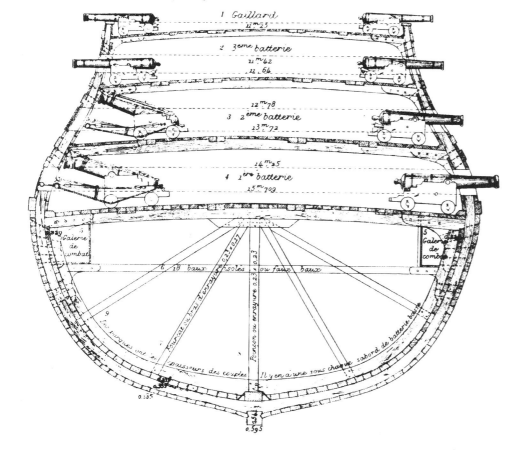

Arrangement of the cannon on a four-deck ship-of-the-line

SHIP'S BOAT: A rowing or sailing boat belonging to a ship and either carried on board or towed behind, and intended for transporting personnel and gear to and from land and between ships. Until the end of the seventeenth century it was often the case that only one boat was carried, and it would frequently be towed behind only being taken on board in strong winds and heavy seas. On large sailing ships two tackles were fixed to the stays, to allow heavy loads to be hauled on board. Similar tackles were also fixed to the lower yards. On schooners and cutters the tackles were fitted to the lowered gaffs. The ship's boats could then be heaved on board by swinging the gaff boom out. Ships with a simple transom stern, such as brigs, schooners and cuters, were sometimes fitted with light, curved stern davits with wooden sheaves let into them, on which the boat could be hoisted and made fast. All these arrangements for bringing the boat and lowering it again were

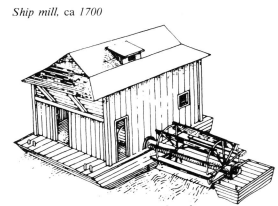

Ship mill, ca 1700

time-consuming, and were therefore not ideal when a lifeboat was required. Folding and swivelling davits first came into use in England around 1800. Both types of davit allowed the boats to be lowered rapidly.

In the seventeenth century, a maximum of two ships' boats were carried on any vessel, but the number then rose to five or six per ship, the boats varying in size. The table below shows the boats carried on board English and French warships at the end of the seventeenth century, according to the ships's rating, the rating denoting the size and armament of the ship.

Rate	Approx displace-ment (tons)	Approx crew strength	Boats
I	1520	600	Longboat, pinnace, jolly boat
II	720	260	Longboat, pinnace, jolly boat
III	550	140	Longboat, pinnace,
IV	290	100	Longboat, pinnace
V	185	60	Longboat

The size of the ships' boats varied depending on the rate of the warship. The longboat was between 7 and 16m long, the pinnace between 6.5 and 11m, and the jolly boat 6 to 8m long. In the heyday of sailing ships, the number of boats on brigs, barques and clippers was again raised, this time by law. The largest and most

Russian shnaika, nineteenth century

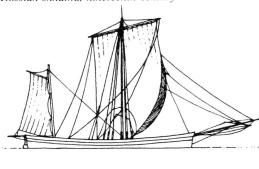

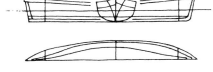

important ship's boat became the launch, followed by the cutter and the jolly boat. The smallest ship's boat was termed the gig. The large, full-bodied launch was the transport boat for goods of all kinds. The cutter was a multi-oared, fast rowing boat which was used in particular for transporting cargo. The short but beamy jolly boat was primarily a work boat, for carrying out maintenance on the ship while the gig's main duty was to carry the captain and the ship's officers, and consequently was often termed captain's gig.

Other small boats were also carried on board for other tasks. The smallest boat of all on board was jokingly termed the MOSES BOAT by the sailors. The boats carried on board were equipped with sails, oars and provisions, depending on their number and size, to make them suitable for crew training, and to operate as lifeboats. The easily handled lugsail was the usual sail fitted, although later on a gaff sail was preferred. On large ships the boats were lashed down on the main midship hatch, or on wooden or metal gratings. When the boats came to be suspended on davits, they were lashed securely in place. In the course of time many improvements were made to the equipment installed for lowering and raising the boats.

SHIP MILL: A vessel anchored in running water, and used to exploit the energy of the current to drive a corn mill. It is said that ship mills were first used by the Romans in 536AD when the Goths besieged Rome, and destroyed the waterways and the land-based mills. The Byzantine General Belisarius ordered mill wheels and mill works to be built on large floating barges, in order to supply the population with flour. Ship mills were employed on many rivers of the world in the late Middle Ages.

A ship mill consisted of two barge-like hulls, firmly anchored at the point where the current was strongest. The larger 'house ship' carried the mill mechanism, the supply of grain, and a mooring for a boat, while the second hull supported the outside end of the paddle wheel shaft. Between the two hulls was the water wheel, half-submerged, and of a width to fit the hull spacing. A ship mill operated on the river Mulde near Eilenburg until 1920, when it was destroyed by fire. In the late 1930s a few ship mills were still to be seen on the Danube near Budapest. The last German ship mill was the Bergschiffs mill near Bad Düben-Alaunwerk. It was still in use after 1945, but was then brought onto land, restored, and set up in Bad Düben as a mill museum. In Roumania 29 ship mills remained in operation in 1957.

SHNAIKA: A Russian nineteenth-century cargo ship from the White Sea region. The ship carried a large square sail on the mainmast, and a gaff sail on the smaller mizzen mast.

SHOAL WATER BOAT: A boat or ship built for coastal work, with a shallow draught

enabling it to navigate shoal waters generally. The shelf area off the North Sea coast stretching from Holland to Schleswig-Holstein is in many places only navigable by very shallow-draught ships (drawing less than 2m), and then only at flood-tide, or along the tidal channels. Among the characteristic shoal water boats which have been developed on the North Sea coast are the TJALK, the KUFF, the SCHMAKE and the SCHNIGGE. At low tide the shoal water boats come to rest on the ground, hence they must be flat-bottomed types. In the nineteenth century the shoal water EWER was developed on the west coast of Schleswig-Holstein and the north Friesian islands, as a specialized form of the north German ewer, usually with a single mast. Shoal water ewers were occasionally built with mizzen masts. The term shoal water boat is nowadays applied to shallow draught cruising yachts, designed for sailing in rivers and estuaries.

SHOE DHONI: A fishing boat from the Godavari Selta, India, whose name refers to the unique shoe-shaped hull. The mast is stepped at about one quarter of the boat's length, and is supported from the front by the deck, which reaches back to that point. The boat also has its maximum beam at this forward point.

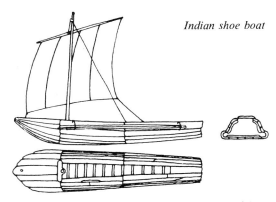

Indian shoe boat

SHRIMP SCHUYT: A small BOMME with a flat transom stern and a rather squat, egg-shaped hull form. The area forward of the mast was covered, and there was a compartment aft of the mast separated and sealed off with a bulkhead, sometimes taking the form of a fish well. The rig consisted of mainsail, staysail and jib. The last sailing shrimp schuyt was wrecked in 1940.

SICKE, *sacksicken*: A two-masted boat from the southern Baltic, with two masts and spritsails. Principal dimensions were 5 to 7m length and 1.5 to 2.5m beam. Depending on the size of the boat, the CLINKER-built hull had three or four strakes. The shorter of the two masts was located far forward. The sicken, a form of fish well connected to the outside, was located in the central section of the boat.

SIDON SARCOPHAGUS RELIEF: A bas-relief picture on a sarcophagus dating from the second or third centuries, showing a Syrian-Roman cargo sailing ship, based on a keel and frames. The sarcophagus was found in the city of Saida (formerly Sidon) on the Lebanese coast, and dates from the time when Lebanon was under Roman rule.

SIXAREEN, *sixern*: An open boat of the Shetlands, employed in the haaf (deep sea) fishery, setting long lines. The sixareen developed during the eighteenth century after Shetland ceased to import all its boats (in pieces for assembly on the island) from Norway, and retained Scandanavian characteristics in its construction. It was a light, fine-ended CLINKER boat with raking curved stem and stern posts. The name derives from the six oars it carried, but it was also propelled by a single large dipping lugsail. The sixareen was around 12m in length, with a beam of 3m and a depth of 1m. It did not have a long life: after some seven years it was dismantled, some of the timber possibly being re-used to make a smaller, four-oared version — the fourareen or fourern.

SIX-MASTER: A general term covering all large sailing ships with six masts, regardless of rig. These vessels were rigged as barquentines or schooners. The barquentine version carried

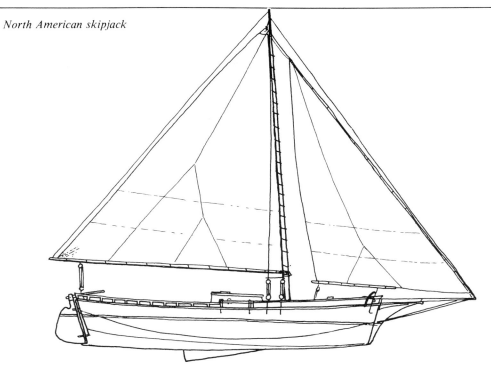

North American skipjack

fore-and-aft sails on the five after masts, with square sails on the foremast. The first six-masted barquentine was built in 1918. The six-masted gaff-rigged schooner carried fore-and-aft sails on all masts.

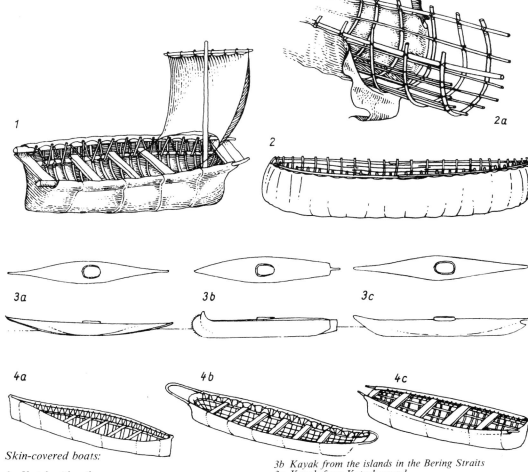

SKAGEN BOAT: Originally an open, two-masted fishing boat, which was also built in a covered version towards the end of the nineteenth century. It was used for fishing with line and driftnet.

SKAITH: *see* LONGSHIP.

SKIFF: A slim, lightweight rowing boat. The name skiff is common in a number of countries for other types of light boat. For example, a small, open, CLINKER-built sailing boat is known as the Orkney skiff ; in North America the term Delaware sturgeon skiff is used for a 7.5m long fishing boat used for catching that fish. This is a two-masted soft-chine keelboat with transom stern, usually rigged with spritsails.

SKIN BOAT: A primitive form of vessel based on a light wooden framework of circular, oval or extended shape, covered with animal skins. Such boats evolved independently in various parts of the world, the frameworks being covered with a variety of materials. The ancient Greeks and Romans carried such skin-covered boats with them on military campaigns. They referred to them as carabia (latin: carabas). The Normans used the words chuile, cyule or ceol, although these terms also applied to other types of boat. *See also* CORACLE, CURRAGH *and* PELOTA.

SKIPJACK: A single-masted, clipper-stemmed, transom-sterned boat from the North American Atlantic coast, used for oyster dredging. The mast rakes aft and sets a lug-of-mutton sail with a staysail or jib running to a short bowsprit. It was 12 to 24m in length. The hull design was adopted for small yachts.

Skin-covered boats:

1   *Umiak with sail*
2   *Chinese skin-covered boat*
2a *Woven framework of a Chinese skin-covered boat*
3a *Greenland kayak*
3b *Kayak from the islands in the Bering Straits*
3c *Kayak from Kotzebuesund*
4a *Greenland umiak*
4b *Umiak from east Greenland*
4c *Umiak from eastern Siberia*

SKULDELEV SHIP: *see* ROSKILDE SHIP.

SLAVE SHIP: Fast, lightly-built brigs or
schooners which carried abducted slaves from
Africa to America, after the slave trade had
been outlawed by all states, and warships
patrolled the coasts. Ships of about 250 tons
cargo capacity crammed in up to 500 slaves
below deck, packed close together, with each
person having his body-width of space to lie
down in. The standard of care was correspondingly low, and in many cases up to 50 per cent
of the slaves died during the crossing.

SLOF: A large, open nineteenth-century
Rhine ship about 45m in length, of simple
design with a folding mast. High washstrakes
were a feature of the vessels, to prevent
flooding when the vessel was loaded.

SLOOP (*naval vessel*): A small cruising ship
which served in the Royal Navy from the later
seventeenth century, formally known as a
sloop of war. They may have originally been
sloop-rigged but from at least the 1680s up to
about 1760 these ships were rigged as a
SNOW, KETCH or BRIGANTINE, and
carried up to 12 six-pounder cannon. Thus
they ranked next after the Sixth Rate ships.
After 1760, 16-gun three-masted sloops were
built. When brigs were introduced into the
navy around 1780, an official line was drawn in
the naval ships' lists between full-rigged 'ship
sloops' and brig-sloops. These latter were
under the command of a commander whereas
gun-brigs were captained by lieutenants.

SLOOP GALLEAS: In the first third of the
nineteenth century a type of sloop was built
with a small mizzen mast, and from it the sloop
galleas was developed around 1850. In its
sloop form the vessel featured a tall mizzen
mast with long topmast, standing further
forward, in addition to the sloop mast. Both
masts were rigged with large, gaff sails and gaff
topsails, plus three square sails on the
mainmast, a staysail and several jibs on the
bowsprit. In the Baltic region the sloop galleas
was a rare ship type.

SLOOP, *schlup, slup*: A single-masted sailing
boat whose name is associated with the
shallop. The characteristic feature of the type
is the sloop rig, consisting of just a main and
foresail, which represents the standard rig for
both modern racing and cruising boats. The
mainsail may be a BERMUDIAN sail or a gaff
sail.
    Sloops were in existence as early as the
sixteenth century, although at this time the
name referred to rowing boats and oared
sailing boats. Later on, the vessels were fitted
with a variety of rigs to suit their many
different applications in trade, fishing and war.
The rig also varied at different periods and in
different regions. In the North and Baltic Seas

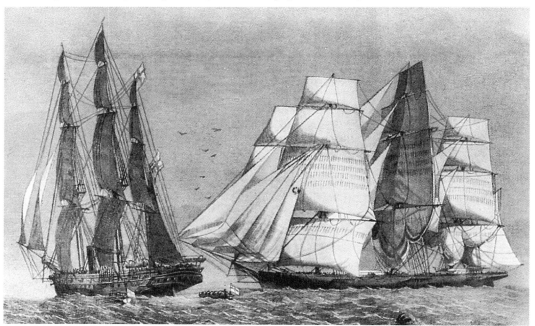

Capture of the slave ship Sunny South *(ex* Emanuela) *by HMS* Brisk, *1860*

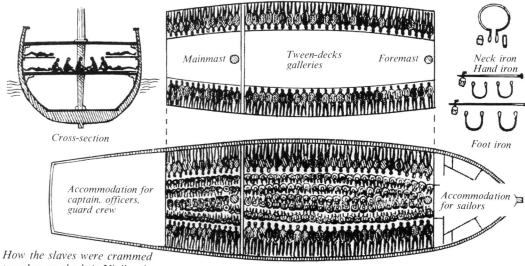

Cross-section

Mainmast   *Tween-decks galleries*   Foremast

*Neck iron
Hand iron*

Foot iron

Accommodation for captain, officers, guard crew

Accommodation for sailors

How the slaves were crammed together on the brig Vigilanti, *captured in 1822*

Plan view of the tween-decks

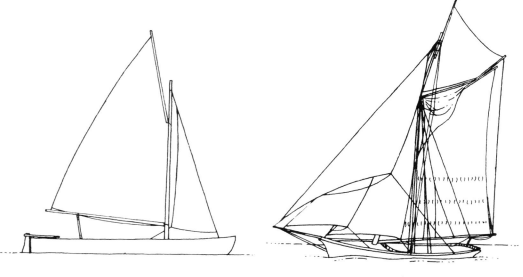

Sloop rig with gunter mainsail   *Earlier rig with gaff topsail*

the terms slop and sloop were particularly common in respect of small fishing vessels, and coastal traders.

SMAKE: *see* SCHMACK.

SMELT EWER: A single- or two-masted fishing ewer used on the lower Elbe for catching smelt, and also known as the Hamen ewer. These ewer were about 14m long and 4.5 in breadth.

SNEKKJA: A medieval ship type with relatively fine lines, used in the northern European region from the tenth to the fourteenth century. It was a rowing vessel and could travel at high speeds. Snekkjas were frequently used in battle in England and other countries. In size, the thirteenth-century snekkja was comparable to the COG, but by the fourteenth century its importance had waned. By that time snekkjas were carried on board large military vessels as ships's boats.

SNIPE: A North American sailing dinghy developed in 1931 with a snipe as sail symbol. Built in hardchine style, the boat is 4.73m long overall, and 4.12m on the waterline, with a beam of 1.52m. The boat is an international one-design class, has 10m² of sail area and is sailed by a two-man crew.

Snow, 1768

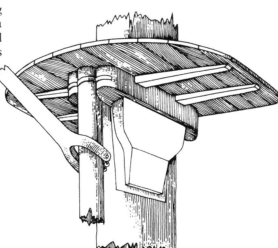

Lower mast with spreader, snow mast and gaff

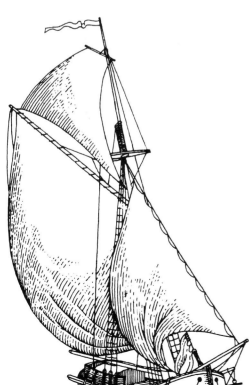

Merchant sloop with gaff topsail

SNOW: A two-masted square-rigged northern European ship of the eighteenth and nineteenth centuries, rigged rather like the BRIG. The mainsail, which was sometimes loose footed, was carried on a snow mast (a light, auxiliary mast) which was located immediately abaft the mizzen mast. The snow mast was a light auxiliary mast for the gaff sail. Various types of fore-and-aft rigged ships were often built with such masts because it simplified sail handling.

SNURREWADEN BOAT: A fishing boat designed for catching flatfish. The snurrewade, or schnurwade, is a type of dragged net specially designed for catching flatfish. Around 1875, coastal fishing in the North Sea was concentrated on catching plaice by means of the snurrewade, and to this end a new ship type with round stem and round, transom-less stern was built, aimed at providing a particularly large deck area. The boats incorporated a large fish well. The two-masted boats were rigged with gaff mainsail and topsail, jib and flying jib plus mizzen sail and mizzen topsail. The vessels were about 15 to 20m long and 4.5 to 5.5m wide.

'SOHAR': *see* BÛM.

SOLING: A one-design racing boat (keel boat), designed by the Norwegian designer J Linge. Since 1972, the Soling has been an

Soling, one-design Olympic class keelboat

Olympic class, and carries a stylized boat Greek letter 'Ω' (Omega) as sail symbol. The boat is 8.15m long overall, and 6.10m on the waterline, with a beam of 1.90m and displaces 1000kg including 580kg of keel ballast. The draught is 1.30m, and the racing crew consists of three men. The mainsail has an area of 15.95m², the foresail 8.35m². The modern one-design class boat is built in plastic only, using the master mould developed by the IYRU (International Yacht Racing Union). It features bulkheads forward and aft to seal off buoyancy chambers, which are filled with foam to increase the buoyancy yet further. The mast is usually made of light aluminium alloy.

SOUTH SEAS BOATS: Vessels of the southern section of the Pacific Ocean, which includes the main areas of Melanesia (region of black islands), Micronesia (region of small islands) and Polynesia (region of many islands); a total of about 3000 islands within an area of about 250,000m², and stretching from New Guinea to the Easter Islands and from Hawaii to New Zealand. Until contact was established with Europeans, the boat- and shipbuilders of the South Seas had nothing but stone-age tools and aids for constructing their vessels. They used a cross-bladed axe (similar to the European adze) to which was clamped a swivelling mussel shell which served as a cutter (usually shells of the giant mussel Tridacna gigas). Holes were bored with drills whose point consisted of a long spiral snail shell. Larger boats were built by teams of men, in which case one person had the permanent task of sharpening the tools.

On islands with plentiful timber the 8 to 12m long boat hulls were usually built as dugouts, with or without side planks bound on. On the Polynesian atolls such as the Tuamotu islands and the Marshall islands of Micronesia, where few trees grew, the hulls were made of thinner and shorter logs. The individual components were usually cut and trimmed so accurately, and the planking components and strakes bound together so carefully, using coconut fibre thongs, that the joints were watertight without additional sealing material, and without recourse to caulking. This was achieved without the use of nails; instead strips of pandanus leaves were laid underneath the planks, which were pressed down onto a seating using cords made of coconut, Lygodium or rutan fibres. Before any long voyage the hull was painted white with a lime-rich liquid gleaned from algae, which protected the vessel from encrustation and simultaneously pacified the Gods.

In the South Seas the dugout with outrigger was the most common type of vessel. The outrigger boats usually featured single outriggers, although double outriggers were preferred in the northern Solomon islands and western New Guinea. To improve their sea-going characteristics, the sides of the dugouts were raised by means of planks fitted onto the main trunk, bound in place with fibres and

Spree cargo kahns

Spree tourist kahns

sealed with resins. As the water resistance of a single outrigger has the effect of making the whole vessel turn, various islands (eg the Marians, Palau, Sandwich and Gilbert islands) developed an asymmetrical boat hull to compensate. The side of the boat furthest away from the outrigger was flatter and had less pronounced curvature than the inside face to compensate for the effect; this solution, rarely used in boatbuilding, is evidence of keen observation. In this respect the single-outrigger boat in particular had a series of interesting features. The outrigger was always fitted on the weather side (the side facing the wind), so that only a small portion of it was submerged, in order to minimize water resistance; because of this, the method of handling the sail differs fundamentally from that used on all other boats. The angled yard spar has one forked end, and it and the steering paddle can be shifted to the other end of the boat when necessary. Thus the vessel can sail in

either direction, with the outrigger always on the windward side. The sails usually consisted of woven matting made of fibres ad strips of leaves from the pandanus palm and the sago tree.

The main forms of sail shape can be differentiated: the triangular (or Oceanic lateen sail), the typical crab's claw shape in its many variants, and the rectangular sail set on a yard. It is possible that the square sail evolved at a later date, under the influence of European vessels. A large movable paddle, similar to a side-rudder, was attached at either end of the vessel to steer it. Another of the South Seas boats is the double-boat, which may have evolved from the outrigger boat or *vice versa*. On these vessels a second buoyant vessel (another dugout) acts in place of the outrigger as stabilizer.

The art of seafaring was quite highly developed among the South Seas tribes, including knowledge of the stars, the weather and the oceans, especially among the Micronesians and Polynesians. For instance, schools of navigation were established on the Marshall islands at an early date. Among the teaching aids used were maps made of palm leaves tied together; sea snail shells bound in place indicated the position of the islands and atolls of the Marshall archipelago, and showed the distances and the courses to be held. One of the most astounding feats achieved by the South Seas islanders is that regular voyages were carried out over the open sea between Tahiti and Hawaii as early as the thirteenth century; a distance of almost 4000km. That various South Sea tribes also knew how to build larger vessels is clear from the reports of G Forster covering the voyages of discovery of J Cook (around 1770). Forster reported warboats with 144 oarsmen, eight to ten helmsmen and about 30 warriors.

SPEEL YACHT: The name given in Holland to the pleasure vessels which began to be popular in the early seventeenth century. They were usually two-masted yachts, the forward mast being stepped right at the bow. The rig consisted of gaff sails with very short gaffs, but no foresails. The transom was very tall and had equally high bulwarks, to protect passengers from the elements. The spiel yachts had narrow leeboards, usually decorated.

SPERONARA: A small, open sailing boat based on the coasts of Sicily and Malta. It was fitted with a mast stepped far forward, rigged with a spritsail. The vessel's origins are lost in the long distant past, but it remained in use into the nineteenth century. There were also two-masted speronaras, known as drahisfas.

SPOON-BOWED SHIP: Ships capable of coping with drift ice, and large yachts with a long, projecting stem, with convex curvature like that of a spoon. Under certain conditions at sea, for example, when there is a steep sea the spoon bow, with its inherent buoyancy, helps to prevent the bow dipping too severely when the vessel pitches. The increased foreward beam at the waterline also improves the vessel's stability.

The first spoon-bow yachts to gain international recognition were designed and built by the American designer NA Herreshoff.

SPREE KAHN: Shallow-draught punted barge which can still be seen on the river Spree in Germany today, especially in the Spree forest region. They are used for carrying passengers and light freights. Originally, these vessels were used to transport vegetables, fruit and other products to Berlin.

SPRIT EWER, sprit kahn: A EWER or KAHN rigged with spritsails. Sprit ewers were first mentioned in Holland at the end of the seventeenth century, but were not in use on the Elbe until the end of the eighteenth century.

Spritsails are easier to handle than the square sails which were standard in northern Europe up to the mid nineteenth century, and

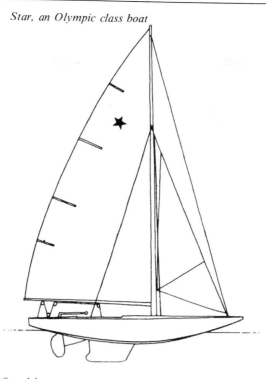

Star, an Olympic class boat

for this reason coastal and river ships, such as the ewers and inland cargo barges, were often fitted with them. Particularly well known were the spritsail cargo barges which carried about 200 tons of coal on the rivers Elbe and Oder. The empty barges were towed upstream from the towpath, and when fully laden required no more than slight thrust from the sail for the journey down the valley, although nimble sail handling was essential in the tricky water conditions. As the public waterways were not marked at the time, pilots were required for each journey. The pilot (known as the haupter or mummenstecker) always sailed in front with a small boat, marking out the navigable stretch with poles (the mummen) stuck in the river bottom. A stockpflücker (stick puller) followed the cargo barges in a second boat and pulled the poles out again. As the waterways were constantly changing, each pilot hoarded the latest knowledge of the waterway as a professional secret. In order to keep the pilot's fees small, sprit cargo barges often sailed in convoy and five to eight sprit barges would be coupled together. The method of marking the waterway was time-consuming, and the barges' speed correspondingly slow, so sails were only set on the front and rear barges on such convoys (known as Elbe-kompanien).

SPRITSAIL BARGE: *see* THAMES BARGE.

SQUARE-RIGGED SHIP: A general term for sailing ships on which the sail-carrying spars are suspended at right-angles to the ship's centreline. The most obvious alternative arrangement is the fore-and-aft rigged ship, whose sails are fitted along the ship's centreline.

Until the Middle Ages, fore-and-aft sails (lateen sails) were preferred in the Mediter-

ranean, and square sails in northern Europe. After this time, more efficient combinations of square and fore-and-aft sails gradually evolved. Eventually, such compromise arrangements predominated, with the result that hardly any large ships rigged exclusively with square sails remained by the time of the heyday of sailing ships. Whether supplementary fore-and-aft sails are fitted or not, the term square-rigged ship is still used for any ship on which square sails are the basic arrangement.

STAATSIE-POON: *see* POON.

STAR: An international one-design keel boat with a bulb keel. It is an open boat of hard-chine SHARPIE type. The first boat was drawn up by the yacht designer W Gardner, and was built in J Smith's boatyard at New York. The first boat was 6m long, and with its relatively low length/beam ratio it earned the nickname bug. Since 1911, the boat has been built to an overall length of 6.90m, which is now standard. The present-day Star is 4.72m long on the waterline, 1.73m in breadth, and 1.015m deep with its 400kg bulb keel. Originally, the Star carried a low gaff mainsail, but in 1921 a bermudian rig was adopted. In 1929, the rig was again modernized, with an extended mast and taller sails. Since that time the sail area has remained unchanged at $26m^2$, and it is especially remarkable that the foresail has remained unchanged through all the boat's stages of development. The sail symbol is a large, red, five-pointed star. The racing crew consists of two persons. A spinnaker and genoa are not permitted for racing.

The Star became internationally popular, and by 1922 a worldwide organization for Star sailors had been established, the International Star Class Yacht Racing Association (ISCYRA). In 1923, the first world championships for the Star class were held. The Star is one of the most long-lived of Olympic class boats. It first took part in the Los Angeles Olympic games of 1932, and was represented at all Olympiads until 1972. In 1979, the Star boat was once more granted the status of an Olympic class boat.

STATE BARGE: Barge used for state occasions, carrying the state coat of arms and

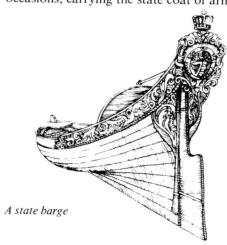

A state barge

rowed by sailors in full dress uniform. The small number of state barges which remained in use until quite recently were mostly copies of historic vessels, decorated with rich carved work and paintings.

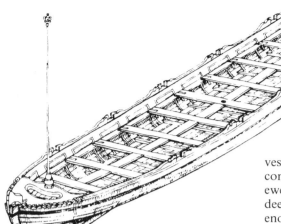

STAYSAIL KETCH: *see* KETCH.

STAYSAIL SCHOONER: *see* SCHOONER.

STAVERSE JOL, *staverse jolle*: A flat-bottomed, sea-going Dutch sailing jolle with a particularly broad bow, but no leeboards. The jolle is 5.50m to 8.50m long, 2.40 to 3.00m in breadth and has a sail area of about 25m². It was a development of a Dutch herring and sardine fishing boat which had been built since about 1870. By about 1950 the last of the staverse jollen had disappeared.

STECKNITZ KAHN: A cargo barge of about 12 tons cargo capacity which was specially tailored to match the conditions and size of the Stecknitz canal. The canal was commissioned by the city of Lübeck and built between 1391 and 1398 as a means of communication between Hamburg and Lübeck, and thus between the North and Baltic Seas. The canal connects the rivers Elbe and Trave. It is 59km long, but only 4.66m wide and 0.9m deep and has 13 locks. Transport of goods on this canal using Stecknitz barges can be traced back to 1820. It was considered to be vital that a short water route should exist between the North Sea and the Baltic, and in consequence an even more direct link was built from the Hamburg end, using the rivers Alster and Beste, between 1525 and 1550. Under the Danish King Christian VII the 45km long Eider canal was built between 1777 and 1785. This connected Rendsburg to Kiel bay at Holtenau, and could be used by ships up to 32m long and 3m draught.

STONE EWER: A north German ewer which was designed especially for transporting bricks, and which thus required particularly strong structural timbers to cope with the compact, heavy cargo, especially when the

vessel was resting on the ground. In comparison with other types of ewer, the stone ewer was short and squat, with a relatively deep draught. The vessels had to be strong enough to rest on the ground at ebb tide with a full load without leaking. Two-masted stone ewers of 15 to 16m length, about 5.2m beam and 1.6m hold depth were built in large numbers in the nineteenth century, especially in Dornbusch, Wischhafen, Gauensiek, Stade and Cranz.

One of the walled locks on the Stecknitz canal

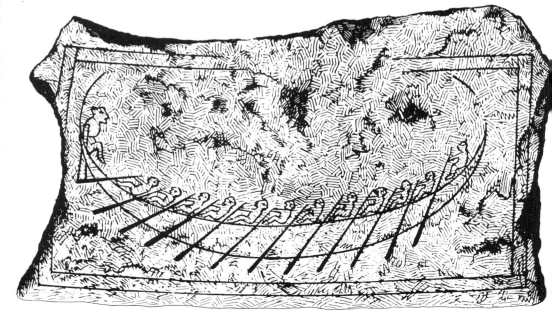

Häggeby stone, Sweden

STONE FISHING BOATS: A small harbour and coastal vessel, fitted with raising booms and grabs to allow it to lift stones from the harbour basin, or waterways leading to it. It represented a specialized forerunner of the floating crane.

STONE TABLET SHIP PICTURES: Ships and runic drawings on individual stones, similar to rock drawings. One of the oldest picture stones found in northern Europe is the Karstad rune stone, which is named after the site of its discovery. It dates from around 1000 BC and was found by a teacher from Nordfjord in Norway. The stone includes a number of representations of double-stemmed ships as well as runes.

The ship picture on the Häggeby stone dates from the ninth century. It is a bold drawing of a schuyt or karfe and a Viking ship with stem and stern or similar design, featuring 12 rows of oarsmen. This stone was formerly the property of the church in the Swedish town of Häggeby, but now belongs to the Stockholm Museum collection.

In a rock grave near Kivik (Skane, south Sweden) stone tablets dating from the early bronze age have been discovered intact. One of these tablets shows a stylized picture of a double-ended ship. Another well-known picture of a ship on a stone is a Scottish example, now stored in the Edinburgh museum. This dates from the second half of the thirteenth century, and shows a ship similar to the cog.

STÖR PRAHM: A flat-bottomed sailing barge of the eighteenth and nineteenth centuries used for transporting timber on the River Stör, and of suitably rugged construction. The vessel had large leeboards and a folding pole mast. The rig comprised spritsail, staysail and jib. The last example was scrapped in 1911.

STRAW EWER: A ewer with leeboards used on the Elbe in the Hanover region. It evolved at the beginning of the nineteenth century and served mainly to carry straw and hay and other agricultural products to Hamburg-Altona from an area stretching from Neuland (Harburg) to Hoopte. The straw ewers were specially fitted out for their particular cargo, and had short decks forward and aft only. The centre section of the vessel was completely open. The boats were up to 20m long and were rigged with a loose-footed gaff mainsail and staysail.

STRUJOK: A small barge used on the Volga in the eighteenth and nineteenth centuries, propelled by a double-ended paddle with lance-shaped blades.

Strumok, Russian river khan of the eighteenth and nineteenth centuries

STRUSE: A ship of the Hanseatic period, especially well known on the River Don. It was employed as a means of transport for grain and other cargoes susceptible to damp. For this reason the deck was sealed with a layer of clay. Two large, loosely suspended oars were used to steer the vessel. There were several strusen in the Swedish fleet around 1630. They were about 16m long and could carry between 40 and 70 tons with a crew of six to nine men. There were also larger, sea-going ships to which the same term was applied as, for example, the 450-ton English warship *Struse of Danzig*, which was built in Danzig (Gdansk) and purchased in 1544.

SURF BOAT: A broad ship's boat of the eighteenth and nineteenth centuries which was used to land or embark passengers on open shorelines. As it had to pass through shallow waters and rough surf, the boat either had a flat keel or no keel at all, had sharp, projecting

Sutton-Hoo ship; excavation site and imprint of ship from the first half of the seventh century

bow and stern, and was built strongly to withstand the inevitable shocks and stresses of its life.

SUTTON HOO SHIP: A ship grave of a king of the Angles, found in one of a series of 11 tumuli near Sutton Hoo, in Suffolk in 1938. This was probably the grave of King Redwald of the Angles, who was buried in the year 630. In spite of the fact that the ship's timbers had rotted away almost completely, systematic investigations of the outline left in the sand allowed experts to reconstruct the dimensions and shape of the ship. The work was made easier by the fact that the position of the rivets was clearly visible. The ship was 27.4m long, 4.3m in width and had a hold depth of about 1.4m. It was built of oak with a keel plank and 26 transverse ribs. The ship was propelled by oars, whose projecting guides were still clearly recognizable. The shape of the ship indicated that it was a transitional type between the NYDAM BOAT and the classic VIKING SHIP. The ship was accompanied by a rich collection of other items, especially weapons and jewellery made of gold and precious stones. This is one of the most important finds ever made in England, and it is now stored in the British Museum.

SVOISKAJA LODKA: A two-masted open cargo barge used on western Russian rivers in the nineteenth century. It had two pole masts each fitted with a simple angled yard sail which could be lowered. The vessel was steered with a rudder fitted with a tiller, the effect of which was reinforced when necessary by a punt pole or long oars operated from the bow or stern.

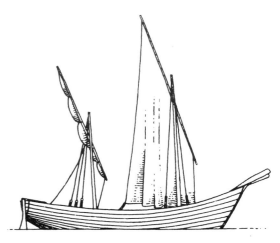

Svoiskaja lodka, nineteenth-century Russian river cargo kahn

T

Tafa'anga, Polynesian outrigger boat

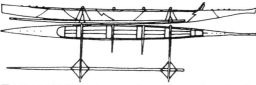

French tartane, ca 1770

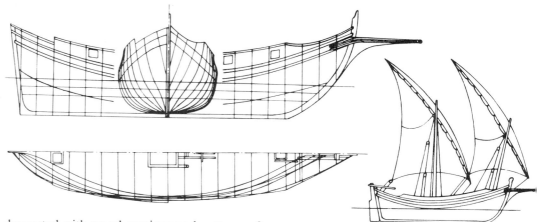

TAFA'ANGA: An outrigger boat 6 to 9m in length, from the Tangan achipelago. It had side planks added to the dugout hull, and the ends were covered in.

TAFOREA: A ship type of the fifteenth and sixteenth centuries which was employed for many purposes. It was built and sailed on the Iberian peninsula and also in France and Italy. As well as ordinary transport tasks, the vessel was used to carry horses and artillery. The type was characterized by a low freeboard. The taforea was said to have sides no higher than those of a GALLEY or GALEOTE.

TAGLERPOLTEN, *tagler:* This term applied to small, single-masted fishing craft used in the Tuck region. Three sizes were built. There were those from 11.5 to 15m long and 5 to 6m wide, others around 10m long and 4 to 4.2m wide, and the smallest versions at about 8m long and 3m broad. The stem was S-shaped, while a centreboard was usually fitted on the larger taglerpolten. The pole mast carried a boomless gaff mainsail with a gaff topsail above it. The long jib boom supported a staysail and a relatively large jib.

Small, roofed tanka

TANKA: A Canton SAMPAN used for a variety of purposes, such as carrying passengers. The central area of the boat is roofed and divided into two compartments — the aft one usually being the living quarters of the tanka owner and his family. The boat is propelled by a bow scull and a stern scull, while a third person fends off collisions with a type of stanchion hook.

TANKWA, *Tanqua:* A simple PAPYRUS raft used on Lake Tana in Ethiopia. The lightweight rafts carry three to four persons, and are propelled by bamboo punt poles. Larger rafts are also built, up to 10m in length, and capable of carrying around three tons.

TARADA: An Iraqi planked boat, similar to the Mash-hûf in design, used in the marches. The boats are carefully built, with the plank seams sealed with natural ashphalt. The boats belonging to tribal leaders are specially decorated with wood carvings and patterns of nails. The name tirada was applied to a boat made from reeds and covered with bitumen: zaima is the more common term for such boats today.

TARIDE, *tareta, tareda, tarta:* A Mediterranean oared sailing ship which was built in large numbers at the time of the Crusades, and which survived from the early Middle Ages until the fourteenth century. In 1246, Louis the Pious of France ordered 12 tarides to be built, each with three sails and 40 oars. There was said to be space on board for 20 horses. The flat-bottomed vessels were stated to be about 36m long, with a beam of about 3.3m. Thirty years later the keel length of a taride under construction in Genoa was stated to be 17m, and the overall length 26.8m, and the beam 8.7m. The ships were more strongly built than the GALLEY and could carry a greater cargo. They were also used in the Sicilian fleet.

TARTANE, *tartana, tartan:* A widely used general-purpose and fishing ship of the Mediterranean and Arabian Gulf regions which survived from the seventeenth to the nineteenth century. The word tartana meaning small ship, which the Italians adopted from the Arabic, refers to the small size of the vessel. The type was basically a two-masted vessel, but single-masted versions were built later. In 1768, F H Chapman described the tartane as a small, two-masted ship with bluff bow, lateen-rigged on both pole masts, and with a strong forward rake on the smaller foremast. In contrast, the drawing by Amiral Paris (1882), prepared rougly 100 years later, shows single-masted Italian tartanes of streamlined form, with long, projecting jib booms, rigged with three foresails and one large lateen sail.

TCHEKTIRME, *tchektima:* A single-masted, full-bodied Turkish coastal vessel, used primarily in the Bosphorus and the Dardanelles. The smaller vessels carried a bermudian mainsail, plus a staysail, jib and outer jib. The larger versions had a lower mast and topmast, rigged with two square sails and a staysail, and a large spritsail rather than a bermudian mainsail. Washboards were fitted to compensate for the low freeboard.

TEA CLIPPER: *see* CLIPPER.

TEK-PAI: A Taiwanese bamboo raft. The number of bamboos varied between six and 14, the thicker ends forming the stern of the raft with a resulting taper forwards, where the bow is curved upwards to ride over the waves. This 'palmised' or 'duck' hull shape is characteristic of a great many types of Chinese craft — rafts and planked boats — and this is taken as evidence that the SAMPAN is descended from a raft. The tek-pai was 6m or more in length with a beam of about 2½m. In addition to a battened matting lugsail, it was equipped with

Tempest; Olympic class keelboat, 1952 and 1976

two pairs of oars, which not only rowed but steered the craft. Three dagger boards were employed. Passengers were accommodated in a wooden tub.

TEMPEST: An open keel boat of 6.70m overall length, 5.87m on the waterline, 1.92m beam, 1.10m draught and with a sail area of 23m², not including the spinnaker of 18.8m². The boat was designed by the English designer, Ian Proctor, and was an Olympic class from 1969 to 1976. The sail symbol is a large black 'T', and the boat carries a two-man crew. A feature of the Tempest is that the keel can be raised in similar fashion to a centreboard.

TENDER: Small vessels which provide a variety of services to larger ships.

TESSACONTER: One of the large ships of the ancient Greeks, said to have been built as a 80-oar vessel under the Macedonian army leader Ptolemeus around 250 BC. The vessel was stated to be 124m long and 17m in breadth, with a height of 21m forward and 23.5m aft. Although these dimensions cannot be proved, it is clear from the number of oarsmen that the vessel was significantly larger than other ships of the time judging by the necessary minimum fore-and-aft spacing of the oarsmen's benches, which was about 1m.

THALAMEGUS: A large, luxuriously appointed Roman houseboat, like that of the Roman Emperor Caligula. *See also* LAKE NEMI SHIPS.

THAMES BARGE, *spritsail barge*: A flat-bottomed, wall-sided cargo vessel with

English three-decker Sovereign of the Seas, *launched 1637. From an engraving by J Payne*

leeboards, setting a large spritsail, foresail and mizzen. Most barges also set a gaff topsail and many set a jib on a bowsprit. Those without a topmast and topsail were known as stumpies. They were very numerous in the nineteenth century and survived to be the last of the sea-going commercial sailing boats in northern Europe. Ranging in size from 13 to 30m in length, they drew less than 2m when loaded, and little more than a metre when unloaded, and could be sailed unballasted. The smallest

carried only 30 tons; the largest, 250 tons. Although primarily associated with the River Thames, they traded as far as the ports of Exeter and Hull, and crossed the Channel to the French, Dutch and German ports.

THERA FRESCO: A fresco named after the island of Thera (present-day Santorini in the Greek Cyclades) on which ships are depicted. Around 1500 BC, a simultaneous earthquake and volcanic eruption caused part of the island to sink below the surface of the sea. The city there was buried, and a covering of volcanic ash made many islands as far as away as Crete uninhabitable for a long period. The city was later partially excavated, and a fresco about 2.5m long and 0.4m high was discovered in a building which is assumed to have been the residence of fleet commanders. The fresco shows several ships of different sizes, all built in the same style, and decorated in festive style with garlands for what was probably a cult celebration.

The vessels have a pointed, upward-curving stempost, similar to ships' sterns shown in ancient Greek pictures. Four larger vessels have a further interesting feature. The stern is fitted with a projecting extension supporting a beam running along the hull. The significance of this extension has not been explained fully though it might have been used for towing tree trunks. The larger vessels are propelled by about 20 men on either side, who appear to be paddling, although oarsmen are clearly distinguishable on one of the smaller boats. There are awnings on the deck for the shelter of travelling priests, officials or merchants.

THREE-DECKER, *three-decked ship*: A sailing ship of the line with three full-length

Thames sailing barge, ca 1910

covered batteries. The first three-decker in the English navy was the *Sovereign of the Seas*, launched in 1637. This ship displaced around 1700 tons and carried 104 guns and a crew of 600 men. The *Victory*, Nelson's flagship at Trafalgar in 1805, was also a three-decker. She displaced around 3000 tons and carried 100 guns and a crew of 850 men. The last English three-decker sailing ship was the *Duke of Wellington*, built in 1852. Later, this vessel was converted to a screw-driven steam ship. The last French three-deckers were even larger. The *Ville de Paris* had a displacement of about 5000 tons and carried 120 guns. The long building times and high costs of construction and maintenance of these large three-deckers meant that they were built in limited numbers. Smaller three-decked ships with around 90 cannon were more generally used in the battle fleets.

Three-masted full-rigged ship Christian Radich, *the Norwegian training ship*

Three-masted barquentine under sail

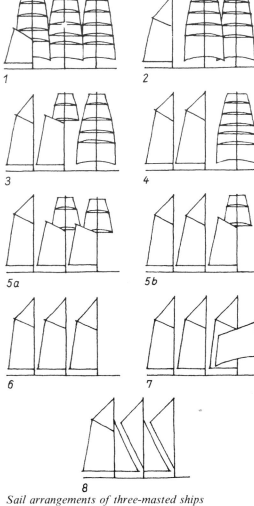

Sail arrangements of three-masted ships

1	Three-masted full-rigged ship or frigate
2	Three-masted barque
3	Three-masted jackass barque or Polka barque
4	Three-masted schooner-barque or barquentine
5a	Three-masted two topsail schooner
5b	Three-masted topsail schooner
6	Three-masted gaff-rigged schooner
7	Three-masted gaff-rigged schooner with square foresa
8	Three-masted staysail schooner

THREE-MASTER, *three-masted full-rigged ship*: A sailing ship with three masts. We can differentiate between three-masted full-rigged ships, on which all three masts were square-rigged, and the three-masted BARQUE, which carried square sails on the two forward masts only, supplemented by gaff or lateen sails on the after mast. Other types of three-masted ship were the three-masted gaff-rigged SCHOONER with gaff sails on all three masts, three-masted topsail schooners with square sails set above the gaff sails on the forward mast, and barquentines with square sails on the foremast and gaff sails on the two after masts. Medieval ships types such as the HULK, CARRACK, CARAVEL and NAO were also three-masted ships.

TIGARI, *gawla*: A hemispherical fired clay vessel of Bangladesh, about 1m in diameter, paddled by and accommodating only one person.

TIKWINKA: A nineteenth-century Russian single-masted cargo sailing ship, rigged with a tall, relatively narrow square sail on a single pole mast which was stepped far forward. The vessel was used on the rivers running into the Black Sea.

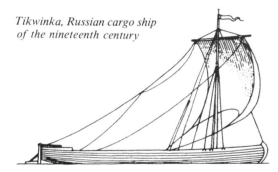

Tikwinka, Russian cargo ship of the nineteenth century

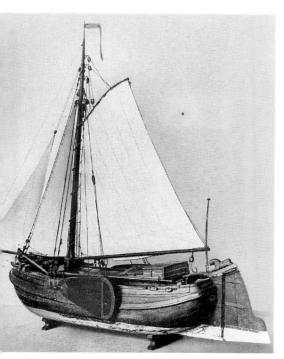

Tjalk with curved gaff, nineteenth century (model)

TIMBER RAFT: *see* RAFT.

TJALK: A typical Dutch shallow-water sailing vessel, whose origins can be traced back to the older BOIER, also a Dutch type, and whose principal characteristics were retained in the succeeding types such as the KUFF TJALK, KUFF, POON and HUKER. Like the boier, the tjalk was full-bodied, with a

Tjalk with spritsail and square topsail, ca 1768

completely flat bottom and no external keel, so that it could rest squarely on the ground when it dried out. Because of its broad beam in relation to its other principal dimensions, and its full-bodied hull, the tjalk only had a small draught, and was therefore ideal for negotiating shallow canals and channels through mudflats.

The term tjalk first appeared in a Friesian

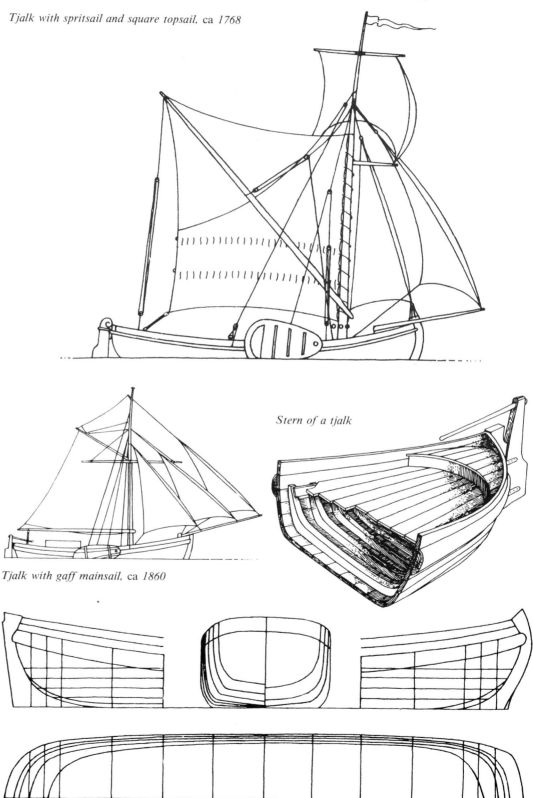

Stern of a tjalk

Tjalk with gaff mainsail, ca 1860

Sheer draught plan of a tjalk, ca 1907

Dutch tjalk yacht

document dated 1673, and in the work *Architectura Navalis* by the Dutchman Nicolaes Witsen in 1690. Many paintings of the sixteenth and seventeenth centuries show the tjalk, depicting the type as a robust, general-purpose ship of simple design. It was clearly in widespread use. The true tjalk rig consisted of a large gaff mainsail with a particularly short gaff and a long main boom, but many variations on this theme evolved up to the nineteenth century. For instance, F Chapman shows a sprit-rigged Dutch tjalk of around 1768. In the nineteenth century, a small tjalk was built in quite large numbers in the east Friesian and Oldenburg region of the Ems. These ships were measured at about 12 registered tons, and had a folding pole mast stepped quite far forward.

The spritsail typical of the nineteenth century was superseded around the middle of the century by a large gaff mainsail with short gaff and long boom, a gaff topsail, and several foresails. As well as the smaller vessels there were also sea-going tjalks with greater sheer, and heck (stern) tjalks with a stern opening for the tiller.

According to H Szymanski, about 160 timber-built and 28 iron tjalks, both sea-going and inland types, were in use in north Germany around 1900. The iron tjalks proved excellent vessels. They were built exclusively in Dutch yards, and in 1928 the German inland fleet still included 189 iron tjalks, with an average cargo capacity of 140 tons.

TJALK YACHT: A single-masted Dutch yacht of the TJALK type which was used for private transport by prosperous Dutchmen. Tjalk yachts were built in large numbers, and

served to carry people to church, on visits, for shopping, and for carrying light cargo. The vessels were up to 15m long, had broad, full-bodied hulls with rounded, decorated bow and stern, and were rigged with gaff mainsail, mizzen and foresails. Because of their pavilion-like superstructures they were also known as paviljoen yachts.

Larger and much more richly decorated tjalk yachts, built with suitably imposing superstructures, were also built, and used mainly as official state yachts.

TJOTTER: A flat-bottomed, single-masted Dutch vessel used as a fishing boat or as a yacht, featuring a long jib boom. It was similar to a fishing boat which had existed since the beginning of the century. In keeping with Dutch tradition, this exceptionally short and broad yacht (4.80m long, 2.50m wide) carried leeboards, and had a relatively large sail area of 25m². It was built after about 1900.

TOMBSTONE SHIP PICTURES: Pictures of ships were often cut into tombstones from ancient times until the Middle Ages, reflecting the social significance of the ship. One picture, showing a large, oared sailing ship with square sails set on a yard, dates from between 1000 and 500 BC, and was found in an ancient Roman Etruscan grave site at Pesaro.

Very informative tombstones were also found during excavations on the highway to Tirer near the old wine-growing town of Neumagen. The pictures on the stones date from the time of the Roman Emperor Constantine (337–280 BC), and show ships on

the Moselle loaded with wine barrels. The boatmen are rowing from a standing position rather than seated, operating the oars with short, jerky strokes. The tomb stones are now stored in the Museum of Saint Germain-en-Laye.

Among the best known northern European tombstones which include depictions of ships are the Gotland stones dating from the Viking period (eighth and ninth centuries). In the case of the Lörbro-Tängelgarda stone, the artist selected ships, battle engagements and sacrifices as his subjects. These pictures provide much information about the development of the sail on ancient Nordic ships.

TORLONIA RELIEF, *Ostia relief*: A marble relief dating from the first or second centuries, discovered in Ostia, the port of ancient Rome (founded in 335 BC, silted up since the fifth century), and named after the Roman Torlonia family of the eighteenth to nineteenth centuries which owned it. The relief shows a typical Roman freight ship, with port equipment and signal fires in the background. The ship shown is a CORBITA, one of the so-called round ships whose primary purpose was to supply Rome with grain. Deck beams can be seen projecting through the ship's sides, which indicates the presence of a deck over the cargo hold to protect the grain cargo.

From the proportions and detail fittings of

Ship on the Lärbro grave stone

the ship the vessel is estimated to have been 25m long and 6 to 7m wide and carrying about 80 to 100 tons. A heavy rudder suspended on a tackle can be made out on the aftership. The tackle was necessary as a means of hoisting the rudder up in heavy seas, to prevent it being damaged. The helmsman operated the rudder from the aft superstructure, which was similar in form to a deckhouse. The types of sail shown are similar to those of other extant Roman ship pictures, such as on the SIDON SARCOPHAGUS, with a large square sail on the mainmast and a triangular topsail above it. The area of the two sails might have been between 150 and 180m². The foremast was raked forward, and also carried a square sail when the vessel was at sea. As the relief picture shows, the foremast was fitted with a block and tackle arrangement at the masthead for loading and discharching cargo.

Roman ships also set a square sail at the bow, the artemon, about 15m² in area, to increase the total sail area. On the relief picture the large square sail depicts the legendary brothers Romulus and Remus and the suckling she-wolf. *See also* OSTIA FRESCO.

TORNADO: A racing catamaran originating in England, and recognized since 1968 as an International one-design class. The Tornado became an Olympic boat class in 1976. It has an overall length of 6.10m and is 5.85 long on the waterline. The vessel is 3.05m wide and has a hull weight of 127kg, a sail area of 21.80m² and is sailed by a racing crew of two men.

TOTORA RAFT: A boat-shaped rush or reed RAFT used by the Indian tribes on Lake Titicaca. At 3821m above sea level the lake is well above the treeline and the fishing vessels used there for centuries have always been constructed of reeds. The rafts are made of

totora reeds which are dried and tied up into bundles, and then lashed together to form a raft of boat-like shape, with a trough and pointed ends. The similarity to the boat-shaped papyrus rafts on the Nile can only be a result of the similar building material. Larger rafts had a bipod mast and a rectangular sail consisting of woven reeds.

TRABAKEL, *trabaccolo*: A sailing ship with two lugsails used in the Adriatic generally, and by the Dalmatians in particular, in the seventeeth and eighteenth centuries. It was an all-purpose vessel employed for coastal work and fishing in the waters between the offshore islands and the mainland. There are certain similarities between this type and the smaller BRAZZERA. Above the large lugsail on each mast was a small square topsail, while the bowsprit supported a large jib. The vessel's length was around 30m and the beam about 6m. A characteristic feature was the stem which curved over and back towards the stern. The boats intended for coastal sailing had a full-length deck between the masts, fitted with a large hatch.

Dutch treck yacht, second half of the eighteenth century

TREBISONDE: A nineteenth-century single-masted cargo ship with square sails whose name alludes to the Turkish merchant city of Trebizond. The vessel plied between Constantinople (Istanbul) and the Black Sea ports.

TRECK SCHUYTE, *treck yacht*: A river boat, schuyte or yacht, which was designed to be

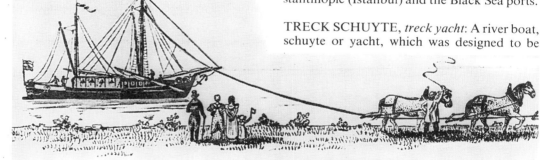
A towed post on the Rhine, ca 1815, also carrying passengers

The Volga towing gang, *painting by Ilja Repin*

Dutch treck schuyt, nineteenth century (model)

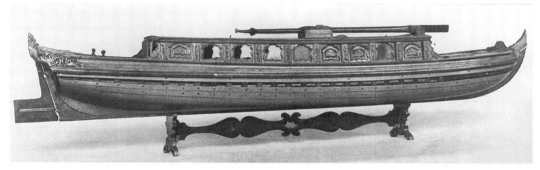

Large Dutch treck yacht, late eighteenth century (model)

pulled along rather than rowed or sailed. The treck schuten could be up to 15m long, and were of quite substantial economic importance for transporting cargo and people (in the latter case the boats were fitted with a cabin) on the many narrow inland waterways of the Netherlands. They were pulled either by manpower or by draught animals.

In the sixteenth, seventeenth and eighteenth centuries there were treck schuten, treck boats and treck yachts on the waterways of most large European cities, varying widely in equipment and decoration, and both privately and state-owned.

TRIAKONTER: A Greek vessel from around 500 BC propelled by 30 oarsmen. Various possible arrangements for the disposition of the rows of oars and rowing seats have been proposed. Generally speaking, these terms referred to the maximum possible number of oarsmen, so we can safely assume that the ships were rowed by 15 oarsmen per side, and hence by a total of 30 oarsmen.

TRIER, *Attic trier*: An ancient Greek oared warship with auxiliary sails and three rows of oars per side, arranged one above the other. A

number of early Greek city states, with Athens taking the leading role, took part in the development of ancient Greek shipbuilding and sea travel. At the time of the Athenian politician Themistocles (524–459 BC) the Corinthian shipbuilder Amenocles modified the design of the large Greek oared PEN-TEKONTER by setting three rows of oarsmen at different levels to form three banks of oars, an arrangement which increased the speed and

fighting power of the vessel significantly.

The probable size of the triers is now estimated to have been between 40 and 45m in length, 4.5 to 5.0m in breadth, and roughly 1m draught. Their dimensions are based on reconstructions, the dimensions of boathouses, and other indirect evidence. The oarsmen in the top row were named thranites, those in the centre row zygites and those of the bottom row thalamites.

The keel of the trier was made of holm oak, and the planking of lighter copper beech or limewood. The fore part of the ship was particularly strongly built, and ended in a bronze or iron-clad ram, known as the embolon. Above the ram was a smaller spur, and between the two was a transverse hole to take a rope. The powerful stem was finished off with a decorated stem head. The stern was spoon-shaped with a forward-curving upper end known as the aphlaston. The trier was steered by steering oars on both sides of the after-ship.

Originally, triers were open vessels, although mats were fitted on both sides of the ship which could be unrolled to protect the oarsmen from sun and bad weather. Later triers were built with a bulwark and a permanent deck to accommodate the soldiers located above the top row of oarsmen. For long voyages the trier set auxiliary sails: a mainsail and a smaller sail on the small, forward-raked bow mast. Masts and sails were taken down before fighting commenced, or removed from the ship altogether.

Triers proved their worth as Mediterranean warships for centuries. Initially, the crew consisted of about 170 oarsmen, 20 sailors and officers, and about 10 marines. The oarsmen were usually thetes, impoverished freemen without property, who allowed themselves to do slave work (ie as oarsmen) for remuneration. In wartime they carried light arms. Heavily armed infantry (the hoplites) formed a small proportion of the soldiers. They were mostly property owners who could afford the equipment, consisting of the large shield, the brazen helmet and breastplate, greaves, a short sword and a long spear.

The Greek trier captain, the trierar, had a

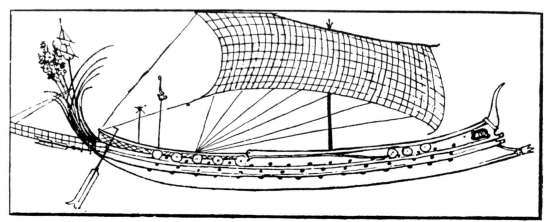

Trier from Delos, from the first century BC

Trimaran Pen Duick

suited to Mediterranean conditions, and in spite of Romans' lack of expeience, they copied the Greek vessels in large numbers in a short space of time, incorporating modifications to take advantage of their advanced constructinal methods, and to suit the battle techniques which had proved successful with Roman land-based troops.

The trireme was a CARVEL-planked vessel based on frames, and was fitted with a mast carrying a large square sail. A Roman innovation was the boarding bridge, which was mounted on the foredeck on a strong mast, around which it could swivel. When an enemy ship was approached, the boarding bridge was dropped down onto it. The spike on the outer end would hold fast in the enemy ship, allowing the Roman warriors, vastly experienced in man-to-man combat on land, to storm over the boarding bridge to engage the enemy in close combat. The Roman triremes were rowed by free Roman peasants and plebeians, rather than by slaves.

first officer, the kybernetes (Greek helmsman) and the keleustes (Greek oar master) at his side. In battle the main tactic of the trier captain was to get into the immediate vicinity of the enemy ship, and either break its oars by running close by (thus rendering it incapable of movement), or ram it broadside on. From our knowledge of the construction and the number of oarsmen, it is estimated that triers could achieve speeds of up to 6 knots.

In succeeding centuries the trier was copied by other Mediterranean nations. The Roman's versions were known as TRIREMEs.

TRIMARAN: A three-hulled vessel. Although multi-hull vessels were known in New Guinea trimarans have been developed during the latter part of the twentieth century as high-performance yachts, particularly for trans-ocean racing. With their central hulls and smaller side floats, light-weight materials and large sail areas, trimarans have come to dominate catamarans and single-hulled yachts.

TRIREME: One of the first of the large Roman warships, based on the Greek TRIER with three rows of oars per side. The Romans began the construction of a major battle fleet at the time of the struggle for Carthage (146 BC). The Greek triers had proved ideally

Roman trireme with boarding bridge

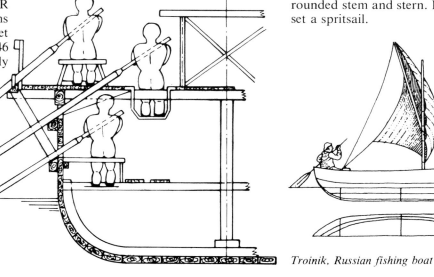

Possible arrangement of oars on a trier

TROINIK: A small northern Russian fishing boat around 5m in length with strongly rounded stem and stern. It could be rowed or set a spritsail.

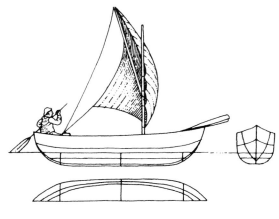

Troinik, Russian fishing boat

TSCHAIKE, *Czaike, zayke*: A lightweight Austrian galley which guarded the Austrian/Hungarian border formed by the rivers Danube, Save and Theis against the Turks. Tschaiken were built in Gmunden in upper Austria between 1530 and 1547 for the Austrian armed forces based on the Danube. During the seventeenth century and up to the mid eighteenth century the types of tschaike in use included the full tschaike of about 24m length, 2.4m beam and 0.5m draught, with 26 oars, and half tschaiken of 12.3m length and about 2m beam, with 20 oars. There were also double tschaiken, about 27 or 28m long. The eighteenth century saw the addition of quarter tschaiken and about 2m beam, with 20 oars. There were also double tschaiken, about 27 or 28m long. The eighteenth century saw the addition of quarter Tschaiken which were built in Gmunden up to 1763/64.

Tschaiken were rigged with square sails, lugsails or spritsails, but in battle the masts were folded down, and the vessels were rowed. Their armaments consisted principally of light guns, mounted in characteristic forked supports, and one or two 7 to 10 pounder howitzers on rotating mounts.

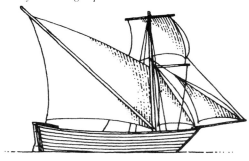

Tsernik, Greek/Turkish sailing ship of the nineteenth century with large spritsail

TSERNIK: A single-masted Greek/Turkish sailing ship of the late nineteenth century, carrying a very large spritsail on a long sprit, and a square sail above it.

TUCKZEESE, *Tuckerkahn*: CLINKER-built fishing boats designed for trawling in sheltered bays. They were mostly covered vessels up to 21m long, 6.5m wide and with a freeboard of 2m. The stem and stern timbers were attached to the keel by means of knees. The after half of the ship was fitted with a dry fish hold and a fish well. The rig consisted of one lugsail, and a staysail. Fishing from tuckzeesen vessels can be traced back to the first quarter of the sixteenth century, and thus represents one of the oldest forms of trawling. *See also* ZEESEN BOAT.

TUNE SHIP: The remains of a Viking ship from the late ninth century, similar to the GOKSTAD SHIP, and found on the eastern coast of the Oslo fjord on the island of Rolvsoy in 1867 under a 5m high tumulus. The upper parts of the ship were badly decayed, but in

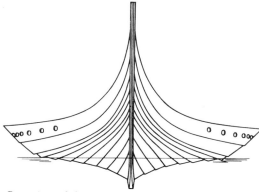

Bow view of the reconstructed Tune ship

The brig Franz und Luise *off Naples*

Tune ship, Viking ship from the ninth century, surviving components

The two-masted schooner, Phoenix

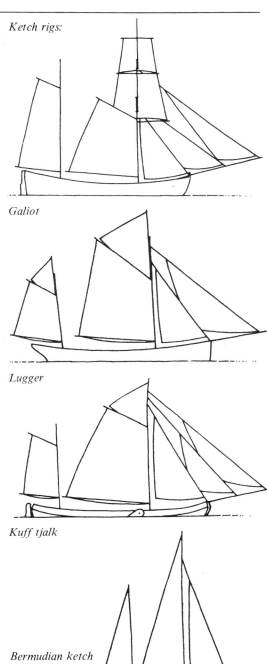

Ketch rigs:

Galiot

Lugger

Kuff tjalk

Bermudian ketch

spite of this it proved possible to reconstruct the vessel in its entirety. The reconstructed ship is now on show in the Viking Museum at Oslo on the Bygdoy peninsula, along with the Gokstad ship and the OSEBERG SHIP. The hull was built of oak, and is 19.8m long and 4.27m in breadth. The draught was relatively shallow, as on all Viking ships. The ship was fitted out for sailing and for rowing, with 11 pairs of oars.

TURTLE: *see* BUSHNELL DIVING BOAT.

TWO-MASTED SHIPS, *two-masted yacht, two-master*: A two-masted ship is one on which the two masts can be of the same height, or either may be slightly taller than the other, Typical two-masted vessels are the BRIG, square-rigged on both masts, the

SCHOONER, the KETCH, and the YAWL. The aftermast is the higher (ie the main mast) in brigs, brigantines and schooners whereas in ketches and yawls the after mast is shorter (ie it is the mizzen).

TURUMA: A Swedish coastal warship designed in the 1770s by F H Chapman. It was a form of coastal frigate with auxiliary oared propulsion. The rig was originally lateen but this was soon changed to a cut-down three-masted square rig without topgallants. They were about 42m long and armed with twenty-four 18 pounders and 16 swivel guns. The 19 pairs of oars were worked on outriggers above the gunports.

12-METRE: Increasingly associated with the America's Cup, the 12-Metre nevertheless was just one of a number racing yachts like the 8-Metre and 6-Metre that evolved as a result of a strict international rule in the 1920s. The '12-Metre' is the resultant of the measurement formula that trades speed producing factors like effective hull length against sail area. The 12-Metre has been the subject of enormous development since 1958 when it was first used in the America's Cup. Roughly 65ft long with a sail area of about 15–18,000 ft^2, the 12-Metre is especially efficient upwind although the constraints of the rule make them inevitably very heavy with up to 80 per cent of their displacement in the keel.

Two of the most famous 12-Metres were the American yacht *Intrepid* which successfully defended the Cup twice, and the winged keel *Australia* II which won the Cup off the Americans in 1983.

UDEMA: A sophisticated galley type warship used in the second half of the eighteenth century in the rocky coastal waters of Sweden and Finland. It featured a type of three-masted POLACRE rig comprising two square sails on the foremast and mainmast and a gaff sail on the mizzen. The ships were about 37m long and 9m in breadth, and could be propelled by 20 pairs of oars when necessary. Armaments consisted of two 18-pounders, nine 12-pounders, two 8-pounders and more than twenty 3-pounders. They were designed by the famous naval architect F H Chapman, but were not very successful since the guns and oars were on the same deck and could not be used simultaneously, which was a great disadvantage in a coastal warship.

UMIAK: A typical skin-covered boat from Greenland, also in common use in the polar regions of North America as far as the Aleutians. A similar boat used off northern Siberia was termed the BAIDARA. The umiak, and the baidara were relatively large, open boats about 10m long and about 1.5m in breadth. They were used when whole families or clans

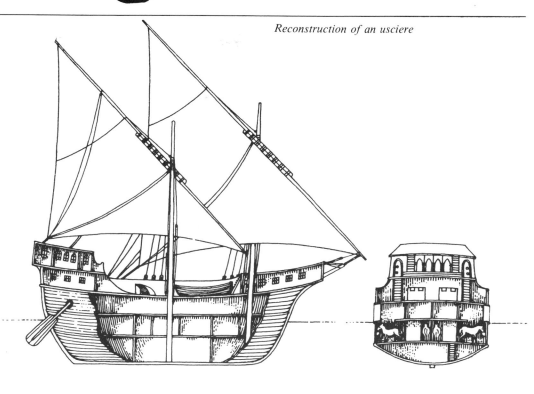

Reconstruction of an usciere

Greenland umiak, skin-covered boat, the Eskimo women's boat

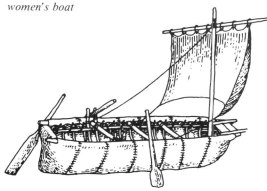

Eskimo summer quarters under an umiak

wanted to move to a new place of residence, or for other transport tasks. They were often rowed or paddled by women, although a small mast with a rectangular sail could be set up forward, the sail consisting of reindeer skins sewn together. The umiaks were accompanied by men in light, fast kayaks.

The larger skin-covered boats were also used for seal hunting and whaling. The boat framework was based on an internal keel, and was built up of twigs and whalebones, bound together with leather thongs or tendons, and then covered with sealion skins or walrus leather. The boat was relatively light in weight. It could be carried on land by six individuals, and could carry 12 persons in the water.

USCIERE, *hussiers*: A full-bodied, two-masted Mediterranean cargo ship, whose predecessor was the Roman horse transport. The hull had openings at the stern and on both sides to allow the horses to enter and leave. The openings could be caulked for sailing. A form of gangplank was carried on board to help the animals reach land. The ships were usually built as two-deckers, and could carry up to 100 horses. More often, however, horses were only carried on one deck, with wagons and war equipment on the other.

UTRECHT SHIP: In 1930, during building works on the Van Hoorne wharf near Utrecht in Holland, the remains of a primitive form of HULK were found in the river bed of what had once been a tributary of the Rhine. The remains were preserved, and are now on show in the Utrecht Central City Museum. Research indicated that the vessel had been built around AD 790.

The overall length of the reconstructed ship is 17.20m, with a beam of 3.60m and a depth of 1.34m. In shape and construction the Utrecht ship differs significantly from Viking vessels dating from the same period. The bottom section of the Utrecht ship has neither keel nor stem or stern timbers, and consists of a hollowed-out oak log 14.30m long and 1.95m wide, with extensions bound onto each end. Each side of the dugout component is fitted with three planks about 0.5m wide. The central planks are semicircular in cross-section, convex face out, similar to a wale or sheer plank.

Viewed from the side and in plan, all the planks have curved runs from end to end of the hull. The top of the side planks are finished off with timbers of semi-circular cross-section, 140×80mm in size.

Thirty-eight ribs were fitted into the hull after planking, to connect the side planks to the bottom dugout section. Treenails were used to fix them. The ribs do not extend over the whole cross-section, but take the form of alternating half-ribs. One rib extends upward from the bottom to slightly more than half the side height while its neighbour stretches downward from the top edge of the planking to a point just below half the side height. There is a socket cut into one rib, located 4.80m from the bow, to accept a small mast. The very forward position of the mast, along with other constructional features, indicates that the vessel had been designed as a towed river ship, as this is the typical position for a towing mast.

The Utrecht ship, represents a basic form of the type of river ship known as the hulk, which was widespread in western Europe in the Middle Ages. The type was known from various pictorial representations before this relic was found. For instance, coins bearing the picture of a hulk-like ship were minted in Dorestad under the French ruler Louis the Pious (814 to 840). A few centuries later the ship was evidently known in England, as it is shown on a christening stone in Winchester Cathedral dating from the year 1180.

UXEL: A Moorish ship which took part in the battles against the Spanish around 1340. The ship was 50m long and 10m wide, and could carry a cargo of 50 horses. Presumably, it was an oared sailing ship, and a forerunner of the Mediterranean GALEASSE in design, with superstructures at the bow and stern as well as amidships. These ships could accommodate about 280 armed men in addition to the crew.

V

VAALER DUGOUT: A dugout found in a former waterway which ran through the Vaaler moor on the Wilsterau, a tributary of the Elbe, in 1878. The vessel was pointed at both ends, and was 12.29m long, 1.3m wide and 0.62m deep. The trunk was hollowed out to a wall thickness of 50mm at the bottom, and 40mm at the sides. Eleven ribs were left projecting in order to stiffen the craft. Between the ribs the wood was left thicker at the top to form a gunwale, with holes drilled through, which could have been primitive oar guides.

V-BOTTOM BOAT, *V-frame boat, V-frame ship*: Any type of boat or ship in which the hull cross-section includes a V-shaped bottom. V-shaped hulls are quite often combined with hard-chine construction, forming the typical single or double-chine cross-section where the bottom meets the sides at or close to the waterline.

VICTORY: Admiral Nelson's flagship. The First Rate, three-decker was laid down at Chatham Dockyard on 23 July 1759 and on 30 October 1760, even before her launch, she became the fifth vessel in the English navy to receive the name *Victory*. On 7 May 1765 the *Victory* was launched, and in 1769 this full-rigged ship-of-the-line underwent sea trials. In 1778, the vessel was first used as flagship of the Channel squadron under Admiral Keppel. The *Victory* subsequently served as flagship under more than a dozen English fleet commanders, the most famous of whom being Admiral Horatio Nelson. The specification of the *Victory* is as follows: Length of hull: 69.0m, length of gun deck: 56.5m; keel length: 46.5m; beam: 17.5m; height of topsides: 10.0m; draught: 6.0m; displacement: around 3000 tons.

The Viking, *a reconstruction of the Gokstad ship in the harbour of Sandfjord before the Atlantic crossing in 1893*

In 1780, the ship was sheathed with 3923 copper plates. After serving under Admirals Howe (1782), Hood (1793), Hotham (1795), and Jervis (1797), mainly in the Mediterranean, the *Victory* was retired from active service and used as a hospital ship for prisoners-of-war for the following two years. During a general refit from 1800 to 1803, the stern was rebuilt, and the former two open stern galleries removed. On 11 April 1803 Nelson hoisted his flag on the *Victory* as Commander of the Mediterranean fleet. The ship at this time was armed with 30 12-pounders on the upper deck, 12 12-pounders on the quarter deck, 2 12-pounders on the forecastle, 2 68-pounder carronades on the forecastle, 30 32-pounders on the lower gun deck, and 28 24-pounders in the middle deck.

The ship carried 850 officers, sailors and marines. During the decisive Battle of Trafalgar, on 21 October 1805, Nelson, on the *Victory*, commanded 27 ships-of-the-line and six frigates to victory against the combined Spanish and French fleet, during which action he was mortally wounded.

After the damage received at Trafalgar had been repaired, the *Victory* again became a flagship, although now classed as a Second Rate, until decommissioned in November 1812. In 1817 the ship was repaired and refitted, and declared a First Rate once more. From 1824 to 1847 the vessel was again in use as a flagship, albeit stationary, flying the flag of the Port Admiral at Portsmouth, and from 1848 to 1869 she served as the stationary flagship of the Commander-in-Chief of the Fleet. After this she became tender to the new flagship until 1891. From 1891 to 1922 the *Victory* was again given the function of stationary flagship, but by then the state of the structural timbers of the ship's hull was so poor that repairs lasting more than six years were required before, in July 1928, the ship once more looked as she had before the battle of Trafalgar. Since that time the *Victory* has been preserved as a museum ship in the oldest dry dock in the world, Dock No 2 in Portsmouth.

VIKING SHIP, *Viking long boat*: A combined rowing and sailing ship used by the Scandinavian Viking peoples. The Viking period is considered to be roughly from the end of the eighth century until part-way into the eleventh century. The tribes living on Zeeland, Skane, Halland and Jutland were known to be good seafarers many centuries earlier, as reported by Tacitus in his *Germania*, written around 98 BC. We know of many voyages of pillage, especially to the coasts of England, from the beginning of the fourth

The Victory, *flagship of the English Admiral Nelson 1803 (model)*

Vikings ships

1   Reconstruction of the Gokstad ship under sail
2   Method of tying the shields in place
3   Plank cleats and rib joints on the Gokstad ship
4   Shutter for the oar ports
5   Method of fixing the shrouds
6   Perforated block
7   Gunwale of the Nydam ship showing plank cleats
8   Hjortspring boat
9   Nydam ship

10   Oseberg ship
11   Steering rudder on the Gokstad ship
12   Plank joint and method of sealing on the Hjortspring boat
13–16   Keel forms
13   Nydam ship
14   Hjortspring boat
15   Kvalsund ship
16   Oseberg ship
17   Steering rudder on the Nydam ship
18   Oar ports and oar blade of the Oseberg ship
19   Centre section of the Gokstad ship with mast socket

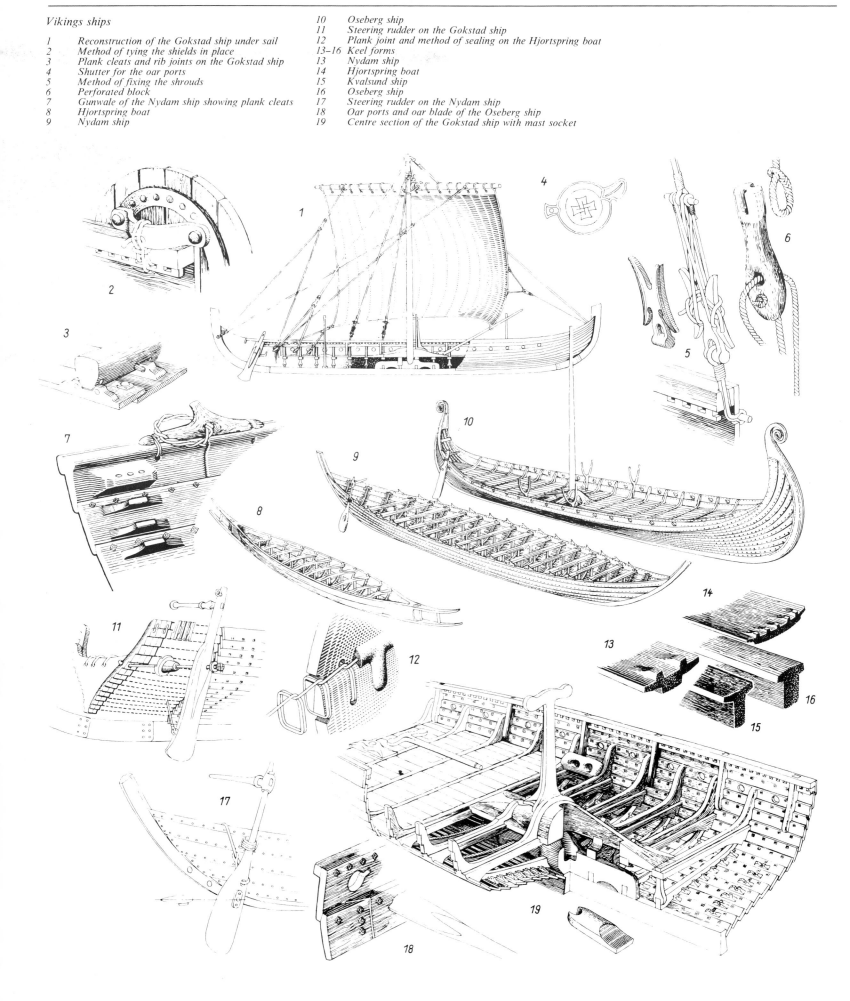

*Seascape with fishing boats, painted by P Umbier
(died 1670),* Museum für Bildende Kunst, Leipzig

The Swedish ship of the line Carl XIII *and the Danish
ship of the line* Danneborg *during a comparative
speed test in 1853.*

The Asia, *an East Indiaman belonging to the English East India Company, off Hongkong, painted by W J Huggins (1781–1845).* National Maritime Museum, Greenwich

Swedish 68-cannon ship, Prins Gustav, *engages Russian ships on 17th July 1788 off Hoghland*

Ormen Friske, a Swedish copy of the Gokstad ship. After several successful sea voyages, the ship was lost during a voyage from Stockholm to Rotterdam

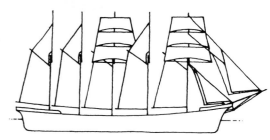

Vinnen rig, combined square and gaff sails

company of F A Vinnen and Co, Bremen, in which square and fore-and-aft sails were combined in a unique arrangement. The Vinnen shipping company had five five-masted gaff schooners built in 1922, which carried three square sails on each of the fore- and middle masts, after the manner of the topsail schooner.

VOTIVE SHIPS, *consecration ships*: Model ships which were presented to churches as gifts, and in some cases they have remained there for centuries.

Votive and consecration gifts have their cult origins in the worship of gods in ancient times. The Greeks and Romans required the assistance of the gods before the start of an undertaking or a battle, in time of danger, or when illness was prevalent, and made solemn vows to pacify the gods' anger. In the Christian world the practice of presenting votive gifts can be traced back to the fifth century. As well as valuable silver and gold items, pictures painted on wood or fabric by sailors, fishermen and merchants were presented as

century until the eighth century. With the formation of kingdoms in the settled regions of southern Scandinavia in the eighth century, large Viking armies landed in England in 825. London was plundered in 836, and Hamburg suffered a similar fate in 845, 857 and 861.

Vikings settled on the Faroe islands around 800, and on the Orkneys and Shetlands in 802. Iceland was discovered, and they began to settle there in 861. According to the Icelandic saga of Erik Raude (written by Hauk Erlendson around 1200), Erik Raude reached Greenland in 983, and his son Leif Erikson reached North America in 1000, landing at the site of present-day Boston, roughly on the 42nd parallel. These enterprises were quite extraordinary for the time, and demanded unusual energy as well as a large number of sea-going ships. During the Viking period the Norsemen refined their skills in shipbuilding, developed over many preceding centuries, to a high level. In addition to the oared longship, which was a very long, narrow warship type, they also built, and were familiar with, beamier oared ships with supplementary sails, and also much broader cargo ships.

Viking ships were usually between 10 and 30m long. The flat-sided warships could hold a crew of more than 100 men. The oarsmen sat closely spaced one behind the other, and operated the relatively short, lightweight oars using a stabbing, jerky technique, or Turkish rowing as it was known on the Mediterranean galleys. Viking ships were steered with a oar

suspended on the starboard side. With an average displacement of 50 tons and their great length, the ships had a relatively small draught, with the result that they could negotiate shallow coastal waters and quite small rivers. One interesting feature was the keel, which projected downward by about 300mm roughly half way along the hull. The tall, curving hull ends and the deeper draught amidships had a favourable effect on the ships' manoeuvrability.

The CLINKER-planking and rib construction typical of the Nordic ships is common to all the ships dating from the Viking era. One of the most important is the GOKSTAD SHIP, discovered in 1880, the OSEBERG SHIP, found in 1904, the TUNE SHIP, and the finds at KVALSUND and ROSKILDE. A number of reconstructions of original ships have been made, among them the *Ormen Friske*, a Norwegian version of the Gokstad ship, which became well known after it completed a voyage from Bergen to North America for the World Exhibition in 1893 under the command of Captain Magnus Andersen.

A later Swedish copy with the same name undertook several successful open sea voyages, but was lost with all hands in 1950 near Helgoland, during a voyage from Stockholm to Rotterdam, for reasons which have remained unexplained.

VINNEN SAILING SHIP: A type of large sailing ship, named after the shipping

Votive ship in the Marienkirche in Robstock

Votive painting by an unknown master, late fifteenth century, in the Artushof at Gdansk

sacrificial gifts after a successful voyage, or after a man had survived a catastrophe.

However, it is the votive or consecration ships which provide most historical information. One of the best known votive ships is the Catalonian NAO, dating from 1450. This is the oldest model ship known which represents the type of vessel used on the early Portuguese voyages of discovery. It was dedicated to a saint, and belonged to the chapel of San Simon of Mataro, on the Catalonian coast, until it was discovered in the late 1920s. Today, the model is on show in the Prins Hendrik museum in Rotterdam. It is 1.23m long and 45cm wide, and is a significant source of historical information. Votive model ships of varying age are among the treasures of many churches on the coasts of seafaring countries, and sometimes deep inland too. Votive ships were also among the items buried in ancient graves. For instance, about 100 small consecration ships were found in a grave in north Jutland, which dated from around 1200 BC. The models were similar to kayaks and were beaten from thin gold sheet and decorated with sun symbols.

Votive ships also had their role in the cult circles of Africa as well as in the Near and Far East. For example, an ancient custom in Japan, still respected today, is to send small model ships with lighted paper lanterns out to sea, at the Buddhist festival of all souls in mid-July.

WAI-PI-KU CH'UAN: A Chinese river boat from Szechwan, designed for travelling downstream on rivers with rapids. Interesting features included the two rudders of different sizes, one for calm water and one for rapids. The large rudder for rapids was a spar up to 15m long, similar to that used on large log rafts. The helmsman stood amidships on a raised bridge above the deckhouse. The boat was pulled back upstream from the bank using ropes.

WARNEMÜNDER JOLLE: A two-masted vessel in which the taller mainmast was stepped at about a quarter of the ship's length, and the shorter after mast at about half the ship's length. Both masts were rigged with spritsails. A bowsprit supported a jib. The term jolle was already in common use at the beginning of the sixteenth century.

Warnemünde jolle with spritsails

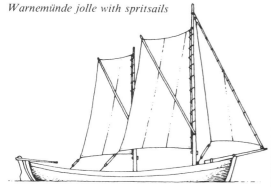

WARNOW PRAHM: A PRAHM lighter, used since the thirteenth century on the rivers of the central Baltic region. Originally, it was a towed vessel, but later versions on the River Warnow had a single mast. Warnow prahms with a simple square sail were still in use at the end of the nineteenth century, as were towed or punted versions. Around 1900, the flat stem and stern, consisting of transverse planking, were superseded by orthodox beam timbers.

The Wasa, *after the raising*

WASA: A Swedish seventeenth-century warship which acquired fame when she sank on her maiden voyage.

On 24 April 1961 the Swedish Royal ship *Wasa* — once the largest ship of the Swedish navy — was finally raised after difficult salvage work, 333 years after sinking on her maiden voyage on 10 August 1628. This was the first time that an original early seventeenth-century ship had been salvaged, and its hull was virtually intact, thus providing an excellent insight into shipbuilding of that era. The ship had four decks, of which the second and third were battery decks for forty-eight 24-pounder guns.

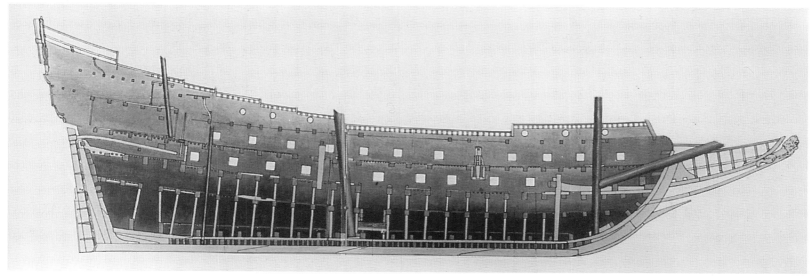

Body plan of the Wasa

A 24-pounder cannon on the lower battery deck of the Wasa

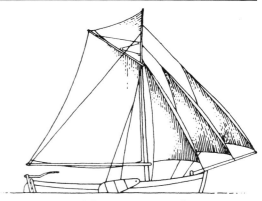

Weser kahn with large gaff mainsail and three foresails

The following cannon were also found: eight 3-pounders, two 1-pounders, one 16-pounder, two 62-pounder and three 32-pounder guns. All the cannon were of bronze. For a ship of 57.0m length, 11.7m beam and about 8.5m freeboard and a sail area of around 380m^2 with a mainmast height above keel of around 49m, she was heavily armed. The crew consisted of 133 men and about 300 marines.

The lower gunports were only about 1.2 to 1.5m above the surface of the water, and in the proceedings of the naval court of September 1628 it is stated that, when the ship was listing strongly to the lee side, a sudden gust caused an extra degree of heel, and the lower gunports dipped into the water; the ship flooded, and capsized. Nobody was blamed by the court. The court also discussed the weight of ballast carried. The ballast found in the salvaged hull was clearly insufficient to give the ship an adequate safety margin against capsizing. The ship simply had inadequate lateral stability.

The *Wasa* had three masts and carried three square sails on the fore- and mainmasts. The mizzen carried a single square topsail above the lateen sail. The bowsprit supported upper and lower spritsails. The stern superstructure of the ship housed the living quarters for the officers on the upper deck. The *Wasa* was richly decorated with sculptures and carved work, as befitted the ship's intended status. The decorations were concentrated round all the galleries on the aftership, on the gun ports and the figurehead. The tools, clothing, personal effects and equipment found provide a vivid picture of the living conditions prevalent on large warships at the time.

WATER BOAT, *water prahm*: Usually a full-bodied auxiliary vessel similar to a PRAHM, fitted with fixed water tanks for supplying fresh water to ships lying in harbour or at the roads. Water boats sometimes had their own

sails, in which case they could also carry out other supply services in similar fashion to the BUM boats.

WESER KAHN, *Bremer kahn*: The Weser or Bremer KAHN was the standard lighter serving large ships on the lower Weser, especially for goods transport between Bremen, Vegesack and Bremerhaven. A few larger Weser kahns were also employed as coastal ships. According to H Szymanski there were 173 Weser kahns based in Bremen in 1840, and the number had risen to 252 in 1866. In 1934, only a handful of obsolete Weser kahns still survived.

The Weser kahn was a vessel with large

American whaler Alice Mandel, *1851, blubber boiler below the forecastle protective deck (model)*

Whale boat, lashed to the davits

leeboards and a mizzen. The kahns could be anything from 12 to 25m long, 4 to 7m in breadth and 1.25 to 2.75m hold depth, with a tonnage between 20 and 120BRT. The vessels had a flat transom, considerable forward sheer and large loading hatches with hatch covers similar to a pitched roof. The crew was from two to four persons, depending on the size of the ship.

WHALING BOAT: Small rowing boats used in the era of the sailing ship for harpooning whales. They were often fitted with an auxiliary sails. The invention of the grenade harpoon by the Norwegian Sven Foyn in 1868, the introduction of harpoon cannon, and the development of reliable ships' engines, resulted in the development of the steam-driven whaling boat which was 30 to 60m long.

WILD WATER CANOE: A specialized vessel for travelling on wild water, such as mountain streams and rivers with waterfalls and obstructions, or for competitions on suitable stretches of water. Wild water racing is held over distances of 4 to 15km in Canadian one-man and two-man boats and in the one-man folding boat. *See also* CANADIAN CANOE.

WILSTERAU EWER: One of the smallest of the north German EWERS, broad of beam and shallow of draught, and suited to carrying freight on the small River Wilsterau. The ewers were built in Wilster, and were about 11 to 15m long, 3 to 3.5m in beam, and had a folding mast.

WISHBONE SAILING SHIP, *Vamarie staysail ship*: A type of rig first used on the American yacht *Vamarie* in 1933, featuring wishbone gaffs. The wishbone rig is only used on two-masted fore-and-aft rigged ships such as staysail schooners or staysail ketches.

With this rig the long edge of the sail runs up the mainmast or foremast from the base of the mast to the masthead. The wishbone gaffs, consisting of two gently curving spars and situated roughly half to two-thirds up the height of the mainmast, run laterally past the one-piece mainsail, and the outer ends join up again. Because the mainsail is stretched up through the wishbone gaff and cannot fall away to leeward the vessel is able to sail particularly close to the wind.

WORK BOAT, *ship's work boat*: A simple, broad rowing boat of small or medium size carried on board ship, and used for work on the ship in port or in the roads.

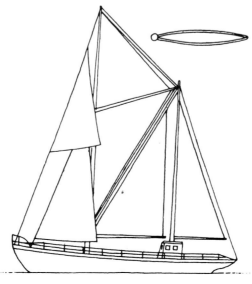

Wishbone ketch

Algerian xebec of the eighteenth century (model)

XEBEC, *schebeck, chebec, shebek*: A three-masted Mediterranean sailing ship of Arab/Turkish origins, which was also propelled by oars when necessary. The type was employed off the Algerian coast by corsairs, and was also used in the French navy and as a French and Portuguese merchant ship. Xebec simply means small ship, although the vessels were large enough to be fitted with 20 to 40 guns on the full-length deck, with oar benches set between them. An armed xebec was up to 40m long and 10m wide, and with a draught of 3m the light, slender design could carry up to 300 tons of armaments and crew. There are various unmistakeable features of the Mediterranean GALLEY to be found in the xebec, which to some extent mark it out as a successor to the galley type. However, the xebec was longer and stronger, more seaworthy, more strongly armed and had an improved sail rig. Although they retained the principle of the galley rig, xebecs had a refined, fully developed hull shape and sail rig, and were the fastest and most manoeuvrable sailing ships of the Mediterranean. These proved to be decisive advantages in naval combat, and as a result Louis XIV (1643–1715) had copies built in France. An authentic model of a French xebec from around 1650 to 1700 is on show in the Paris Maritime Museum. Even in the eighteenth century it was considered an honour for a French naval officer to serve on a xebec.

Both the Arab/Turkish type and the early French version were lateen-rigged on three pole masts. After 1750, some xebecs were rigged with a combination of sails, with lateen and square sails on extended masts. The ships were term polacre-rigged xebecs or half-xebecs, and carried either square sails on the mainmast only, or on both forward masts, backed up by a square topsail on the mizzen. A characteristic feature is the structure projecting far forward beyond the stem, later extended further by a bowsprit and jib boom. As a result, it was possible to step the forward mast far forward, close to the stem. The forward mast was also raked forward strongly, in order to exploit the ship's length to the full. In a similar manner, an extended, raised after gallery, projecting far out astern, made it possible to step the smaller aft mast well aft. These features assisted considerably in handling. A few Swedish xebecs were built in the Baltic, and also some Russian ones, these latter about 35m in length, with 40 oarsmen and 32 to 50 guns. Half-xebecs were also built. They were about 23m long.

Xebec

1   Spanish xebec, 1735
2   French pinke after Lascallier, 1790
3   French polacker-xebec, 1679
4   Various mastheads
5   Shroud tackle with toggle

6   Masthead with halyard for the lateen yard, parrel, upper
       backstay blocks and bunt line guide blocks
7   French xebec, eighteenth century
8   Hull section close to the mainmast
9   Sheer draught plan of a French xebec

Y

Dutch yacht ca 1800 *(model)*

Yacht I

1 Dutch state yacht, ca 1680
2 Dutch state yacht with spritsail, early seventeenth century
3 Stern of a state yacht
4 Besan yacht
5 Retractable bowsprit on a cutter

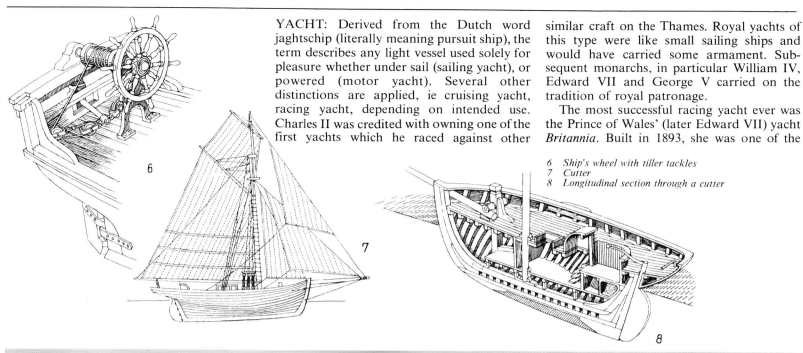

YACHT: Derived from the Dutch word jaghtschip (literally meaning pursuit ship), the term describes any light vessel used solely for pleasure whether under sail (sailing yacht), or powered (motor yacht). Several other distinctions are applied, ie cruising yacht, racing yacht, depending on intended use. Charles II was credited with owning one of the first yachts which he raced against other similar craft on the Thames. Royal yachts of this type were like small sailing ships and would have carried some armament. Subsequent monarchs, in particular William IV, Edward VII and George V carried on the tradition of royal patronage.

The most successful racing yacht ever was the Prince of Wales' (later Edward VII) yacht *Britannia*. Built in 1893, she was one of the

6 *Ship's wheel with tiller tackles*
7 *Cutter*
8 *Longitudinal section through a cutter*

Three-masted schooner Creole

Two-masted schooner yacht America, *1851 (model)*

Small bermudian-rigged cruiser

Yacht II

1	Scandinavian merchant jackt, ca 1840, view of hull	5	Jullanar, *England, 1875*
2	Rig of a Scandinavian merchant jakt	6	Gloriana, *designed by Herreshoff, ca 1900*
3–6	Plans of yachts (development of lines)	7	Sail plan of the schooner Meteor V
3	Short Foot, *England, early nineteenth century*	8	Modern yacht with sloop rig
4	Schooner America, *USA, 1851*	9	Comparison of gaff and bermudian rig

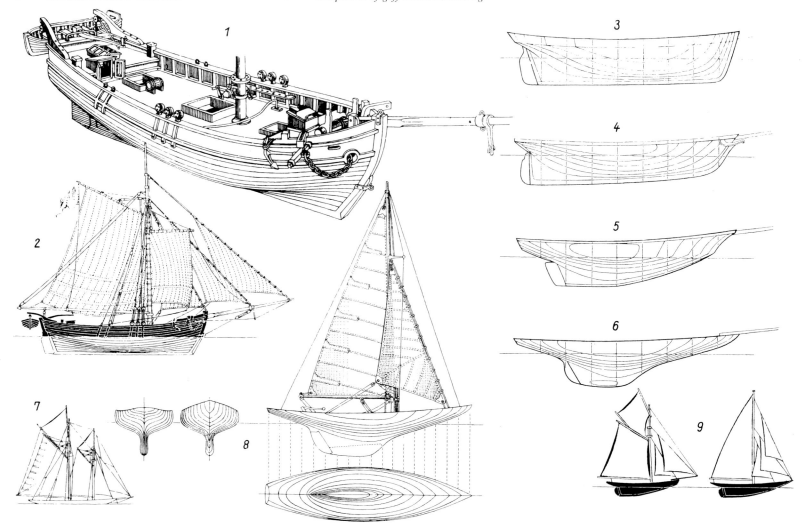

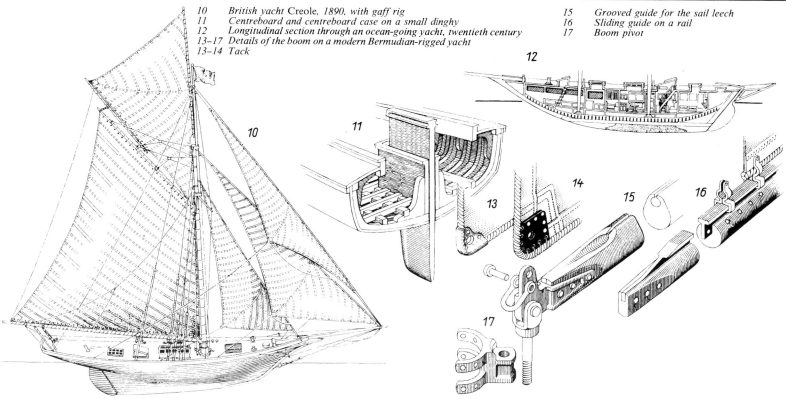

10 British yacht Creole, 1890, with gaff rig
11 Centreboard and centreboard case on a small dinghy
12 Longitudinal section through an ocean-going yacht, twentieth century
13–17 Details of the boom on a modern Bermudian-rigged yacht
13–14 Tack

15 Grooved guide for the sail leech
16 Sliding guide on a rail
17 Boom pivot

America's Cup yacht
Shamrock V

largest of the prewar racing yachts and her presence at local regattas round the British Isles kept the sport alive for over 40 years.

Yachting has always thrived under the patronage of royalty and the wealthy and the term has connotations of affluence, although nowadays the term yacht, suitably qualified, can be applied to almost every size and type of pleasure craft from small keelboat up to the largest motor yacht.

YASSI-ADA SHIP: The reconstructed wreck of a Byzantine cargo ship from the seventh century BC. In 1958, a shipwreck dating from the fourth century BC was discovered at Yassi-Ada in the Mediterranean, and when a further ship was found in the same vicinity, a group of archaeologists from the University of Pennsylvania investigated the find and reconstructed the ship, the work lasting from 1961 to 1964. The reconstruction showed that the vessel was very full-bodied, with a length of 18.9m and beam of 5.2m. From the pieces found, it was possible to determine that the ship had had a fixed, full-length deck. There was a cooking area which was roofed over with flat tiles, some of them perforated to allow smoke to escape. The parts of the cooking area indicated that a fireplace made of tiles had stood on a thick layer of clay, reinforced with iron bars. Various pieces of domestic equipment were found, made of stone, terra cotta, glass and metal; among them a mortar and pestle, pots of various size and shape, copper kettles and eating utensils.

One of the most interesting finds was a metal sliding balance, which indicates that this was a merchant ship. The scales probably hung below the deck, while their inscription 'Naukleros Georgios' implies that they were the property of the ship's patron Georgios. The reconstruction built from the pieces salvaged by the research group shows the construction of the ship's hull, and the transverse stiffening timbers in the region of the cooking area. Since relatively few wooden parts survived, the suggested hull form can only be given limited historical credence.

YAWL: Another term derived from the Dutch jol(le) used to describe in particular a two-masted sailing yacht whose after mast is mounted aft of the rudder post. The small mizzen is often no more than a balancing sail but has been used as a way of getting around particular racing rules which rate multi-masted craft more favourably. One of the most famous and successful yawls of recent years was Carleton Mitchell's *Finisterre*, three time winner of the Bermuda race. The term yawl is also applied to a kind of ship's boat or sailing- or fishing-boat.

Yawls with their small mizzen masts stepped right aft

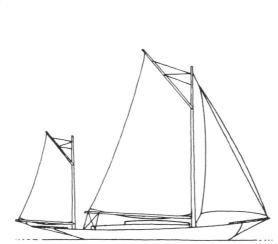
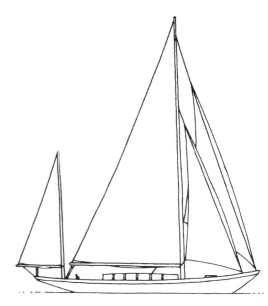

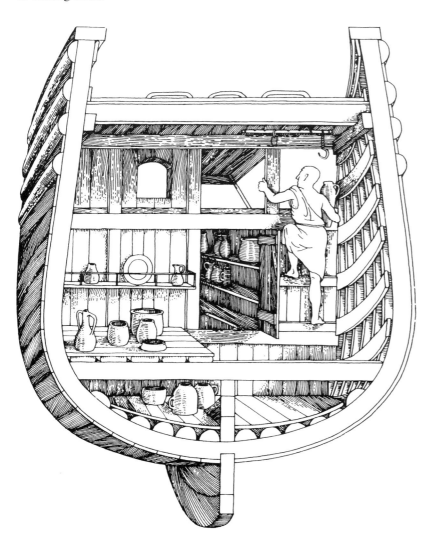

Reconstruction of a Byzantine transport ship from the seventh century BC based on the wreck found near Yassi-Ada

Zaruks under sail today

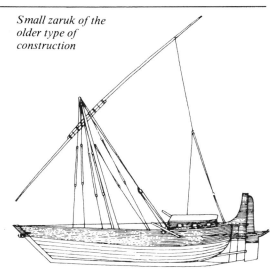

ZEESEN BOAT, *zees boat, zees kahn*: One of the best known of the Baltic fishing vessels which operated in bays and sheltered waters until the mid twentieth century. The vessel was about 10m long and was used for trawling for pike-perch and eels. The wooden boats were quite heavily built, and carried a 6m long bowsprit, with a stern boom projecting roughly the same distance astern.

Fishing was carried out using the zeesen, a

ZARUK, *zaruke*: A single-masted Arab DHOW once common on the Red Sea and in the Gulf of Oman. The older types exhibited typical dhow features, such as a flat keel along about one third of the ship's length, with long, projecting stem and stern timbers curving upward towards the hull ends. In a way, the hull was reminiscent of the design of early Egyptian sea-going ships.

The smaller zaruks were predominantly used close to the coast for transporting freight and fishing, but the larger versions gained notoriety as smugglers' and slave dealers' ships in the nineteenth century.

The base of the mast, which was raked forward by about 10 to 15 degrees, was located about half-way along the hull, and was supported by means of two or three pairs of shrouds, and by forestays and backstays on the larger vessels. The angled yard was always made of two spars lashed together, and carried a large settee sail. An Arab speciality was the method of operating the rudder. There was no tiller, instead there was a type of yoke fixed to the bottom of the rudder. On later, smaller vessels, about 15m in length, European influence diluted some of the typical dhow characteristics, in particular the keel, which is now longer and flat, and the additional deadwood on the afterbody used to increase the lateral resistance.

Large zaruk from the Gulf of Oman

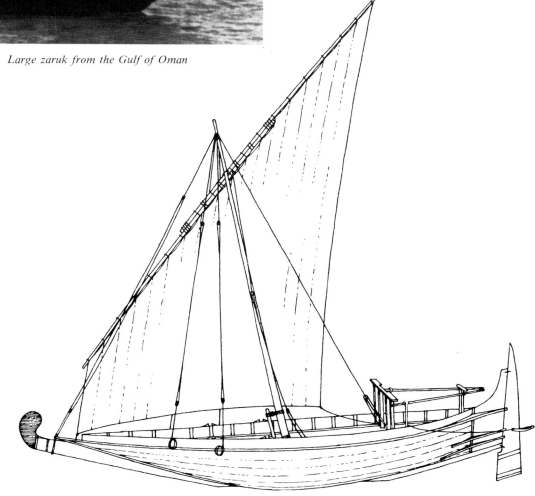

Old zeesen boat with topsail

type of trawl net without otter boards.

The rigs of the zeesen boats of the Darsser cove and Rügen differed from the zees kahns based in the Oder bay. The Oder bay vessels usually carried fixed lugsails on the main and mizzen masts, in contrast to the gaff mainsails on the mainmast and fixed lugsail on the mizzen carried by the Mecklenburg zeesen boats.

Partly to maintain a tradition, and partly because of the fine sailing characteristics of the rugged, broad, roomy, wooden zeesen boats, the vessels which still survive have become popular yachts on the Darsser and Bostetter bays.

ZIEGE: The term applied to a single-masted river ship used for sailing on the river Weichsel in Poland from the sixteenth to the eighteenth centuries. The vessels were about 7 to 10m long, of full-bodied hull form, and carried a square sail.

ZILLE: A full-bodied freight barge which has been in use on inland waters for centuries. The timber-built, flat-bottomed, open vessels, sometimes fitted with a short deck at the after end, were towed, and usually carried no sails. There have been various suggestions as to the origin of the vessel's name. It may be related to the Anglo-Saxon and Norman ciula (keel), or it may originate from the Danube region, where flat-bottomed barges belonging to Danube ships were called züllen. At a later date, long Danube ships were referred to as zeile.

In a *Dictionarium* which was published in Frankfurt am Main in 1696, Hulsius describes zillen as ships which were made from trees 80

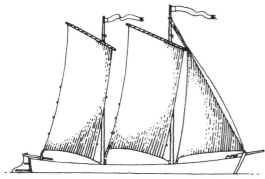

Zeesen boat with fixed lugsails

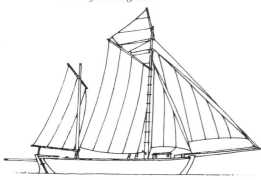

Zeesen boat with gaff mainsail and fixed lugsail

Zeesen boats racing on the Darsser Bodden

Flat-bottomed Dutch zomp

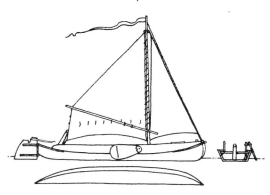

feet long. He states that the term züllen originated in the sixth century (Battle of Ravenna). Today, the zille is still occasionally encountered, serving as a houseboat on the Havel and the Elbe, and very rarely as a cargo-carrying vessel.

Zillen were also used for transporting tree trunks. Some of the trunks would be coarsely hewn and joined together to form a rough zille, which would then be loaded with the remaining logs. At the vessel's destination this temporary hull would be dismantled and the structural timber sold. This procedure was known as zillenschlächterei — slaughtering the zillen.

ZOMP: A Dutch single-masted, flat-bottomed cargo vessel with a length of 12 to 15m. The type was first built in the seventeenth century, and had the following features: a completely flat bottom, sides joined to it with sharp bilges, and curving upwards at either end to a tall stem and stern. In order to increase useful draught midships, extra planks were added to the top strake on both sides to form washboards. The bottom edge of these plates was cut to follow the deck sheer, then simply curved to follow the curvature of the boat as seen from above. As well as raising the freeboard, these planks also served as support for the leeboards. The sternpost was vertical and carried a relatively large rudder. The stem was curved, with the upper part running back towards the boat.

The term zomp was also applied to a Swedish sea fishing boat from the Stockholm region, for which drawings, drawn by Chapman in 1768, have been published. Some vessels were 13m long and 3.75m wide, while others were smaller at only 5.4m long and 1.8m wide. Both sizes of boat were built on a keel with a pointed stern, and were often stern-heavy on account of the fish well located in the after section of the hull. The rig consisted of gaff mainsail and staysail. The larger zomps had loose washboards, suspended on the gunwales on hooks, to help prevent spray entering the boat. The forward part of these vessels was covered, and there was a small cabin built around the mast.

ZUIDERSEE Q-75 BOAT: When the Zuidersee was reclaimed, the Dutch arch-aeologist Van Der Heide discovered the remains of a twelfth-century boat in sector Q 75. Although the only parts of the vessel which had survived were parts of the boat's bottom, impressions in the earth indicated a completely flat bottom and CLINKER-planked sides. The sides were not stiffened by means of ribs, and the floor timbers which join the floor to the sides were extended up the sides, alternately to port and starboard. This design feature differs from that used in the hulk found at Utrecht (*see* UTRECHT SHIP) and the ancient Scandinavian ships.

ZULU: A Scottish fishing vessel with two masts rigged with lugsails, and introduced around 1880. The hull had slim fore- and aft sections, a vertical stem and a stern inclined at about 45 degrees. A jib was set on the long bowsprit. The sheet of the mizzen sail was made fast to a stern boom.

Swedish 60-cannon ship Wasa. *This ship was built in 1778, 150 years after the foundering of her better known predecessor.*

The shipyard situated on the small island of Onrust, near Batavia, in 1699. Between the seventeenth and nineteenth centuries this yard was an important base for the East Indies company, with its shipbuilding stocks, saw mills, cranes and arsenal

A Japanese picture of the Schallach, *an East Indiaman which put into Japan between 1741 and 1744. It was built in 1735 for the Dutch East Indies Company.*

ÅKERLUND, H.: Fartygsfynden i den forna hamnen i Kalmar. Uppsala 1951

ÅKERLUND, H.: Nydamskeppen. En studie i tidig skandinavisk skeppsbyggnastkonst. Göteborg 1963

ANGELUCCI, E.; CUCARI, A.: Ships. MacDonald and Jane's. London 1977

ARCHENHOLZ, J.W. von: Die Geschichte der Flibustier. Tübingen 1803

ARCHIMEDES: Werke, mit modernen Bezeichnungen, herausgegeben und mit einer Einleitung versehen von Sir T. L. Heath. Berlin 1914

ARENHOLD, L.: Die allmähliche Entwicklung des Segelschiffes von der Römerzeit bis zur Zeit der Dampfer. In: Jahrbuch der Schiffbautechnischen Gesellschaft, Vol 7, Berlin 1906

ARENHOLD, L.: Die historische Entwicklung der Schiffstypen vom römischen Kriegsschiff bis zur Gegenwart. Verlag von Lipsius und Tischer. Kiel und Leipzig 1891

ASSMANN, P.: Seewesen. In: Denkmäler des klassischen Altertums. München 1887

BAASCH, E.: Hamburgs Convoyschiffahrt und Convoywesen. Hamburg 1896

BALLARD, G. A.: The Egyptian Obelisk Lighter. In: The Mariner's Mirror 33 (1947), University Press Cambridge. P 158–164

BALLARD, G. A.: The Transporting of the Obelisks at Karnak. In: The Mariner's Mirror 6 (1970), P 246–273, 307–314

BALMER, H.: Die Romfahrt des Apostels Paulus und die Seefahrtkunde im römischen Kaiserzeitalter. Bern, Münchenbuchsee 1905

BARNETT, R. D.: Early Shipping in the Near East. In: Antiquity 32 (1958) 57, P 220–230

BATHE, B., u. a.: Der Segelschiffe große Zeit. Edited by J. Jobé. Delilus, Klasing & Co. Bielefeld, Berlin 1967

BAUMGARTEL, E. J.: The Cultures of Prehistoric Egypt. Edinburgh 1947

BELL, C. D. J.: The Obelisk Barge of Hatshepsut. In: Ancient Egypt, 1934, P 107–114

BELL, C. G. J.: Ancient Egyptian Ship Design; Based on a Critical Analysis of the XIIth Dynasty Barge. In: Ancient Egypt, 1933, P 100–111

BERQUEMAN, A.: Les Musées Belges de Marine. Librairie Encyclopédie. Brüssel 1943

BETHGE, H.-G.: Der Brandtaucher. Ein Tauchboot – von der Idee zur Wirklichkeit. VEB Hinstorff Verlag. Rostock 1968

BEYLEN, J. van: Schepen van de Nederlanden. Van de late middeleeuwen tot het einde van de 17e eeuw. Amsterdam 1970

BILDLEXIKON, NAUTISK. Tre Tryckare (Cagner & Co.). Göteborg 1963

BI-TASCHENLEXIKON SCHIFFBAU/SCHIFFHART. VEB Bibliographisches Institut. Leipzig 1982

BOECKH, A.: Urkunden über das Seewesen des attischen Staates. Berlin 1840

BOTTA, S. E.; FLANDIN, E.: Monuments des Ninivé. 5 Vol Paris 1849

BREUSING, L.: Die Lösung des Trieren-Rätsels. Bremen 1889

BRIX, A.: Praktischer Schiffbau. Bootsbau. Hrsg.: Akademischer Verein «Hütte». Ernst & Sohn. Berlin 1921

BROGGER, A. W.; SHETELIG, H.: The Viking Ships. Their Ancestry and Evolution. Oslo 1951

BROGGER, A. W.: Winlandfahrten, 1939

BUSLEY, C.: Schiffe des Altertums. In: Jahrbuch der Schiffbautechnischen Gesellschaft. 20. Vol Berlin 1919, P 187–279

BUSLEY, C.: Schiffe des Mittelalters und der neueren Zeit. In: Jahrbuch der Schiffbautechnischen Gesellschaft. 21. Vol Berlin 1920, S. 602–699

CANBY, C.: Geschichte der Schiffahrt. Editions Recontre u. Erik Nitsche, International. Lausanne 1962

CATALOGUE of the Henry Huddleston Rogers Collection of Ship Models. Annapolis, Maryland, 1954

Beschrijvende CATALOGUS der Scheepsmodellen en scheepsbouwkundige Tekiningen 1600–1900 in het Nederlandsche Historisch Scheepvaart Museum. Scheepvaart Museum. Amsterdam 1943

Chapelle, H. I.: The History of the American Sailing Navy. New York 1949

CHAPMAN, F. H.: Architectura Navalis Mercatoria. Stockholm 1768

CHAPMAN, F. H. af: Architectura Navalis Mercatoria. Robert Loef Verlag. Burg bei Magdeburg 1957

CHAPMAN, F. H. af: Architectura Navalis Mercatoria. Nachdruck. VEB Hinstorff Verlag. Rostock 1970

CHAPMAN, F. H. af: Tractat om skeppsbyggeriet tillaka med förklaring och bevis öfver Architectura Navalis Mercatoria. Stockholm 1775

CHATTERTON, E. K.: Sailing Models Ancient & Modern. London 1934

COUSTEAU, J.-Y.; DIOLÉ, P.: Silberschiffe. Tauchen nach versunkenen Schätzen. München, Zürich 1972

CRAEMER, H. A.: 5000 Jahre Segelschiffe. München, Berlin 1938

CRONE, G. S. E.: Nederlandsche jachten, binnenschepen, vischvaartuigen en darmee verwannte kleine zeeschepen 1650–1900. Swets & Zeitlinger. Amsterdam 1926

CRUMLIN-PEDERSEN, O.: Cog – Kogge – Kaag. Froek af en frisisk skibstypes historie. Helsingor 1965

CULVER, H. B.: The Book of Old Ships and Something of their Evolution and Romance. Garden City Publishing Comp., Inc. New York 1935

CULVER, H. B.; GRANT, G.: Forty Famous Ships. Doubleday, Doran & Co. New York 1936

CURTI, O.: Schiffsmodellbau. Eine Enzyklopädie. VEB Hinstorff Verlag. Rostock 1972

CUTLER, C.: Greyhounds of the Sea. The Story of the American Clipper Ships. Annapolis, Maryland; United States Naval Institute, 1985

DAENELL, E.: Die Blütezeit der deutschen Hanse. Hansische Geschichte von der zweiten Hälfte des 14. bis zum letzten Viertel des 15. Jahrhunderts. 2 Vols Berlin 1905/06

DEBUS, K., et al.: Kreuzersegeln. Sportverlag. Berlin 1965

DELBRUECK, R.: Südasiatische Seefahrt im Altertum. In: Bonner Jahrbücher 155/6, 1955/56, P 8–58 & 229–308.

DUDSZUS, A.: Schiffe des Altertums und der Antike. In: Seewirtschaft 14 (1982) 1–11

DUDSZUS, A.; DANCKWARDT, E.: Schiffstechnik – Einführung und Grundbegriffe. VEB Verlag Technik. Berlin 1982

DÜMICHEN, J.: Die Flotte einer ägyptischen Königin aus dem 17. Jahrhundert v. Chr. Leipzig 1868

DUHAMEL DE MONCEAU, H. L.: Eléments de l'architecture navale ou traité practique de la construction des vaisseaux. Paris 1752

DURON, M.; ROUGERON, R.: Encyclopédie des bâteaux. 1978

ECK, O.: Seeräuberei im Mittelalter. München, Berlin 1940

EDEY, M.A.: Anfänge des Seehandels. Amsterdam 1974

EICH, L.; WEND, J.: Schiffe auf druckgraphischen Blättern. Ausgewählte Meisterwerke des 15. bis 17. Jahrhunderts. VEB Hinstorff Verlag. Rostock 1980

EICHLER, C.: Vom Bug zum Heck. Seemännisches Hand- und Wörterbuch. Klasing & Co. Bielefeld, Berlin 1954

EICHLER, C.: Yacht- und Bootsbau für Bootsbauer, Konstrukteure und Segler. Vol 2 Delius, Klasing & Co. Bielefeld, Berlin 1966

EINBAUM – DAMPFLOK – DÜSENKLIPPER. Urania-Verlag. Leipzig, Jena, Berlin 1969

EISENLOHR, A.: Ein mathematisches Handbuch der alten Ägypter. Leipzig 1877

ENCYKLOPEDIE, MARITIEME. Redaktion J. v. Beylen, 7 Vol De Boor, Bussum 1970/73

ERBRACH, R.: Forschungen aus der Blütezeit des Baues hölzerner Segelschiffe im 19. Jahrhundert. In: Jahrbuch der Schiffbautechnischen Gesellschaft, Vol 45, Berlin 1951, P 288–299

EWE, H.: Schiffe auf Siegeln. VEB Hinstorff Verlag. Rostock 1972

FALK, H.: Altnordisches Seewesen. Heidelberg 1912

FAULKNER, R. O.: Egyptian Seagoing Ships. In: The Journal of Egyptian Archaeology 26 (1940), P 3–9

FELDHAUS, F.M.: Die Technik der Vorzeit, der geschichtlichen Zeit und der Naturvölker. Leipzig, Berlin 1914; Reprint 1970

FIMMEN, D.: Die kretisch-mykenische Kultur. Leipzig 1921

FINK, G.: Die Hanse, Leipzig 1939

FIRCKS, J. von: Wikingerschiffe. Über ihren Bau, ihre Vorgänger und ihre eigene Entwicklung. VEB Hinstorff Verlag. Rostock 1979

FLAMM, O.: Schiffbau. Seine Geschichte und seine Entwicklung. Berlin 1907

FLIEDNER, S.: Die Bremer Kogge. Bremen 1968

FONSECA, Q. da: A caravela portugesa e a prioridade técnica des navegaçoes Henriquins. Imprensa da Universidade. Coimbra 1934

FRANZ, K.: Die ägyptische Gestaltung des Seeschiffes. Berlin 1927

FRANZÉN, A.: The Warship Wasa. Stockholm n.d.

FRIEDERICI, G.: Die Schiffahrt der Indianer. Stuttgart 1907

FRIEDRICHSOHN, J.: Geschichte der Schiffahrt. Hamburg 1800

FURTTENBACH, J.: Architectura navalis/Das ist von dem Schiffsgebäu/Auf dem Meere und den Seekusten zu gebrauchen. Ulm 1629 (Germanischer Lloyd 1956)

GELOICH, I.: Studien über die Entwicklungsgeschichte der Schiffahrt. Laibach 1882

GEORGEN, O.: Geschichte des Kriegsschiffbaues vom Altertum bis zur Einführung der Dampfkraft. Der Zirkel. Architekturverlag GmbH. Berlin 1919

GERDS, P.; GEHRKE, W.-D.: Und am Bug der Greif. Ein Beitrag zur Geschichte der Rostocker Schiffahrt. VEB Hinstorff Verlag. Rostock 1977

GJESSING, G.: Die Wikinger-Schiffsfunde. Oslo 1951

GOEDEL, G.: Etymologisches Wörterbuch der deutschen Seemannssprache. Verlag von Lipsius und Tischer. Kiel, Leipzig 1902

GRAESER, B.: Seewesen der alten Ägypter. Berlin 1869

GÜNTHER, H.: Die Eroberung der Tiefe. Stuttgart 1928

HAACK, R.: Über attische Trieren. In: Zeitschrift des Vereins deutscher Ingenieure 39 (1885), P 165–174

HABACHI, B.: Two Graffiti at Sehel from the Reign of Queen Hatshepsut. In: Journal of Near Eastern Studies 16 (1957), P 88–104

HACKNEY, N. C. L.: Mayflower. VEB Hinstorff Verlag. Rostock 1978

HÄGG, E.: Under tretungad flagga. Vår seglande orlogsflotta och dess män 1750–1900. Aktiebolaget Svens Litteratur. Stockholm 1941

HÄPKE, R.: Der Untergang der Hanse. Bremen 1923

HAGEDORN, B.: Die Entwicklung der wichtigsten Schiffstypen bis ins 19. Jahrhundert. (Veröffentlichungen des Vereins für Hamburgische Geschichte, Vol 1) Verlag von Karl Curtius. Berlin 1914

HAHN, E.: Die Entwicklung des Schiffes und der Schiffahrt nach wirtschaftsgeschichtlichen Gesichtspunkten dargestellt. In: Zeitschrift des Verbandes deutscher Diplom-Ingenieure 2 (1911), P 617–624

HARDEN, D.: The Phoenicians. London, New York 1962

HARDY, A.C.: The Book of the Ship. London 1947

HAUSEN, J.: Schiffbau in der Antike. Beitrag zur Geschichte des Schiffbaus. Konstruktion und Festigkeit der Schiffe in der Antike. Koehlers Verlagsgesellschaft m.b.H. Herford 1979 (Diss. TH Aachen 1977)

HEINSIUS, P.: Das Schiff der hansischen Frühzeit. (Quellen und Darstellungen zur hansischen Geschichte. Hrsg. vom Hansischen Geschichtsverein. Neue Folge, Vol XII). Verlag Hermann Böhlaus. Weimar 1956

HENNIG, R.: Abhandlungen zur Geschichte der Schiffahrt. Jena 1928

HENRIOT, E.: Geschichte des Schiffbaues. Urania-Verlag. Leipzig, Berlin 1955

HENRIOT, E.: Kurzgefaßte illustrierte Geschichte des Schiffbaus von den Anfängen bis zum Ausgang des 19. Jahrhunderts. VEB Hinstorff Verlag. Rostock 1971

HENRIOT, E.: Kratkaja illjustrirovannaja istorija sudostroenija. Izdatel'stvo Sudostroenie. Leningrad 1974

HERMAN, F.: Seeräuberei im Mittelmeer. Lübeck 1815

HEYERDAHL, T.: Expedition Ra. Im Papyrusboot über den Atlantik. Verlag Volk und Welt. Berlin 1975

HEYERDAHL, T.: Kon-Tiki. Verlag Volk und Welt. Berlin 1949

HISTROIRE DE LA MARINE. Illustration. Paris 1939

HOBBS, E. W.: How to Make Clipper Ship Models. Brown, Son & Ferguson, Ltd. Glasgow 1938; reprinted 1948 and 1952

HOECKEL, R.: Fleute Derfflinger 1675 Robert Loef Verlag. Burg bei Magdeburg 1947

HOECKEL, R.: Fregatte Berlin 1674 Robert Loef Verlag. Burg bei Magdeburg 1947

HOECKEL, R.: Jacht Bracke 1678. Robert Loef Verlag. Burg bei Magdeburg 1948

HOECKEL, R.: Hamburgisches Konvoischiff Wappen von Hamburg 1667–1683. Robert Loef Verlag. Burg bei Magdeburg 1958

HOECKEL, R.: Modellbau von Schiffen des 16. und 17. Jahrhunderts. VEB Hinstorff Verlag. Rostock 1965

HOECKEL/JORBERG: Amerikanische Kriegsbrigg 1810. Robert Loef Verlag. Burg bei Magdeburg 1957

HÖHLER, F.: Das Brandskogen-Boot und der Versuch seiner Nachbildung. In: Mannus. Zeitschrift für deutsche Vorgeschichte 30 (1938), P 193–203

HÖHLER, F.: Plankenschiff oder Spantenschiff? In: Schiffbau, Schiffahrt und Hafenbau 37 (1936), P 289–294

HÖVER, O.: Von der Galiot zum Fünfmaster. Unsere Segelschiffe in der Weltschiffahrt 1780 bis 1930. Angelsachsen-Verlag GmbH. Bremen 1934

HÖVER, O.: Deutsche Hochseefischerei. Oldenburg 1936

HÖVER, O.: Von der Kogge zum Klipper. Zur Entwicklung des Segelschiffes. Karl F. Wede Verlag. Hamburg 1948

HÖVER, O.: Deutsche Seegeschichte. Rütten & Loening Verlag. Potsdam 1942

HÖVER, O.: Älteste Seeschiffahrt und ihre kulturelle Umwelt. Hamburg 1948

HORNELL, J.: The Boats of the Ganges. The Fishing Methods of the Ganges. In: Memoirs of the Asiatic Society of Bengal. Vol. VIII, No. 3, Calcutta 1924 P 171–230

HORNELL, J.: Water Transport, Origins and Early Evolution. Cambridge 1946

HORNSTEIN, A. von: Schiffe und Schiffahrt. (Hallwa-Taschenbücherei, Vol 53). Bern 1957

HOWARTH, D.: Sovereign of the Seas – The Story of British Seapower. London 1974

JAHNKUHN, H.: Haithabu. Ein Handelsplatz der Wikingerzeit. 1954

JAL, A.: Glossaire nautique. Firmin Didot Frères. Paris 1848

JOHNSON, G.: Ship Model Building. Cornell Maritime Press. 1953

KAHLER, P.: Das türkische Seehandbuch des Piri Reis (Bahrije) für das mittelländische Meer vom Jahre 1521. Berlin, Leipzig 1926

KATZEW, M. L.: Das Schiff von Kyrenaia. In: G. F. Bass: Taucher in die Vergangenheit. Unterwasserarchäologen schreiben die Geschichte der Seefahrt. Luzern, Frankfurt 1972, P 49–53

KEMP, P. K.; KEMP, P.: Famous Ships of the World. Frederick Müller, Ltd. London 1956

KERCHOVE, R. de: International Maritime Dictionary. Nostrand. Princeton, New Jersey 1961

KLEBS, L.: Die Reliefs des Alten Reiches. Heidelberg 1920

KLEBS, L.: Die Reliefs und Malereien des Mittleren Reiches. Heidelberg 1922

KLEBS, L.: Die Reliefs und Malereien des Neuen Reiches. Heidelberg 1924

KLEM, K.: De Danske Vey. Host & Sons. Kobenhavn 1941

KLOESS, H. K.: Über Schiffsformen und ihre Entwicklung. In: Jahrbuch der Schiffbautechnischen Gesellschaft. Band 45

(1951), P 33ff.

KOEHLER, P.: Die Basler Rheinschiffahrt vom Mittelalter bis zur Neuzeit. (Schriftenreihe der Basler Vereinigung für Schweizerische Schiffahrt, Vol 1). Basel 1944

KÖSTER, A.: Modelle alter Segelschiffe. Verlag Ernst Wachsmuth AG. Berlin 1926

KÖSTER, A.: Seefahrten der alten Ägypter. In: Meereskunde, Heft 175

KÖSTER, A.: Das antike Seewesen. Berlin 1923

KÖSTER/NISCHER: Das Seekriegswesen bei den Griechen. Das Seekriegswesen bei den Römern. In: Handbuch der Altertumswissenschaft, begründet von Iwan v. Miller, hrsg. von Walter Otto. 4. Abt., 3. Teil, 2. Band: Heerwesen und Kriegsführung bei Griechen und Römern. München 1928

KOHLHAUER, E.: Die griechischen und römischen Schiffe. Leipzig 1903

KONIJENENBURG, E. van: Der Schiffbau seit seiner Entstehung. Internationaler stäniger Verband der Schiffahrtskongresse. Brüssel 1913

KOPECKY, J.: Die attischen Trieren. Leipzig 1890

KORTH, J. W. D.: Die Schiffbaukunst oder die Kunst, den Bau der Kriegs-, Kauffahrtey- und anderer Schiffe nach theoretischen und praktischen Regeln auszuführen. Paulische Buchhandlung. Berlin 1826

KOZÁK, J.; POSPISIL, P.; RADA, M.: Taschenatlas der Schiffe. Werner Deusien. Hanau 1975

KRÄMER, W.: Die Geschichte der Entdeckungen unserer Erde. Leipzig, Berlin 1971

KRÁSA, M.: Das Lächeln von Angkor. Artia Verlag. Prague 1962

KUNSTGESCHICHTE DER SEEFAHRT. Hrsg. v. Hans-Jürgen Hansen. Gerh. Stalling Verlag. Oldenburg, Hamburg 1966

LAAS, W.: Die großen Segelschiffe. Verlag von Julius Springer. Berlin 1908

LÄCHLER, P.; WIRZ, H.: Die Schiffe der Völker. Traum, Geschichte, Technik. Walter-Verlag. Olten/Freib. 1962

LAIRD CLOWES, G. S.: Sailing Ships. Their History and Development. Ministry of Education, Science Museum, Her Majesty's Stationery Office. London 1932

LAMBOGLIA, N.: Albenga. In: J. du Plat Taylor: Marine Archaeology. London 1965, P 33–66

LANDSTRÖM, B.: Das Schiff. Vom Einbaum zum Atomboot. Rekonstruktionen in Bild und Wort. C. Bertelsmann Verlag. Gütersloh 1961

LANDSTRÖM, B.: Die Schiffe der Pharaonen. Altägyptische Schiffbaukunst von 4000 bis 600 v.u. Z.C. Bertelsmann Verlag. Gütersloh 1974

LANDSTRÖM, B.: Segelschiffe. Von den Papyrusbooten bis zu den Vollschiffen in Wort und Bild. Bertelsmann Lexikon-Verlag Reinhard Mohn. Gütersloh 1969

LANITZKI, G.: Amphoren, Wracks, versunkene Städte. VEB F. A. Brockhaus Verlag. Leipzig 1980

LA RONCIÈRE, C. de; CLERC-RAMPAL, G.: Histoire de la Marine Française. Librairie Larousse. Paris 1934

LAUGHTON, L. G.: Old Ships, Figure-Heads and Sterns. London 1925

LA VARENDE, J. de: Die romantische Seefahrt. Rowohlt Verlag. Hamburg 1957

LECHLER, J.: Die Entdeckung Amerikas vor Kolumbus. Leipzig 1939

LEIF, H.: Bordbuch des Satans. Eine Chronik der Freibeuter vom Altertum bis zur Gegenwart. München 1959

LEMKE, H.: Die Reisen des Venezianers Marco Polo im 13. Jahrhundert. (Bibliothek wertvoller Memoiren, Edited by Dr. D. Schultze.) Hamburg 1907

LEWIS, E.V.; O'BRIEN, R.: Schiffe. Rowohlt Taschenbuch Verlag GmbH. Reinbek bei Hamburg 1973

LLOYD, C.: Schiffe und Schiffsvolk. Eine bildgeschichte von den Winkingern bis zur Gegenwart. Hamburg 1962

LOON, H.W. van: Männer und Meere. Siebentausend Jahre Seefahrt. Ullstein Verlag. Berlin 1936

LUBBOCK, B.: The China Clippers. Brown and Ferguson, Ltd. Glasgow 1919

LUBBOCK, B.: The Colonial Clippers. Brown and Ferguson, Ltd. Glasgow 1924

LUBBOCK, B.: The Opium Clippers. Brown and Ferguson, Ltd. Glasgow 1933

LUBBOCK, B.: The Down-Easters. Brown and Ferguson, Ltd. Glasgow 1930

LUBBOCK, B.: The Blackwall Frigates. Brown and Ferguson, Ltd. Glasgow 1924

LUBBOCK, B.: The Last of the Windjammers. 2 Vols Brown and Ferguson, Ltd. Glasgow 1927/29; auch 1948

LUCININOV, S. T.: Junyj modellist-korablestroitel' (Der junge Modellschiffbauer). Sudpromigiz. Leningrad 1963

LUSCHAN, F. von: Über Boote aus Baumrinde. In: Aus der Natur. Zeitschrift für alle Naturfreunde. III. Jahrgang, 1. Halbband. Leipzig 1907

MACINTYRE, D.; BATHE, B. W.: Kriegsschiffe in 5000 Jahren. Verlag Delius, Klasing & Co. Bielefeld, Berlin n.d.

MARSDEN, P.: A Roman Ship from Blackfriars. London 1966

MARTIN, J. H.; BENNETT, G.: Das große Buch der Schiffe. Südwest-Verlag. München 1978

MAYDORN, D.: Der Brandtaucher. Das erste deutsche Unterseeboot Wilhelm Bauers. (Meereskunde, Vol 15, Part 167). Verlag Mittler & Sohn. Berlin 1926

MICHAELSEN, H.: Riesenschiffe. In: Meereskunde, Part 3, Berlin 1914

MIDDENDORF, F. L.: Bemastung und Takelung der Schiffe. Springer Verlag. Berlin 1903; Manualdruck 1921

MOELLER, C.; ROELOFFS, R.: Cyclus von Schiffen aller seefahrenden Nationen. Hamburg 1839/40; Nachdruck 1954

MOLL, F.: Das Schiff in der bildenden Kunst. Vom Altertum bis zum Ausgang des Mittelalters. Kurt Schweder Verlag. Bonn 1929

MOLL, C.; SZYMANSKI, H.: Zur Vorgeschichte des germanischen Schiffbaues. In: Beiträge zur Geschichte der Technik und Industrie. Jahrbuch des Vereins deutscher Ingenieure, 11 Vol Berlin 1921

MOLLEMA, J. C.: Geschiedenis van Nederland ter Zee. 4 Vols N.V. Uitg. Mij. Joost van den Vondel. Amsterdam 1939/42

MONDFELD, W.: Die arabische Dau. VEB Hinstorff Verlag. Rostock 1979

MONDFELD, W.: Die Schebecke und andere Schiffstypen des Mittelmeerraumes. VEB Hinstorff Verlag. Rostock 1974

MONDFELD, W. zu: Historische Schiffsmodelle. Das Handbuch für Modellbauer. Mosaik Verlag. München 1978

MOORE, A.: Sailing Ships of War 1800–1860, including the Transition to Steam. Halton & Truscott Smith, Ltd. London; Minton, Balch & Co. New York 1926

MORRISON, J. S.: The Greek Trireme. In: The Mariner's Mirror 27 (1941), P 14–44

MOSCATI, S.: Die Phöniker. Zürich 1966

MÜLLER, C. G. D.: Anfangsgründe der Schiffbaukunst. Hamburg 1791

MULACH, G. A.: Die Schiffahrt im Bild. 2 Vols Dieck & Co. Stuttgart 1925/26

MULACH, G. A.: Die Schiffahrt im Wandel der Zeiten. Dieck & Co. Stuttgart 1925

MULACH, G. A.: Das Segelschiff im Bild. Dieck & Co. Stuttgart 1926

NANCE, R. M.: Sailing Ship Models. A Selection from European and American Collections with Introductory Text. Halton & Truscott Smith, Ltd. London 1924

NEUKIRCHEN, H.: Häfen und Schiffe. VEB Hinstorff Verlag. Rostock 1974

NEUKIRCHEN, J.: Krieg zur See. Deutscher Millitäverlag. Berlin 1966

NEUKIRCHEN, H.: Seefahrt gestern und heute. Transpress VEB Verlag für Verkehrswesen. Berlin 1971

NEVERMANN, H.: Schiffahrt exotischer Völker. Druck- und Verlagsanstalt H. Wigankow. Berlin 1949

NÖRLUND, P.: Die Wikingersiedlungen in Grönland. 1937

NOOTEBOOM, C.: Eastern Diremes. In: The Mariner's Mirror 35 (1949) 4, P 272–275

NORDÉN, A.: Brandskogs-skeppet. In: Fornvännen, 1925, P 376–391

NORDÉN, A.: Die Schiffbaukunst der nordischen Bronzezeit. In: Mannus. Zeitschrift für deutsche Vorgeschichte 31 (1939), P 347–398

NORDÉN, A.: Bronsalderns skeppsbyggnadskonst i Norden. In: Teknisk tidskrift 1925, P 45ff

NOUR, M. Z.; ISKANDER, Z.; OSMAN, M. S.; MOUSTAFA, A. Y.: The Cheops Boats. Part 1. Cairo 1960

OLECHNOWITZ, K.-F.: Der Schiffbau der Hansischen Spätzeit. (Abhandlungen zur Handels- und Sozialgeschichte, Vol 3). Hermann Böhlaus Nachfolger. Weimar 1960

THE OXFORD COMPANION to Ships & the Sea. Edited by Peter Kemp. Oxford University Press. London, New York, Melbourne 1976

PAGEL, K.: Die Hanse. Georg Westermann Verlag 1952

PÂRIS, E.: Segelkriegsschiffe des 17. Jahrhunderts. Von der Couronne zur Royal Louis. VEB Hinstorff Verlag. Rostock 1975

PÂRIS, E.: Souvenirs de Marine. 6 Vols. Gauthiers & fils. Villach 1882/1908

PÂRIS, E.: Souvenirs de Marine 1882–1892. Edited by Winter. Robert Loef Verlag. Burg bei Magdeburg 1956

PÂRIS, E.: Souvenirs de Marine 1882–1908. Edited by Von E. Henriot. VEB Hinstorff Verlag. Rostock 1962

PÂRIS, E.: Die große Zeit der Galeeren und Galeassen. Hrsg. v. L. Eich, E. Henriot und L. Langendorf. VEB Hinstorff Verlag. Rostock 1973

PATAKY, D.; MARJAI, J.: Schiffahrt und Kunst. Corvina-Verlag. Budapest 1973

PETREJUS, E. W.: Ships of All Ages. A Set of Sixteen Marine Drawings. Series A-D (Nbrs. 1–64). De Esch, Ltd. Hengelo

PLASSMANN, J. O.: Wikingerfahrten und Normannenreiche. Jena 1929

PLEYTE, C. M.: Het Schip van Brugge. In: Abhandlungen der Société d'Emulation. Brügge 1936

PLISCHER, H.: Christoph Columbus. Leipzig 1926

PLISCHER, H.: Entdeckungsgeschichte vom Altertum bis zur Neuzeit. (Wissenschaft und Bildung. Band 290) Leipzig 1933

PLISCHER, H.: Vasco da Gama. Der Weg nach Ostindien. (Alte Reisen und Abenteuer) Leipzig

PLISCHER, H.: Fernão de Magelhães. Die erste Weltumseglung. Leipzig 1922

PÖRTNER, R.: Die Wikinger Saga. Düsseldorf, Wien 1971

POLYBIOS: Historien. In: J. Rehork: Geschichte im Altertum I-XII. V. Hamburg 1944, P 27 bis 126

RABBENO, G.; SPEZIALE, G.-S.: Die Forschungen im Nemi-See in ihrer Bedeutung für die Geschichte der Schiffbaukunst. In: Jahrbuch der Schiffbautechnischen Gesellschaft 33 (1932), P 248–279

RADUNZ, K.: Vom Einbaum zum Linienschiff. Streifzüge auf dem Gebiet der Schiffahrt und des Seewesens. Urania-Verlag. Leipzig, Berlin 1912

RAHDEN, H.: Die Schiffe der Rostocker Handelsflotte 1800–1917. Hinstorff Verlag. Seestadt Rostock 1941 (Veröffentlichungen aus dem Rostocker Stadtarchiv, Vol 2)

REHM, A.: Schiff und See. Seestadt Bremerhaven. Eine fröhliche Verklarung für Küstenbewohner und Landratten. Nordwestdeutscher Verlag Ditzen & Co. Bremerhaven 1971

REINCKE, H.; SCHULZE, B.: Das hamburgische Konvoyschiff Wappen von Hamburg III. Hamburg 1952

RISSE VON SCHIFFEN des 16. und 17. Jahrhunderts. Edited by L. Eich. VEB Hinstorff Verlag. Rostock 1979

RITTER, H.: Mesopotamische Studien. Arabische Flußfahrzeuge auf Euphrat und Tigris. In: Der Islam. Zeitschrift für Geschichte und Kultur des Islamischen Orients. Vol IX, Part 2, P 121–143. Straßburg 1918

RITTMEISTER, W.; MAHLAU, A.: Die Schiffsfibel. L. Staackmann Verlag. Leipzig 1939

RÖDING, J. H.: Allgemeines Wörterbuch der Marine. In allen 4 europäschen Seesprachen nebst Vollständigen Erkläningen. Licenciat Nemnich. Hamburg; Adam Friedrich Böhme. Leipzig 1793/94

ROGERS, H. H.: Collection of Ship Models. Anapolis, Maryland; United States Naval Academy Museum, United States Naval Institute 1954

ROMALA/ANDERSON: The Sailing Ship. Six-thousand Years of History. London 1926

ROSENBERG, G.: Hjortspringfundet. (Nordiske Fortidsminder. Vol III, Part 1.) Nordisk Forlag. Kobenhavn 1937

RUDOLPH, W.: Boote, Flöße, Schiffe. Edition Leipzig. Leipzig 1974

RUDOLPH, W.: Handbuch der volkstümlichen Boote im östlichen Niederdeutschland. Akademie-Verlag. Berlin 1969

RUDOLPH, W.: Die Insel der Schiffer. Zeugnisse und Erinnerungen von rügischer Schiffahrt. Vom Beginn der Entwicklung bis 1945. VEB Hinstorff Verlag. Rostock 1962

RUDOLPH, W.: Segelboote der deutschen Ostseeküste. (Deutsche Akademie der Wissenschaften zu Berlin. Veröffentlichungen des Instituts für deutsche Volkskunst. Vol 53) Akademie-Verlag. Berlin 1969

SALONEN, A.: Die Wasserfahrzeuge in Babylonien. In: Studia Orientalia 8 (1939) 4

SCHÄUFFELEN, D.: Die letzten großen Segelschiffe. Delius & Klasing. Bielefeld, Berlin 1969

SCHARFF, A.: Das Schiff im vorgeschichtlichen Ägypten. In: Der Erdball. Illustrierte Zeitschrift für Länder- und Völkerkunde 5 (1931), P 412–418

SCHELTEMA, A. von: Der Osebergfund. Leipzig 1938

Alte SCHIFFSMODELLE aus dem Hause der Schiffergesellschaft in Lübeck. 12 Tafeln mit Erläuterungen herausgegeben von Professor Dr. Franz Schulze. Verlag von Bernhard Nöhring. Lübeck

SCHIFFSRISSE ZUR SCHIFFBAUGESCHICHTE. 1. Part Holländische und deutsche Schiffe 1597–1680. Ed. by R. Loef. Robert Loef Verlag. Burg bei Magdeburg 1956

SCHIFFSRISSE ZUR SCHIFFBAUGESCHICHTE. 2. Part: Englische und amerikanische Schiffe 1577–1810. Ed. by R. Loef. Robert Loef Verlag. Burg bei Magdeburg 1956

SCHLETTE, F.: Germanen zwischen Thorsberg und Ravenna. Urania-Verlag. Leipzig, Jena, Berlin

SCHMÖKEL, H.: Ur, Asur und Babylon. Drei Jahrtausende im Zweistromland. Zürich 1955

SCHWABE, H. R.: Die Entwicklung der schweizerischen Rheinschiffahrt 1904–1954. (Schriftenreihe der Basler Vereinigung für schweizerische Schiffahrt. Vol 4) Basel 1954

SCHWARZ, T.: Die Entwicklung des Kriegsschiffbaues vom Altertum bis zur Neuzeit. 2 Vols Leipzig 1909/12

SEEFAHRT. NAUTISCHES LEXIKON IN BILDERN. Delius, Klasing & Co. Bielefeld, Berlin 1963

Der geöffnete SEEHAFEN…Hamburg 1902; Nachdruck der Seiten 29–175, besorgt von der Schiffbautechnischen Gesellschaft. Schiffbautechnische Gesellschaft. Hamburg 1954

SEEMANNSSPRACHE. Wortgeschichtliches Handbuch deutscher Schifferausdrücke älterer und neuerer Zeit. Ed by F. Kluge. Halle (Saale) 1908

SPENGEMANN, F.: Petroleumklipper. Bremen/St. Magnus 1951

SPENGEMANN, F.: Von Vegesacker Reedern, Schiffen und Kapitänen. Schiffsgeschichtliche Beiträge. Bremen/St. Magnus 1956

SPENGEMANN, F.: Aus der Segelschiffahrtszeit. Landbotenverlag. Bremen 1948

SPENGEMANN, F.: Bremens Segelschiffe. Bremen 1956

STEIN, P.: Zur Geschichte der Piraterie im Altertum. Bernburg 1894

STEINDORFF, G.: Das Grab des Ti. Leipzig 1913

STEINHAUS, C. F.: Die Schiffbaukunst in irhem ganzen Umfange. 2 Vols Hamburg 1848

STEINMANN, A.: Das kultische Schiff in Indonesien. Zürich 1939

STENZEL, A.: Seekriegsgeschichte in ihren wichtigsten Abschnitten mit Berücksichtigung der Seetaktik. 6 Vols Hahn-Verlag. Hannover, Leipzig 1907/11

STENZEL, A.: Deutsches seemännisches Wörterbuch. Mittler & Sohn. Berlin 1904

STEVENS, J. R.: Old Time Ships. Toronto 1949

SUDER, H.: Vom Einbaum und Floß zum Schiff. Die primitiven Wasserfahrzeuge. (Veröffentlichungen des Instituts für Meereskunde an der Universität Berlin. Neue Folge. B.: Historisch-volkswirtschaft-

liche Reihe. Part 7.) Berlin 1930
SVENSSON, S.; MACFIE, G.: Segal durch Jahrhunderte. Delius, Klasing & Co. Bielefeld, Berlin 1961
SZYMANSKI, H.: Der Ever der Niederelbe. Hansischer Geschichts-verein. Lübeck 1932
SZYMANSKI, H.: Alte Schiffstypen Niedersachsens. In: Neues Archiv für Niedersachsen, Part 13, P 667–711. Walter Dorn Verlag. Bremen 1949
SZYMANSKI, H.: Deutsche Segelschiffe. Die Geschichte der hölzernen Frachtsegler an den deutschen Ost- und Nordseeküsten vom Ende des 18. Jahrhunderts bis auf die Gegenwart. (Veröffentlichungen des Instituts für Meereskunde an der Universität Berlin. Neue Folge. B.: Historisch-volkswirthschafliche Reihe. Part 10) Berlin 1934; Reprint: Verlag Egon Heinemann. Norderstedt – Hamburg 1972
SZYMANSKI, H.: Die Segelschiffe der deutschen Kleinschiffahrt. In: Pfingstblätter des Hansischen Geschichtsvereins. Blatt XX. Lübeck 1929

TARN, W. W.: The Greek War Ship. In: Journal of Hellenic Studies 25 (1905), P 76–93
TENNE, A.: Kriegsschiffe zu Zeiten der alten Griechen und Römer. Oldenburg 1915
THIEL, H.: Vom Wikingerboot zum Tragflügelschiff. Verlag Junge Welt. Berlin 1966
TIMM, W.: Kapitänsbilder. Schiffsporträts seit 1872. VEB Hinstorff Verlag. Rostock 1971
TIMM, W.: Vom Koggen zum Fünfmaster. Schiffsdarstellungen aus 10 Jahrhunderten nordeuropäischer Segelschiffahrt. Verlag der Kunst. Dresden 1962
TIMM, W.: Schiffe und ihre Schicksale. Maritime Ereignisbilder. VEB Hinstorff Verlag. Rostock 1976
TIMM, W.: Kleine Schiffskunde. Segelschiffs-darstellungen aus zehn Jahrhunderten. Verlag der Kunst. Dresden 1968
TIMMERMANN, G.: Vom Einbaum zum Wikingerschiff. Vergleichende Betrachtung der Bodenfunde von Schiffen als Grundlage der Schiffsgeschichte. In: Schiff & Hafen 8 (1956), P 130–138, 218–226, 336–342, 403, 412, 431, 545–549, 602–612

TIMMERMANN, G.: Entwicklung des Schiffbaus seit den ältesten Zeiten. In: Jahrbuch der Schiffbautechnischen Gesellschaft 49 (1955), P 110–118
TIMMERMANN, G.: Zeichnerische Festlegung der Schiffsform in der Vergangenheit. In: Schiff & Hafen 13 (1961), P 43–47
TIMMERMANN, G.: Vom Pfahlewer zum Motorkutter. (Schriften der Bundesforschungsanstalt für Fischerei, Hamburg. 3. Band) Westliche Berliner Verlagsgesellschaft Hennemann KG. Berlin 1957
TIMMERMANN, G.: Schiffsmodelle. Eine Geschichte der Schiffbaukunst. Urbes Verlag. Hamburg 1958
TIMMERMAN, G.: Die nordeuropäischen Fischereifahrzeuge, ihre Entwicklung und ihre Typen. (Handbuch der Seefischerei Nordeuropas. Vol XI, Nachtragsband, Part 4.) E. Schweizerbart'sche Verlagsbuchhandlung (Nägele und Obermiller). Stuttgart 1962
TIMMERMAN, G.: Deutsche Seemannsausdrücke. Hamburg 1953
TRANSPRESS-LEXIKON SEEFAHRT. Transpress VEB Verlag für Verkehrswesen. Berlin 1977
TREBITSCH, R.: Fellboote und Schwimmsäcke und ihre geographische Verbreitung in der Vergangenheit und Gegenwart. In: Archiv für Anthropologie, Ed by J. Ranke und G. Thilenius. Neue Folge, Vol XI. Braunschweig 1912

VOCINO, M.: La Nave nel Tempo. Max Bretschneider. Rome 1942
VOGEL, W.: Geschichte der deutschen Seeschiffahrt. I. Vol: Von der Urzeit bis zum Ende des XV. Jahrhunderts. George Reiner. Berlin 1915
VOGEL, W.: Zur nord- und westeuropäischen Seeschiffahrt im frühen Mittelalter. 1917
VOIGT, C.: Von den Krieggschiffen Kurbrandenburgs. In: Schiffbau, Schiffahrt und Hafenbau 31 (1930), P 394–397
VOIGT, C.: Niederländischer Schiffbau im 18. Jahrhundert. In: Schiffbau, Schiffahrt und Hafenbau 27 (1926), P 739–742
VOIGT, C.: Schiffs-Ästhetik. Die Schönheit des Schiffes in alter und neuer Zeit. Verlag

der Zeitschrift »Schiffbau« Reinhold Strauss KG. Berlin 1922

WÄTJEN, H.: Aus der Frühzeit des Nordatlantik-verkehrs. Studien zur Geschichte der deutschen Schiffahrt und deutschen Auswanderung nach den Vereinigten Staaten bis zum Ende des amerikanischen Bürgerkrieges. Feliz Meiner Verlag. Leipzig 1932.
WAGNER, W.-D.: Die Fregatten »Peter und Paul« und Heiliger Paul. VEB Hinstorff Verlag. Rostock 1965
WARNER, O.: Große Seeschlachten. Gerhard Stalling Verlag. Oldenburg, Hamburg 1963
WENZEL, H.: Mare aeternum. Edition Leipzig. Leipzig 1969
WESTPHAL G.: Lexikon der Seefahrt. Hamburg-Kl. Flottbek 1968
WINTER, H.: Das Hanseschiff im ausgehenden 15. Jahrhundert. VEB Hinstorff Verlag. Rostock 1968
WINTER, H.: Die Kolumbusschiffe von 1492. VEB Hinstorff Verlag. Rostock 1960
WINTER, H.: Wappen von Hamburg (1669) und Berlin. VEB Hinstorff Verlag. Rostock 1967
WINTER, H.: Der holländische Zweidecker von 1660/1670. VEB Hinstorff Verlag. Rostock 1967
WITSEN, N.: Aeloude en hedendaegsche Scheeps-Bouw en Bestier. Christoffel Cunradus. Amsterdam 1671
WOSSIDLO, R.: Reise, Quartier, in Gottesnaam. Da Seemannsleben auf den alten Segelschiffen im Munde alter Fahrensleute. VEB Hinstorff Verlag. Rostock 1952

YK, C. van: De neederlandsche Scheepsbouw-Konst opengestelt. C. B. G. Müller. Amsterdam 1697

ZIEBARTH, E.: Beiträge zur Geschichte des Seeraubs und Seehandels im alten Griechenland. (Hamburgische Universität. Abhandlungen zur Auslandskunde. Vol 30) Hamburg 1929
ZIMMERMANN, P.: Rheinschiffahrt. Zürich 1950

Beaufort Force	Wind speed in knots	Description of wind	Sea equivalent in open ocean
0	Less than	Calm	Sea like a mirror.
1	1–3	Light air	Ripples with the appearance of scales are formed but without foam crests.
2	4–6	Light breeze	Small wavelets, still short but more pronounced. Crests have a glassy appearance and do not break.
3	7–10	Gentle breeze	Large wavelets. Crests begin to break. Foam of glassy appearance. Perhaps scattered white horses.
4	11–16	Moderate breeze	Small waves, becoming longer: fairly frequent white horses.
5	17–21	Fresh breeze	Moderate waves, taking a more pronounced long form; many white horses are formed. (Chance of some spray.)
6	22–27	Strong breeze	Large waves begin to form; the white foam crests are more extensive everywhere. (Probably some spray.)
7	28–33	Near gale	Sea heaps up and white foam from breaking waves begins to be blown in streaks along the direction of the wind.
8	34–40	Gale	Moderately high waves of greater length; edges of crests begin to break into spindrift. The foam is blown in well-marked streaks along the direction of the wind.
9	41–47	Strong gale	High waves. Dense streaks of foam along the direction of the wind. Crests of waves begin to topple, tumble and roll over. Spray may affect visibility.
10	48–55	Storm	Very high waves with long overhanging crests. The resulting foam in great patches is blown in dense white streaks along the direction of the wind. On the whole the surface of the sea takes a white appearance. The tumbling of the sea becomes heavy and shocklike. Visibility affected.
11	56–63	Violent storm	Exceptionally high waves. (Small and medium-sized ships might be for a time lost to view behind the waves.) The sea is completely covered with long white patches of foam lying along the direction of the wind. Everywhere the edges of the wave crests are blown into froth. Visibility affected.
12	64–71	Hurricane	The air is filled with foam and spray. Sea completely white with driving spray; visibility very seriously affected.

APPENDIX TWO
WIND STRENGTH AND WAVE HEIGHT

Wind strength (Beaufort)	Characteristic wave height in metres			Characteristic wave period in seconds		
	Western Baltic	North Sea	North Atlantic	Western Baltic	North Sea	North Atlantic
3	0,45	1,00	1,70	2,9	4,6	6,3
4	0,60	1,40	1,95	3,4	4,9	6,5
5	0,85	2,00	2,40	3,8	5,4	6,9
6	1,20	3,00	3,10	4,4	6,1	7,4
7	1,60	4,00	4,00	4,8	6,8	8,0
8	1,95	5,60	5,25	5,3	7,7	8,5
9	2,50	6,60	6,45	5,8	8,4	9,1
10	3,15	7,20	7,45	6,0	9,0	9,6
11	3,80	7,50	8,40	6,3	9,6	10,1
12	4,30	7,70	9,20	6,5	10,3	10,6

1854	GREAT REPUBLIC 1854	Four-masted barque 1904
Length at the load waterline	89,0m	95,0m
Maximum beam	15,35m	14,0m
Depth	12,0m	8,5m
BRT	4000 BRT	3054 BRT
Displacement	5375 m³	6500 m³
Tonnage	3000 t	5400 t
Degree of fullness of the displacement (block coefficient)	0.458	0.7
Midsection area below water	80,4m²	88,5m²
Degree of fullness of the midsection	0.837	0.94
Foremast sail area	1191m²	854m²
Mainmast sail area	1286m²	855m²
Third mast sail area	923m²	866m²
Jigger mast sail area	263m²	207m²
Bowsprit sail area	457m²	241m²
Total area, minus staysails and studding sails	4120,m²	3023m²
Staysails	561m²	–
Studding sails	700m²	–
Total area	5381m²	3023m²
Centre of effort of sails, height above DWL	25,0m	24,0m
Centre of effort of sails, distance forward of midsection	4,0m	5,10m
Sail area/m²	66,92	34,2
Crew strength in individuals	15	32
Sail area per man	47m²	95m²

Development of principal dimensions, tonnages, sail rigs and crew strengths of typical four-masted ships, built 50 years apart, comparing the *Great Republic* built in 1854, and a four-masted barque built in 1904.

APPENDIX FOUR
SAIL AREA AND DISPLACEMENT OF SIGNIFICANT SAILING SHIP TYPES

Sailing ship type	Sail area in m_2	Displacement in tons
Two-masted topsail schooner	ca 400	200...400
Two-masted fore-and-aft schooner	300... 650	200... 400
Schooner brig	500... 600	250... 550
Brig	600... 800	400...1000
Three-masted barquentine	1000...1500	700...2300
Three-masted barque	1500...2000	1400...4500
Three-masted full-rigged ship	1800...2500	2500...6500
Four-masted barque	2500...3000	4300...8500
Four-masted full-rigged ship	3000...4000	6000...10,000
Five-masted barque	3500...5200	8000...10,000
Five-masted full-rigged ship	6000	10,800
Six-masted fore-and-aft schooner	3200	550...9000
Seven-masted fore-and-aft schooner	3800	10,000

APPENDIX FIVE
RATING OF WARSHIPS AROUND 1800

Rate	Displacement in tons	Number of guns	Number of crew	Length 1st Deck	Dimensions in feet Beam 1st Deck	Depth 1st Deck to Keel
1.	2000...2164	100...130	850...900	178...186	50...52	20...24
2.	1650...1950	84... 90	750...850	164...178	48...50	19...21
3.	1200...1660	64... 80	520...750	148...170	42...48	16...20
4.	700...1000	44... 60	380...500	124...156	36...46	14...18
5.	650... 730	32... 40	200...300	120...144	32...38	12...15
6.	400... 630	20... 28	150...200	108...124	28...24	10±12

APPENDIX SIX
LIST OF FOUR-MASTED SAILING SHIPS LOST OR ABANDONED IN 1891 AND 1892, BASED ON CIRCULAR NO. 2104 OF THE INTERNATIONAL TRANSPORT INSURANCE ASSOCIATION, DATED 20TH JANUARY, 1893.

Ship No.	Name	Shipping Company	Shipyard	Year built	Dimensions in feet			BRT	Fate
					L	B	D		
1	ROMSDAL	J. & A. ALLAN Glasgow	R. Steele Greenock	1877	275,9	41,1	23,5	1887	On the voyage Chittagong — Dundee. Cargo: jute. Last seen 31st October 1891.
2	BEN DOURAU	WATSON BROS.	H. Mourray & Co., Pt. Glasgow	1881	280,4	40,2	23,6	1950	On the voyage San Francisco — Channel. Cargo: grain. Last seen 24th April, 1892.
3	FALLS OF EARN	Ship Falls of EARN Co. (Lim.) (Wright a. Breakenridge, Glasgow)	Russel & Co., Greenock	1884	302,6	42,1	24,5	2386	On the voyage Penarth — Acheen. Cargo: coal. Last seen July 1891 in Olehleh harbour.
4	DUNKERQUE	A.D. BORDERS ET FILS, Bordeaux	Russel & Co., Glasgow	1889	329,8	46,2	24,9	3152	On the voyage Cardiff — Rio de Janeiro. Cargo: pit-coal. Last seen 1891.
5	STANLEY	SHIP STANLEY Co. (Lim.) G.M. Steeves	Russel & Co., Glasgow	1889	278,1	41,9	24,4	2210	On the voyage Philadelphia — Hiogo. Cargo: petroleum. Abandoned at sea, March 1892.
6	INVERT-ROSSACHS	D. BRUCE & Co., Dundee	Russel & Co., Glasgow	1891	305,0	43,2	25,3	2710	On the voyage Philadelpha — Calcutta. Cargo: petroleum. Abandoned at sea, March 1892.
7	NATION	W. THOMAS & Co., Liverpool	W. Boxford & Sons, Sunderland	1891	294,0	43,0	24,0	2540	On the voyage Rangoon — Bremen. Cargo: rice. Last seen 24th March 1892.
8	ASHBANK	A. WAIR & Co., Glasgow	Russel & Co., Greenock	1891	278,6	42,0	24,2	2292	On the voyage Algoa bay — Newcastle, NSW Cargo: ballast. Last seen 31st May, 1892.
9	THRACIA	W. THOMSON & Co., Liverpool	R. Duncan & Co., Pt. Glasgow	1892	282,0	42,0	24,0	2000	On the voyage Greenock — Liverpool. Cargo: ballast. Capsized off Port Erin in August 1892.
10	MARIA RICKMERS (5 Master)	RICKMERS REISMÜHLEN, Reederei und Schiffbau A. G., Bremerhaven	Russel & Co., Greenock	1892	375,7	48,0	25,4	3822	On the voyage Saigon — Bremen. Cargo: rice. Last seen 24th July 1892.